T0399906

Residential Architecture as Infrastructure

This edited collection provides an up-to-date account, by a group of well-informed and globally positioned authors, of recently implemented projects, public policies and business activities in Open Building around the world.

Countless residential Open Building projects have been built in a number of countries, some without knowledge of the original theory and methods. These projects differ in architectural style, building industry methods, economic system and social aims. National building standards and guidelines have been promulgated in several countries (Finland, China, Japan, Korea), providing incentives and guidance to Open Building implementation. Businesses in several countries have begun to deliver advanced fit-out systems both for new construction and for retrofitting existing buildings, demonstrating the economic advantages of 'the responsive, independent dwelling.' This book also argues that the 'open building' approach is essential for the reactivation of the existing building stock for long-term value, because in the end it costs less.

The book discusses these developments in residential architecture from the perspective of an infrastructure model of built environment. This model enables decision-makers to manage risk and uncertainty, while avoiding a number of problems often associated with large, fast-moving projects, such as separation and distribution of design tasks (and responsibility) and the ensuing boundary frictions.

Residential Architecture as Infrastructure adds to the Routledge Open Building Series, and will appeal to architects, urban designers, researchers and policymakers interested in this international review of current projects, policies and business activities focused on Open Building implementation.

Stephen H. Kendall, Ph.D., R.A. is Emeritus Professor of Architecture at Ball State University and co-founder and vice president of the Council on Open Building. Dr. Kendall's career in architectural practice, research and education spans more than 40 years. His research focuses on the Open Building approach needed to make buildings more adaptable, easier to customize to meet changing preferences and thus more sustainable. His work recognizes the increasing size and complexity of projects and the dynamics of living environments, the workplace and the marketplace where design must go beyond short-term uses and where control is distributed not only during initial planning but also over time.

Open Building

The Routledge Open Building Series is a library of titles addressing the Open Building approach to architecture and urban design. It offers an international perspective, providing theory, design methods, examples of construction techniques, manufactured products and many realized projects. These titles augment a growing literature in sustainability and resilience in the built environment by focusing on the fourth dimension.

Open Building advocates separation of design tasks: the design of what is shared and what will last, and the design of what belongs to individual occupancies and is expected to change more quickly. This is both a social/political and a design skills issue. Urban design projects, office buildings, shopping centers and laboratories are examples of separation of design tasks. The same should become the norm in multi-unit housing, healthcare and educational facilities and other project types making up our everyday world. The Open Building approach addresses how to establish the boundary between what is shared and what is decided independently; how to separate the distribution of utility lines between the two; how to evaluate a building's or urban design's capacity to accommodate a variety of interventions initially and over time; and what shared patterns, types and systems help designers cultivate coherent variety. More generally, Open Building helps design professionals work with change and to cooperate in the flowering of everyday environment.

This series provides answers to these questions, and more, and is designed to be the go-to resource for anyone seeking to understand and practice Open Building.

The Appearance of the Form
Seven Essays on the Position Designing takes Between People and Things (Routledge Revivals)
N. John Habraken

Supports
An Alternative to Mass Housing (Routledge Revivals)
N. John Habraken

Healthcare Architecture as Infrastructure
Open Building in Practice
Edited by Stephen H. Kendall

Residential Architecture as Infrastructure
Open Building in Practice
Edited by Stephen H. Kendall

For more information about this series, please visit:
https://www.routledge.com/Open-Building/book-series/OB

Residential Architecture as Infrastructure

Open Building in Practice

EDITED BY STEPHEN H. KENDALL

Routledge
Taylor & Francis Group

LONDON AND NEW YORK

Routledge
OPEN BUILDING SERIES

First published 2022
by Routledge
2 Park Square, Milton Park, Abingdon, Oxon OX14 4RN

and by Routledge
605 Third Avenue, New York, NY 10158

Routledge is an imprint of the Taylor & Francis Group, an informa business

British Library Cataloguing-in-Publication Data
A catalogue record for this book is available from the British Library

Library of Congress Cataloging-in-Publication Data
Names: Kendall, Stephen H., editor.
Title: Residential architecture as infrastructure : open
building in practice / edited by Stephen H. Kendall.
Description: Abingdon, Oxon ; New York : Routledge, 2022. |
Series: Open building |
Includes bibliographical references and index.
Identifiers: LCCN 2021013420 (print) | LCCN 2021013421 (ebook) |
ISBN 9780367863135 (hardback) | ISBN 9780367863159 (paperback) |
ISBN 9781003018339 (ebook)
Subjects: LCSH: Architecture, Domestic—Planning. |
Architectural design—Methodology. | Architecture and society.
Classification: LCC NA7115 .R47 2022 (print) |
LCC NA7115 (ebook) | DDC 728—dc23
LC record available at https://lccn.loc.gov/2021013420
LC ebook record available at https://lccn.loc.gov/2021013421

ISBN: 978-0-367-86313-5 (hbk)
ISBN: 978-0-367-86315-9 (pbk)
ISBN: 978-1-003-01833-9 (ebk)

DOI: 10.4324/9781003018339

Typeset in Univers LT Std
by Newgen Publishing UK

This book is dedicated to the many too-often unsung pioneers around the world who are implementing the Open Building approach to the design of residential projects. But most important, the book is dedicated to John Habraken, whose insights in the late 1950s grew into a fundamental rethinking of the role of architects in cultivating everyday built environment.

Contents

Preface

This book was preceded by another book on the same subject titled *Residential Open Building* (Kendall and Teicher, 2000). Both have their roots in the concept first spelled out in *Supports: An Alternative to Mass Housing* (Habraken, 1962, 1972, 1999, 2020). Habraken proposed separating the design of what all dwellings share (the support) from the individual, independent dwelling units (the infill) in large projects. This concept was worked out at the SAR (Stichting Architecten Research in Eindhoven, NL) in the mid 1960s in what was the first serious effort at design methodology for architecture. It was a response to the widely experienced fact that the 20th century spawned an unprecedented period of rapid urban growth and a coarsening of the urban fabric. No longer was the single, independent dwelling the basic cell of a regenerative fabric. Instead, large buildings holding sometimes hundreds of dwellings became the basic building block, decision-making and economic 'unit.' They were rigid, 'lumpy,' unibody constructions, regulated and financed as such. While that trend had already been set a century earlier, it was from the early 1900s onward that residential construction on a massive scale became an important subject for professional design. This happened in many countries, independent of political economy. Administrators of government subsidies and pension funds expected architects and engineers to tell them how to build large numbers of dwellings as a secure investment.

For the first time in the history of human settlement, everyday environment became a professional product. Architects and their clients thought that the best way to do this was to design floor plans and stack them and arrange them into large buildings, and then to construct everything at once. This is now considered the proper formal way to make much of our contemporary urban environment (with the exception, notably, of office buildings and shopping centers, explained later).

Everything else, the improvised products of a millennia-old way of incremental urban growth and transformation, in which each dwelling is the basic unit of transformation, is still alive in a primitive but productive way. This is evident around most mega cities today in a process known as 'informal settlements' and is the everyday reality of people working to improve their own living places, even in societies dominated by the professional culture.

It's interesting that while the dominance of the professional class grows, concerns for sustainability and resilience have increasingly come to the forefront. Discussion of circular economy and 'circular building processes' are now heard. For the first time in human history the world is facing an existential crisis of man-made climate change, due in large measure because of the inability of society – and those in positions of power – to see the big picture or take measure of the long-term implications of today's actions.

> The modern market economy, which rewards corporations for short-term profits and aggressive cost cutting, is also part of the problem. Its incentive structure all but ensures that companies in the business of producing our building stock will end up selling services and buildings that will only shift the burden to future generations. The market loves to reward corporations for risk-taking when those risks are largely borne by other parties, like customers or taxpayers. This is known as 'privatizing profits and socializing losses.'

Over more than a century the formal way of delivering and renewing our building stock has become a complex network of technical and design professionals as well as government administrators, politicians and financial institutions. Despite efforts that remain at the margins, this way of working has failed to properly harness the power of industrial production, logistics, data management software in its products or to accept a possible active role for inhabitants in large projects in the process. The result is that, while everything else today can be made in large quantities for less money and at higher quality, serving an increasingly sophisticated user-dominated market at all income levels, dwellings for those same societies are more expensive every year. This cannot continue to be blamed on regulations and bureaucrats.

Meanwhile, buildings for other purposes, such as commercial office buildings, shopping centers and transit lounges in airports, have successfully applied what we now know of as the Open Building approach. Professionals who developed such projects never heard of Open Building, but they found the principle of separating design decisions the most efficient way to get the job done. They saved time and money. And, while architectural quality is often in question, these building types have the inbuilt capacity for incremental renewal that is arguably a crucial characteristic of a renewable and sustainable built fabric.

But it is also the case that a substantial part of the problems we face lies in our inability to incrementally renew our residential built fabric to meet the challenge of sustainability. This is why this book focuses on the Open Building approach to large residential projects. Other books have appeared focused on healthcare architecture and more will be coming focused on educational facilities. To make the argument more accessible, I use the word infrastructure to describe the method of large building design planned for incremental renewal, because it is familiar, while Open Building is generally not familiar. But they are equivalent terms. This is explained in Chapter 1.

Selecting authors for this book

In selecting authors to contribute to this book, I found myself asking why we should expect the process of built environment transformation to be less riddled with conflict, waste and exorbitant costs than it is. Perhaps expecting otherwise is naïve, given how many players are involved, how resistant current habits are to change even when we learn more, how rapidly standards of building performance change, how quickly user preferences shift, and recognizing how deeply entrenched decision-making is among parties with competing and conflicting interests and no motivation to change habits.

Naïve or not, visions of doing a better job drive those whose work is collected in this book. Their voices are varied and are fortunately not alone. Their work is mirrored by many other building professionals, researchers and managers around the world who haven't capitulated to cynicism or ignorance, but who work with their feet on the ground and their minds in a constant learning mode. We should hope for a sustainable building stock less burdened by incessant and tiresome conflict and rising costs. This requires new attitudes and skills to make building stock transformation effective and equitable – as well as producing excellent if not delightful architecture.

While technical issues are discussed in these chapters, the core challenges, not surprisingly, are essentially political, economic and organizational, and reside in the ecology of decision-making in the building industry, in changing minds and in rebalancing the distribution of control in housing processes. It is clearly not easy for clients, users, financial institutions, public sector regulators or design service providers doing large residential projects to move beyond the tradition of detailed programming, fixed floor plans and governance structures that attempt to prevent change. Given this, what should the professions do? Is it even worthwhile for architects to learn new skills and attitudes if those who we think need them and must eventually demand them and pay for them have yet to realize the needed paradigm shift? My experience in teaching architecture students is that it is not difficult to teach new skills associated with the Open Building approach. Good designers in practice can, if they want to, learn the skills even more quickly. Architects designing office buildings, shopping centers and airport concourses already do this, but don't have a name for it. Yet what good is it if an architect has learned new skills if their clients have not recognized the need to ask for them, or if old attitudes, regulations and financing tools block better ways of working? Between the lines, and sometimes explicitly, the chapters in this book hint at these questions and the problem of changing attitudes and minds – our own and others.

The chapters, in diverse fashion, touch on several assumptions about residential architecture:

1. incremental change in the residential building stock, whether in the short term or over generations, is continuous but not random;
2. decision-making control is never unified, but is distributed among many players, including users; the professions have to do a better job managing distributed control, cooperating with each other, and enabling and encouraging harried, everyday citizens to play a decisive role in the flourishing of built environment;
3. unless everyday citizens 'take matter(s) into their hands' in the mutation of their dwellings in large projects, the power of industrial production – so evident in all other spheres of life – will be unable to drive down costs;
4. changes in regulations, financing and in building industry practices are needed to assure long-lasting buildings and building complexes planned for incremental renewal and the independence of each dwelling in large buildings; and
5. new professional skills are needed, suited to these realities.

Separating design tasks is the central theme of the Open Building approach to the design of built environment. Whether the separation is accomplished under one party's control, or when control is distributed among several parties is a secondary issue. The approach is inescapably political; but it is also about design skills and ways of building, regulatory and financing methods. It is, at root, about professional methods.

Understanding residential architecture – and the building stock as such – as part of a broadened idea of infrastructure is the key to implementing it, and key to this is the recognition of a fit-out level and the importance of a residential fit-out industry capable of working in that space. In its final chapters, the book focuses on the emergence of a distinct infill industry, delivering just-in-time independent dwellings, harnessing advanced manufacturing and logistics by profitable enterprises. It is also the means by which Open Building will become cost competitive with the traditional way of building. This is the focus of the last part of the book.

While this latter part of the book is one of advocacy, it is not blind to considering why this transformation is so difficult, and consequently enumerates a number of reason that the emergence of an infill or fit-out industry is so slow in coming.

References

Kendall, Stephen and Teicher, Jonathan. (2000) *Residential Open Building*. London: Spon.

Habraken, John. (1962) *Supports: An Alternative to Mass Housing*. (Originally published in Dutch under the title: *De Dragers en de Mensen*. Amsterdam: Scheltema en Holkema). First English-language edition (1972) London: The Architectural Press, and New York: Praeger. Reprint of the 1972 English edition (1999) U.K., Urban International Press, edited by Jonathan Teicher. Reissue of the English edition (2020) with a new forward by the author. Routledge Open Building Series REVIVALS, edited by Stephen Kendall.

Contributors

Jia Beisi holds a Bachelor of Architecture from Nanjing Institute of Technology (NIT China) and a Postgraduate Diploma from the Swiss Federal Institute of Technology (ETH Zurich). He obtained a Ph.D. in Architecture History and Theory in 1990 through a joint program of NIT and ETH Zurich. Since January 1996, he has been Associate Professor at the University of Hong Kong. Besides design studio, he teaches courses in History of Chinese Architecture and Housing in Urban development in the Department of Architecture, and was coordinator of programs of the BAAS or MArch. He is the joint coordinator of W104-Open Building Implementation in the International Council for Research and Innovation in Building and Construction (CIB). He has published four books and more than 53 papers in international and/or national journals including *Open House International*, *Landscape Research*, *Habitat International*. Since 2008 he has also been the Director and Partner of the Architectural design office Baumschlager Eberle Hong Kong Ltd., having led and/or participated in project design for a number of projects including housing, shopping malls, institutional buildings, urban design and hotels.

Frank Bijdendijk studied Architectural and Urban design in Delft (NL). After service in the Royal Dutch Air Force, he was Project Manager at Bredero's Bouwbedrijf in Utrecht for several multifunctional projects. He later became Technical Director of Lunetten B.V. in Utrecht for the development of the residential area called Lunetten (6000 houses, shopping center, offices, schools etc.), and from 1982 to 2012 was Managing Director of the Housing Association Het Oosten (from 2008 on Stadgenoot) – managing 36,000 dwelling units in Amsterdam. In 2012 he started his own independent consultancy in real estate and became Founder and President of the National Renovation Platform (100+ members out of the complete real estate sector) and a member of the board of commissioners of many companies. In 2016 he joined the Board of Inspiration of a young company called Re-Born, Circular Real Estate. He is the author of many books; inventor and developer of Solids=Function-dynamic real estate; winner of several awards bearing a Royal distinction; and owner of a hydro-electric power plant, producing green energy.

Liu Dongwei earned his Ph.D. in Architecture from Tsinghua University. He currently serves in a leadership role in a number organizations, including: Chief Architect of China Institute of Building Standard Design and Research; Chairman of the Architectural Design Standardization Committee of the Ministry of Housing and Urban–Rural Development; Vice Chairman of the Industrialization Branch of the China Engineering Construction Standardization Association; and Vice Chairman of the Architectural Industrialization Committee of the China Architectural Association. He has been engaged in scientific and technological research in the field of construction for many years and is committed to research and practice directions of national construction engineering construction standards, construction industrialization and industrialization technology, affordable housing, aging society living, and green sustainable settlements. He is responsible for the Sino-Japanese cooperative JICA China New Housing Technology Research Project, China–Japan Housing Technology Integration Project, and China's Centennial Housing Demonstration Project. He has edited more than ten national industry standards and atlases and published many academic monographs and dozens of papers.

Carolin Franke is a Practicing Architect at ILO Architects Ltd. in Helsinki, Finland. She is currently working with the cultural project of Cable Factory and its extension of the Dance House Helsinki. For the 16th International Architecture Exhibition Biennale Architettura in Venice, Italy she was part of the Design Team of Talli Architects Ltd. Other former employers include Architecture Workshop Finland Ltd. and Sauerbruch Hutton architects. In 2015 she wrote her Master Thesis titled 'Raw Space Housing' at Aalto University in Helsinki, focusing on the implementation and challenges of individual and adaptable housing solutions. She studied in Dresden (Germany), Haarlem (Netherlands) and Helsinki (Finland).

John Habraken is Emeritus Professor of Architecture at the Massachusetts Institute of Technology, where he served as Head of the Department of Architecture from 1975 to 1981. Under his leadership, the Master of Science in Architecture Studies program (S.M.ArchS) was launched, a research-based program for students with professional degrees in architecture or urban design, the first such degree program in the United States. Prior to that, he was First Chairperson and Professor, Department of Architecture and Urban Design, Technical University Eindhoven, from 1967 to 1975. He received an honorary Doctorate from this University in 2005. From 1965 to 1975, he was Director, Stichting Architecten Research (SAR – Foundation for Architectural Research), a non-profit research organization charged with the development of design methods to facilitate implementation of the 'support/infill' approach in housing. From 1986 to 1990, he was a Board Member of Infill Systems BV, a corporation for the development of infill systems in housing and was President and CEO of Matura International BV in the Netherlands from 1990 to 1994.

John Habraken has lectured around the world, received numerous awards, has written ten books and a number of major research reports and has authored more than 100 papers and book chapters, many translated into other languages. Publications on his work have appeared in English, Dutch, German, Italian, Spanish and Japanese. In 2010 he launched a website Thematic Design (www.thematicdesign.org) for students and professionals, focused on cultivating the everyday built environment.

Stephen H. Kendall is Emeritus Professor of Architecture at Ball State University. He earned a professional degree from the University of Cincinnati, a Master of Urban Design from Washington University in St. Louis, and a Ph.D. in Design Theory and Methods from MIT under the direction of Professors John Habraken and Donald Schön. Prior to his 35-year academic career, which included teaching in the U.S., Japan, The People's Republic of China, the Republic of China, South Africa, Indonesia and Italy, he designed hospitals, schools and residential buildings as a registered architect, and built small residential buildings as a design/builder. His research and writing focus on the Open Building approach to a resilient building stock. He has written more than 45 papers and book chapters; co-authored *Residential Open Building* (2000); and has authored numerous technical reports and funded research projects, most recently for the US Department of Defense Health Agency on Healthcare Facilities Designed for Flexibility. His edited book *Healthcare Architecture as Infrastructure: Open Building in Practice* (Routledge) was published in 2018. From 1996–2016, he was senior joint coordinator of the CIB W104 international network. He co-founded the Council on Open Building (http://councilonopenbuilding.org) in 2017. Its mission is to expand sustainability and resilience practices to include planning and designing neighborhoods and buildings for incremental upgrading and for diverse and evolving uses.

Soo-am Kim is a Senior Research Fellow at the Korea Institute of Civil Engineering and Building Technology. His fields of expertise are architectural planning, long-life housing, and remodeling and maintenance of buildings. His accomplishments include: research on standardization and infill design of housing, development of housing performance certification systems and long-life housing certification systems, study of Hanok, planning design technology and institution of house remodeling. His current research focuses on the construction of a long-life housing demonstration complex of 116 households in two buildings with the project of 'Development of cost-saving long-life housing supply model and field test', a national R&D initiative. He is also involved in Smart house planning research, and development of a remodeling certification system.

Yongsun Kim studied in the Graduate School of Engineering, the University of Tokyo from 2001 to 2005; since 2007 he has been a Researcher in the Graduate School of Frontier Sciences, the University of Tokyo, where his major research field is building construction systems and architectural renovation.

Nadezhda Koreneva is a Russian architect. She is co-founder of an architectural studio KRNV, based in Moscow, which works with residential environments, on the architectural and urban design levels. The office works on design projects on each stage from masterplan to infill layout. She graduated from the Department of Architecture and Urban Planning in VSTU and completed the educational program New Leaders of Territorial Development in MARCH and RANEPA. Her Ph.D. dissertation develops new strategies for Open Building in the context of Moscow.

Caroline Kruit is a freelance media consultant, editor, publisher and art director with a background in building engineering and journalism. Caroline is editor in chief for Openbuilding.co, a platform initiated by Dutch architects and engineers who incorporate the principles of Open Building and circularity in buildings and city planning.

Kazunobu Minami received his Ph.D. from The University of Tokyo and a S.M.Arch from the Massachusetts Institute of Technology. From 1981, he worked for the Japanese Government as an architect for 24 years. Since 2005, he has been a Professor of Architecture at Shibaura Institute of Technology in Tokyo. He served as a joint coordinator of CIB W104–Open Building Implementation from October 2003 to 2010. He has lectured widely in various countries and has published many peer reviewed papers at international conferences.

Yoshiro Morita is a Professor in the Department of Architecture, Tokyo Polytechnic University, Japan. His major research fields are building construction systems, building production and housing. His publications include *A Guide to the Industry of Architecture* (co-authored, Shokokusha, 2017); *Box Delivery Industry: Talk with Architects and Building Engineers of Prefabricated Houses in the Early Phase* (co-authored, Shokokusha, 2013), and *Sustainable Site Design: 100 Cases* (co-authored, Shokokusha, 2008).

Amira Osman is a Sudanese/South African Architect/Lecturer/Researcher. She is a Professor of Architecture at the Tshwane University of Technology. Amira studied at the University of Khartoum in Sudan in 1988 (B.Sc.), 1996 (M.Sc.). She obtained a diploma from the Institute for Housing Studies in Rotterdam (IHS) in 1992 and a Ph.D. in Architecture from the University of Pretoria in 2004. Dr. Osman was one of the conference conveners for the World Congress on Housing in 2005 at the University of Pretoria and the convener of the Sustainable Human(e) Settlements: The Urban Challenge, 2012, hosted by FADA, University of Johannesburg and its partners. She also served as UIA 2014 Durban General Reporter and head of the Scientific Committee for the International Union of Architects (UIA) and the South African Institute of Architects (SAIA). She currently jointly coordinates the international network for Open Building CIB104. She previously worked as a Senior Researcher at the Council for Scientific and Industrial Research (CSIR) in Pretoria (2010–2012) where she collaborated with a team from the Department of Human Settlements, SAIA and other councils and private sector representatives in the development of ten points for sustainable human(e) settlements which she proceeded to disseminate widely.

Li Shanshan is an Assistant Professor at the School of Architecture and Urban Planning, Beijing University of Civil Engineering and Architecture. Her research focuses on the development of Open Building practices in China which continues her Ph.D. dissertation in 2015 (A View of Flexible Housing in China, University of Turin in Italy) and the design and index system of long-life sustainable housing within family life cycle, which is supported by a grant from the National Nature Science Foundation of China (2020–2022).

Hyeon-jeong Yang is a Research Specialist at the Korea Institute of Civil Engineering and Building Technology. Her fields of expertise are: Architectural Planning, Interior Architecture (Smart Housing) and Long-life housing and remodeling. Her accomplishments include development of a smart home service process, Han-style interior design research, and Elderly housing research. Her current research focuses on the development of a cost-saving long-life housing development model and construction of a demonstration complex, Research on a remodeling certification system, AI integrated Smart Housing Platform and Services Technology.

Wu Zhichao earned her Ph.D. in Architecture from the University of Tokyo. She is Associate Researcher (Senior Engineer), currently Deputy Chief Engineer of China Building Standard Design and Research Institute Co. Ltd., External Master's Degree Supervisor of Beijing University of Civil Engineering and Architecture, Expert Committee Member of China Engineering Construction Standardization Association, and Prefabricated Building Expert member of the Industrial Technology Innovation Alliance. She is one of the authors of 'SI Housing and Housing Construction Model – Theory, Methods and Cases'; 'SI Housing and Housing Construction Model System – Technology and Illustrations'; 'A Century of Housing-Research and Practice of China's Future-oriented Green and Sustainable Housing Construction.' She participated in the compilation of the Chinese Building Code 'Design Standards for Prefabricated Residential Buildings'; 'Technical Standards for Prefabricated Concrete Buildings'; 'Technical Standards for Prefabricated Steel Structure Buildings'; and 'Evaluation Standards for Prefabricated Buildings' among other publications and reports.

Summary of the chapters

Part 1 Residential open building projects in a number of countries
This part of the book highlights a selection of projects in the Netherlands, Finland, Russia, Hong Kong and the global South. The cases all address the fact that while Open Building is often mistakenly understood as simply a technical strategy for building design and construction, it is equally a socio/political issue and one involving new attitudes and skills. While the approach addresses technical issues (such as 'disentanglement,' 'capacity analysis,' 'interface standards' and the like), the approach is more focused on two basic tenets: separation of design tasks and cooperation among designers. This suggests new roles, attitudes, methods, governance structures and business opportunities, which are briefly outlined in each chapter. These chapters also discuss barriers to more widespread implementation of residential open building in the situations in which the authors work.

Chapter 1 Basic principles of an infrastructure or Open Building model of residential architecture

An infrastructure model of managing large, complex systems is introduced and discussed as a natural response when projects – buildings and neighborhoods or building complexes – become ever larger and involve an increasing number of players. This is what the Open Building approach is aimed to address. When that happens, centralization of control doesn't work, and tasks are separated. Control is distributed and design tasks (as well as the work of construction, management, finance, regulation and upkeep) are 'partitioned'. The goal of task separation is to reduce risk to any one party, to keep the system operational while parts are put off-line for replacement or upgrading, and to assure optimal capacity to meet evolving technical or performance standards, to spur innovation, to meet user expectations and to lower costs.

Developments toward Open Building are urgently needed to reduce costs. The means to achieve this goal is to make each dwelling in a multi-occupant or attached building typology fully independent. Each dwelling should be able to adjust, be replaced or altered independent of other dwellings in the same building. This is the same independence we take for granted in detached dwellings, the most prevalent typology everywhere in the world. Detached dwellings are attractive in part because they reduce potential points of friction between neighbors and enable independent action and responsibility in the context of a 'commons' that respects community norms. With increased density, more technical, social and legal boundary frictions arise. Enabling the independence of each dwelling helps to establish dwellings as the basic cell in a living urban fabric capable of regenerating itself over time.

Chapter 2 Open Building's recent developments in the Netherlands

A recent surge in residential Open Building projects in the Netherlands initiated by a growing number of architects and clients signals a potential turning point in residential architecture in the country where the Open Building concept was born. This chapter discusses a number of such projects, discusses the challenges their architects face and demonstrates how these developments fit well into the circular economy discourse.

Chapter 3 Open Building in Finland

Open Building research in the latter part of the 20th century led to projects in Finland that were some of the earliest to be realized in the private sector by for-profit developers. Linked to data-management tools, these projects had an influence that has led to more being built, and to the publication of guidelines linking sustainability and the Open Building approach. This chapter tells the story of these developments, presents several exemplary projects, and discusses barriers to and opportunities for further projects to be realized in Finland.

Chapter 4 Quality control by levels: steering the design process using BEA's Project Book

Architectural design is object-oriented and involves decision-making on form, space and the organization of technical systems. It is also a process of decision-making by all the involved parties including potential users throughout the entire life of the building. This chapter discusses the design process and Project Books of Baumschlager Eberle Architects (BEA), both of which are based on a classification of five social-spatial levels: urban public spaces; permanent (base) building structure/ mechanical systems; facades; functional layouts; and interior fit-out per occupant. The five levels of BEA's design process enlarge the social and functional capacity of buildings to accommodate multiple uses over time, including but not limited to residential occupancies.

Chapter 5 Open Building in Russia

Over the past 100 years, there have been many global, radical political turns and economic crises in Russia. These transformations have greatly influenced contemporary Russian spatial principles of urban design and development. There are two principal phenomena which now set the stage for developments toward Open Building in Russia.

The first is the 'free plan apartment.' This approach operates at the level of the real estate investment in buildings. This is a trend to build essentially empty residential buildings in which decisions about apartment layouts and equipment are made separately, in a second stage. This part of the chapter discusses the advantages, limitations and legal obstacles using real projects to illustrate the issues. The second phenomenon is the 'free plan neighborhood.' This operates at the level of urban design and involves developers filling-in empty or 'left-over' spaces left in the typical 20th-century urban residential development schemes. With no clarity about how to steer development at this level of intervention, many problems are occurring while the process of land surveying and illegal invasions by developers is taking place. This chapter discusses both phenomena and suggests broad remedies.

Chapter 6 Open Building in the global South

Several decades ago, the Open Building approach attracted a substantial interest in so-called 'developing countries.' Investigations in 'slum upgrading,' 'informal settlements,' and 'user participation' could be found in South America, South Asia and Africa. This chapter reassesses the role that the Open Building approach can offer in the 'global South' by presenting a range of projects which have been conceptualized and built with no reference to Open Building as a concept. However, these projects are based on the idea of encouraging long-lasting residential architecture planned for change. The chapter is premised on the belief that there is a need for new forms of governance and regulatory frameworks that allow for experimentation and testing out of alternative forms of delivery. This is especially important in the countries of the global South considering unique socio-economic conditions as well as a large degree of informality in residential development processes. The possible implementation of Open Building in the countries of the global South is discussed by analyzing several case studies based on the basic principles of Open Building.

Part 2 The policy environment for residential Open Building

The adoption of policies and industry guidelines providing incentives and standards for widespread implementation of residential Open Building can be a significant turning point toward Open Building implementation. This part of the book reviews several such proposed and actual policies.

Chapter 7 The future of Open Building resides in the existing stock

This chapter argues that the future of Open Building lies in the reactivation of the existing building stock. The investments made over decades in the building stock worldwide cannot be thrown away. Using evidence from economic and demographic analysis, this chapter argues for systematic methods of renewal.

Chapter 8 Japan's Act Concerning the Promotion of Long-Life Quality Housing

After decades of research and hundreds of realized S/I (Skeleton/Infill) projects, in 2009, the Japanese central government began implementing an act providing incentives to developers to build long-lasting residential projects. By the end of March 2019, more than one million such dwellings have been realized, both single-family and multi-family. This chapter tells the story of developments leading up to the 2009 law and prospects for the future of Japanese housing in the spirit of the Open Building approach.

The Japanese Government, universities and industrial corporations have collaborated at various times in advancing housing standards, particularly the longevity and adaptability of the building stock. Adaptable infill systems like movable partitions and movable storage are examples of design solutions to make housing units fit for the changes of life over several decades of residency. Longer life housing with adaptable infill, which preserves buildings by encouraging them to adapt to change, is at the heart of housing solutions for a sustainable future because it significantly reduces the waste of materials for building construction. A number of recent technical innovations show the potential for even greater flexibility in both the new and existing housing stock. Innovative technologies are expected to become the most essential force for the development of housing in Japan, and the tradition of collaborative relations among the government, academia and industry in Japan will continue to be the most effective way to promote innovation in the house-building and construction industries.

Chapter 9 Research, development and implementation of long-life housing in China

In 2018, the China Institute for Building Standard Design and Research issued guidelines for the design of long-lasting housing. This capped several decades of experimental projects and a fundamental reassessment of traditional methods of designing multi-unit housing projects which are now viewed as producing premature and widespread obsolescence, social disruption and waste. Trends in demographics, economic investments and the urgency of building sustainably indicate that the Open Building approach (identified by other names in China) is an important development to be taken seriously.

Chapter 10 Korea's 100-year housing program
For over a decade, Korean research units in the public and private sectors have been working to shift the paradigm of housing production in Korea from one based on the tradition of defining functions first, then building to suit, to one with a long view. Recognizing evolving technical standards, user requirements, household formation and the imperatives of investing sustainably, prototype projects and design and construction guidelines are coming to be recognized as representing an important shift in the way housing is financed, built and renewed in Korea.

Part 3 Developments toward a fit-out industry: the key to residential Open Building
The Open Building approach was initially formulated with a goal of harnessing the power of industrial production in the housing process in the service of 'the natural relationship.' This was the idea of the independent dwelling unit which was not at root a technical idea but a proposition for separating design tasks. But, unlike the widely heralded 'industrialized housing' movement, Open Building theory posits a clear distinction between the processes of industrial production and the process of building, while showing a clear relationship and complementarity between these two enterprises. This part of the book briefly reviews this subject and shows how a residential fit-out industry has the potential of utilizing industrial production in a new way in the realization and continual reactivation of buildings. The chapters also show barriers to the emergence of this kind of product/service industry.

Chapter 11 Infill systems: a new industry
The idea of harnessing the powerful capabilities of industrial production in the service of the 'natural relation' was first posited in *Supports*, published in 1961. Early work at the SAR in the 1960s focused on dimensional and positional coordination and other agreements that would encourage independent producers to manufacture products that would go together to make what were then called 'detachable units.' The basic principles of an infill industry, addressing both social and technical issues, are summarized here in a set of illustrations produced in 1994.

Chapter 12 How housing renovation is meeting the challenge of oversupply of dwelling units in Japan
In the last decade, a number of real estate companies in large Japanese cities have begun to find it profitable to retrofit individual apartments or condominium dwelling units in well-situated multifamily buildings. They 'gut' out the old interior, and in a matter of a few weeks, completely 'refresh' the interiors with new floor plans, including all of the piping, wiring and other

technical equipment, without disturbing other occupied units in the building. This chapter discusses why this is happening and gives examples of companies providing this service, while also discussing why this trend is slow to take hold.

Chapter 13 Dualities of interior decoration companies in China

There is a long tradition in China for small to medium sized enterprises to provide the service of customized interior apartment decoration, in both new construction and in redecorating existing units. In the last five years, a few companies have gone to scale in providing this service. One such company can now out-fit an apartment in seven days with a trained team of four installers. This company has completed over 80,000 such units in the last few years. This chapter discusses how this tradition of small-scale interior decoration may be slowly leading to a sophisticated, factory-based 'industrialized' interior fit-out industry, while clearly showing the barriers to this more advanced way of working.

Chapter 14 Developments toward a residential fit-out industry: the key to a sustainable housing stock

This chapter argues that a residential fit-out industry is a logical extension of the already massive remodeling industry that exists in most countries. But, because the existing building industry is unable to break out of its obsolete habits, a fit-out industry of many competitive, certified companies will probably only come into being by outside actors entering the stage. In the same way that Henry Ford basically invented an automotive industry, before a network of roads, highways and expressways came into being to support the automobiles being produced, someone or some company will need to develop a successful residential fit-out service. This will stimulate competition which in turn will lower costs, and will put residential base buildings in demand as the pragmatic basis for a regenerative residential building stock.

Acknowledgments

I would like to acknowledge first of all the authors who took time from their busy professional lives to write chapters for this book, not expecting financial compensation but being generous enough to contribute to the expansion of the knowledge base of our professions. Their willingness to work with me through several drafts and to provide images for their chapters is very much appreciated.

For the longest time, the residential open building approach has been criticized as being too complicated, too expensive, and unworkable if not simply unnecessary. The chapters in this book give evidence otherwise.

Part 1

Residential Open Building projects in a number of countries

This part of the book explains how the basic principles of infrastructure design can be effectively applied to the design of large residential projects. The word infrastructure is familiar, although in architecture it refers only to the utility systems, not the entirety of a building. Chapter 1 explains how the basic principles of infrastructure planning – which are equivalent to the Open Building approach – can be extended to support the design of large residential projects.

The chapter then highlights a selection of recent projects in the Netherlands, Finland and Russia, and the global South. The cases all address the conundrum that while Open Building is often mistakenly understood as a technical methodology for building design and construction, in which the term 'flexibility' is too often used, it is also a socio-political issue. While the approach does address technical issues (such as 'disentanglement,' 'capacity analysis,' 'interface standards' and the like), in fact the approach is more focused on two basic tenets: separation of design tasks, and cooperation among designers. This suggests new roles, attitudes, methods, governance structures and business opportunities, which are briefly outlined in each chapter.

DOI: 10.4324/9781003018339-1

Chapter 1

Basic principles of an infrastructure or Open Building model of residential architecture

Stephen H. Kendall

In the early decades of the 21st century, breakthroughs in progress toward Open Building implementation are urgently needed to assure the capacity of the residential building stock to regenerate itself, cell-by-cell or one-dwelling-at-a-time. This is the best way to achieve the sustainability and resilience of the everyday environment.

To achieve this goal, each dwelling in a multi-occupant or attached building typology needs to be fully independent. This is not a matter of so-called flexibility, which is a largely technical way of describing things. Rather, it is first of all a matter of separated design tasks, which, because we are discussing buildings, inevitably involves technical matters, but is fundamentally about new patterns of decision-making. Independent dwellings mean that each should be able to adjust, be replaced or altered independent of other dwellings in the same building. This is the same independence we take for granted in detached dwellings, the most prevalent typology everywhere in the world. Detached dwellings are attractive in large part because they are independent and enable independent action and responsibility in the context of community norms, conventions and regulatory instruments, with reduced points of friction between neighbors. With increased density, more technical, social and legal boundary frictions arise. Enabling the independence of each dwelling in large projects helps to establish dwellings as the basic cells in a living everyday environment.

Residential architecture is arguably the most important application of the Open Building approach – and evidently the most difficult to achieve. It concerns the bulk of the built environment; it most directly touches the daily lives, habits, attitudes and aspirations of all of us. Residential Open Building is also the most complex among all project types, both organizationally, economically, socially, and technically. Large multi-dwelling projects have more territorial subdivisions, more regulatory burdens, with more interwoven and usually entangled mechanical, electrical and plumbing systems per m^3 than other building types. People need (and want) to live together, but also need their autonomy, sense of personal space, achievement and responsibility, while also living in a supportive 'commons.'

DOI: 10.4324/9781003018339-2

There is overwhelming evidence that the seemingly innate need to shape our personal environments to suit our individual preferences remains alive even if it is suppressed or denied. This need is evident, if we just look around, independent of income, household structure and culture. Achieving a balance between individual responsibility and a supportive commons is never easy, because change – and expressions of individual preferences – can be unsettling, the more so in large buildings inhabited by hundreds of households where consensus and predictability are also needed. In contemporary societies in most countries, finding this balance can often be the source of tension and conflict, particularly in times of rapid social and technical changes. In part this is because of the hegemony of professionals who do not want to relinquish control of the design of the built environment once they have gained it. But it is more than that: fear of 'the different other' also accounts for some of the difficulties in living close together. Recognizing these difficulties, the default response of those who invest in, design and manage multi-occupant buildings today is to institute regulatory measures and make design and construction decisions that thwart dwelling independence – and that block or greatly inhibit incremental change and variety – even while installing more amenities in the 'common' sphere in what I consider an implicit strategy of pacification. Sometimes this strategy is explicit. The Open Building approach offers a way to release some of these tensions, and to save money in the process.

Others have sought to make each dwelling unit in a multifamily structure independent (e.g. Boosma, et al., 2000; LeCorbusier and Jeanneret, 1946; Matsumura, 2019; Parman and Bender, 1976). However, as far as I know, only the adoption of the Open Building approach has succeeded, producing countless projects around the world. Many of those initiating such projects do not even know of this worldwide phenomenon and use various names to describe what they are doing.

The perspective put forward in this book asks readers to set aside the long-held concept that large multifamily housing projects are best produced as unitary entities or investments, designed and accounted for as a whole. This unitary way of seeing such complex buildings is obsolete and too costly. It is a remnant of the now obsolete functionalist ideology. In the interest of a regenerative built environment, in which independent dwellings find their place in the normal functioning of everyday built environment, this book hopes to contribute to the ongoing work of many practitioners and clients alike to cultivate a sustainable, resilient built environment, planned for incremental change.

We should think of our homes as a legacy to future generations and consider the negative environmental effects of building them to serve only one or two generations before razing or reconstructing them. Homes should be built for sustainability and for ease in future modification.
(From *Healthy Housing Reference Manual*,
National Low-Income Housing Coalition, USA)

A central premise of this book, explained in different voices and in varied contexts, is that individual freedom and responsibility normally associated with the detached dwelling need not – and indeed cannot – be allowed to be forfeited under the pressures of density and the forces pushing for uniformity. With world population expected to grow from 7 billion in 2020 to 9.7 billion by 2050, societies across the globe will need to build more compactly and more sustainably and more affordably, with a greater commitment to equity and long-term value. In doing so, societies will have to harness the initiative of individual households at all income levels in more effective ways, as well as the power of industrial production, matched by action of both public bodies and private entities, to lower the cost of housing. We will need everyone's active involvement to balance individual enterprise with collective action to make the built environment thrive, and to reactivate existing environments for long-term value.

A radical proposition

This book adds to the growing literature on the Open Building approach to the design of large and complex buildings. This approach springs from the book *Supports: An Alternative to Mass Housing* (Habraken, 1972), as noted in the Preface, first published in Dutch in 1961, in English in 1972 and 1999, and reissued in 2020 (Routledge Open Building Series – Revivals). *Supports* offered a fundamentally new insight: a way of seeing the built environment and of the role of professionals – and everyday citizens –in its cultivation. John Habraken had the ability to imagine a different world. That book and the ideas in it, written by an architect, are unabashedly political, because they deal with governance or decision-making, that is 'who controls what, and when' in the making of built environment. Habraken asserted that the housing shortage for ordinary citizens, which the 'mass housing' of the time sought to overcome, could not be accomplished until dwellers were reintroduced as active decision-makers. **He proposed not another design solution, but a redistribution of control.** This was radical at the time and was widely condemned as being impractical and too expensive, although no one would argue against the idea of people deciding on their own dwellings.

As an answer to 'who controls what, and when' in housing, Habraken suggested the distinction and separation of two design tasks. One was the design of **supports**, having to do with all that is shared among many inhabitants of a project. The other task was the design of independent dwellings in such **supports. This is not to be confused, as it so often is, with the 'initial construction phase' and the 'completion of a project,' a technical distinction in the building process that has no bearing on decision-making matters.**

Habraken proposed that the full power of industry could best be exploited in housing processes when independent dwellings could become a new market and could drive industry's productive power in a new, disintermediated way (Ryan, 2000). He argued that the uniformity and rigidity of 'mass housing' was not a technical problem but resulted from marginalizing users/inhabitants. It matters little if this marginalization occurred in government or private market housing processes producing large housing projects. The elimination of independent dwellings in large projects, he argued, thwarted the exercise of household economic decision-making power, thus inhibiting the full potential of industrial capacity to meet that individual demand. This ultimately suppresses competition and raises costs.

This formulation of an approach to large housing projects – two distinct design tasks and the full utilization of industrial capability serving individual demand for independent dwellings – constitutes what is usefully understood as an infrastructure model of built environment. In fact, a diagram of a highway viaduct and the vehicles that use it appeared in one of Habraken's early essays. This book aims to show that an infrastructure model extended into the very fabric of large residential buildings can be the basis for inspiring and varied architectural developments, not to mention driving down costs.

While the present book focuses on residential architecture, the proposition that an infrastructure model of built environment makes sense as a governance and planning structure encompasses all major project types – housing, educational and healthcare facilities, laboratories and places of work and commerce (Kendall, 2018).

The book also pays attention to barriers to wider implementation of the Open Building approach to residential architecture, barriers both technical, political, social and in the regulatory environment. Residential Open building faces very strong resistance for varied reasons, more than in other kinds of real property. Some of this story is told in each chapter related to its own country or region and is summarized in Chapter 14.

Infrastructure planning with a view to the long term occurs every day, cognizant that no one has a crystal ball to predict the future, and that in a polycentric political and economic milieu, no one can control everything, but that cooperation is needed, nonetheless. In fact, we should assiduously work to assure that continued aggregation of power by large 'powers' never overwhelms small-scale initiative and fine-grained patterns of control in infrastructure systems in general and residential development in particular. This would constitute a dictatorship of and rigidity in the built environment, which is clearly unacceptable and untenable, not to mention ultimately far too unwieldly and costly. Evidence of the continued power of small-scale initiative is discussed in several chapters, including evidence that the remodeling industry, in both the DIY (do-it-yourself) and professional sectors, often surpasses yearly expenditures compared with new construction.

Redistribution of control in housing remains radical today, in a worldwide professional culture that believes in its own superiority on all things having to do with design and building. It is time we recognized the hubris in this presumption and busied ourselves adjusting our attitudes and skills to meet the real challenges of everyday built environment.

A long view

There can really be no question that built environments that remain alive for a long time transform part-by-part, usually slowly, and not once but over and over. This reality is invisible to anyone invested only in a particular moment. It is a decidedly long view, something admittedly elusive in a culture with a short attention span and incentives to match, insensitive to the lessons of history and focused on singular or special building projects. Too often, we fall into the trap of thinking that once a project is 'done' under our watch, that it will and should never change – if it changes, we think we failed. But all we have to do is look again 5, 10, 20 or more years later, unless what has been built has already been demolished. Now, at least 50% of architect's commissions are for converting, adding to or otherwise adapting existing buildings.

Certainly, a functionalist ideology is at the center of the problem, emblematic in architectural education worldwide, when 'programs of requirements' are given to kick-off student designing, thus planting seeds that are reinforced by clients who, because of complex forces they have to work with, maintain short-term views of their, and societies', interests.

> Our growing culture of internal change behind retained façades is doing more, for it is beginning to herald the end of the single building as the basic unit of the urban environment, and the beginning of the rule of general-purpose serviced floor space. Take the nineteenth-century façades of the derelict banks in London's Old Broad Street, for example. That part of the City will still be present in a hundred years. But behind these same façades there will be no more wooden floors or high clerk's tables, nor even any party walls. Instead there will be glass partitions and levels of office floors with a central atrium, cruising over the old divisions between properties.
> (From Martin Pawley, "Polemic: The Age of the Serial Identity Building," in *World Architecture* 65 (April 1998), p. 26.)

Many argue that planning for incremental change costs more. But that is short-sighted and not fact based. What once was considered exorbitantly costly is now normal. Once upon a time, after many urban conflagrations, some argued that fireproof construction be required by law. This was fought as being too expensive and an invasion on the rights of personal property, but insurance companies insisted, and laws were changed. More expensive but fireproof buildings are now the norm. Similar arguments surrounded the imperative to build earthquake resistant buildings; this too is now an enforceable regulation, and public outcries are heard when poorly constructed buildings collapse. Currently there are disputes that net-zero buildings are too expensive. That too is fast becoming mandatory in many places for the reason that the earth's future depends on it. This book argues that planning buildings for incremental change – to be reprogrammable and continually adaptable – must become the next imperative across all building types. It is already conventional in office buildings, shopping centers and even airport concourses where Open Building is a pragmatic and cost-saving way of working. Several chapters in Part 2 show that governments are in fact moving to provide incentives and guidance in making long-life housing normal, but clearly not without difficulty. The sustainability and resilience of built environment as such is at stake.

Residential real estate as infrastructure

A significant literature exists in many fields – including economics, ecology, business and engineering – addressing infrastructure in the built environment (Ainger et al., 2014, Hayes et al., 2019). Road networks at different scales, railway lines and irrigation systems come to mind, as do potable water and sewer systems and communication networks. They all serve multiple users and frame physical conditions for inhabitation and use. These are large capital assets whose design and use stretch over large territories and continue in operation over long periods of time, and whose parts are incrementally upgraded while the whole system remains in operation. Control of their design, construction, use and adjustment is distributed and guided by both long-held conventions and explicit regulations. Governmental entities as well as private parties and, in recent years, public/private partnerships are involved in complex and changing patterns of initiative, financing and management of such infrastructure systems.

From the perspective of design, construction, management and use, infrastructure is organized on a hierarchy of 'levels' of intervention. These levels are related to each other in a particular way. That is, a 'higher level' constrains 'lower levels' which can change or be replaced without causing higher levels to shut down or be altered (Habraken, 1998, 2002). In a transportation system, a highway is such a 'higher level' offering capacity for (and constraining) 'lower level' physical systems – i.e. vehicles of various kinds. There are other relations between levels. For instance, highways are located in, cross and are funded by various political jurisdictions, with all the negotiations and evolving standards we are familiar with, but are then occupied by private vehicles, new versions of which are regularly introduced. Highway construction and automotive standards and regulations are therefore distinguished according to levels, as are the specialists designing, financing, building and maintaining them. It may take time, but the clarity of these 'levels,' their interfaces and disentanglement lend infrastructures longevity at the same time that they enable incremental renewal and innovation.

Increasingly, large buildings serving multiple and changing users show similar characteristics by offering space for customized user settlement. Shopping centers and office buildings, for instance, have behaved this way for more than a half-century. We also see residential buildings (Kendall, 2017; Kendall and Teicher, 2000), hospitals (Kendall et al., 2014), and educational facilities (Dale and Kendall, 2018) shifting toward this mode. For everyday users, such buildings are experienced as 'wholes' – the building as entirety or the spaces occupied as a unity – yet the processes by which they come to be and by which they transform follow a levels or infrastructure model.

Aside from important questions of architectural quality and 'the love-ability factor' (the enduring and deep resonance of a building or place with its local culture), the implications of an infrastructure model for regulation, financing, policy making and for innovation in the building industry are important.

Base buildings: a new infrastructure

In large buildings, we are seeing a tendency to separate a 'base building' from 'fit-out' and 'fit-out' from 'FF&E' (fixtures, finishes and equipment). This separation into three 'levels' is also known by other names, but whatever the words used, the distinctions are increasingly conventional – internationally – and are mirrored in the real property and building industries' practices, methods and incentive systems.

For example, commercial office buildings use these distinctions inter-nationally. Tenants lease space in buildings in which the layout for each is custom designed and individually adaptable over time, and in which furnishings and equipment are updated frequently. Private and govern-mental institutions owning (or leasing) large buildings likewise make these separations to accommodate ongoing relocation, reconfiguration and re-equipping of functional units. Large architecture, engineering, construc-tion and product manufacturing companies have distinct divisions to ser-vice the design and construction of base buildings. Other companies operate exclusively at the level of the fit-out; some design, produce and install propri-etary product-solutions (Kendall, 2013); still others concentrate on equipment and furnishings. This may have had its birth in the office market in the 1960s (Propst, 1968) or even earlier. Tenants own or lease fit-out partitioning and equipment, and if owned, can sell it to the next users, or may clear out the space when they leave, increasingly aided by parts prepared for disassembly or recycling, or sold into a secondary market as part of a circular economy (McDonough and Braungart, 2002), leaving spaces to be fitted out anew by the next occupant.

Another example is shopping malls, either free-standing or incorporated into mixed use developments, including airport concourses. Developers – public, private or public–private partnerships – build large structures giving attention to public or common spaces and functions (such as parking and public facilities, various amenity spaces, etc.) and shared utility systems.

Retail space is left empty. Overall architectural, technical, space and signage standards are established and documented in detailed tenant handbooks that themselves are periodically updated. This enables retail chains to lease space and bring in their own designers and fit-out services in a process that enables rapid turnaround of space for new occupancies, without disturbing the longer-lasting and shared infrastructure, public space or neighboring users. In recent years, with the advent of e-commerce, many such commercial real estate properties are undergoing substantial turnover and transformation, but always maintain an infrastructure model of design decision-making in doing so.

This way of constructing and using built space constitutes a substantial market, which, in turn, has given rise to increasingly profitable and well-organized supply chains serving the demands for tenant "fit-out" (Kendall, 2013). All decision-levels include finance companies, product manufacturers, design and engineering firms, construction companies, equipment suppliers and a host of others.

There is good reason to believe that innovation in services, products, finance and management has flowered because of this model, because it is easier to innovate on parts of a complex system when the "whole" system is disaggregated or "de-integrated" (but held together by smart agreements and interfaces), as in any well-functioning infrastructure.

Why has this trend emerged?

The emergence of this infrastructure or Open Building model for buildings lies in a convergence of three dominant characteristics of everyday contemporary built environment. First is the increasing size of buildings, sometimes serving thousands. Second is the dynamics of the workplace and the marketplace where use is increasingly varied and changing. Third is the availability of, and demand for, an increasing array of equipment and facilities serving the inhabitant user. In that convergence, large-scale real estate interventions make simultaneous or unified design of the base building and the user level impractical. User-level decisions can be and are effectively deferred and inevitably change over time in any case. This is what drives the very large and growing remodeling and renovation sector of the building industry, which now includes vertically integrated companies. Social trends towards individualization of use make functional specification increasingly personalized and changing, across income levels. Greater complexity and variety of places of work, healing, commerce, dwelling and education demand adaptation by way of architectural components with shorter use-life, such as partitioning, ceilings, bathroom and kitchen facilities, specialized equipment, and so on.

This separation of base building from fit-out, and fit-out from equipment – observable everywhere in the world while using diverse terminology – includes utility systems as well. Adaptable and accessible piping, air handling and wiring systems on the equipment and fit-out levels, for example, connect to their counterpart and more fixed ('higher level') main lines in the base building, many of which connect to the next higher-level infrastructure serving a district (an 'urban fabric' level), an entire city or region. Here again, control is usually distributed hierarchically, not unified; for practical – if not political – reasons it would be very unusual for one party to control all levels. In this process we see a significant contrast between what is to be done on the user level (the unit of occupancy) on the one hand and what is understood to be part of the traditional long-term investment and functionality of the building or urban fabric.

This is the reason for the emergence of the base building as a new kind of architectural infrastructure. The distinction here is best understood as happening between 'levels of intervention' as is always the case when we compare infrastructure with what it is serving. In the case of buildings, the comparison has multiple dimensions, including those in the following table:

Base building	Infill or fit-out
Longer-term use	Shorter-term use
Shared-service related design	User-related design
Heavy construction	Lightweight components
Long-term investment	Short-term investment
Equivalent to real estate	Equivalent to durable consumer goods
Long-term financing	Short-term financing

Residential real estate will benefit from adopting this model

Aside from the more conventional application of this distinction in the office and retail real estate sectors, separation of design tasks is gradually becoming evident internationally in residential multi-unit construction. The following chapters offer a small selection of such cases. Multi-unit or mixed-use buildings are most prevalent in urban and peri-urban contexts, and while not the dominant type of residential construction (single-family detached or attached types still dominate), they are an important part of the overall residential market across all income levels. Changes in demographics, building and energy-efficiency standards and household preferences are forcing the emergence of a shorter use-life fit-out level. From this perspective, the fit-out level (floor plans, kitchen and bathroom fixtures and equipment, furnishings and finishes) is usefully distinguished from the more permanent base building.

When this distinction is recognized, construction of residential base buildings can start before detailed fit-out design has been finalized, allowing a substantial shortening of the project critical path without incurring risk. In current practice, it is not exceptional that a two-to-five-year period elapses between initiating the planning process for a large residential or mixed-use project and full occupancy. The evidence is that market-driven requirements evolve during the design phase and are to some extent obsolete when the building is first occupied. If a base building is conceived of as a project by itself, construction can commence and unit sizes and floor plans can be deferred (if they are correctly disentangled), without disturbing the construction schedule of the base building.

In luxury residential projects it is not uncommon today that different firms are hired to design the base building and the fit-out of individual units of the building, as well as in mixed-use commercial or office projects. While commencing a complex project without having all of the details fixed might appear to increase risk, the opposite is evident: using infrastructure principles helps manage uncertainty, reduces risk to investors, users, and service providers, and saves money. What is available to wealthy residents should be available to everyone.

Some implications of adopting an infrastructure model of buildings

In the literature on real property and real estate, real property assets including healthcare and educational facilities are usually described as what I would call 'lumpy' assets (Geltner and de Neufville, 2017). They are seen as largely indivisible or unitary economic entities, to be juggled and financed as 'wholes.' The adoption of an infrastructure or 'levels of intervention' model of the building stock supports the actual granularity – or deeper hierarchy of 'wholes within wholes' – of built environments.

The use of levels, evincing territorial/hierarchical depth, can, but need not, result in a shift from unified control to divided control. A single party may still design all or several levels in this model, with the consequence of centralizing risk and expanding the management responsibility of the single party. For instance, one party can control the base building, fit-out and furnishings. Frank Lloyd Wright was famous for such unitary design control in his projects. But he was not alone: this was the ideal in Modernist ideology and still persists.

Figure 1.1
A levels or infrastructure model of the built environment (from Habraken, N.J. *The Structure of the Ordinary: Form and Control in the Built Environment*. MIT Press, 1998)

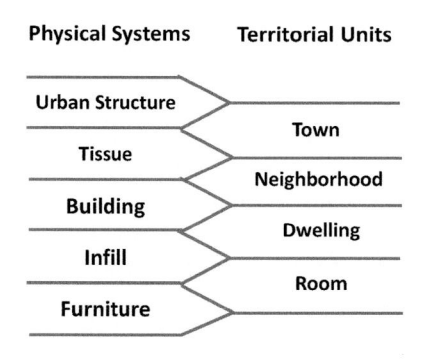

Physical Systems   Territorial Units

Urban Structure

           Town

Tissue

           Neighborhood

Building

           Dwelling

Infill

           Room

Furniture

But using levels also enables well-organized control distribution and the separation of design tasks, which is, in fact, the more pragmatic approach in large projects. Separating design tasks or control is evident when the design control of an urban tissue belongs to an urban design firm, while design of individual buildings is distributed to different design firms. Another example is evident when we see that part of a real property asset is owned by one party (or the collective of individual owners), and the many spaces served by it (or that occupy it) are each controlled by independent parties. This can happen either through distributed ownership as in condominiums, through leasing or 'granted rights' agreements, or in the case of individual departments of an organization such as an academic medical center, when each functional unit may serve as a decision unit or profit center.

Divided or distributed control – either through separated contracts or in unified contracts mandating clear separation and monitoring of design tasks – produces interfaces and the need for cooperation and clear agreements (Emmitt and Gorse, 2009). But tacit interfaces exist in any case, even in situations of 'integrated' or 'unified' control, between designers in a team, between architect and engineer, and between the design team, client and builder, or between client and designer where a handshake once sufficed. The presence of interfaces can result in boundary frictions even if such boundaries are conventional but are more likely to cause problems when they are not explicitly recognized, which can happen with new players, with unconventional practices, or in uncertain, litigious times. The addition of decision-makers distributes risk but also adds organizational complexity. Divided control also effects design processes, construction cost accounting and schedule, facility management, investor risk, financing, building regulations, and many other aspects of the behavior of the building stock.

None of this is new, but at the same time this ecology remains astonishingly obscure. An infrastructure model for buildings, however, when explicitly adopted and normalized, should encourage the development of industry-wide interface standards, product innovation and new methods and skills. These are slow to evolve in what are now excessively entangled, conflictual and overlapping relations among the players in the building sector and the parts controlled by each agent, an ecology that has grown historically but in an unplanned way that is now showing signs of stress (Kendall, 1990).

Independence of individual units of occupancy in an infrastructure model

When control is distributed and design tasks separated, situations of conflict can naturally arise as already noted. This is most evident when autonomous or independent action is sought at each level, as happens when an occupant of a multi-story building wants to rearrange their space and doing so causes disturbance of those occupying space beside or below them. These conflicts have greater clarity in multi-occupant buildings since 3D property demarcation came to be formally used (Paulson, 2007). But even when clear accounting of 3D property is in effect in legal documents, technical entanglement persists, particularly in respect to the utility systems that cut across territorial boundaries, despite the use, in some cases, of utility "easements" inside buildings (Easements, 2018).

There are familiar examples of solutions to these situations of conflict. For example, in electrical utility (and communication) systems, the introduction of standard power outlets and plugs has enabled equipment to be disentangled and achieve autonomy, and with it a new distribution of control. Liberating electrical equipment (refrigerators, computers, surgical equipment, etc.) from the electrical circuitry that powers them – by developing "plug-in" connections with standards governing interfaces and products – stimulated the development of many hardware solutions, which proliferated once standards associated with them were established (albeit not yet a single international standard). Developments in wireless and battery-powered technology may further mitigate such entanglement problems.

Far less advanced are drainage piping systems that carry both black and gray water from individual plumbing fixtures to the 'higher-level' parts of these drainage systems – the 'public' infrastructure elements (both in buildings and at the urban level) and waste treatment facilities. In multi-occupant buildings, several territorial boundaries are typically crossed between the individual fixture and the pipes in the street. Problems easily arise when drainage pipes serving a dwelling unit's fixture pass through another territory (i.e. in the ceiling of another unit of occupancy) before entering the 'common' piping in the base building. This technical/territorial entanglement, while conventional, is counterproductive, leads to decision-making rigidity during design, and legal/social conflict during maintenance and use (e.g. acoustical disturbances), waste of resources and cost increases.

But, despite the availability of an increasing array of technical solutions, the most important first step is recognition of the territorial hierarchy implicit in the infrastructure or Open Building model as shown in Figure 1.1. When that recognition informs decision-making and legal documents, technical solutions can be found to enable greater autonomy or independence at each level.

Legal implications of the infrastructure model

It is clear that there are legal implications of the infrastructure model in real estate transactions. These will be undoubtedly different from the legal implications of, for example, a highway system and the vehicles using it; or in a public utility such as electric power distribution. In the infrastructure model of buildings, as explained above, we understand the distinction of a permanent part (base building) from the more changeable part (the fit-out) and the even more mutable FF&E. But what is the legal status of a part of the whole (e.g. the fit-out or equipment) that can be altered, removed and replaced without disturbing the base building? In respect to the residential building stock and the building stock in general, these questions deserve much more careful scrutiny than is possible here and are certainly going to vary depending on the legal tradition in force. But some basic issues can be discussed briefly.

Real property vs. real estate

A passage quoted here explains the dilemma faced by decision-makers, designers and policy makers in setting up real estate developments for inevitable change.

> Real estate professionals, investors, and even homeowners need to be able to understand and differentiate between types of property that may be involved in a real estate transaction. The first big distinction ... is the difference between real property and real estate.
>
> You can think of *real estate* as land, the natural resources that are on or under it, and any man-made structure that is permanently attached to it ... any type of development on land that changes its original state and increases its economic value is considered an improvement. *Real property is a broader concept than real estate*. Real property is a concept that not only includes real estate but also a bundle of rights related to the real estate. In other words, real estate is a term that defines a set of physical things, while real property is a concept that includes those things plus the legal rights attached to it. Some common real property rights include ownership, possession, and use and enjoyment.
>
> *Real Property vs. Personal Property*
> If a piece of property (e.g. a chair, a car, etc.) is not real property (real estate is real property), it is personal property. In other words, personal property is all property that is not real property. If it's not land, and the natural resources on or under it or the man-made stuff *permanently affixed* to the land, the property is personal property. Sometimes movable personal property is called a 'chattel'.
>
> *When Personal Property Becomes Real Property*
> Sometimes personal property can become real property and real property can become personal property. Let's consider ... a house to see how a piece of personal property can become real property. Let's say that ... a new Jacuzzi bathtub has been installed in a bathroom. The tub has become a *fixture*, which is a piece of personal property that has been permanently attached to real property and becomes part of it. *We call this transformative process of personal property becoming part of real property annexation*. Fixtures may not be removed before closing a sale because they are considered an improvement to the real property (Real Estate vs. Real Property: Differences and Terms, 2016).

Now, let's take a moment to *distinguish between fixtures and trade fixtures*. In commercial real estate, trade fixtures are fixtures that are used in a trade or business. Unlike regular fixtures, it's generally lawful for a trade fixture to be removed, or severed, from the real property. For example, a bookstore's bookcases affixed to the walls of retail space rented in a mall is a trade fixture. The business may remove the bookcases after the lease is up, but it will have to compensate the landlord for any damage caused to the retail space by removing the trade fixtures.

(Squillante, 1987)

A number of questions arise from this 'lesson' that relate to the infrastructure model. How is it determined which parts are to be classified as 'real property,' as 'fixtures' and as 'trade fixtures?' How has this determination changed over time and why? Commercial real estate has a classification called "trade fixtures" but apparently residential properties do not, at least in the United States. This suggests that if a healthcare facility is classified as commercial, then the autonomy of the various levels in the infrastructure model can be legally justified. But the literature shows that definitions of what is a fixture and a trade fixture are confusing, as the citation below indicates.

To understand the law of fixtures, one must know its origins. The history of the law of fixtures involves several theories. English law follows the maxim "quicquid plantatur solo, solo credit" (whatever is fixed to the earth goes to the earth), whereas American law uses several different tests to determine whether an object should be classified as a fixture. These tests are vague and subjective and result in inconsistencies when applied to substantially similar fact patterns. It is therefore understandable that one commentator has observed that "to attempt to discover an all-inclusive definition for a 'fixture' or to posit tests for fixtures in all circumstances is not a profitable undertaking."

(Squillante, 1987)

This soliloquy shows that clarity in respect to the legal basis for implementing an infrastructure model in the building stock is sorely needed.

Technical implications of the infrastructure model
Improving technical interfaces between levels of intervention in building design is also critically important. This is one of the most important aspects of applying an infrastructure or Open Building model, requiring an exploration of new conceptual, management and technical solutions, and associated design skills.

Several examples illustrate this point. Highway design has, for example, successfully addressed the interface between levels. Roads are designed with lanes of a certain width and weight limits, designed to accommodate a specific range of vehicles, but not just any vehicle. Vehicles are designed accordingly; new versions of such vehicles adhere to these constraints; sometimes an entirely new class of vehicles requires that road designs follow new design criteria.

An example of a situation in which the infrastructure model has not been resolved in building design is in the sanitary waste systems in multi-unit buildings. In conventional practice, the sewage piping serving fixtures in a unit of occupancy on a given floor penetrates into the ceiling space of the occupancy below. The same thing can be observed in wood and steel framed construction and is therefore not based on a specific technology but on ignorance of territory and the importance of independent units of occupancy.

A solution to the placement of sanitary waste piping and cabling that meets the criteria of autonomy of individual units of occupancy is shown in Chapter 2, Figures 2.12B and 2.13D. In that case, the occupant is responsible for the installation of a thin raised floor under which horizontal utility lines are routed. Other 'above slab' floor systems solutions are possible and in use internationally and some are discussed in other chapters in this book. (Chapters 8, 12 and 14). New advances in separating gray and black water piping, and methods for allowing gray water drain lines to be 0-slope, help make this solution even more feasible. See Chapter 8 for an example from Japan, and Chapter 14 for an example from the Netherlands.

Cycles of retrofitting: evidence of a living building stock

Retrofitting of existing buildings now accounts for almost 45% of total architectural services in the United States and is projected to remain at this level for some time (Billhymer and Riz, 2015; Ma et al., 2012; Paradis, 2016). Investments in housing renovation per year often exceed investments in new construction. In the United States, of the investment in home improvements, 45% was for interior work in 2017 (American Housing Survey, 2018). Internationally, similar trends are evident. Recent governmental incentives in many countries to retrofit existing buildings are related to the necessity to reduce energy consumption and waste, but beyond that purpose, retrofitting existing buildings is valued to offset normal depreciation, increase property value, preserve historic neighborhoods, accommodate evolving functional requirements and meet societal or demographic trends.

For any given multi-occupancy residential (or mixed use) building, gut-retrofitting of individual occupancies is required – in general – at 20 to 30-year cycles, if not sooner. This means entirely cleaning out all interior, non-loadbearing walls, all equipment, cabinets, finishes, electrical and HVAC equipment. Upgrading of some major 'common' parts also occurs – façades, roofs and building-level mechanical, electrical and plumbing (MEP) systems for example – at similar cycles. In intervening years, incremental or piecemeal rehabilitation or repair is usually done to replace obsolete parts in order to sustain building performance and to meet changing building codes, living standards and demographic shifts. These incremental repairs are often made in two domains of responsibility and investment: the 'common' parts serving all occupancies, and parts in 'individual' occupancies. However, building industry statistics do not reflect this accounting, but instead reflect the essentially technical view of buildings as made up of many parts associated with the building trades, not reflecting the different life cycles or the separation of a base building and a fit-out level of intervention.

There is strong evidence that gut-retrofit and incremental repair will both be optimized when a clearer separation is made between the 'common' parts (aka 'base building') and the 'individual' parts (aka 'fit-out'), and when this distinction is reflected in government statistics. Any entanglement or overlap of these two domains of work causes friction and raises costs and may necessitate the entire building to be vacated and upgraded in its entirety, with significant loss of income to the owner, or force premature demolition.

Summary

In developing multi-unit residential and mixed-use projects, there are always reasonable expectations to assure short-term return on investment (ROI). Public agencies often face pressures not unlike private enterprise or public/private partnerships in this respect although their time horizons should ostensibly be much longer. We should not try to convince developers to ignore short-term ROI. That said, it can reasonably be argued that long-term ROI must become an important criterion for evaluation in the built environment across all project types, both public and private, as we move toward a sustainable circular economy. But it is also clear that this is a very difficult goal to achieve, because of the high degree of uncertainty in the mid- to long-term future (De Neufville and Scholtes, 2011).

This produces a dilemma. A central tenet of residential project planning for at least a half-century, at least as advocated in the participatory planning literature, has been the proposition that user participation is vitally important to a built environment in which citizens have real and enduring interest. Engaging user requirements in front-end decision-making in all building types is stressful, however, even when the client demands it. This difficulty arises because users come and go, change their minds, make choices based on different conceptual schema, disagree on priorities, and there are usually simply too many participants. And when they are not financially vested, their voices are easy to ignore.

Many methods of eliciting consensus among users and their requirements have nevertheless been put to use in programming building projects, led by marketing professionals who conduct focus groups, and otherwise classify the buying or renting public into specific 'user cohorts.' In an effort to reduce uncertainty, the 'end user' is one of the first to be excluded or generalized into 'user classes.' As a result, attempts at early specification of user-level requirements has become the Achilles heel in planning large projects – floor plans drive larger decisions, but should not. Furthermore, data shows that buildings begin to change as soon as they are occupied, often driven by changing marketing requirements, if not changing regulations and performance requirements. So even if it were possible to base initial design decisions on user requirements, they are short-lived. This is why resistance to listening to users remains strong, unless they are co-investors; but even then, the next users' preferences are not, and cannot be, heard, under current practices.

In large residential projects, investors and developers need to acquire land, seek financing, deal with local regulations and site/climate constraints and construction in all kinds of weather and labor conditions. These processes will likely become more complex and more constrained by regulations and face continued changes in technology and skilled labor shortages.

Given the already arduous path to developing sites and constructing buildings, investors wanting to keep their options open and yet build for the long haul can look to adoption of an Open Building model as one helpful tool. Advanced off-site production of various kinds – what may be called prefabrication, kitting or product bundling – can offer new levels of quality and cost control, and just-in-time customized solutions for what goes into buildings to make space habitable – across project types. But it is important to adopt these techniques according to the levels model, which, today, is generally not the case. Instead, these off-site production techniques still serve a unibody model of development.

This is where an infrastructure or Open Building model can help. Using levels of intervention to guide separation of design tasks and to foster collaboration is the future. The opportunities for the infrastructure model to inspire a new architecture and urbanism in which evolving functions find their place are of the most profound significance and await further study, elaboration and discussion. The opportunities in an infrastructure model are also auspicious for those who initiate projects – both private and public – and for those that regulate, finance, build and manage them. These too await more systematic study and evaluation.

Are our professional skills up to the task?

How are our professional skills adjusting to this dynamic way of seeing architecture and urban design? How do we 'hand-off' a project to other architects who follow us in cultivating a particular place? Will 'big data' help as we employ simulation tools to support multidisciplined planning for change? Are we fully exploiting the power of mass-production in the service of buildings planned for change and user control of everything 'behind their front door?' How will increased computational power assist coordination among diverse and changing casts of players? Can sophisticated supply chains and logistics be organized to serve the independent dwelling, supported by new data-management tools? Is our historically highly disaggregated (fragmented) building industry able to become more efficient, or do entirely new players need to enter the game to change the rules? What can history teach us about planning for change? What public policies, financing and regulatory instruments are needed? Why are governance structures – for example those instantiated in so-called 'common interest communities' – blocking capacity for change? Can we, in other words, organize our professional practices to design reprogrammable buildings of the highest quality that invite variation and change in a way that is both efficient and economically attractive?

My hope is that readers will come away sharing the recognition that we are in a hopeful transition phase. The 'we' I refer to includes the design professions, certainly, but also our clients, their financiers, and those operating in the construction, regulatory/policy-making sector, as well as new generations of students in design schools. This transition is not smooth but is, I believe, inevitable. The rough sailing should not be particularly surprising. We face uncertain times. Decision-making is increasingly dispersed and unfolds over time yet faces ever larger and powerful players with hegemonic tendencies and short-term perspectives (both public and private).

Distribution of resources is clearly out of balance and inequitable. Governance structures are slow to adjust to new realities, which can be a useful restraint on often chaotic change, but also confound needed redistribution of resources, control and initiative. Building users often prefer personalized solutions and experiences at various 'price points,' (witness the DIY and remodeling industry's magnitude) but are sadly pacified and convinced by a building industry that reduction of inhabitant freedom and responsibility assures sustained property value. And we have at our disposal a daunting technical repertoire and technical mastery that have expanded with incredible rapidity in the last 50 years, making choice more complex and agreement more arduous.

This is a confusing and contentious – and often litigious – time in the building and real property industries in most countries. Residential multifamily projects such as condominiums, with divided control as their essence, are particularly prone to legal disputes because, in part, individual dwellings are insufficiently independent – a problem for which architects are at least partly to blame. At least in the United States, architects hesitate to work on such projects out of fear of ongoing legal disputes that translate into very high malpractice insurance premiums. New players enter the development game, frequently displaying the hubris of believing that they can remake the industry with little or no deep understanding of what happened before or without sending out thought probes into the future or around the world – witness the curious renewed love affair with 'prefabrication' and 'modular construction' as if they were something new. The sense is a breathless rush of invention and innovation as a key to success. While aversion to risk and new approaches are understandably high, at the same time pressures are strong to find ways of building more at lower cost, and at higher quality, and managing divided control of complex residential property assets over time.

Despite all of the attempts at innovation over recent decades, housing costs are not decreasing. Housing affordability, no matter how defined, is a crisis we can't ignore. No other industry could survive if its products did not both improve in quality and decrease in cost.

International and national advocacy of Open Building implementation

A number of formal organizations were launched in the Netherlands starting in the 1980s to advocate for Open Building implementation. These included the Open Building Foundation (SOB) and OBOM (Open Building Development Model), a research group at the Technical University Delft. SAR-International Network was launched to lend structure to the informal, worldwide network of those who adhered to the SAR ideas. They are chronicled in *Housing for the Millions: John Habraken and the SAR (1960–2000)* (Boosma et al., 2000). But after a period of time, these organizations receded from an active role and were disbanded.

In the belief that these ideas needed a more formal international platform, an Open Building Implementation network was formed in 1996, under the umbrella of CIB. CIB stands for the International Council for Research and Innovation in Building and Construction (https://cibworld.org). At the time of this writing, this Open Building network (CIBW104) has more than 300 people in its contact list from more than 20 countries, and has accumulated a substantial record of published, academic peer reviewed papers, presented at yearly conferences in many countries around the world since its founding.

In 2017, the Council on Open Building (www.councilonopenbuilding.org) was launched in the U.S., with the goal of expanding the sustainability agenda to include the principle that buildings and neighborhoods must be planned for incremental change, based on the principles of separating design tasks and cooperation among designers. In 2019, the Council held an international conference – Open Building for Resilient Cities – with peer reviewed papers from many countries and moderated panels with many U.S. and international practitioners in housing, healthcare and educational facilities design. The Council is actively organizing professional conferences, seminars, interdisciplinary design exercises and case studies demonstrating that the principle of separation of design tasks is already conventional in some project types (e.g. urban design, commercial and retail real estate) but needs to become a general practice in all large, complex real property investments. As of this writing, a number of large architectural and engineering firms in the U.S. and some prominent clients are engaged in the Council. A series of design workshops and roundtable meetings are ongoing in 2021, organized in four 'strands': urban design, healthcare, educational facilities and housing.

At about the same time (2019), a group of architects in the Netherlands organized themselves into a cooperative network (www.openbuilding.co) that is active in organizing research, teaching and other promotion activities around the theme of Open Cities, Open Architecture and Open Systems. The members of this group are actively pursuing these principles in practice, primarily in housing, and sometimes combining the roles of architect and developer. Many of the recent projects of members of this group are reported on in Chapter 2.

In China, a large but still informal network of architects, government agencies, and researchers continue to write, produce design guidelines, and build projects in the long search for 100-year housing, planned for incremental change. This work started in the 1980s with early contacts with John Habraken, and continues up to the present, as reported on in Chapters 9, 13 and 14.

Japan, another incubator of the Open Building approach (called S/I or skeleton/infill housing there), experienced a very large and deep commitment of government agencies, university researchers and private corporations in experimental residential projects between the late 1970s and 2000. Many hundreds of projects are on record, implemented by various governmental agencies and private developers. Some of this is the subject of Chapters 8, 12 and 14, but this commitment has now somewhat waned.

A network of researchers in what is called the global South continues its work to find breakthroughs and to collaborate with government agencies and practitioners in working toward Open Building implementation under circumstances very much different from the initiatives in the so-called developed world. This story is told in part in Chapter 6.

The chapters in this book represent, therefore, only a small selection of developments toward residential Open Building. As explained throughout the book, residential Open Building remains the most complex, controversial and difficult building type for Open Building implementation.

Authors in this book share the observation with many others that contemporary housing as it exists today is the result of an outdated professional culture that has little incentive to change its ways. They all know that it is always a risk for individuals, companies, regulators and financial bodies to change their way of working and there is no reason to do so as long as they are making money. The problem is not technical but social and political, and of professions unwilling to give up power developed and organized in a particular way over a long period.

Without users being able to control their own fully independent dwellings in large projects, there is a different culture; innovation in building products and processes is retarded, reaching a circular economy is more difficult, and large building companies will be less likely to figure out less expensive ways of working.

References

Ainger, C. and Fenner, R. (2014). *Sustainable Infrastructure: Principles into Practice* (Delivering Sustainable Infrastructure Series). London: ICE Publishing (Thomas Telford. Ltd).

American Housing Survey (2018). Available at: www.census.gov/programs-surveys/ahs.html

Billhymer, L. and Riz, D. (2015). Retrofits and the first benefits of integrated design. *Design Intelligence*, September 28.

Boosma, K., van Hoogstrarwn, D. and Vos, M. (2000). *Housing for the Millions: John Habraken and the SAR (1960–2000)*. Rotterdam: NAI Publishers, pp. 78–80.

Dale, J. and Kendall, S. (2018). An Open Building approach to school design. AIA Knowledge Community Committee on Architecture for Education. *Learning by Design*, pp. 6–8. Available at: www.learningbydesign.biz

De Neufville, R. and Scholtes, S. (2011). *Flexibility in Engineering Design*. Cambridge, MA: MIT Press.

Easements (2018). Available at: https://real-estate-law.freeadvice.com/real-estate-law/zoning/easement.htm (sourced April 28, 2018).

Emmitt, S. and Gorse, C. (2009). *Construction Communication*. New York: John Wiley & Sons.

Geltner, D. and de Neufville, R. (2017). *Flexibility and Real Estate Valuation under Uncertainty: A Practical Guide for Developers*. London: Wiley Blackwell.

Habraken, N. J. (1972). *Supports: An Alternative to Mass Housing*. New York: Praeger (first English edition).

Habraken, N. J. (1998). *The Structure of the Ordinary: Form and Control in the Built Environment*. Cambridge, MA: MIT Press.

Habraken, N. J. (2002). The uses of levels. *Openhouse International*, 7(2), pp. 9–20.

Hayes, S., Desha, C., Burke, M., Gibbs, M. and Chester, M. (2019). Leveraging socio-ecological resilience theory to build climate resilience in transport infrastructure. *Transport Reviews*, 39(5), pp. 677–699.

Kendall, S. H. (1990). Control of Parts: Parts Making in the Building Industry. Unpublished PhD Dissertation, MIT Department of Architecture.

Kendall, S. (2013). The next wave in housing personalization: Customized residential fit-out. In B. Piroozfar and F. Piller, eds., *Mass Customization and Personalization in Architecture and Construction*. London: Taylor & Francis, pp. 42–52.

Kendall, S. (2017). Four decades of open building implementation. *Loose-Fit Architecture: Designing Buildings for Change* (guest edited by A. Lifschutz), 87, pp. 54–61.

Kendall, S. (2018). *Healthcare Architecture as Infrastructure: Open Building in Practice*. London and New York: Routledge. Additional resources are available at www.thematicdesign.org and in the Routledge OPEN BUILDING Series.

Kendall, S. and Teicher, J. (2000). *Residential Open Building*. London: Spon.

Kendall, S., Kurmel, T., Dekker, K. and Becker, J. (2014). Healthcare facilities designed for flexibility the challenge of culture change in a large U.S. public agency. *Proceedings, International Union of Architects Congress, Durban, South Africa*.

LeCorbusier and Jeanneret, P. *Algiers Plan* (1946). *Oeuvre Complete, 1929–1934*, 4th ed. Zurich: Editions d'Architecture.

Levy, M. and Panchyk, R. (2000). *Engineering the City: How Infrastructure Works, Projects and Principles for Beginners*. Chicago, IL: Chicago Review Press.

Ma, Z., Cooper, P., Daly, D. and Ledo, L. (2012). Existing building retrofits: Methodology and state-of-the-art. *Energy and Buildings*, 55(12), pp. 889–902.

Matsumura, S. (2019). *Open Architecture for the People*. London: Routledge, p. 31.

McDonough, W. and Braungart, M. (2002). *Cradle to Cradle: Remaking the Way We Make Things*. New York: North Point Press.

Paradis, R. (2016). *Retrofitting Existing Buildings to Improve Sustainability and Energy Performance*. Washington D.C.: National Institute of Building Sciences.

Parman, J. and Bender, R. (1976) The townland system: An American framework. *Industrialization Forum*, 7(1), pp. 27–32.

Paulson, J. (2007). 3D Property Rights: An Analysis of Key Factors Based on International Experience. Doctoral Thesis in Real Estate Planning Real Estate Planning and Land Law, Department of Real Estate and Construction Management, School of Architecture and the Built Environment, Royal Institute of Technology (KTH), Stockholm, Sweden.

Propst, R. (1968). *The Office: A Facility Based on Change*. Elmhurst, IL: The Business Press.

Real Estate vs. Real Property: Differences & Terms. (2016). Study.com, 21 September. Available at: study.com/academy/lesson/real-estate-vs-real-property-differences-terms.html

Ryan, C. (2000). How disintermediation is changing the rules of marketing, sales and distribution. *Interactive Marketing*, 1, pp. 368–374.

Squillante, A. M. (1987). The Law of Fixtures: Common Law and the Uniform Commercial Code-Part I: Common Law of Fixtures. New York: *Hofstra Law Review*, 15(2), Article 2.

Chapter 2

Open Building's recent developments in the Netherlands

Caroline Kruit

A new generation of architects and engineers adopt and adapt the rules of play

At the start of the 21st century, the need for affordable housing in the Netherlands was as urgent as it was 20 years later, as this chapter was being written. Not only did the housing stock not match the demand; post-WWII developments were degrading and deteriorating areas, and the rigid design of the buildings made them hard to adapt to new demands and regulations. In part to address these issues, new areas were designated by many municipal governments for urban development: former industrial areas, older neighborhoods and plots just outside city limits. It is in these new development areas that some of the work reported on here is being undertaken.

Although the Netherlands is the cradle of *Supports: An Alternative to Mass Housing* (Habraken, 1972), which developed into what has become known as the Open Building approach, the current generation of architects has had little to no formal education on this way of working. Therefore, it is all the more surprising that over the past two decades a number of architects and developers have found the principles of Open Building to be key instruments for the development and design of residential projects. During the major economic crisis at the end of the first decade of the 21st century and in the midst of a climate crisis, young architects have initiated, developed and designed residential buildings that are setting an example and represent a promise for a future long lasting and sustainable building stock attuned to evolving user requirements.

In 2019 14 architects and engineers founded OpenBuilding.co, a platform for sharing research and practical know-how. Initiated by Marc Koehler, principal of Marc Koehler Architects and Superlofts.co, this collective not only intends to share knowledge about Open Building with their peers, but also to put the topic on the agenda of policy makers, investors and project developers.

This chapter reports on key developments of Open Building in the past 20 years and cites several recent built projects by the members of the

DOI: 10.4324/9781003018339-3

OpenBuilding.co network. The chapter concludes with observations on forces within the Dutch society, and the regulatory, financing sectors and building industry that continue to block more widespread implementation of residential Open Building.

Building on new ground(s): Multifunk on IJburg by ANA Architects

- Project location: IJburglaan, Steigereiland IJburg, Amsterdam, the Netherlands.
- Chronological information: start of project 2001; start of construction 2003; completion 2004.
- Project design team: ANA Architects, Jannie Vinke, Marcel van der Lubbe, Gert Anninga, Jolein Feteris, Franziska Brockdorf, Johan Rooijackers, Marie-Louise Mejlholm, Nicole Finke, Christina Eickmeier, Floortje Keijzer; Technical design: Gert Anninga, Jolein Feteris, André van der Kruk.
- Number of dwelling units: 88; commercial space: 3500 m^2; daycare for kids: 400 m^2.
- Ratio of parking spaces per dwelling unit: 106 parking spaces incl. commercial parking spaces.
- Project site and building area: site area: project site: ca. 7200 m^2, building area (footprint): 4100 m^2, total m^2 in building: 20,000 m^2 (including parking).
- Project client: Lingotto Vastgoed (project developer)/Ymere (housing corporation).
- New construction.
- Structure type: base building: concrete structure with longitudinal bearing walls and a load-bearing façade, generous floor height, floors and walls with so-called fontanelle cutouts in floors (easily filled or closed) and walls for vertical and horizontal connections including staircases for multi-level apartments or offices, and vertical mechanical shafts at frequent intervals along the central corridor for connection points for infill installations. (Note: some of these floor openings have been filled with concrete since completion, impairing the flexibility of the building.)
- Installation utilities: energy: city heating, installation connected to central shafts, distribution in top-floor layer of units; water/sewer/sanitary: separated sewer systems (rainwater separated from sewer); heating: floor heating, installation connected to central shafts, distribution in top floor of units.
- Infill system/approach: the dwellings were delivered including layout. Housing corporation Ymere supplied partition walls constructed in metal studs: 300 mm cavity walls 300 mm (140/20/140). The walls have double sheeting inside the dwellings (gypsum sheet on top of a fermacel sheet) to allow the residents to put paintings/artwork on the wall.

In Amsterdam the development and realization of IJburg – a masterplan comprised of new, man-made islands in the Lake IJsselmeer immediately to the north-east of the city – finally started in 1999 after decades of planning. The masterplan for IJburg showed a wide variety of housing typologies and functions. Citizen participation, not only for the buildings, but also for the public spaces, was brought to bear. Multifunk, one of the first projects on IJburg, was developed by Lingotto and the housing corporation Ymere (see Figure 2.1). The idea was a multi-use building, allowing different configurations in the floorplan and a variety of functions. ANA Architects were responsible for the design. Completed in 2004, the majority of dwellings in Multifunk were two-bedroom apartments – the common typology for young families, the main target group for IJburg. Retail spaces occupied the ground floor. ANA Architects made numerous drawings for different typologies and lay-outs, to show the capacity of the building – for its residents (to adapt to new demographics, for example) and the housing corporation (should the target market, function and/or economic situation change). In 2014, at its ten-year anniversary, ANA Architects made a thorough evaluation of the process, design and use of Multifunk (Vinke and van der Lubbe, 2014). The most important conclusion was that the offered capacity had not been used so far – not by the residents nor by the housing corporation – which is remarkable as a major economic crisis unfolded during the first ten years of its existence. The openings in the floors, originally closed with removable construction elements, were closed with concrete, as they were considered acoustic 'leaks' by a building manager who wasn't aware of the flexible, 'open' concept of the building.

Figure 2.1
The Multifunk project in its context on the IJburg (Photography by Luuk Kramer)

Redeveloping harbor areas: Schiecentrale in Rotterdam by Mei Architects & Planners

- Project location: Schiehavenkade, Rotterdam, the Netherlands.
- Chronological information: start of project 2002; start of construction 2006; completion 2008.
- Project design team: MEI Architects and Planners: Robert Winkel, Robert Platje, Hennie Dankers, Eelco Dekker, Frank Aarssen, Jack Bouwer, Erwin Verhoeve, Maurice de Ruijter, Bart Spee, Jack Hoogenboom, Mirjam van Dam, Joanne Wienk, Leah Wiederholdt, Meike Stoetzer, Richel Lubbers, Michel Zaan, Jane Nagtegaal.
- Number of dwelling units: the total of 55,000 m² floor space allows for 7000 m² office space and 156 living–work units (with flexible layout) and 20 ground-based dwellings over 3.5 floors. Other amenities within the building volume: a supermarket (2000 m²), a gym (600 m²), 400 parking spaces and a semi-public roof space of 3000 m². The building also includes a sun terrace, playground and day-care facilities.
- Ratio of parking spaces per dwelling unit: 400 parking spaces (ratio 2.56), parking garage is a public garage.
- Project site and building area: project site = building area = 5775 m²; total m² in building: 55,000 m².
- Project client: Ontwikkelingsbedrijf Rotterdam, Proper Stok, PWS.
- New build adjacent to (towards) a monument.
- Structure type base building: concrete core, concrete portals and columns. Façade: aluminium and glass, lightweight concrete cladding, composite storage boxes, metal mesh railings for balconies and façade elements.
- Installation utilities: compact solid core per unit, with electricity/heating, toilet, shaft and connections for kitchen and bathroom, vertical and horizontal distribution within unit. District heating (city heating), underfloor heating & cooling, cold and heat storage.
- Infill system/approach: metal stud partition walls. Loft layout individually by users/inhabitants.

Between 2000 and 2004, the Dutch government allocated a significant budget to encourage product innovation and project development. One of the grants offered by the ministerial departments of Economic Affairs and VROM (Volkshuisvesting, Ruimtelijke Ordening en Milieu – Housing, Spatial Planning and the Environment) for the building industry was the so-called IFD grant. IFD stands for Industrial, Flexible and Demountable (remountable) methods for building. In effect, it encouraged project teams to adopt building methods very similar to the principles of Open Building: it promoted industrialization, capacious base building structures and reconfigurable infill. The project Schiecentrale in Rotterdam received an IFD grant in 2004. Developed by Proper Stok developers and the housing association PWS, the building was designed by Mei Architects and Planners. Schiecentrale, a large development on the shores of the Maas river with over 80 residents – working and/or living side by side – was completed in 2008 (see Figure 2.2).

The base building consists of a concrete structure with wide columns (vertical slabs) and large span floor slabs. Separation walls between the dwellings and/or offices are made with double metal stud walls in between the vertical slabs. Most of the infill walls are built with metal stud walls as well. The support or base building installations are vertically distributed through shafts in the compact core with the stairs and elevators, and horizontally via the ceilings in the communal hallways. Connected at regularly placed meter boxes, the infill or fit-out installations are distributed for each legal unit (or: apartment right) via the raised floors and – in some cases – a secondary wall layer. The building is connected to the city heating system, with low temperature floor heating distributed in the anhydrite (self-leveling) top floor screed per bay.

The municipality allowed a double function for the use of the upper floors: living or working. In the 12 years since its opening, there have been many changes in residents and uses, but the combination of work and living is still working. Architect and developer Robert Winkel, principal of Mei Architects and Planners, has lived and worked in Schiecentrale from the very start. He himself has demonstrated the capacity of the concept. He started as the resident of a modest apartment, incorporating his office into his living quarters after a few years. Recently he changed and extended the apartment to a family home, moving his offices to another floor in the same building (see Figure 2.2 A).

Recently, MEI Architects and Planners have completed a number of other projects that exemplify both Open Building principles and adaptive reuse. An exhibition at OMI (Office of Metropolitan Information) in Rotterdam highlighted their work recently:

Figure 2.2
Schiecentrale in its context (Photography by Ossip van Duivenbode and Ronald Tillemans)

29

Figure 2.2A
**Schiecentrale:
capacity for
variety of
uses and
layouts
(Photography
by van
Duivenbode
and
Tillemans)**

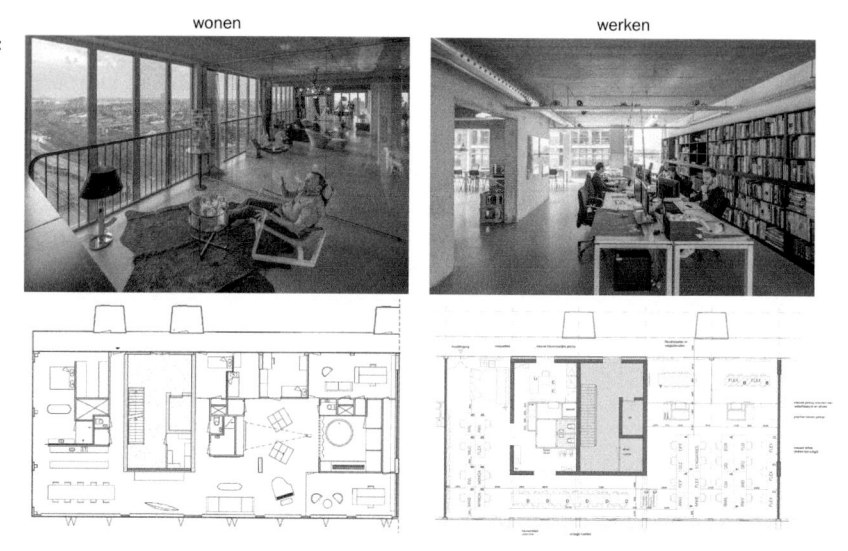

wonen   werken

At OMI, Mei presented their Rotterdam projects through models, drawings and photos. The exhibition showcased their work and methods, a special combination of renovation, conversion and renewal. Whether it is about the transformation of the pre-war Fenix warehouse or Jobsveem, restoration of De Lijnbaan or the new buildings at the historic location of the Schiecentrale; Mei knows how to give a unique interpretation to different periods of the city.

Solids in Amsterdam

- Project location: IJburglaan, IJburg, Amsterdam, the Netherlands.
- Chronological information: start planning phase 2005; start of construction 2008; completion 2011.
- Project design team: Baumschlager Eberle Architekten and Inbo Architecten (Kees Brons, Piet van der Ploeg, Tako Postma).
- Number of dwelling units: standard mid-income rental apartments, current number unknown; top floors are currently in use as a hotel (since 2018, 67 rooms) with retail in plinth/ground level.
- Ratio of parking spaces per dwelling unit: unknown.
- Project site and building area: 7287 m² useable space for different functions.
- Project client: Kristal Projectontwikkeling (project developer), Stadgenoot (housing corporation).
- New construction.
- Structure type: concrete core, loadbearing columns in façade, concrete floors.

- Installation utilities: horizontal piping installation and piping layout per dwelling is installed in a raised floor, eight shafts for vertical distribution per floor clustered around elevator/stair core.
- Infill system/approach: no standard infill provided; clear separation of infill and support; current infill materials unknown.

In the first decade of the 20th century Frank Bijdendijk, the director of the housing corporation Stadgenoot in Amsterdam, developed an experimental concept for multifunctional buildings for the rental market, following Open Building principles. Two projects were realized. The base building or infrastructure of these projects, which he called Solids, was designed for an economic and technical lifespan of at least 200 years. Stadgenoot, as the owner of the infrastructure, introduced a new business model to rent out the empty spaces in units, offering the floor space to the highest bidders during internet-based auctions. The tenants were to design and build the infill or fit-out of their spaces. Working and living were permitted, with a wide range of layouts and apartment sizes possible. The buildings had generous dimensions, open floor plans, and a classic, high-quality, load-bearing façade. In close cooperation with the municipality, the regulations for installations, interior fit-out and use were loosened. The tenants had to comply with the rules either for utility buildings or dwellings, using raised floors of their own choosing to accommodate the different installations for each function. As the rules for dwellings are looser in some regards (as is the amount of installations needed) the floors in tenant spaces were 15 cm (6 inches) lower than the floors in the communal areas for horizontal distribution of installations to points of use in each dwelling.

Initially, banks agreed to give mortgages to these new fit-out owners, the costs of which would be tax deductible like they are for owners of private detached homes. Implemented on a national scale in the Netherlands, where the majority of households rent their homes, the proposed change in tax deductibility could have been an incentive for unit-by-unit renewal and renovation for a large part of the existing multifamily housing stock. However, Dutch tax law was overhauled at about the time these projects were under construction, and the deduction eliminated, setting a financial barrier for the tenants and undermining the concept of the solids (Habraken, 2003).

Solid 1 on IJburg (see Figures 2.3, 2.3A, 2.3B), designed in 2004 by Baumschlager Eberle Architekten and completed in 2011, did not attract enough tenants to maintain a healthy operating model, due in part to the change of the tax law. The other Solid that was realized, Solid 11 in Amsterdam-West by Tony Fretton and Inbo Architects, attracted a more promising group of residents when it was rented out after completion in 2011 (see Figure 2.3C). Like in most European countries, the Dutch real estate market crashed in 2008, putting the concept of the Solids under pressure from the very start. Both Solid projects were partly rented out to hotel chains, with the tourists causing nuisance to the other tenants and scaring off potential residents.

Figure 2.3
**Solid 1 IJburg
in its context
on the Ijburg
(Photography
by Inbo)**

Following a report by Inbo Architects in 2013 (Wallagh, 2013), the housing corporation decided to cancel the Solids experiment, reportedly having invested more than double the budget of a regular project into each building until that moment. Part of the IJburg Solid was filled in and rented out as standard middle-income apartments. The business model and idea of Solids – investment in a long-term base building of high quality, with spaces leased and infill owned with tax-deductible mortgages – was eagerly observed in the building industry. From the start of the development, each step towards realization and – later – exploitation of the Solids was reported. Needless to say, the difficulties of the Solids business-model experiment (especially when the tax law was changed undermining the financial model) did not pass unnoticed by the architects, investors–developers and policymakers working on similar projects and ideas, that were met with more skepticism (or even resistance) than before.

New initiatives building on the 40-year legacy of Dutch Open Building

To accommodate freedom for future residents to create their own living environment in large buildings, architects developed buildings that allowed different dwelling typologies within the same base building or support. But for the current generation of Dutch architects the term Open Building was fairly new – it had not been part of their education, or only as part of the national architectural history. Open Building was a child of the 1960s, steadily

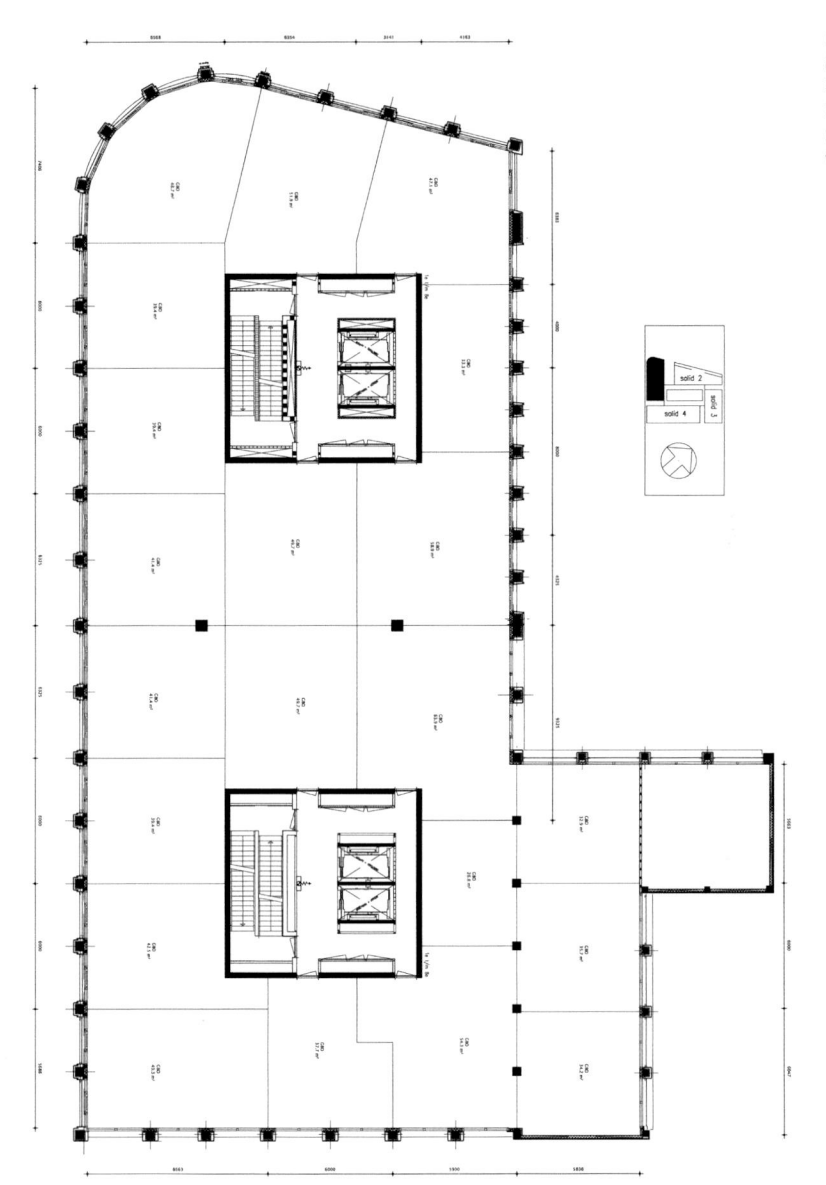

Figure 2.3A
**Solid 1
IJburg base
building plan
(Courtesy of
the Architect)**

growing until the 1980s with a few notable projects such as the Molenvliet, Lunetten and Pelgromhof projects by architect Frans van der Werf, but it largely receded from the spotlight after that. With more popular and urgent reading material – looking for arguments and innovations to answer the questions and ambitions on the topic of sustainable building – the writing of Stewart Brand and the principles of circularity as published by the Ellen

Figure 2.3B
**Solid 1
IJburg
empty
tenant
space ready
for infill
(Photo credit
Stephen
Kendall)**

Figure 2.3C
**Solid 11 in
its context in
Amsterdam
West (Photo
credit
Stephen
Kendall)**

McArthur Foundation (Ellen McArthur Foundation, 2018) were the starting points of many research and design projects. The studies led to building principles that show superficial similarities with the principles John Habraken describes in *Supports* (Habraken, 1972) and subsequently developed as a set of design methods by the SAR and supported by further technical studies at OBOM at TU Delft in the 1980s (Habraken, 2003) under the direction of Professor Age van Randen: strong, sturdy and capacious buildings that literally offer space to independent dwelling units and their living requirements, co-created with residents and fitted out with infill systems supplied by the building industry. Many early developments in Houthavens and most of the residential buildings in Buiksloterham discussed below fit this description. It was only after completion of the buildings and talking about it among peers, that the architects realized that what they were doing already had a name and precedents: Open Bouwen (Open Building).

New development areas opened up in Amsterdam

Just before the housing prices started falling at the end of 2008, the Amsterdam municipality had assigned two new areas for residential development: Houthavens, a former harbor area in the western part of the city and Buiksloterham, an industrial district in Amsterdam North on the other side of the river IJ from Amsterdam city center. As with IJburg and the harbor areas in the east, the municipality aimed for diverse and affordable dwellings, a high density of residential buildings and high-quality architecture. In the light of another crisis – the climate crisis – the masterplans and tender requirements also included a significant ambition for sustainable building and energy efficiency. While most commercial developers were suffering from the economic recession, new forms of commissioning were conceived. With so-called CPC groups (Collective Private Commissioning – CPO in Dutch) architects tried to claim the plots in Houthavens and – later – in Buiksloterham. In a CPC group, future residents organize themselves in a foundation or association to be able to realize non-profit joint homes through new construction or refurbishment of existing buildings. In the case of De Hoofden, the initiative for the formation of CPC groups was taken by the architects.

Building with and for groups of private clients: CPC De Hoofden

- Project location: Plot 1&2, Haparandaweg, Houthavens, Amsterdam, the Netherlands.
- Chronological information: start project 2011; start of construction 2014; completion 2016
- Project design team: Lead Architect: Marc Koehler Architects (MKA); collaborators: De Hoofden collective (MKA along with de Architekten Cie, Thijs Asselbergs, Space Encounters and Hootsmans Architectuurbureau). In collaboration with contractor Era Contour. Residents involved from the start of the project.
- Number of dwelling units: Plot 1: 29 units; Plot 2: 25 units.
- Ratio of parking spaces per dwelling unit: Plot 1: 18 spaces (ratio 0,6); Plot 2: 18 spaces (ratio 0.72); Total 36 spaces (0.6).
- Project site and building area: Plot 1 site area: 1242.3 m², Plot 1 building area: 1242.3 m² (building footprint), Plot 1 building excluding mezzanines and garage: 3723 m², Plot 1 building including mezzanines and garage 5017 m²; Plot 2 site area: 984 m², Plot 2 building area: 984 m² (building

footprint), Plot 2 building excluding mezzanines and garage: 2198 m^2, Plot 2 building including mezzanines and garage 4220 m^2.

- Project client: Private commission by cooperative of homeowners 'De Hoofden.'
- New construction.
- Structure type: base building: an open structural framework 5 m high and 5.7 m wide bays, made of in-situ concrete; façade: a prefabricated system with a steel beam, aluminum framed, triple glazed window, plus integrated electric sunscreens, CO_2-directed vents and rainwater drainage. Façade openings are customized to each unit layout. The protruding concrete frame shields balconies for privacy and prevailing weather conditions.
- Installation utilities: The vertical structural core has stairs, elevator, and two large and one smaller shaft in the concrete core. A technical space accommodates the CO_2 directed mechanical ventilation unit, which has air extraction points in the ceiling and inlet grills in the façade. Floor heating/cooling distribution units are both included in the base building (for underfloor heating and cooling in the dwellings). Supply points for services are located in the entrance hall of each floor. Residents further fit out and customize their own dwellings with installations, including a power system (powerlines are extended through the interior walls and cross laminated timber (CLT) mezzanine floors).
- Infill system/approach: Residents fit out and fully customize their own dwellings with interior walls, CLT mezzanine floors (suspended from the ceiling with steel rods), custom designed/made sanitary and kitchen installations. Each dwelling is unique.

Architects and architectural firms had a very hard time during the financial and economic crisis of 2008–2012. It is estimated that more than half of architects lost their jobs. New partnerships among architects were formed to jointly face the crisis. Architects found ways to create their own work. CPC commissions offered new opportunities. The group of architects calling themselves De Hoofden (a collaboration of Marc Koehler Architects, Architectuurcentrale Thijs Asselbergs, Architekten Cie., ILA, Hootsmans Architectuurbureau, the residents of the listed building De Hoofden at the Herengracht in Amsterdam) decided to build for CPC groups on three plots of Houthavens (see Figure 2.4). The projects are co-created with future residents, using meetings, consultations and online communication to discuss design (of the individual dwellings, the façade, collective areas and functions), choices for materials, financial planning and collective purchases (for solar panels and services, collective furnishings, but also for individual fit-out). Each plot has its owners' association and board, and monthly fees for maintenance of the common areas and elements (similar to the U.S. condominium), with regular meetings for all individual clients – and future

Figure 2.4
De Hoofden in Houthavens (Photography by Marcel van der Burg)

residents – from the very start of the project. Before the actual building starts, these groups have found a community spirit that will carry them through a long period of decision making.

From building with a group of clients to developing a brand and community: Superlofts

- Project location: Plot 4, Haparandaweg, Houthavens, Amsterdam, the Netherlands.
- Chronological information: start project 2012; start of construction 2015; completion 2016.
- Project design team: Marc Koehler Architects (lead architect for base building and façade), in collaboration with contractor Era Contour. Residents involved from the start of the project.
- Number of dwelling units: 19 residential units.
- Ratio of parking spaces per dwelling unit: total: 18 spaces (ratio 0.95).
- Project site and building area: site area: project site 824 m², building area 824 m², building excluding mezzanines and garage 2315 m², building total, including mezzanines and garage 3921 m².
- Project client: private commission by cooperative of homeowners.
- New construction.
- Structure type: the base building consists of an open framework of 5 m high spaces, made of in-situ concrete. In Plot 4, the design of the framework was improved with a structural bay of 6.6 m that provided more generous and flexible floorplans flooded by daylight (in comparison with Plot 1 and 2). Moving the smart main core to the façade allowed for more diverse and modular combination of loft types; façade: a prefabricated system with a steel beam, aluminum framed, triple glazed windows, plus integrated electric sunscreens, CO_2 directed vents and rainwater drainage. Façade openings are customized to each unit layout. The protruding concrete frame shields balconies for privacy and prevailing weather conditions.
- Installation utilities: similar to projects on Plots 1 and 2 (above).
- Infill system/approach: similar to projects on Plots 1 and 2 (above).

Figure 2.5
**Superlofts
in the
Houthavens
area of
Amsterdam
(Photograph
by Marcel
van
der Burg)**

CPC De Hoofden in Houthavens is often referred to as 'the first Superlofts' (see Figure 2.5). The organizational and structural concept that was established for this development was improved and repeated on a fourth plot in Houthavens by Marc Koehler Architects. Called Superlofts, the building is (like its predecessors) built with a concrete structure with floor heights of almost 6 meters designed to accommodate multiple dwelling configurations and a mezzanine floor. Each floor of the building is divided in five legal units grouped around a core with common installations and vertical circulation (fire stair and elevator). Each unit has its own front door and electrical meter. Residents can choose one, two or more 'legal' units to create their living space. The smallest dwelling is just over 40 m^2 on its main floor (430 ft^2) and has a double height: a mezzanine can add at least 20 m^2 (215 ft^2) of living space (see Figure 2.5A). The layout and interior design are up to each resident: in a manual the governmental regulations, collective ground rules and technical constraints are described. In most cases the buyers of the dwellings work with an architect (from within the Superlofts network, but not necessarily Superlofts staff). The online Superlofts community is growing with each location, with the Superliving part of the website as a source of inspiration and exchange of ideas, building tips and even digital drawings of building elements.

The Superloft concept shows that the role of the leading architect in projects following Open Building principles is a complex one. First and foremost, the architect is the coordinator: the architect connects people to the wish of building their own home and to the people who will develop an individual design and build (or contract-out) their dwelling. The architect needs to translate people's ideas and wishes to a design that will form the infrastructure or base building for individual dwellings and a grid and rules of play upon which others can design the infill. The leading architect has to translate the basic principles, wishes and regulations to a building concept and present the building proposals to supervisors, co-creators, building contractors, and so on. Some architects working on CPC projects will call themselves editors or screenwriters. Others feel they are entrepreneurs before real estate professionals, using their skills and craftmanship while meeting the restrictions of building regulations and financing. They use their skills to communicate with all stakeholders: from the insecure first-time buyer of a home to the contractor who is skeptical of new ways of delivering projects. In many of the projects described in this chapter, the architect is a master builder too: knowing about every building element or material, all parts of the fit-out, every detail of the base building.

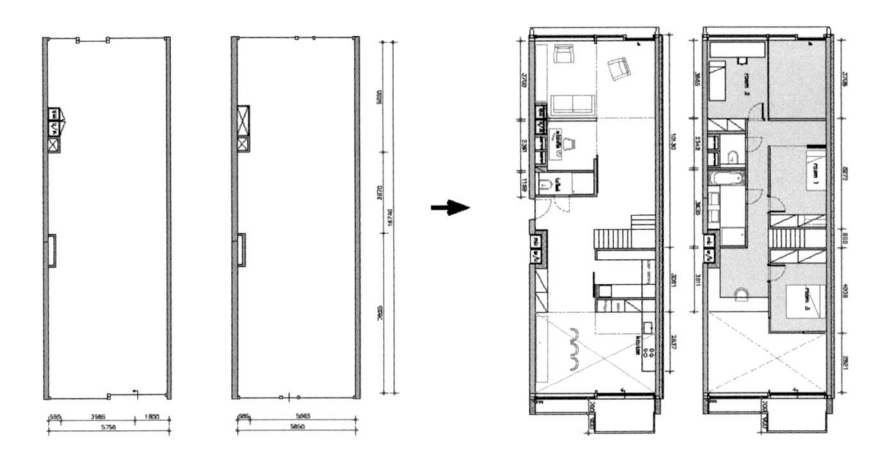

Figure 2.5A
Superlofts raw space and infill (Courtesy of Marc Koehler Architects)

The people that live in Superlofts are a diverse group of people, connected by the wish to create a unique home in the heart of a new development area close to the city center. They are pioneers of all ages. Superlofts Houthavens turned out to be a solid investment, despite financial difficulties at the start of the project. Obtaining a mortgage for a new, sustainable housing concept with independently decided infill proved to be a difficult task for many prospective buyers, as the average building price was higher and there were no existing benchmarks for the (residual) value of certain investments. These hurdles led to another new role for the architects: personal financial advisor.

New criteria matched with Open Building principles: Patch22, Amsterdam by Frantzen et al.

- Project location: Johan van Hasseltkade, Christoffelkruidstraat, Buiksloterham, Amsterdam, the Netherlands.
- Chronological information: design phase 2009–2010; start construction December 2014; base building finished March 2016; first inhabitant summer 2016.
- Project design team: Frantzen et al. architecten, project architects Tom Frantzen, Karel van Eijken, contributor Laura Reinders. The homeowners design and build the infill (with or without an architect).
- Number of dwelling units: 33 living-working units, 600 m^2 commercial space.
- Ratio of parking spaces per dwelling unit: 37 parking spaces (ratio 1.1).
- Project site and building area: gross floor area 5209 m^2, lettable floor area: 4295 m^2.
- Project client: Lemniskade projecten (project developer), Tom Frantzen and Claus Oussoren.
- New construction.
- Structure type: concrete core, timber laminated columns and beams, SlimLine prefabricated lightweight structural floor system using castellated steel beams and concrete slab on the bottom; façade: timber frame construction with double façade with indoor balcony on street/waterside.
- Installation utilities: central city heating, water and electricity per dwelling with main connection and meters in central room on ground floor; distribution via vertical shafts per legal unit; raised floors for horizontal distribution with maximum flexibility in floor layout.
- Infill system/approach: clear separation of infill and support. Partition walls with Soundbloc metal stud frames. Homeowners design and construct their own space plan and infill.

Tom Frantzen is another architect that – in the midst of the economic crisis – decided to create his own development opportunities by starting a real estate company: Lemniskade Projecten. With Patch22, a residential building on plot 22 of the new Buiksloterham development, Frantzen and his real estate partner Claus Oussoren won the tender on criteria of sustainability in 2009. Completed in 2015, Patch22 has won international awards for its sustainability concept (see Figure 2.6). It is a very energy efficient building with renewable materials and incorporating capacity for variation and change in function and layout. It received the Golden Pyramid, a Dutch award for inspiring leadership in real estate. The seven-floor building is suited for living, working and – to some extent – the 'making' industry. Frantzen wanted a building that will last a very long time: hence its capacity for variable and changing functions and layouts (see Figure 2.6A). Even during a financial crisis, Frantzen found buyers by creating a website for the project and using social media campaigns: pioneers wanting to invest time, energy and money in creating their own living space in this future residential area in Amsterdam.

The base building of Patch22 has a main load-bearing structure of wooden beams arranged in a diagonal pattern exposed on the façade, with a concrete stair/elevator core and a composite floor system called SlimLine Floor (www.slimlinebuildings.com) (see Figure 2.6B). This concept uses castellated steel beams and a concrete ceiling, manufactured in precast elements, with a top subfloor of choice installed after installations are placed. For noise reduction (Buiksloterham still has some industrial activity) and a coherent

Figure 2.6
Patch22 in its context in a former industrial area (Photography by Luuk Kramer)

Figure 2.6A
Patch22 base building ready for infill decisions (Photography by Luuk Kramer)

Figure 2.6B
**Patch22 with
the slimline
floor system
(Photography
by Tom
Frantzen)**

appearance of the building as a whole, the balconies are fully glazed with operable panels. Every floor is divided into eight legal units around a concrete core with stairs and elevator and vertical installations. Each of the eight units has a front door. The buyers design and build their own living space: the dwellings are sold without the infill (or infill installations). Frantzen was able to incorporate numerous innovative building elements in the building and convinced the municipal supervisors that placing the electrical meter boxes for all apartments in the lobby on the ground floor would increase future flexibility. The construction floor-to-floor height is 4 m (13 ft). With the SlimLine Floor system, cables and pipes can reach every point in the apartment (or even on the balcony, where one resident has decided to locate the bathtub).

A dream home for all: BlackJack in Amsterdam by BNB Architects and BO6 Architects

- Project location: Ridderspoorweg, Buiksloterham, Amsterdam, the Netherlands
- Chronological information: start of project April 2013; start of construction December 2014; completion September 2015
- Project design team: the supporting construction and installation principle: BNB architects (Dirk Jan van Wieringhen Borski) and Rene de Prie architect. Size of the dwelling/commercial spaces, façade design and floorplan are determined individually the buyers, assisted by BNB architects or their own architect. Installation design: individually by the buyers, assisted by BNB architects.
- Number of dwelling units (upon completion): 28 residential units, 12 commercial units. (hotel/offices/restaurant/gallery), 4 working–living units. These numbers have changed since completion.
- Ratio of parking spaces per dwelling unit: 1 parking space per 160 m^2.
- Project site and building area: site area: Project site 1705 m2, building area 535 m2, total m2 in building 5115 m2.
- Project client: private commission by cooperative of homeowners.
- New construction.
- Structure type: base building: prefab concrete lightweight floors (CD20 system) and concrete columns; façade: glass and aluminum.

- Installation utilities: heating: aquifer thermal energy storage, floor cooling and heating, heat recovery; energy: photovoltaic cells 250 LG Neon 300 Wp, total capacity 64200 Wp.
- Infill system/approach: the base building has substantial capacity by using columns to enable variable unit sizes and layouts, and multiple entrances and shafts per floor, as well as multiple installation sleeves and a grid of pipe sleeves in the floor supporting variable layouts. The size of the apartments, individual floorplans, walls, electricity and pipes are custom planned and changeable in time.

Next to Patch22, on plot 21 of Buiksloterham, is BlackJack, a ten-floor, energy-neutral building with a fully glazed façade (see Figure 2.7). This CPC project was initiated and organized by BNB Architects and BO6 Architects, who had earlier experiences with developing a business center building for a corporation of businesses on IJburg (CBC – collective business commissioning). Before starting talks with prospective buyers, the architects developed a script and design for the base building. In their opinion, the location needed a building with a strong character, a uniform appearance on all floors, independent of what the residents do with their living space behind the façade. The façade is part of the base building. On each floor a 2 m (6.5 ft) deep balcony with glass railings surrounds the building. By placing the core with elevator, stairs and vertical support installations at the rear (north side) of the building, the floors for occupancy are u-shaped. A hallway on each floor around the core leads to a maximum of eight front doors – with six legal units per floor, each unit about 45 m^2 (484 ft^2). It is possible to combine units in a vertical and horizontal way (see Figure 2.7A).

Figure 2.7 **BlackJack in its context – PATCH 22 to the right (Photography by Luuk Kramer)**

BLACKJACK FLEXIBILITY

Because of the flexible hull and flexible logistic dwellings can be made from 25m2 uptil 300m2. They can shrink or grow in time without making big changes. It is also possible to change from dwellings to workspaces or offices.

BlackJack - bnb architects

200m2
150m2
100m2
45m2

Figure 2.7A
BlackJack diagram of its capacity to accommodate a variety of dwelling sizes (Courtesy of BNB Architects)

The base building is a structure with concrete columns and a light concrete floor system called CD20 that allows openings for stairs. Each dwelling has a certain freedom in layout, limited by building regulations and the several designated areas for sanitary units and kitchens (of which multiple possibilities are prepared for, equipped with preset cables and drainage pipes in the concrete floor. Following the script and order of registration, the buyers were able to decide on the size and location of their dwellings, as well as their interior layouts. A mixed and multicultural group applied for living on this location: singles, couples, families, retirees. As it happens, the one buyer with a dream of living in a penthouse in Amsterdam on a small budget, is living his dream in BlackJack, in a 45 m² (484 ft²) studio on the top floor, with a grand view of Amsterdam across the river IJ.

Building a grid for a neighborhood: Schoonschip by Space&Matter

- Project location: Johan van Hasseltkade, Buiksloterham, Amsterdam, the Netherlands.
- Chronological information: in 2009 the idea was born, after that it took Schoonschip years to form the group, get the location and make everything needed legally possible; start of construction 2018; completion 2020.
- Project design team: Space&Matter for urban planning and plot passports. A large number of different architects and different builders/contractors for the dwellings. The collective of homeowners decided about the image quality plan and the whole look and feel of the area. They are organized in a foundation: Stichting Schoonschip.
- Number of dwelling units: 30 plots/floating dwellings shared by 45 households; 1 shared space for the residents, the jetties are also shared space.
- Ratio of parking spaces per dwelling unit: none; the collective shares electric cars that are parked in the public domain.
- Project site and building area: project site: 6200 m² in the Johan van Hasselt Canal, the dwellings are generally between 90 and 150 m², the largest is 240 m².
- Project client: CPO Schoonschip (Collective Private Ownership).
- New construction.
- Structure type: timber frame constructions on a floating base of concrete.
- Installation utilities: energy efficient equipment, full insulation, passive solar heating, heat pumps, solar boilers. Energy surpluses from households are handled through a smart grid (every dwelling is connected to this smart grid: an energy system that optimizes the supply and demand of sustainable energy at a local level on the basis of intelligent technology for hardware and software). Some of the other solutions

applied: sedum roof, rainwater harvesting, water-saving showers, water-saving vacuum toilets and use of wastewater.

- Infill system/approach: individual approach per plot. Timber frame is most commonly used.

The water channel in front of Patch22 and BlackJack is called Johan Van Hasseltkanaal-West and leads to the River IJ (and ultimately to the North Sea). Since the start of the development of Buiksloterham as a residential area, plans for a floating community on this location were submitted. In the course of recent years, the neighborhood Schoonschip ('clean ship', or 'to come clean' in a figurative way) is docked at this quay (see Figure 2.8). The procedures and social components of Schoonschip resonate with the Open Building approach: floating homes, connected to an urban plan. The jetties connect to 30 (leased) water plots, 46 (owned) dwellings and over 100 residents. The residents themselves developed every part of the process, and together with the various experts they involved, have created a sustainable infrastructure and community. They commissioned the architects of Space&Matter to develop an urban masterplan: a grid and so-called plot passports for the floating homes. This allowed each resident to choose their own architect to design their house.

Schoonschip has only one connection to the energy grid, and shared water, sewer and waste systems. Residents profit from the energy generated by the solar panels and heat pumps allocated to each dwelling. The collective is able to trade and store that energy through a smart grid. They share electrical cars and bikes, have developed a central community boat, and try to improve the water quality through floating gardens. Half of the dwellings are shared by two households, making Schoonschip financially feasible for more

Figure 2.8
Schoonschip: the cluster of houses in the water near Patch22 and TOPUP (Photography by Jan Willem Sieburgh)

people, making a serious attempt to make their ecological footprint as small as possible.

New ways of commissioning: Crowdbuilding and Smartlofts by Space&Matter and Smartlofts JFK, Amsterdam

- Project location: President Kennedy Plantsoen, Amsterdam, the Netherlands.
- Chronological information: start of project June 2013; start of build July 2015; completion November 2016.
- Project design team: architect base building Space&Matter. In collaboration with the cooperative, contractor Vink Bouw and developers OPEN Development and Crowdbuilding. Representatives of the cooperative were involved in monthly work meetings. All future residents were given the opportunity to develop their housing design with Space&Matter: some residents designed their own layout or had their own architect. The plan was developed together with construction, building physics and installation consultants.
- Number of dwelling units: 36 residential units, 2 big shared spaces for the residents.
- Ratio of parking spaces per dwelling unit: indoor garage with 16 parking spaces (ratio 0.44).
- Project site and building area: project site 1000 m², building area 3800 m².
- Project client: cooperative of future residents.
- Refurbishment: the transformation of a former Municipal District Office.
- Structure type: base building: the existing concrete skeleton is re-used; façade: combination of new stucco and masonry.
- Installation utilities: the building is almost self-sufficient and equipped with 300 PV panels on the roof and supplied with a heat pump. Vertical distribution through core. The installations in the dwellings are customized to the wishes of the owners.
- Infill system/approach: the construction team took up the design with the residents' group, with each dwelling fitted out to individual layout and wishes.

Space&Matter initiated the platform Crowdbuilding, taking their experience with Schoonschip to other locations and forms of co-creating and co-living by first assembling a group of residents with a shared ambition. The separate dwellings within Crowdbuilding projects are designed by residents and their own architect, creating space individually within a quasi-base building development. With the concept of Smartlofts, the same architects attract target audiences to (existing) buildings and involve the future residents in the design process. One of the examples of this approach is the project JFK Smartlofts, where a former municipal office building was refurbished and is currently an apartment building with 36 residential units, the infill of each unit co-created with the future resident (see Figure 2.9).

Figure 2.9
**JFK
Smartlofts –
a building
transformed
in co-creation
with future
residents,
in its
Amsterdam
context
(Photography
by Luuk
Kramer)**

Although the approach of Crowdbuilding and Smartlofts may be different (finding a group of clients versus offering a communal building/location for communal use), both initiatives enhance the idea of an offered shared infrastructure in which each resident can realize their individual program for living (and/or working).

Writing scenarios for architectural decisions: Schetsblok in Amsterdam by ANA Architects

- Project location: Poeldijkstraat, Amsterdam, the Netherlands.
- Chronological information: start of project 2013; start of construction 2016; completion 2018.
- Project design team: ANA Architects (Jannie Vinke, Marcel van der Lubbe, Bas Hoevenaars, Joeri van Wijk, Jilles van Eibergen Santhagens) in cooperation with the collective of future homeowners.
- Number of dwelling units: 25 residential units.
- Ratio of parking spaces per dwelling unit: 16 parking spaces (ratio 0.64).
- Project site and building area: site area: Project site 650 m², building area 650 m², total m² in building 3.600 m².
- Project client: Foundation 4 Winden (representative body of future homeowners), Kondor Wessels Vastgoed (developer).
- New construction.
- Structure type: base building: concrete floors and columns; façade: timber framing filled with insulation, aluminum window frames.

- Installation utilities: energy: PV-panels and municipal grid; water/sewer/ sanitary: municipal grid; heating: district heating.
- Infill system/approach: non-loadbearing block walls for the partition walls and internal layout; homeowners designed their own space (with/ without an architect) and used their own contractors.

The idea of co-creation with residents is becoming more popular in the Netherlands. The role of the architect as an intermediary between the wishes of the inhabitants and the design of their living space may be traditional, yet the tools and language used are significantly changing. The project Schetsblok by ANA Architects (see Figure 2.10) was awarded with the Dutch Building of the Year Award 2019, the jury praising it as a project 'with potential for the future, in which careful thought was given to what consumers want today: freedom of choice, affordability, sufficient outdoor space.' The assignment for the project was given by Stichting De Vier Winden, a foundation representing future buyers. The future residents were intensely involved in the design process. ANA Architects wrote the script and administered the rules. In preparation for the talks with the residents, multiple layouts were designed by the architect, only to end up drawing another proposal following the clients' wishes: not one of the proposed floor plans was adopted exactly as drawn. For the façade a scenario with different horizontal and vertical grids was written. Once the plans were decided upon, the residents were able to compose 'their' part of the façade using the palette of elements, materials and colors selected by the architects. With design rules for adjacent apartments, the residents had to tune in with their future neighbors, which meant that complex discussions took place among as many as four other residents whose façades abut to any one unit's façade. This project follows the principles of Open Building

Figure 2.10
Schetsblok in its context (Photography by Luuk Kramer)

Figure 2.10A
**Schetsblok
second floor
layouts
showing
capacity of
the base
building
(Courtesy
of ANA
Architects)**

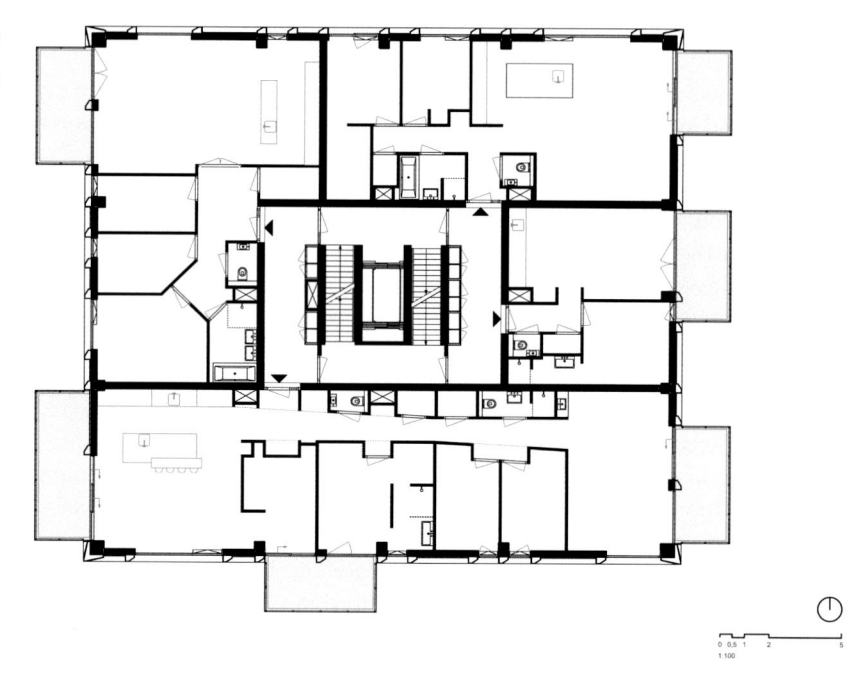

regarding the involvement of residents in creating their own living environment, with the idea of a fixed base building infrastructure and variable and independently decided infill (notably including façade elements) as the basis for future changes (see Figure 2.10A). In this case, the layout of the apartments is customizable and changeable over decades, but the façade as initially designed is fixed for decades to come and could be considered as a part of the base building: new residents will not be able to change that in the foreseeable future.

Strategies for façades

Within the OpenBuilding.co group of architects there is ongoing research and discussion on the topic of the façade. Three different approaches are under study: the *Collage* (Silodam, De Hoofden Houthavens), the *Silhouette* (BlackJack, Patch22) and The *Grid* (Schetsblok, Smartlofts, Superlofts). The key distinction among these approaches is the question of initial design (incorporating wishes/demands of the individual owners), control (who decides), adaptability over time, and the design of the façade in the light of ambitions towards circularity and adaptability. In contrast to these approaches, the façades of the Solid projects discussed above are entirely base building decisions, initially and over time.

Starting with the *Collage*, this approach is seen on different levels of intervention: that of the neighborhood and of the building. The *Collage* enhances the idea of placing different materials, grids and rhythms in one design, to express the notion of individuality and different functions behind that façade. If a change of function or regulations implies the replacement of part of the collage with new façade elements, it will not disturb the overall character of the building. In most cases, the architect responsible for the base building will also design the façade and write possible scenarios for future change. What happens in the more distant future is another topic for discussion.

With the strategy of the *Silhouette*, the façade is regarded as part of the base building and built to last several generations of owners and users. Nevertheless, the stakeholders in the design process have a voice (regarding architecture, materials and functionality), but ultimately the architect of the base building is responsible for its design. *Silhouette* façades incorporate flexibility of use behind the first, with the outer layer of the façade addressing the scale of the building. In the case of BlackJack and Patch22, the glass balusters and balconies create that uniform, outer layer. With both projects, it allows the users of the buildings to create different functionalities or uses behind that outer layer, that will not be visible at street level.

When creating a façade following the strategy of the *Grid*, the architect of the base building designs scenarios for the infill of a detailed grid: drawing different compositions and palettes of materials, colors and details that are able to coexist harmoniously within one façade. The buyers of the different dwelling rights have the last say on which palette is chosen. The architect's role is scriptwriter, an advisor to the buyers/users in most cases, and the director of the final composition (responsible for the building permit). This is the approach taken in the pioneering Papendrecht/ Molenviet project of Frans van der Werf in the late 1970's. This strategy asks for leniency of the regulating parties on different levels and moments: often the building permit is granted before the final design of the façade is made. As for changes in the façade when new users or second buyers are introduced, the procedures are not that open to change till now. That is exactly the point where Open Building principles and the wish for circularity in building elements will meet in future discussions. The first pilot projects with 'façades as a service' (offering relatively short-term and flexible lease contracts to building owners) are currently in development. These are interesting developments for Open Building, especially for the *Collage* and *Grid* strategies as mentioned above.

Taking circularity to the next stage: Project CiWoCo in Amsterdam by GAAGA

- Project location: Boterbloemstraat, Ridderspoorweg, Buiksloterham, Amsterdam, the Netherlands.
- Chronological information: start of project 2015 Q4; start of construction 2018 Q2; completion 2019 Q1.
- Project design team: Architect GAAGA (Esther Stevelink, Arie Bergsma, Maaike van der Veer) in collaboration with the client (Coöperatie BSH20E, involved in the design and construction process from an early

stage), OntwerpJeWoning for process management, constructor Vink Bouw, structural engineer Van Rossum and consultants NIBE, Hiensch Engineering, MoBius Consult, 3B Bouwondersteuning.

- Number of dwelling units: 12 living–working units (including 8 apartments, 3 terraced houses and 1 studio). Each of the dwellings includes an additional and undefined living and/or working space. This undefined space has a separate front door and can be used for example as a home-based office, guest room or room for elderly parents.
- Ratio of parking spaces per dwelling unit: 12 spaces (ratio 1.0).
- Project site and building area: site area: project site 759 m², building area 709 m² on ground floor (including parking space), 420 m² on first floor, total m² in building 1500 m².
- Project client: Collective Private Commissioning by Coöperatie BSH20E.
- New construction.
- Structure type: base building: load bearing structure of prefabricated concrete with demountable joints. The base building itself is recyclable and can become a source of urban mining; façade: re-used Azobe wood of former sheet pilings formerly used along Dutch waterways. The wood is placed within steel frames. A total of 90% of the building materials can be reused or recycled.
- Installation utilities: energy: PV panels on the roof; water/sewer/sanitary: municipal grid; heating: district heating as a heat source for the floor heating system in the dwellings, in a light-weight concrete screed.
- Infill system/ approach: infill walls are lightweight (metal stud) and are separated from the load bearing structure. Flexible and adaptable installations that are separated from the load bearing structure (in partition walls and suspended ceilings in common areas).

Buiksloterham is a neighborhood in Amsterdam on the forefront of new developments: not only in CPC projects, but also in sustainable and circular building. The previously mentioned Patch22 project shows a base building in timber and concrete, and changeable infill. The project CiWoCo on plot 20E, just around the corner, takes demountability and recycling further. This CPC-project designed by GAAGA architects is composed of lightweight, prefabricated, demountable elements – for infill *and* base building. The project was completed in 2018 and has won several awards in the field of architecture and sustainability (see Figure 2.11). The base building is a composition of prefabricated lightweight concrete elements that are connected using so-called dry joints. The base building is therefore demountable (or adjustable) as well. All installations are 'add-on' systems, nowhere integrated with the façade or support and therefore easily adaptable. The general distribution of water, electricity and sewerage is handled via suspended ceilings of the communal hallways. The infill installations are distributed from meter boxes in each legal unit and hidden behind secondary walls.

CiWoCo stands for Circulair Woonwerk Complex (circular living–working complex). The building comprises three ground-level homes and eight apartments, connected by an inner courtyard garden on top of a parking garage. The apartments are for living and working, each with its own entrance (for legal and tax purposes). With a strict separation of base building and infill, the building offers capacity for adjustments in layout or use in the future (see Figure 2.11A). The architectural design, the base building and fit-out, the layouts, the different flows in materials, energy and water are meticulously thought out, with short-term and long-term scenarios. Most of the used materials are renewable or are (partly) recycled. For example: the compartmentalized and demountable wooden façade is made from hardwood that was used as sheet piles in the harbor area. Sawn into thin battens and placed upon a framed façade element, this material adds character and color to the project. The panels fit perfectly in the postindustrial surroundings

Figure 2.11
CiWoCo courtyard (Photography by Marcel van der Burg)

Figure 2.11A
CiWoCo Capacity Diagrams (Courtesy of GAAGA Architects)

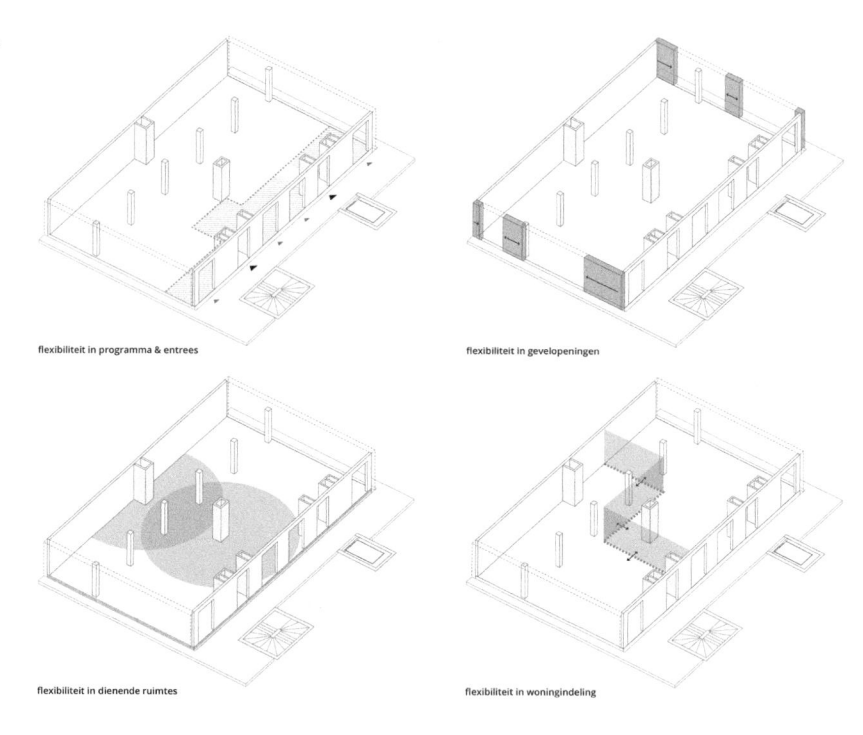

flexibiliteit in programma & entrees

flexibiliteit in gevelopeningen

flexibiliteit in dienende ruimtes

flexibiliteit in woningindeling

but should the need for replacement arise (new function, new regulations or merely the need for more windows), the panels are easily replaced.

Another real estate boom changes it all again?

Ironically, since the economy has gained momentum and the real estate market started to recover (starting in 2013 and moving faster than before), the commercial development companies have taken control of the land issues and tenders again. Even with successful Open Building projects to show, in new developments, CPC-groups and development companies with a sustainability agenda as a top priority find it difficult if not impossible to be competitive. Whereas ten years ago CPC-groups (and their willingness to invest) were welcomed to contribute to the development of new neighborhoods and new levels of sustainable innovations, the upturn in the economy combined with an unabated need for affordable housing seem to contradict with making investments for a future beyond the next government term.

Lessons learned: TopUp by Frantzen et al.

- Project location: Fonteinkruidstraat, Johan van Hasseltkade, Amsterdam, the Netherlands.
- Chronological information: start of project 2014; completion of the base building and façade 2019.

- Project design team: Frantzen et al. architecten, project architects Tom Frantzen, Karel van Eijken, contributor VNDP Amsterdam/Enschede. The homeowners design and build the infill (with or without an architect).
- Number of dwelling units: 14 living-working apartments, 3 commercial spaces.
- Ratio of parking spaces per dwelling unit: 49 parking spaces in separate construction.
- Project site and building area: site area: 4844 m^2 + 1346 m^2 parking garage; lettable floor area: 3981 m^2 + 49 parking spaces.
- Project client: Lemniskade projecten (project developer), Tom Frantzen and Claus Oussoren.
- New construction.
- Structure type: concrete vertical core, timber laminated columns and beams, precast CD20 lightweight concrete floor elements; façade: timber frame construction with double façade with indoor balcony on street/waterside.
- Installation utilities: central city heating, water and electricity per dwelling with main connection and meters in central room on ground floor; distribution via vertical shafts per legal unit; thin raised floors for horizontal distribution.
- Infill system/ approach: clear separation of infill and support. Partition walls with fully insulated metal stud construction with double sheeting. Residents design and construct their own fit-out.

In 2016, Tom Frantzen and his development partner Claus Oussoren developed the plot adjacent to Patch22. The site was occupied by an abandoned communication center with round concrete structures to house the huge cable reels. To use as much of the existing structure for the base building as possible, Frantzen designed a structural concept based upon the one in Patch22, planned it on top of the existing foundation and called the new building TopUp (see Figure 2.12). Instead of the SlimLine floor system, TopUp used the CD20 system (light weight precast concrete floors) in combination with a laminated timber column structure and timber frame construction for the façades of the base building. The strategy for the base building installations was copied in part from the Patch22 project: using the vertical core of the building for distribution to the different dwellings, placing the required meter boxes on ground level. Dwelling-specific installations were routed under a thin raised floor of 15 cm (6 inches), one of several available in the market. The height of the thin raised floor was set by the slope of the drainage pipes from toilets placed at expected distances from the vertical pipe shaft of the base building. Timber was used for the infill of most the dwellings, each dwelling being individually designed by the owner and/or his or her architect.

Again, the architect–developer opted for the division of the available floorspace in a number of legal units (12 per floor) to give the prospective buyers the opportunity to create custom-made dwellings (see Figures 2.12A, 2.12B, 2.12C). The municipality prescribed a combination of working and

Figure 2.12
TopUp (right) Patch22 (middle) BlackJack (left) (Courtesy of the architect)

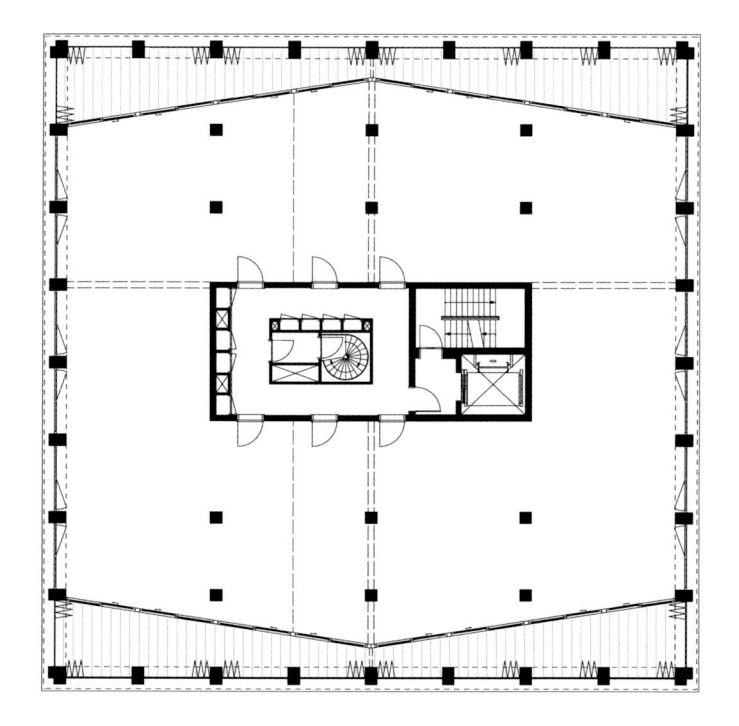

Figure 2.12A
TopUp typical open base building floor plan (Photography by Isabel Nabuurs)

Top-Up typical floor plan without division walls

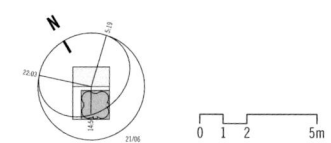

Figure 2.12B
TopUp base building space ready for infill decisions (Photography by Isabel Nabuurs)

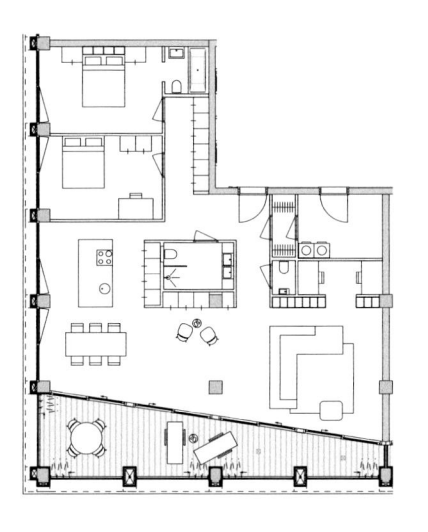

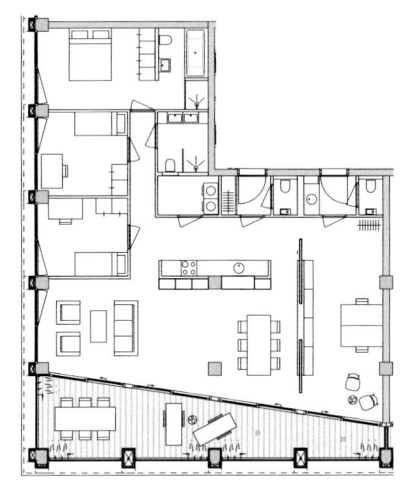

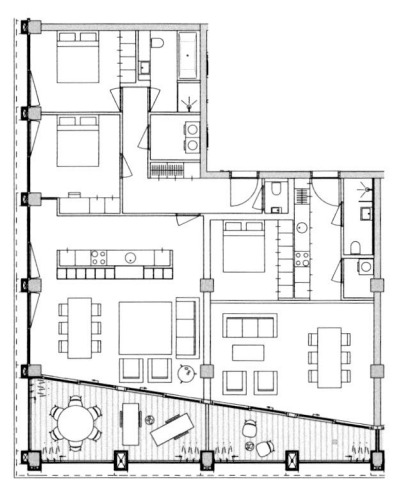

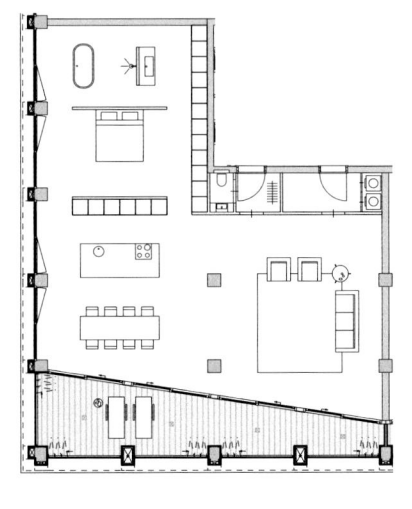

Figure 2.12C
TopUp several possible infill layouts (Courtesy of Frantzen et al.)

living, with most of the offices/retail functions on the ground floor. At least 10% of the floor space on the different floors had to be dedicated workspace. With 12 units per floor (and 12 front doors), the arrangement followed the scenario of Patch22. But with the increasing value of the land price (and the ground lease fees rising accordingly) and the different fee distribution formulas per floor and function, the municipality was less flexible in approving the number of legal units and the variations in use, looking for short-term yield of new developments. Moreover, because of the high land price, the dwellings on the ground proved hard to sell for a competitive price, pushing the margins of the project to an uncomfortable level. Even with an award-winning, successfully used proof of concept next door, this project shows that for each deviation to the 'conventional' both developer and architect need to be prepared for a long process to be able to accomplish their (short-term and long-term) goals with Open Building. TopUp offers at least as much capacity, and is as sustainable and energy efficient as Patch22, offering its residents freedom to design their own infill.

Open Building and the timber revolution: stories by Olaf Gipser Architects

- Project location: Ridderspoorweg, Buiksloterham, Amsterdam, the Netherlands.
- Chronological information: start of project 2016; start of construction 2018; completion base building Q4 2020, completion individual apartments 2021.
- Project design team: Olaf Gipser Architects (architectural design) with Alferink van Schieveen (structural design), Bureau Veldweg (fire safety), Constructie Adviesbureau Geuijen (mass timber structure), Derix Gelijmde Houtconstructies (mass timber engineering), Heutink Groep (contractor), LBP Sight (acoustics), Pirmin Jung (mass timber structure, acoustics), Smartland (vegetation) with The Royal Ginkel Group. The cooperative of future homeowners were involved from the start of the project.
- Number of dwelling units: 29 apartments, many registered as living–working units; 5 commercial units.
- Ratio of parking spaces per dwelling unit: 40 parking spaces for cars (ratio 1.2), 86 spaces for bicycles.
- Project site and building area: site area: project site 1210 m^2; building area 1210 m^2; Total m^2 in building 5500 m^2.
- Project client: private cooperative building initiative (CPO) in collaboration with contractor (risk-taker) and architect. The ground was given by the Municipality of Amsterdam as ground lease ('*erfpacht*') on the basis of a competitive selection procedure with focus on the initiative's participative decision-making processes and sustainability ambitions.
- New construction.

- Structure type: prefab concrete (11 meter high plinth), floor and wall CLT-structure with prefab concrete core above the plinth up to 45 meters. Floors with a foam concrete layer for improving acoustic insulation; façade: timber frame façade with timber window frames and hydro-thermally treated, fireproof, grey-washed timber cladding, light-weight steel structure for balcony and vegetation perimeter zone; 57 double-height vegetation units.
- Installation utilities: energy: roof solar panels; water/sewer/sanitary: municipal grid, computer-controlled irrigation system for vegetation units; heating: district heating in combination with floor heating in the dwellings; ventilation: mechanical ventilation with heat recovery units, in combination with natural ventilation.
- Infill system/approach: dwelling unit layouts are individualized (light-weight walls, certain flexibility of installation re-arrangement), unit sizes (combinable units, redundancy of front door openings on floor levels), and function (ceiling height 3 meters, combinable units, partial functional double coding living/working). Infill of dwellings customized by homeowners.

Buiksloterham in Noord-Amsterdam remains a building site in 2020. One of the projects that is currently (2020) under construction is 'Stories' on plot BSH20A, designed by Olaf Gipser Architects for and with a CPC-group (see Figure 2.13). Its completion is due in 2021. Although the name refers to the narratives of the future residents, this building is telling the Dutch construction industry new stories as well. It is the first building in the area constructed with CLT (cross-laminated timber) upon a concrete plinth of three levels. The wooden structure reaches to 45 m (148 ft), with two floor levels in a double height (regular 2.87 m, double 6.12 m) (9.4 ft and 20 ft respectively) The mass

Figure 2.13
Stories rendering of the project (to the right is BlackJack) (Rendering by WAX)

Figure 2.13A
**Stories
rendering of
the project's
base
building CLT
structure
(Courtesy of
Olaf Gipser
Architects)**

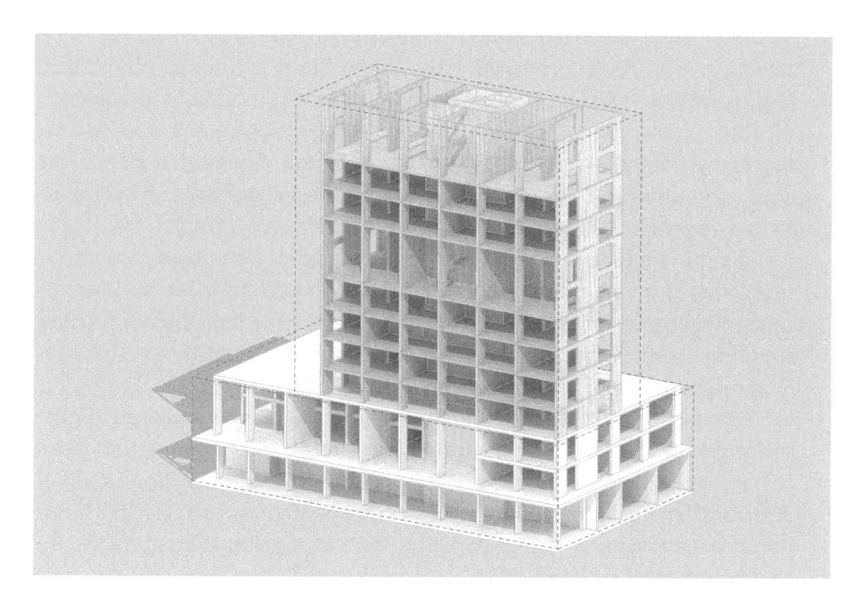

Figure 2.13B
**Stories
rendering
of a typ-
ical base
building
floor
(Courtesy of
Olaf Gipser
Architects)**

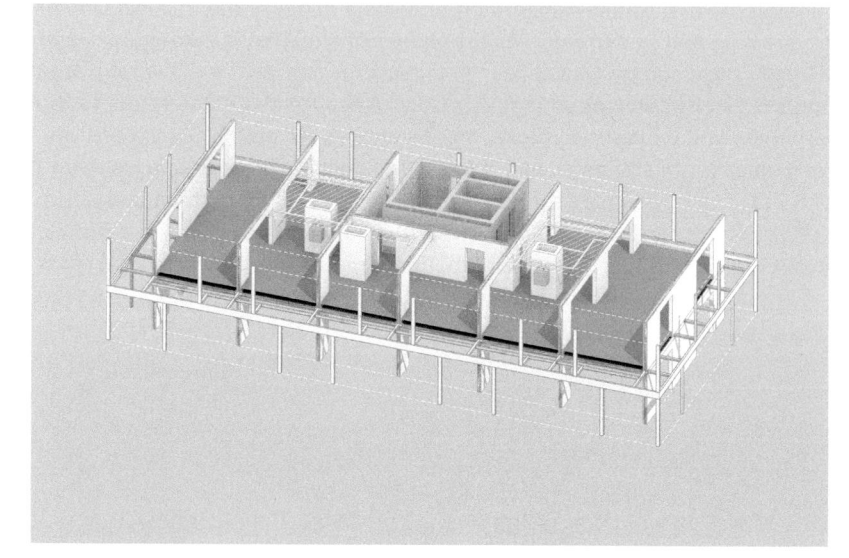

timber construction follows the bay width of 4.50 m (14.75 ft), with a floorplan spanning over six adjacent bays (see Figure 2.13A. The load bearing CLT walls have large openings that allow for spatial connection across the bays, facilitating variable sizes of units of occupancy, and for one to six individual units per floor (see Figure 2.13B, 2.13C, 2.13D). In its current configuration, the building has 27 residential and 7 commercial dwellings, ranging in floor space from 43 m^2 (463 ft^2) to 187 m^2 (2012 ft^2) The separation of the dwellings as well as the individual fit-out walls are constructed with CLT.

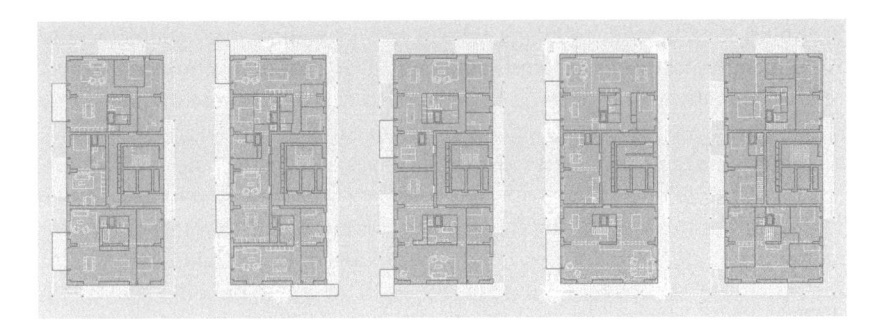

Figure 2.13C
Stories drawing showing the capacity of a typical floor (Courtesy of Olaf Gipser Architects)

Figure 2.13D
Stories infill installations (Photography by Olaf Gipser)

The support installations are incorporated in the concrete core with stairs and elevator. From there, via a meter box for each legal unit, the distribution of pipes and cables is conducted under a thin raised floor: a limestone gravel mass layer for acoustic insulation, a thermal insulation layer, a floor heating layer and a top floor. The structural CLT floor elements are exposed as ceilings. For fire proofing and acoustic measures, the interior walls are clad with plasterboard. The wooden structure is enveloped by a steel construction with balconies and huge planters featuring trees up to 6 m, shrubs and plants as partitioning between the different bays and units, giving the residents the opportunity to partition the 'wooden' façade according to each unique layout without disturbing the characteristic appearance of the building.

Sharing know-how and research: OpenBuilding.co

To share research results, know-how and to have a stronger voice in convincing peers and stakeholders of the advantages of Open Building, 14 architects and engineers started the collective OpenBuilding.co in 2019. The Founding Partners of OpenBuilding.co strongly believe in the benefits of co-creation, designing long-lasting buildings with a strong architectural character and using reconfigurtable fit-out under the control of the tenants or buyers.

Their manifesto shows three themes, each of which can be addressed by or combined with certain principles of Open Building as described, in part, by John Habraken: Open Cities, Open Buildings and Open Systems. The partners invest time and energy on joint research on contemporary topics like new business models for (open) building development (towards a circular economy and building industry), the possibilities of Open Building in timber (for structural purposes, infill systems or in modular building concepts), the use of tools like parametric design, virtual reality and augmented reality in the processes of co-creation, design and building fabrication. In September 2019 the Open Building Academy started with students from the Amsterdam University of Applied Sciences and Delft University of Technology. OpenBuilding.co is preparing events and a communication campaign addressing governmental and municipal policy makers – making them aware of the advantages of Open Building in long-term planning.

Open Building in the era of sustainability and social cohesion

Open Building has been given a new face and contemporary definition in the light of the recent projects in Amsterdam and Rotterdam. The legacy of John Habraken is being adopted by a new generation of architects and adapted to meet the needs, ambitions and technological developments of this era. And although the committed 'Open Building' architects sometimes encounter resistance while initiating, incorporating or defending Open Building principles (often on the basis of costs and short-term investment strategies of lending institutions), the future promises change for the better. The idea of Open Building as a way to create accommodating, coherent and strong cities, neighborhoods and communities designed for change has been awarded on several occasions. The governmental publication 'Nederland Circulair in 2050' (Nederland Circulair, 2016) articulates issues and opportunities that can be addressed with solutions following the principles of Open Building. Recent buildings are proof of that.

One million homes in the foreseeable future

Delft University of Technology has issued the program '1MHomes' – one million homes – to address the housing crisis, aiming to reach the goals of the Paris Climate Agreement at the same time. The ambition is to develop scenarios to scale up the production of housing, using all (digital communication/technological) tools available while creating livable sustainable cities and healthy environments. Open Building will undoubtedly play a role in these developments. Collaboration with other universities and academies is planned.

The Open Building movement in the Netherlands today is not limited to the works and writings of John Habraken, his contemporaries, his students and the 14 partners in the new collective that put Open Building on the international architectural agenda during the World Architecture Festival in 2019. Open Building could become the new standard for building in the Netherlands, as journalist Elsbeth Grievink stated in her article 'Introducing flexible housing' (Grievink, 2020) in the financial newspaper *Het Financieele Dagblad* on February 5, 2020:

> It seems a matter of time before open building becomes the norm. But there is work to be done. In order to gain acceleration in circular construction methodologies, regulations have to change. Buildings that are designed to be taken apart – sooner or later – also require new forms of financing.

Open Building also needs a new or different attitude towards project development and architecture. The projects in this chapter are the proof of concept: the principles of Open Building offer sustainable solutions for the cities, buildings and building systems of the future. As momentum for Open Building is increasing, policymakers have to be made aware of the long-term benefits. But like in the 1960s, it takes more than thorough research and a number of prototypes to change the habits of the building industry. Yet, it does seem that these recent projects have made a sustainable landing in fertile soil.

References

Ellen McArthur Foundation. (2018). *Principles of circularity*. Ellen Mc Arthur Foundation. Available at: www.ellenmacarthurfoundation.org/circular-economy/concept

Grievink, E. (2020). Nieuw: maak kennis met flexibele huizen. *Het Financieele Dagblad*, February 5.

Habraken, J. (2003). Open Building as a condition for industrial construction, in *The Future Site: Proceedings, 20th International Symposium on Automation and Robotics in Construction*, ISARC, Delft. Editors: Ger Maas and Frans van Gassel.

Habraken, N. J. (1972). *Supports: An Alternative to Mass Housing*. London: Architectural Press.

Nederland Circulair 2050. (2016). Published by the Ministry of Infrastructure and Water Management, Ministry of Economic Affairs and Climate Policy, Ministry of Foreign Affairs, Ministry of Interior and Kingdom Relations. Available at: www.rijksoverheid.nl//circulaire-economie

SlimLine Floor. Developed by SlimLineBuildings. Available at: www.slimline buildings.com/slimline-concept

Vinke, J. and van der Lubbe, M. (2014). Learning from Multifunk: een onderzoek naar flexibele en multifunctionele gebouwen. Amsterdam: ANA Architects. Available at: www.ana.nlwww.ana.nl

Wallagh, G. (Inbo Architects) (2013). *Solids: De onbekende toekomst huisvesten*. Amsterdam: Platform31.

Chapter 3

Open Building in Finland

Carolin Franke

A brief introduction to the Finnish housing system

A brief overview of the Finnish Housing system helps to place the projects and discussion in this chapter into context. About 85% of the Finnish population (5.5 million) live in towns or cities. Of this, 1.5 million people live in the Helsinki metropolitan region, which consists of the cities of Helsinki, Espoo and Vantaa. In recent years, as much as 90% of new housing construction has been concentrated in main city regions (KTI Finland, 2019). This chapter focuses on the Helsinki metropolitan region, since first, the vast majority of newly built housing projects are situated there and, second, because the city follows its own specific housing development strategy.

The city of Helsinki is in a unique position vis-à-vis urban development and housing policy because it owns land which it leases to housing development companies. In this way, the city enables long-term control over the built environment and can actively influence the quantity and quality of its housing. When a residential block is being situated on a city plot, the building owner will pay a monthly rent to the city. This rent can be adjusted by the city over time. Some plots or even entire urban districts are reserved for especially innovative housing concepts for which applications can be made for building sites. When handing a plot to a developer for a standard housing project, the city can demand from the developer to build a certain percentage of their projects as social housing in order to keep the social context stable and to avoid income segregation in a given area of the city.

Currently, there are three new neighborhoods under construction: Jätkäsaari (home to 21,000 residents by 2030) (City of Helsinki, 2018a), Kalasatama (25,000 residents by 2040) (City of Helsinki, 2018b) and Kruunuvuorenranta (13,000 by 2030) (City of Helsinki, 2019a). All these districts have a wide range of dwellings: city-owned rental flats, right-of-occupancy dwellings (a mix between rental and owner-occupied housing built with State subsidy) (City of Helsinki, 2019b), student flats, communal houses for senior citizens, privately funded rental flats and owner-occupied dwellings, which create a good base for a diverse housing stock (*Finnish Architectural Review*, 2016). The standard

DOI: 10.4324/9781003018339-4

in new residential construction is high. All dwellings allow for healthy and safe living environments that meet high energy efficiency standards. However, projects that enable or explicitly plan for individuality and adaptability-over-time are still rare. An attempt is made later in the chapter to explain why this is the case.

Ownership of dwellings is very popular in Finland: 66% of Finnish people live in dwellings that they own (Rakennusteollisuus, 2019a). In the construction of new multi-story housing blocks for ownership, a certain number of inhabitants are known to the developer before the beginning of construction. In Finland, there is a Housing Transactions Act, a law which protects the inhabitants before the building has commenced construction. In most residential blocks the developer will sell the units before construction. This is a good indicator of interest on the market and avoids new housing blocks being left empty. The buyers are backed up by the housing sales act. They will pay a rather small amount of the total cost before construction begins in order to reserve the unit; the rest is then paid during and after completion. This gives risk assurance to the bank providing the loan. Not all the units must be sold upfront. Usually, the developer can decide how many can stay unoccupied and often the developers also keep apartments to rent them out. Before the developer can apply for a loan from the bank, they will need to present a variety of documents such as building permission, tender (bid) drawings, security certificates, financial plans, detailed construction documents, etc. This system usually allows for a certain degree of adjustment and alteration in the fit-out of the dwellings, concerning surface materials for example. However, overall the degree of user control is low and standard solutions do not allow much capacity for variability or change, either initially or over time (Rakennusteollisuus, 2019b).

'Communal construction' (Co-op development) is an approach to Open Building (OB) which represents positive progress regarding self-determination and distribution of decision making. In this case, a group of citizens forms a housing company and applies to the city of Helsinki for the right to rent a building plot. This company can then apply for a unified loan to the bank. Adjustment in laws during the last few years make it significantly easier to receive a loan as a building co-op. The housing company hires a project manager and design team, and the group itself decides to which degree every single party is involved in the decision making. This approach is illustrated later in this chapter in the *Aikalisä* housing for seniors' project.

History of residential Open Building in Finland

The principles of OB were first studied in Finland in the 1990s. However, the concept did not spread widely within Finnish housing design practice for a number of years. Architect Ulpu Tiuri was among the first to study OB implementation in the Finnish context. In 1997, she described the Finnish housing market as follows:

During the past decades, in Finland and elsewhere, apartments have been built mainly to accommodate the needs of average inhabitants who appear as statistical figures in the building process. The future dwellers have been looked upon as members of different demographic categories – such as families with children, or elderly people – having common needs while the different values affecting choices in housing within these groups have largely been ignored. The differentiating values and parallel ways and styles of life require that future housing design be complex and able to adapt to unforeseen changes.

(Tiuri, 1997, p. 93)

Tiuri saw the need for change in housing design in order to accommodate specific user groups. However, in 2014, almost two decades after Tiuri's evaluation, the editorial of the *Finnish Architectural Journal* describes the Finnish housing market in the following way:

Finnish residential housing production has been criticized for monotony – and for good reason. A puffy block of flats with five to eight stories and as many apartments per stair landing as possible is what fulfills the requirements of today's market economy realism.

(Mukala, 2014)

This description indicates little has changed in Finland regarding housing prepared for change and variability. But fortunately, this is not the whole story. There have been a number of successful residential projects which exemplify the application of the OB approach, as several realized projects shown in what follows indicate.

The beginnings of OB in Finland: the 1990s

In 1993 the city of Helsinki and the National Technology Agency TEKES organized an OB Technology competition for a block of flats in the area of Herttoniemenranta, Helsinki. The aim of the competition was to find new solutions towards citizen-oriented homes with the capacity to change over time. Esko Kahri ("Kahri and Co architects" at the time) submitted one of the winning proposals and built a block of rental dwellings together with VVO as the developer. Kahri was among the first architects in Finland to work in practice with the OB approach. He first encountered Habrakens' support principles in the mid-1980s. He had great interest in these ideas and following his competition success, was awarded the opportunity to realize his first OB project.

The competition entry was a block of rental dwellings with approximately 100 units. Future inhabitants were able to choose from a variety of apartment layouts (their fit-out or infill). Rents were individually determined, depending on each fit-out. Dividing walls within the units were of light construction and could be altered to form new room layouts in a short time.

According to Esko Kahri, there was a supportive climate for residents' influence in the 1990s. VVO and Kahri realized several residential OB housing blocks during that time. In 1998 they realized a block of flats in Helsinki Pitäjänmäki consisting of over 200 flats, ranging from rental, ownership, and right-of-occupancy apartments (Rakennusteollisuus, 2019a). As reported by architect Kahri, this was the point when existing planning tools at the time came to their limit. The building process had been chaotic and costly. The large number of moving parts within the building process was too much to handle. At the time, there was no good system of coordinating a large variety of apartment fit-out schemes. According to Kahri, the biggest lesson learned from this project was that there must be a system to coordinate the inhabitants' individual wishes and furthermore how to communicate these to the developer and constructor. Additionally, cost estimation must also be clear in communication among all the parties.

Developments in the first decade of the 21st century

In 2001 Helsinki City and the Finnish Technology Agency arranged a second OB competition in Helsinki, this time in the neighborhood of Arabianranta – a newly developing residential area along the seashore about 5 km from Helsinki city center. For their winning competition entry, Ark Open (formerly Kahri & Co.) architects, in cooperation with SATO (a developer), Tocoman (a data management company) and TEKES (the National Technology Agency), developed an online project management system called *PlusHome* for dwelling unit sales, customer service, and material quantities. This system allowed the smooth communication of every party's interests and needs. The main features of the *PlusHome* project were the use of OB methods (i.e. separation of design tasks), a variety of layouts and apartment sizes, as well as a selection of surface materials, fixtures, and appliances, from which the future residents could choose. The online system allowed inhabitants to see an instant updating of costs according to their individual choices. Architects were able to use a 3D modeling system and could work online, collaborating with all parties, calculating quantities and costs, adapting to sellers and users' decisions. This allowed user decision making in a very time efficient and cost-controlled manner. As the project was successfully implemented and finished in 2005, SATO started shifting their own housing developments towards OB principles. Between the years 2005 and 2013, SATO realized together with architect Esko Kahri seven projects with over 700 dwelling units using the PlusHome concept. The Pilot project *PlusHome in Arabianranta* is presented later in this chapter. The online system developed for *PlusHome* at the beginning of the 2000s was far ahead of its time. Even today, building information technology (BIM) is rarely used to its full potential. In non-residential projects in Finland, it is very popular to use BIM-models for participating designers such as architects, HVAC, electrical and structural engineers but it is less commonly used in residential construction. The thinking in construction is still rather traditional and the need for BIM often not seen. This point is discussed later on in this chapter.

Another project which exemplified the OB principles was rising almost at the same time (2007–09). The *Tila* project was realized by SATO developers and designed by architect Pia Ilonen. The core idea of her approach: future inhabitants would be provided with a 5 m (16.4 ft) high raw-space unit of either 50 m^2 (538 ft^2) or 102 m^2 (1100 ft^2). The small units could be merged, or larger units separated in the future according to the inhabitants' demands (from a legal perspective this is not difficult). During the first phase, the base building is designed and erected. According to Finnish regulations, a dwelling must be habitable at the moment of sale. In a standard housing project, that means a finished bathroom and a kitchen are in place. After long negotiations between the architect and the city officials, it was sufficient to provide a bathroom and plumbing and ventilation outlets to which a kitchen can be attached later. The *Tila* project as well as *Harkko*, the second raw space project by Pia Ilonen are presented in detail in the project presentations of this chapter.

Re-thinking the city: the Helsinki urban housing program

In 2009, the City of Helsinki launched the *Re-thinking Urban Housing Program*. It aimed to increase the quality and appeal of living in blocks of dwellings as well as to integrate new personalized design solutions. The goals include solutions that enable dwellings to change over time and thus be sustainable. The program provides guidance from city experts for developers to support their effort towards new design solutions. For residents, the program aims to provide better housing alternatives and a larger variety of housing types. With these measures, the city hopes to achieve more diverse and qualitatively better housing. By 2019, the city has carried out about 30 such projects, mainly on city-owned land but also some on private plots. The projects have covered all forms of occupancy and are coordinated by a city working group consisting of members of the City Executive Office and the Urban Environment Division (City of Helsinki, 2019c).

One recent example of the *Re-thinking Urban Housing Program* is a housing district in the neighborhood of Kalasatama, a former harbor area that is being converted into a new residential and business district situated about 4 km (2.5 miles) from Helsinki city center. The area consists of three separate buildings which all feature user-influenced and life span housing solutions. Underground parking facilities, as well as the courtyard on the street level, are spaces shared by the inhabitants of all buildings (ArkOpen, 2017).

Building I: the *Neo-urban apartment block* consists of 42 ownership dwellings sized 34–135 m^2 (365–1453 ft^2). The concept was developed by architect Pia Ilonen (formerly Talli, now ILO Architects). It is based on the traditional spatial idea of arranging several equal rooms around a central hallway. Kitchen and bathrooms are readily installed at the time of purchase, otherwise, the use of spaces is not predefined but rather can be used according to personal preference and need. In this concept, although not giving any more responsibility or decision-making power to the inhabitants, as in any ordinary residential project in Finland, the inhabitants are provided with an adaptable dwelling out-of-the-ordinary, simply achieved by spatial design solutions without the need for structural or mechanical, electrical or plumbing changes to the property.

Building II: the *Gallery House* by Ark Open architects hosts 77 social dwelling units sized 32–80 m^2 (344–861 ft^2). All rental units, as well as common spaces, are arranged around a central, multi-story enclosed open gallery space that allows a visual connection between neighbors of different floors. This creates a space for community interaction. The design of the Gallery House was intended to be participatory with a high degree of variability regarding the combination of apartments. The floor plans allow for alterations. Apartment dividing walls are non-load bearing and the floor areas of wet spaces are able to be adjusted, as horizontal drainage pipes are located above the concrete slab rather than being cast inside or placed underneath in the ceiling space of the unit below. Common vertical shafts with plumbing, water, ventilation, and electricity are housed outside the units, accessible for service from the open gallery. In this way, apartments can be combined in the future. The adaptable nature of the project offers the possibility to combine small apartments into larger units and in the ability to adjust the floor plans of the apartments. The Gallery House floor plate is deeper than required in the town plan, therefore a change of town plan had to be applied for. During these two years of research and adjustment, SATO had changed its company strategy from user-involvement and adaptability to ready-made rental units. This resulted in a loss of user decision-making and reduced adaptability even if the intention remained positive.

Building III: the *Townhouses* designed by PORTAALI Architects Ltd (now part of Ark Open) target a more demanding group of inhabitants, providing customized small-scale housing in an urban context. All townhouses have a private yard and roof terrace. The original idea was to sell the townhouse units as raw space, following the separation of support and infill that is central to the OB approach, while providing future residents with a selection of dwelling layouts. In addition, it was intended that users would participate in the façade design. Unfortunately, just like in the *Gallery House* the developer decided during the planning process to pull back on a number of user-decision features. Ultimately, fixed apartment layouts were provided, and inhabitants could choose from a set of surface materials and fixtures, similar to standard multifamily housing projects in Helsinki (Kahri et al., 2011).

These projects demonstrate a range of attempts and solutions aimed at creating diverse neighborhoods while working to avoid social segregation. The loss of capacity for user-control of the fit-out, on the other hand, can be seen in various well-intended housing projects. In most cases, the reasons can hardly be influenced by the architects/planners, but rather originate from developers' decision making, as will be discussed further on.

Recent Open Building projects in the Helsinki area

After her initial research in the 1990s and 2000s, architect Ulpu Tiuri continued working on a variety of OB housing projects. In 2005 the Kaivomäki housing block for elderly people was completed. This housing project, located in Helsinki's neighboring city Espoo, is a combination of sheltered elderly housing and independent small rental units for senior citizens. The building is adaptable: floor layouts can be changed according to demand and three rooms for elderly people can be merged into two independent units. This alteration had already happened once during the planning phase, as there was a higher demand for independent units. Throughout the past years, Tiuri worked with several building co-ops. One of them, Aikalisä, has realized housing for elderly people (presented among the project presentations of this chapter). Currently Casa Urbana, another building co-op, is under construction. In this project, inhabitants can choose between different floorplan layouts and surface materials during the planning phase. In her work with building co-op's, every inhabitant meets twice with the architects an hour each time. During these meetings, one architect discusses possible changes to the proposed floor plan with the inhabitant while the second architect is updating the computer model simultaneously. If more time is needed, inhabitants have the possibility to purchase it for an additional fee.

In 2014 Esko Kahri was requested by the Ministry of the Environment to prepare practical guidance forms on adaptable housing in cooperation with Building Information Ltd. (Rakennustieto). Building Information Ltd. is a publishing house owned by the Building Information Foundation RTS, a private, non-profit organization which is aiming to foster good planning and building methods, as well as property management practices (Rakennustieto, 2017). The guidelines published by Building Information Foundation Ltd. include general information on the terminology of adaptable residential design. Reference projects are presented, and guidance is given regarding the roles of the parties involved in the construction process, planning of the building process, spatial design solutions and information regarding building systems and technical implementation. The recommendations given by Building Information Ltd. are widely used by Finnish building professionals and could help improve the organization and realization of OB projects.

In 2017 *Oikos and Logos* a housing project by architect Tuomas Toivonen and the Lehto group was built in Latakartano, Helsinki. Latakartano is situated about 11 km (6.8 miles) from the city center, next to the research fields of the Helsinki University campus in Viikki. The aim of *Oikos and Logos* was 'to build inexpensive, adaptable apartments in a good location and to develop a replicable housing typology along with a cost-efficient construction method – a pilot project for low-cost construction (Toivonen, 2019). The building is structured very rationally; the measurements of the circulation and technical cores are as minimal as regulations allow. The single staircase is in the center of the building and lit by a roof window. The apartment dividing walls are load-bearing concrete; window openings follow the standard brick size and are the largest standard window size. The wet spaces are located in the same position on all floors, and a minimal bathroom–kitchen module is installed to every apartment. Otherwise, the apartments have a raw space character; different floor plan layouts, as well as materials, could be chosen by the inhabitants. Different from all other projects mentioned in *Oikos and Logos*, the floors were cast in-situ. Pre-cast hollow core slabs could not be used as there would have been too many openings within the slabs. The building frame was erected with continuous vertical voids, in which prefabricated technical units, consisting of installations for bathrooms, kitchens, ventilation, electricity and water were installed towards the end of the construction process. Outer walls are prefabricated concrete elements, standard in Finland with a brick façade. The apartment price was 20% below the market price. This project is interesting in the sense that it allows more user control than an average residential project and addresses the issue of affordability at the same time.

As presented above, several exciting multi-story housing projects following the principles of OB can be found in Helsinki starting from the 1990s. During the last few years, building co-ops have been rising and in the latest architectural competitions like *Asuntoreformi 2020* or the competition for *Vantaa Kivistö*, entries feature solutions that present a high degree of long-term adaptabilty, showing that there is interest in the topic. The development of OB projects is slow but ongoing, yet financial pressures, lack of communication between parties, and other challenges have been slowing down progress and will be evaluated further at the end of this chapter.

Built projects

Arabianranta: PlusHome pilot project
- Project location: Kaj Frankinkatu, Helsinki, Finland.
- Chronological information: completed in 2005.
- Project design team: architects Esko Kahri and Petri Viita (Kahri and Co.), Juhani Väisänen and PlusHome Ltd. project team authors Esko Enkovaara and Timo Taiponen.
- Number of dwelling units: 77.
- Ratio of parking spaces per dwelling unit: unknown.
- Project site and building area: site area: 3900 m^2, floor area 6600 m^2.
- Project client: private developer SATO
- New construction.
- Structure type: steel frame, hollow core slabs.
- Installation utilities: horizontal piping installation and piping layout per dwelling is installed in a 'wet zone' in an 'upside-down floor system', with adaptable electric distribution system in all partition walls.
- Infill system/approach: clear separation of infill and support. The information system was developed to coordinate inhabitants, designers, client and developers.

In 2002 the second technology competition Arabianranta was organized by the city of Helsinki. The winning PlusHome proposal was developed by architect Esko Kahri (Kahri and Co.) and Tocoman data-cost office with SATO as developer. On that basis, Kahri and Tocoman founded the PlusHome company and together with SATO started a continuing working relationship with a focus on customer orientation and implementation of OB principles. PlusHome consists of three levels: a building envelope that allows variations of apartment sizes, different layout options within the fixed apartment sizes and a selection of surface materials and fixtures that inhabitants can choose from. Whereas all other projects presented work mainly with spatial solutions in this chapter, the PlusHome concept is the most technical, using a high degree of variability through technical solutions.

The pilot project is located in the neighborhood of Arabianranta. This new housing area along the seashore was developed starting in 2000. It is located about 5 km (3 miles) from the city center. This project consists of one six- and one five-story high building with 77 for-sale dwellings ranging in size between 39 and 125 m^2 (420–1345 ft^2). There is an 84 m^2 (904 ft^2) commercial space on the street level, as well as seven street-level workshop spaces for artisans, four of which are connected directly to the dwellings above by internal stairs. Storage spaces, laundry and technical spaces are located on the ground floor. Two saunas are situated on the rooftop with views over the sea. These latter spaces were required in the neighborhood plan (see Figure 3.1).

The structural frame differs from traditional building methods in Finland. Here the load-bearing walls are the longitudinal outer walls, instead of the inner cross-walls dividing the apartment units. This allows a higher degree of longitudinal variation of unit sizes within the support (see Figure 3.2). The

Figure 3.1
Arabianranta PlusHome exterior photograph (Photograph by Esko Kahri)

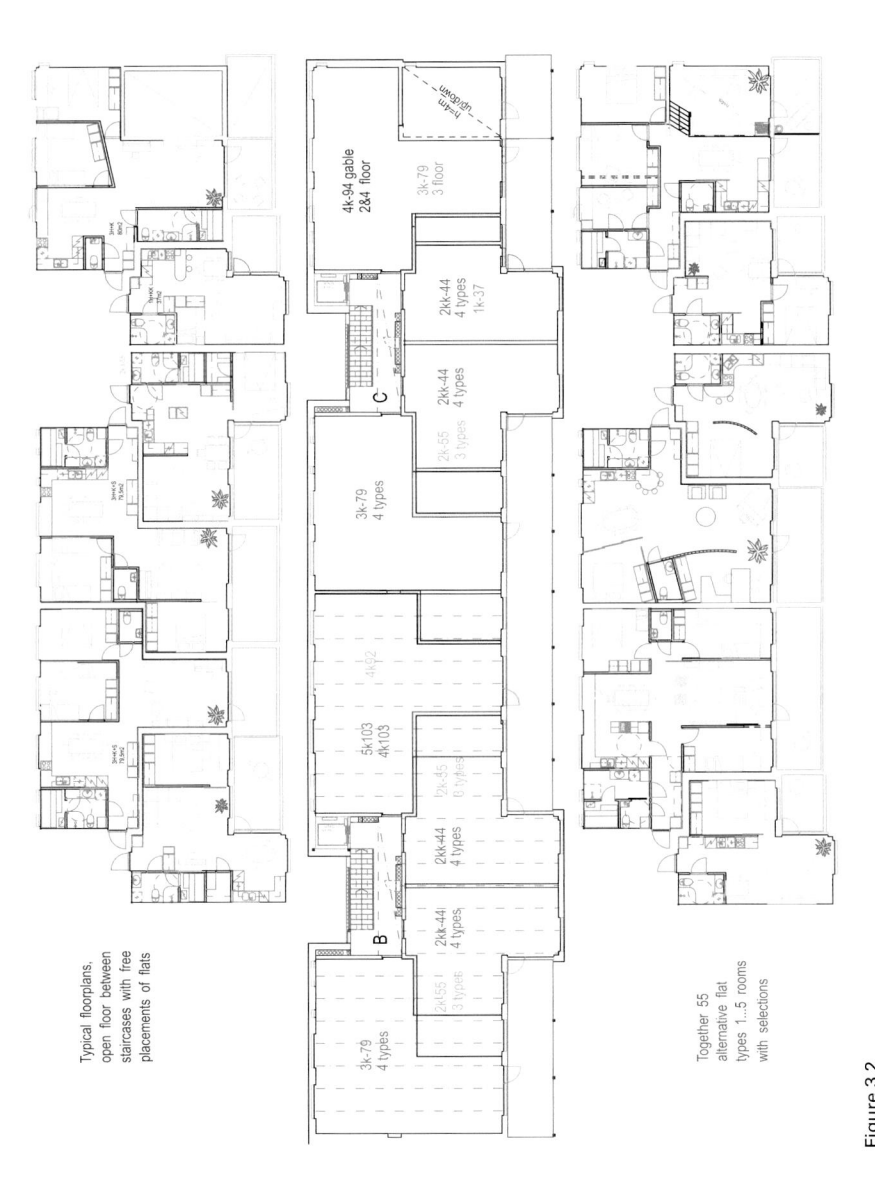

Typical floorplans, open floor between staircases with free placements of flats

Together 55 alternative flat types 1...5 rooms with selections

Figure 3.2
Arabianranta PLUSHOME floor plan variations (Source: Esko Kahri)

outer walls are made of steel frames connected to Z-formed steel beams, on which the precast concrete floor slabs bear. Most of the slabs are hollow-core concrete slabs with a 10 m (32.8 ft) span, which is popular in Finland. In the 'zones' where wet spaces are considered likely, a special slab is used in order to allow plumbing to be accessible from the top – i.e. from the spaces served. It uses steel beams with regular holes for horizonal piping, a concrete 'bottom' slab providing fire and acoustical separation, and a removable top slab. The hollow-core slabs, steel frame outside walls, vertical piping in staircases and horizontal zones make the basic structure renewable. An accessible hollow profile at the top of interior non-load-bearing metal-stud/gypsum board walls allows free placements of electrical and low-voltage wires which run down inside the walls to switches and plugs, allowing easy change or addition of terminations later. The exterior load-bearing steel frames allowed for off-site fabrication in large elements, as well as an almost unlimited option of window placements. Walls between apartments are light construction with double plasterboards. The façades are red brick or clad with thermal plastering; some parts use profiled metal plates. Large balconies for each dwelling, running across the south façade of the building, have shading elements on rollers to allow occupants to freely position them as desired.

Besides the steel building frame (which received an award from the Finnish Steel Industry Association), the main innovation was the information system developed by IT and data consulting company Tocoman, which ensured good management of the project (see Figure 3.3). The system allowed the architect to work on the model, real-time project quantity and cost information and an online platform for inhabitants. Residents could choose between different dwelling sizes and variations up to six months after construction of the support started. The building would 'fill-up' following the sequence of inhabitants' choices. After that inhabitants had another three months to

Figure 3.3
**Arabianranta
PlusHome
project data
management
scheme
(Photograph
by
Esko Kahri)**

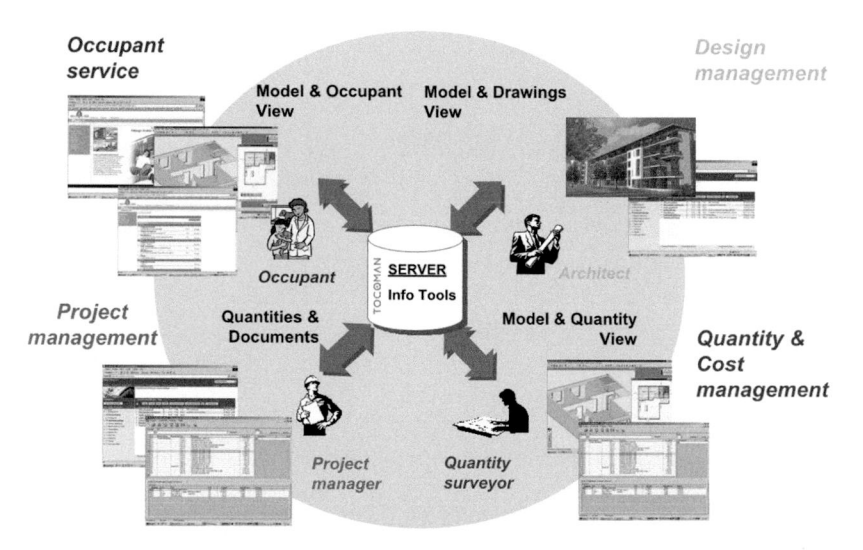

choose surface materials and fixtures while seeing an instant cost estimation of their choices. After selections, quantity information was automatically collected and delivered to the contractors. This system allowed smooth implementation on a rather large scale.

Between 2005 and 2013, PlusHome together with SATO realized seven OB projects with over 700 dwellings, although with a more traditional building envelope than in the pilot. Customer satisfaction has risen, and the concept has been well accepted. The end to PlusHome came with the change of direction from the developer's side towards 'standard rental flats,' parting ways with PlusHome. Tocoman is still in business, but not with PlusHome. However, they have been developing the software further and are selling it under the name BIM3.

Tila

- Project location: Posliinikatu 3, 00560 Helsinki, Finland.
- Chronological information: support: 2007–09 construction, infill: 2010 – ongoing.
- Project design team of support: architects Pia Ilonen, Sami Vikström (Talli architects), Design team of infill: inhabitants.
- Number of dwellings: at the moment of sale and currently: 39 dwelling units total. Possibility for division of large apartments into two 50 m² (538 ft²) apartments, estimated total would be 46 units.
- Ratio of parking spaces per dwelling unit: 0.64.
- Project site and building area: building FA 4.360 m², GFA 3.050 m² + max 1.780 m² gallery space.
- Project client: private developer SATO.
- New construction.
- Structure type: concrete prefabricated frame: bearing walls mainly between units, hollow core concrete floor slabs.
- Installation utilities: shafts outside the dwellings are part of the support. The fixed location of bathroom cells (with a number of layout options) adjacent to the vertical shafts made it possible to distribute ventilation and other installations inside units independently; kitchens were more freely positioned with connections provided in the wall of the bath-unit.
- Infill system/approach: raw-space concept – clear separation of support and infill, where inhabitants are not involved in the support phase and are the only decision makers during infill.

Tila is a neo-loft project developed by architect Pia Ilonen (ILO architects, formerly Talli) (see Figure 3.4). The concept is based on the OB approach, in which inhabitants are provided with a largely empty dwelling unit. Within this unit, inhabitants can choose to subdivide and later adjust the space as needed. The concept defines a clear division into two tasks and phases, support and infill. Whereas the support is developed and constructed almost entirely without

Figure 3.4
Tila exterior photograph (Source: Pia Ilonen)

user participation, the inhabitants purchase a Loft-style dwelling unit that can be designed according to each households' preferences and is entirely independent of architect and developer during the second infill phase. This is a perfect example of the principle of separating design tasks that is a basic principle of the OB approach. The emphasis on DIY (do it yourself) is key in this project. And just like in the original loft idea, the possibility is there to mix dwelling functions within the provided space, as well as to subdivide it.

The Tila apartment block consists of 39 apartments with 5 m (16.4 ft) double-high spaces. The standard apartment size is a 50 m² (538 ft²) module, two of which could be joined together into a 102 m² (1098 ft²) unit. Between 102 m² units, walls are load-bearing; these larger units can be subdivided later. All apartments have private balconies across the entire south façade. The first-floor dwellings have an additional space on the ground floor, which means that the dwellings are three levels when a mezzanine floor is built. The ground floor space can be used for semi-public uses, such as offices, but have most commonly been used as private bedrooms till now. The top floor dwellings are different from the others. They are 81 m² (872 ft²) L-shaped units with an 'inboard' terrace. Storage spaces and a common laundry room are located on the ground floor (most residents install laundry equipment in their dwellings); common space and sauna are located on the top floor. These latter spaces are required by the cities town plan and are part of every new housing project. The circulation works through the main staircase and elevator and access balconies. Access balconies are not very common in Nordic countries due to the cold climate, but in this project, the generous dimensions of the access balconies give a feeling of a single-family home within a multi-unit residential building, because residents can use a 'margin' of the access balcony for benches, plants, children's tricycles, and so on. Along the railings a light-art project was installed which reacts to people's movement and makes the access balcony pleasant to walk along.

During the first phase of construction, the building envelope with all its necessary structures, circulation, and public spaces was realized. The elevator can accommodate a standard sheet of gypsum wallboard which is most commonly used for light division walls (important for subsequent installation of the infill or fit-out). The building is constructed rather traditionally in a Finnish context: a prefabricated concrete structural frame, bearing walls mainly between the apartment units, hollow core slabs and a brick façade. The balconies are a steel structure anchored to the ground.

Due to Finnish regulations, to obtain a certificate of occupancy, the dwelling units have to be habitable when sold. This requires that bathrooms (but not kitchens in this case) are installed. Inhabitants could choose from nine different bathroom layouts. Bathrooms were prefabricated off-site and installed as single units, but according to architect Pia Ilonen, that was not any more efficient than site-built bathrooms and would not be repeated during the next projects. Kitchen plumbing, electrical and ventilation outlets are provided on the outer side of the bathroom walls and allow for a variety of kitchen layouts. A number of electric outlets are placed along the unit dividing walls and the walls of the bath unit. According to Finnish law, newly constructed housing projects are required to provide a mechanical ventilation system. In this project, each apartment unit has its own heat exchanger located in the technical shaft on the access balcony side of the building. At the moment of purchase, the apartment unit is efficiently ventilated. However, as soon as closed rooms are built, ventilation has to be taken care of by the inhabitants. The apartments of 5 m (16.4 ft) height allow for a gallery or mezzanine floor. The residents were given the opportunity to purchase a gallery floor structure including stairs and railing upon moving in. As a rule, only two-thirds of the floor area can be overbuilt with this floor, in order to preserve the loft character in the future. Twenty-six homes were sold with a gallery floor already in place, 13 decided to buy the space raw. Dividing walls were left as exposed concrete and basic linoleum flooring was installed. After the first phase was finished, city officials inspected the building and the building was handed over to the housing company formed by the shareholders (inhabitants). At that moment the architect and developer left the scene. Architect Ilonen had prepared a small booklet for residents consisting of guidelines regarding legal matters concerning further construction.

The second phase gives all decision-making power to the inhabitants. Every individual can decide how to proceed independently. Bring their espresso machine and mattress and start living, as the architects suggest or start designing and building their home according to their preferences, meeting their own budgets, preferences and capabilities. Some hired interior designers, some planned and built themselves. Some turned their neo-lofts into luxury space, some finished them DIY with a low budget. All inhabitants

Figure 3.5
**Tila infill –
infill is
left to the
inhabitant
(Photograph
by Pia
Ilonen)**

Figure 3.6
**Tila floor
plan 3rd
floor
(Source: Pia
Ilonen)**

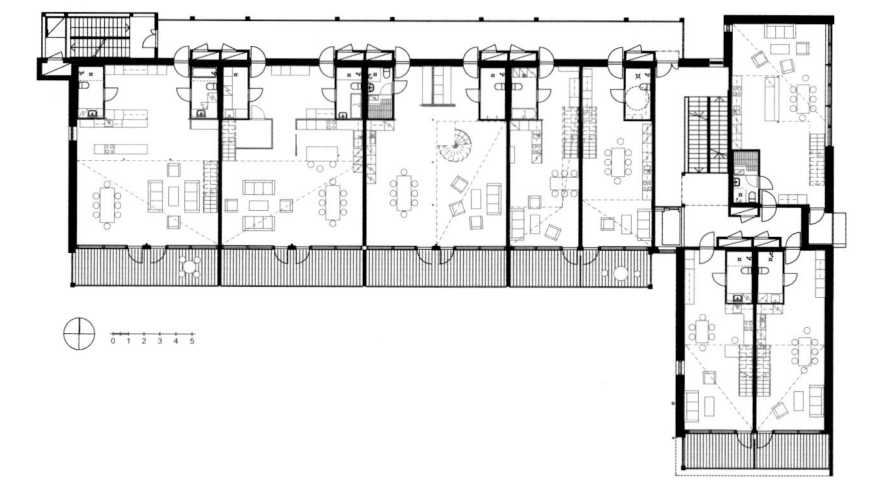

Figure 3.7
**Tila floor
plan 3rd
floor gallery/
mezzanine
(Source: Pia
Ilonen)**

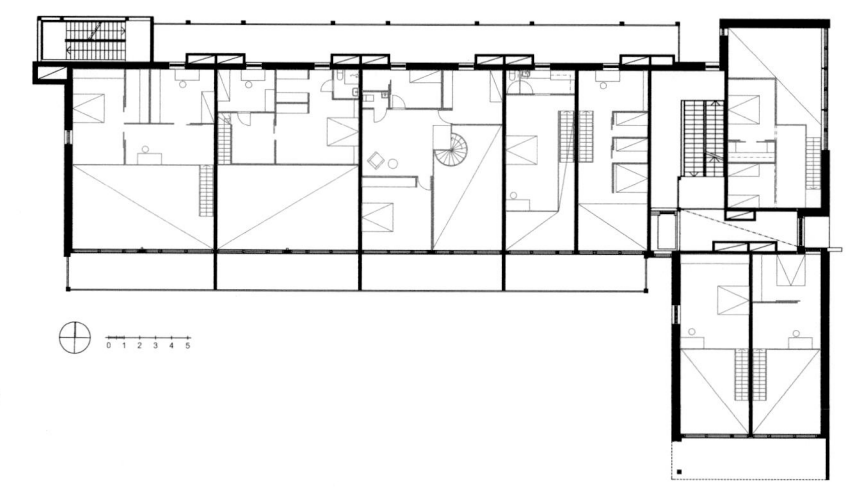

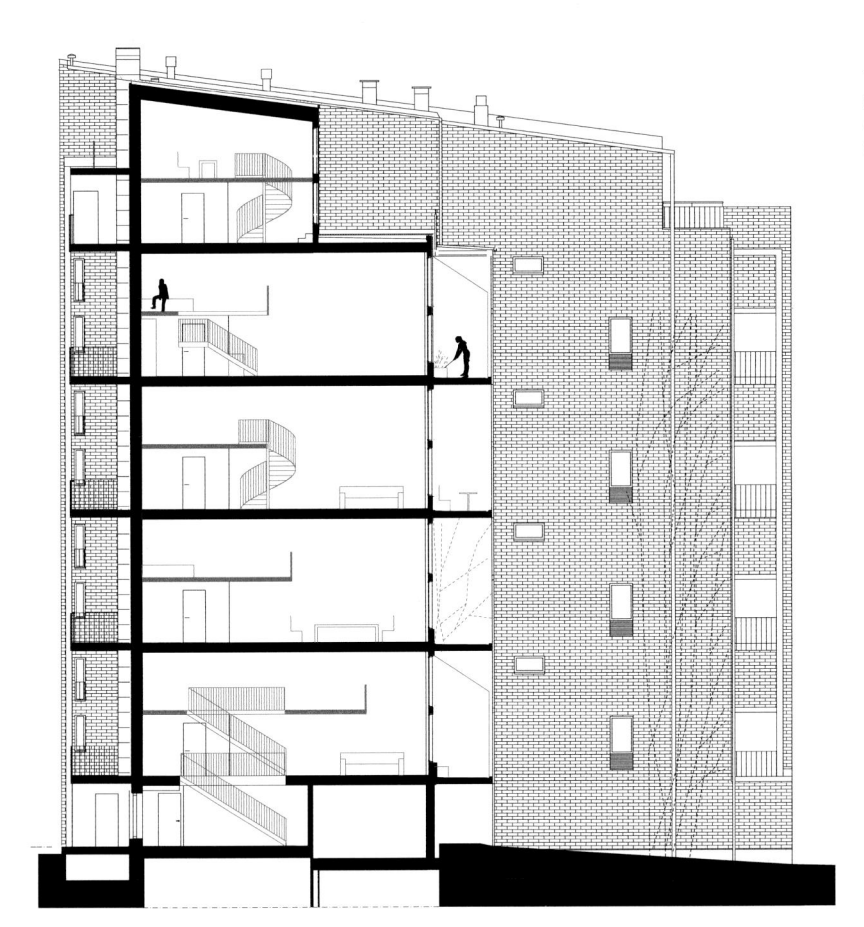

Figure 3.8
Tila cross section (Source: Pia Ilonen)

started building right away, and a great communal sense was formed through it, organizing building materials together, asking the neighbors for help and advice (see Figure 3.5, 3.6, 3.7, 3.8).

Harkko

- Project location: Saaristolaivastonkatu 2, 00590 Helsinki, Finland.
- Important chronological information: construction of support completed in 2019, infill 2019 – ongoing.
- Project design team: architects Pia Ilonen and Anu Tahvanainen (Talli architects).

- Number of dwelling units: 53.
- Ratio of parking spaces per dwelling unit: 0.64.
- Project site and building area: plot: 2373 m², FA 5048 m² + 1136 m² max gallery space.
- Project client: private developer EKE.
- New construction.
- Structure type: steel frame structure, outer walls, and staircases prefabricated concrete elements, hollow-core slabs.
- Installation utilities: vertical shafts outside the dwellings are part of the support. The fixed location of wet spaces made it possible to distribute ventilation and other installations inside units independently.
- Infill system/approach: raw-space concept – clear separation of infill and support, where inhabitant is not involved in the support phase and the only decision maker during infill

Harkko is the second of Pia Ilonen's neo-loft projects, also referred to as the raw space concept. The idea is the same as in the previously mentioned Tila project. For Harkko, the architect worked with EKE as a developer who also functioned as the builder in this project (https://ekerakennus.fi/eke-loft/).

The project is situated on the coastline of Kruunuvuorenranta, a new residential area that used to be a former oil port. The island is situated right across the sea from the Helsinki City Center and offers beautiful views. The strategy in this new residential area is to create a compact and dense area with a large variety of housing, providing residents with a commercial center hosting necessary public functions while preserving its natural environment (see Figure 3.9).

Figure 3.9 **Harkko exterior (Photograph by Pia Ilonen)**

Figure 3.10
**Harkko
infill by
inhabitants
(Photograph
by Pia
Ilonen)**

The Harkko block has 53 dwelling units varying in size from 51 to 90 m^2 (550–968 ft^2). The building is terraced from three to six stories high. Some of the second-floor units have an additional space on the street level, which means they occupy three floors if the gallery or mezzanine floor is built. Storage, laundry, technical and common spaces are located on the ground floor. The sauna is located on the top floor with a common terrace and beautiful views. The second- to fourth-floor dwellings are studios with a room height of 5 m (16.4 ft). This allows residents to build a gallery or mezzanine floor of two-thirds of the floor area. The fifth- and sixth-floor apartments have a room height of 3 m (9.8 ft) which is more generous than usual in the Finnish context. The difference in height and unit shape comes from the city requirements in the neighborhood plan. Every dwelling unit has its own private terrace. The dwelling shapes differ by location within the building. The windows are wooden; doors to the balconies and terraces are sliding. The units are accessed through staircases, elevators and access balconies (see Figures 3.11, 3.12).

The residential block is a steel frame structure, outer walls and staircases are made from prefabricated concrete elements commonly used in Finland, walls between apartments are concrete blocks. As in the Tila project, the elevator is dimensioned so that standard gypsum board panels and other construction materials for infill can be easily transported. Façades are dominated by brownish brick and wooden elements on the balconies which were demanded by the city plan but also function for sun shading. The technical installations are accessible from the access gallery which allow easy maintenance without disturbing the residents.

As in the first neo-loft project, the building envelope with all its necessary requirements, vertical circulation, and common spaces are finished first (see Figure 3.11). During the first phase, the apartment units are equipped with bathrooms; inhabitants could choose from a selection of bathroom layouts. In addition, it was possible for inhabitants to choose a built-in gallery or mezzanine floor including stairs and railings (see Figure 3.10). As in the first project, choices were provided. Most of the inhabitants chose to purchase a ready-built gallery floor. Apart from that the units were left only with basic linoleum flooring and either unfinished or white painted walls. Required

Figure 3.11
**Harkko
support
plan (empty
units)
(Source: Pia
Illonen)**

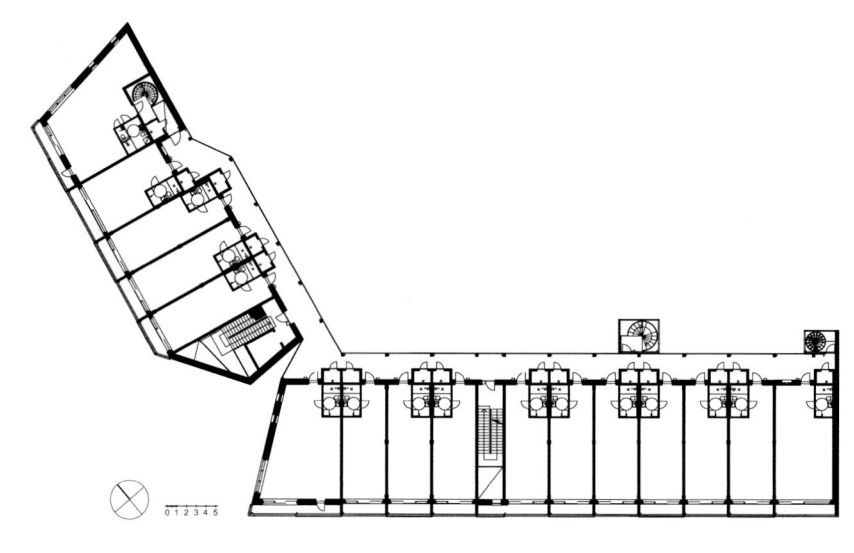

Figure 3.12
**Harko
section
showing
infill
(Source: Pia
Illonen)**

Harkko_section A_FURNISHED_1-250

mechanical installations were provided in the bathrooms and main space; electrical outlets were placed along walls; kitchen outlets for water, drainage and ventilation are located on the outer side of the bathroom unit. If the inhabitants plan to make changes, for example, build a gallery or mezzanine floor or a second bathroom on the upper floor, they must apply for a building permit. This is a standard procedure and would be the same if making alterations to an older building.

After the support was built, the developer and architect handed over the building to the housing company. This is the beginning of the infill and up to all individuals on how to proceed. Pictures document the fit-out installed by the first inhabitants and interviews with several families had been conducted in the Tila project. However, the documentation seems too little, in order to research the decisions of inhabitants within their raw space unit. Therefore, in Harkko the aim is to document the process of people's actions well and follow up on changes in the future after first occupation.

Similar to the Tila project, the community plays a very important part in Harkko. Even before moving in, residents managed to connect via social media to exchange knowledge, ask questions, or file complaints together.

A lesson learned from Harkko was that all designers and parties involved have to be educated in what the project is about. There is a common misconception of raw space lacking well-planned details. When aiming to sell a unit as a raw space, a lot of planning is required from the architect's side. One has to think about possible wishes and outcomes from the inhabitant's side and offer capacity for as many design solutions as possible. Rather than designing one perfect floor plan, one has to design a space with the capacity for a variety of floor plans according to different living concepts, even accepting that inhabitants may do something entirely unexpected. In addition, technical details have to be well executed: where the electrical outlets are placed, how the ventilation system functions, which side of a concrete element is the visible one etc. Everybody has to be in agreement; execution is even more important than in a project that leaves no control to occupants.

Aikalisä housing for seniors
- Project location: Livornonkatu 8, 00220 Helsinki, Finland.
- Chronological information: construction completed in 2015.
- Project design team on support level: Ulpu Tiuri and Jukka Lommi, architects/Arkkitehtitoimisto Tiuri & Lommi Oy; project design team on infill level: Ulpu Tiuri and Antti Vainio, architects/Arkkitehtitoimisto Tiuri & Lommi Oy.
- Number of dwelling units: 41 of various sizes ranging from 36 m^2 to 106 m^2 (388–1141 ft^2).
- Ratio of parking space per dwelling unit: 0.7 parking situated in a common underground parking facility.
- Area of the building site 1195 m^2, total floor area of the building 4495 m^2.
- Client and owner: As Oy Helsingin Aikalisä (Aikalisä Housing Company).
- New construction.
- Structure: concrete prefabricated frame: bearing walls mainly between units, hollow core slabs
- Installation utilities: vertical shafts inside the dwellings are part of the support. The fixed location of wet spaces made it possible to distribute ventilation and other installations inside units independently.
- Infill system: infill decisions were made when construction started; state of the art technology was used for both support and infill; infill can be altered independently for each unit.

Figure 3.13
**Aikalisä
exterior
street side
(Photograph
by
Ulpu Tiuri)**

Aikalisä is a project designed by architect Ulpu Tiuri (Tiuri & Lommi architects). The project addresses a movement in Helsinki: building cooperatives where a group of people work together to construct their own homes (see Figure 3.13).

The concept of co-op housing is especially strong because it is inclusive for all demographics with the advantage of being part of a vibrant community. In the case of the Aikalisä project, it has been a group of senior citizens joining forces and making the decision to build a home for themselves. At least one inhabitant in each apartment must be a minimum of 55 years old.

There is public as well as private senior housing on the market in Finland with varying quality standards. However, individual housing projects that respond to user preferences and involving the seniors into the design process are rare. In this case, the residents' group hired a project manager and the design team and formed the housing company Aikalisä, with which they were able to apply for a plot from the city of Helsinki. Helsinki city supports these kinds of initiatives and granted a rental plot in the newly developed housing area of Jätkäsaari. Jätkäsaari is a peninsula not far from the center of Helsinki which served as a container harbor for the city until 2008. By 2030, it will be home to 21,000 residents and 6000 employees, providing all public infrastructure.

Motivations for senior residents to join this project varied. Some had sold their houses in neighboring cities because they find it easier to maintain an apartment, others want to live closer to the city with better infrastructure and services or would like to live closer to their families, while others seek a community of people in the same age group (Jompero, 2015). The demand is high: all 41 dwellings in Aikalisä were immediately booked when the project started in 2010. The residents financed the project themselves since the bank had refused to give a mortgage for a project of this kind. Since then, in 2016, there was a change in the law concerning loans for building a co-op, that allows groups of individuals trying to build together to have easier access to a construction loan.

The decision making is clearly separated between support and infill. However, in the building process, there is no such division, as the infill is already designed by the time construction begins. In the support phase, decisions concerning the common spaces – like the sauna, laundry and club room which are typical for Helsinki – had to be made. As the residents were looking for a strong community spirit, they decided to realize more common space than required by the neighborhood plan. The first floor has the entrance hall, multipurpose space, laundry, drying room and wheelchair cleaning facilities. The top floor has a sauna, gathering space and common kitchen.

At first, the building envelope was built, including vertical circulation, façades, balconies, vertical shafts and placement of wet spaces. The building frame is constructed from prefabricated concrete elements, load-bearing walls dividing the apartment units and hollow core slabs, which are all standard solutions in Finland. The façade materials are brick and ceramic tile on the top floors and courtyard side. The spatial design of the support and window placement was designed to allow a large variety of floor plan layouts. Vertical shafts inside the dwellings are part of the support. The fixed location of wet spaces made it possible to distribute ventilation and other installations inside units independently.

For each unit, several floor plan options were created as a starting point for individualized design (see Figure 3.14). Two meetings of one hour were reserved for each inhabitant to discuss the individual infill with the architects. To make these meetings efficient, the inhabitants met with two architects, one who would discuss with the inhabitant about their visions, with the second one instantly updating the BIM-model according to the inhabitant's requirements. The second meeting would be a couple of months later, allowing design solutions to be revised. In this way, the architect didn't have to spend additional time after every meeting. If the inhabitant needed more time, they could choose to pay an additional fee for further consultation. According to the architect Ulpu Tiuri, the building costs and total costs for the occupants were considerably lower than the price of condominiums sold in the area. There are no special solutions ensuring adaptability during the life span of the building. But all apartments can be altered like in any other existing building.

After Tiuri's research on fit-out technical solutions from the 1990s, she shows in this project that OB principles can be achieved with ordinary technical solutions, simply by spatial qualities. However, she is still hoping that

Figure 3.14
Aikalisä floor plans (Source: Ulpu Tiuri)

more adaptable technical systems will come to Finland at some point and when that happens, a clear separation of decision-levels will already be state of the art in the building process.

Summary

All projects presented above approach OB implementation in a different way.

PlusHome achieved a high degree of user-participation and adaptability with an unusual (for Finland) building frame and a digital platform to efficiently coordinate all parties involved in the building process. The inhabitants were involved in the decision-making process but remain anonymous to the planners. In contrast, Aikälisä focuses on a close relation between the planners and inhabitants in order to achieve the most suitable design solutions for each individual. In addition, the inhabitants can influence the design of common spaces. The structure of the building is standard, and no special technical solutions were applied. Tila and Harkko on the other hand are the projects separating the support and infill clearly from each other, giving the inhabitant full freedom within their own spaces. Äikälisä, Tila and Harkko achieve the OB principles rather by spatial than technical solutions. The one thing that all projects have in common is that they are exceptional on the Finnish housing market. The reasons for that are evaluated in the following section.

Why aren't more OB projects being built?

This section discusses the reasons that so few OB projects are being realized in Finland. The observations are based on the author's experiences and observations as well as conversations with parties involved in housing production.

A reoccurring pattern in the cases outlined has been that within an organization there is usually one person or a small group of people – no matter whether from the clients', developers' or planners' side – interested in supporting consumer-orientated design solutions with a high degree of long-term adaptability. Most of those projects were driven by an idealistic individual who invested out-of-the-ordinary energy and time in convincing and energizing all parties involved. This needs dedication and can't be accepted as a sustainable process for implementing OB projects.

Education of architects and planners

From the very beginning, housing design planned for change is seldom taught in Finnish Graduate Schools of Architecture, which means knowledge about this approach to housing has to be gained from personal interest, studies or work experience. This slows down adoption. Additionally, more research on the topic is needed. Currently, more money is invested in energy efficiency and the building alone than in housing research. This concerns all planners involved, i.e. architects, and electrical, HVAC and construction engineers.

Speaking from the author's point of view as an architect, housing planned with the capacity for user control and change needs more planning than standard 'rigid' housing. A shell of a building has to be designed, which allows for a variety of fit-out solutions rather than just one; the process of 'capacity analysis' is not yet well understood. The possible needs of inhabitants must be considered. Unfortunately, financially it rarely makes a difference for planners if we are creating innovative housing projects or following standard design solutions. This is a clear indication that effective design methods – which already exist – need to be more widely learned, to convince all parties that OB does not cost more.

Financing and the inhabitant

A main OB principle is the distribution of decision making, including the inhabitants. The highest degree of decision-making power the inhabitants can gain today is by starting a building cooperative. Until 2016 banks would not loan money to co-ops before construction, which meant a large financial burden for inhabitants. After the change in the law, banks now support projects realized by co-ops financially from the start of the planning phase. The positive impact of community planning shows mainly on the amount and size of common spaces. Regarding the individual dwellings, inhabitants generally still seem to have a fear of individualism. Individual solutions are associated with longer planning time and higher costs.

Developer and constructor

The main reason why fewer OB projects have been built in Finland is that developers have not been in favor of them. Developers are aiming to make a profit in the short term. For developers, uncertainty is the enemy. Many architects believe that the fit-out is the most profitable part of a building for the developer, which would mean, i.e. that raw space projects make less profit and are therefore less in the interest of developers. However, there is no empirical research to back up this belief. From an economic point of view, there is currently no argument in Finland for why developers should build more OB projects.

Tools

A well-functioning project management system is crucial in order to realize OB projects. Building Information Modelling (BIM) is not yet standard in Finnish housing construction. If used at all, its main purpose is the coordination and clash detection between designers. Besides the coordination of designers, BIM can also help to improve communication and collaboration between all parties involved, to estimate costs, improve scheduling, and to strengthen facility management. Online platforms linked to BIM can be used for user-participation. Further, the success of the PlusHome methodology needs to be reintroduced. As a result, the argument of increased cost and inefficiency of OB projects could be reduced.

To summarize, there is good reason to believe that it is important to communicate the need and potential of OB housing projects in general. In addition, tools for coordinating the realization of the built project must be further developed and put into use.

References

ArkOpen. (2017). *Helsinki Seaside Open Housing.* [Online]. Arkopen. Available at: www.arkopen.fi/en/helsinki-seaside-open-housing/ (Accessed: 12 November 2019).

City of Helsinki. (2018a). *Jätkäsaari.* [Online]. Uutta Helsinkiä. Available at: www.uuttahelsinkia.fi/en/jatkasaari (Accessed: 12 November 2019).

City of Helsinki. (2018b). *Kalasatama.* [Online]. Uutta Helsinkiä. Available at: www.uuttahelsinkia.fi/en/kalasatama (Accessed: 12 November 2019).

City of Helsinki. (2019a). *Kruunuvuorenranta.* [Online]. Uutta Helsinkiä. Available at: www.uuttahelsinkia.fi/fi/kruunuvuorenranta (Accessed: 12 November 2019).

City of Helsinki. (2019b). *Right-of-occupancy housing.* [Online]. Hel. Available at: www.hel.fi/helsinki/en/housing/housing/occupancy/#c9347bb4 (Accessed: 21 January 2020).

City of Helsinki. (2019c). *Re-thinking Urban Housing.* [Online]. Hel. Available at: www.hel.fi/kanslia/re-thinking-urban-housing (Accessed: 12 November 2019).

Jompero, S.J. (2015). *Uusi asumisen tyyppi vetää maalta kaupunkiin Ehtona meillä oli 55 vuoden ikä* [Online]. Helsingin Uutiset. Available at: www.helsinginuutiset.fi/artikkeli/322908-uusi-asumisen-tyyppi-vetaa-maalta-kaupunkiin-ehtona-meilla-oli-55-vuoden-ika (Accessed: 12 November 2019).

Kahri, E., Anttonen, S., Enkovaara, E., Ilonen, P., Kämäräinen, J. and Viita, P. (2011). *Asukasnäkökulma kaupunkiasumiseen.* 1st ed. Helsinki: Rakennustieto Oy.

KTI Finland. (2019). *The Finnish Property Market*. 1st ed. [Online]. Available at: https://kti.fi/wp-content/uploads/The-Finnish-Property-Market-2019.pdf (Accessed: 12 November 2019).

Mukala, J. (2014). Community and housing. *Finnish Architectural Review*, 111(4), p. 16.

Rakennusteollisuus. (2019a). *Lukuja-asumisesta*. [Online]. Rakennusteollisuus. Available at: www.rakennusteollisuus.fi/Tietoa-alasta/Asuminen/Lukuja-asumisesta/ (Accessed: 12 November 2019).

Rakennusteollisuus. (2019b). *Laki suojaa asunnonostajaa*. [Online]. Rakennusteollisuus. Available at: www.rakennusteollisuus.fi/Tietoa-alasta/Asuminen/Laki-suojaa-asunnonostajaa/ (Accessed: 12 November 2019).

Rakennustieto. (2017). *Building Information*. [Online]. Rakennustieto. Available at: www.rakennustieto.fi/index/english.html (Accessed: 12 November 2019).

Sinnemäki, A. (2016). Monipuolista asuntopolitiikkaa. *Finnish Architectural Review*, 113(4), p. 79.

Tiuri, U.T. (1997). *Asunnon muunneltavuus ja avoin rakentaminen*. 1st ed. Espoo: Helsinki University of Technology, Department of Architecture (p. 93).

Toivonen, T. (2019). Memorandum. *Finnish Architectural Review*, 116(3), pp. 34–39.

Chapter 4

Quality control by levels
Steering the design process using BEA's Project Book

Jia Beisi

Introduction

Architectural design is object oriented and involves decision making on form, space, and the organization of technical systems. It is also a process of decision making by all the involved parties, impacting potential users throughout the entire life of the building. Design decisions based on an integrated conceptual framework are fundamental to any built environment that is constantly evolving with time and that is expected to have a long life.

This chapter introduces a design management tool based on the concept of Open Building and the architectural debates on "infrastructuralism." The former deals with an understanding of social–spatial levels of intervention in built environments; the latter proposes that buildings based on an infrastructure model will be more sustainable and resilient. These observations are the basis for Baumschlager Eberle Architects (BEA)'s design process and its "project books." These projects books are organized on a classification of five social–spatial levels, namely, urban public spaces, building structure and service system, building façade, functional layout, and interior fittings. After a brief introduction of BEA's international network of offices, this chapter investigates two recently completed projects, followed by an analysis of the concept, framework, contents, and management of the project book and the design process of the two buildings. The skills needed for handling the complexity in the design process between the design qualities at the five levels are addressed. The five levels of BEA's design process enlarge the social and functional capacities of buildings to accommodate multiple uses, including but not limited to residential.

Baumschlager Eberle Architekten (BEA), founded in 1985 in Austria's Vorarlberg, the western-most federal state of Austria, is well known (Baumschlager 2020). The firm uses a clear and systematic approach to design and builds landmark structures around the world. BEA has 11 independent offices in eight countries in Europe and Asia, with design teams drawn from around 270 firm members from 21 countries communicating in 19 different

DOI: 10.4324/9781003018339-5

languages. Their presence on the ground helps broaden their understanding of local conditions and cultural specificities and helps them stay close to their clients. In addition to residential and office projects, they work in the fields of education and culture, health and sports, transport and traffic, and are active in the full breadth of planning the built environment, managing interior and landscape design projects as well. Because sustainability is the most important contribution a building can make in terms of ecology, economy, and cultural value, BEA designs buildings to meet a number of sustainability criteria relating to resources and energy, quality, and functional neutrality.

> What does sustainable architecture mean? In a global scene, we have to look at the problems and what we have. We need to look at buildings as a process. We need correct and complete information about people, energy, and resources. On this basis, design is about creating buildings that will last for at least 200 years rather than creating new things.
> (Dietmar Eberle: Lecture delivered at HKU on 24th October 2003)

The architectural characteristics of BE projects can be summarized as having a "strict economy with respect to material and artistic/architectonic means and a keen sense of cultural and social responsibility" (Frampton 2003, p. 19). In their own words, they gained a wide knowledge of buildings, especially in terms of housing, and they paid strict attention to ensuring that highly skilled craftsmanship is applied with respect to the materials used and the quality of construction.

However, some aspects of their work have not been thoroughly studied and properly presented, namely, the issues of design methodology, although they have been frequently mentioned by Eberle in his speeches. Eberle is aware of John Habraken's work in methodology and is knowledgeable about the technological developments in housing since the 1960s. However, in considering those features of Open Building that are represented in their work, they seem directly generated from experience and the immediate reality that they are dealing with every day. Firmly rooted in practice, they have demonstrated a particular skill in which capacity for changing uses, sustainable building, a high level of craftsmanship, and the beauty of architecture are expertly combined in reasonably priced, simple, and compact buildings. Their experience and know-how are significant for researchers and practitioners with respect to the implementation of the Open Building approach.

BEA architects examine every aspect of a building project in all its complexity at the design and planning stages. This groundwork forms the basis for clear and logical decision making, ensures quality throughout the construction process, and guarantees transparency and trust. At the core of this process is their project book.

> To ensure that all the projects move forward in a clear and transparent manner, that the right things are done at the right time and that the core

idea is implemented in accordance with the brief, we have developed our own process methodology and our own tool: the **project book**.

(BEA Office Profile 2020, emphasis in original)

It combines the creative and management processes in one communication tool and documents every stage of a project. It allows the architects to integrate the client's and users' evolving requirements and other professionals' work at any time and to make adjustments as necessary, thereby underpinning architectural quality assurance.

Concept of levels and the BE Project Book

Thinking in terms of levels of intervention, urban tissue is a higher level that represents common values and serves the broad community. Elements such as streets, plazas, pedestrian networks, shopping malls, community centers and schools, drainage systems, and power supply are civilized infrastructures. Stan Allen summarized the seven characteristics of infrastructure, which he believes that new architecture interventions can incorporate (Allen, 1999, pp. 54–55). Infrastructure prepares the ground for future building and creates the conditions for future events. The provision of services supports future programs and the establishment of networks for movement, communication, and exchange. They are flexible and anticipatory. Infrastructure work recognizes the collective nature of the city and all built form, and allows the participation of multiple actors. Infrastructure creates a directed field where different architects and designers can contribute, but it sets technical and instrumental limits to their work. Infrastructures accommodate local contingency while maintaining overall continuity. Although static in and of themselves, infrastructures organize and manage complex systems of flow, movement, and exchange. They create the conditions necessary to respond to the incremental adjustments in resource availability and modify the status of inhabitation in response to changing environmental conditions. Infrastructures allow detailed design of typical elements or repetitive structures, facilitating an architectural approach to urbanism.

However, infill, supports, and infrastructure by themselves do not answer questions of quality or perception of space. A sense of space is largely from visual perception and comforts obtained by the human body. Although a building is a highly complex web of many individual components, it is immediately absorbed and with all the human senses: when one steps into the space of a street or a square, he/she forms an intuitive impression of its appearance and scale, triggering a subconscious chain of associations without consciously grasping every detail. Atmosphere involves a mix of sensory perceptions, such as seeing, hearing, smelling, and touching. This mood will frequently determine whether we use a space intuitively in a relaxed way and feel comfortable in relation to it. All these factors are based on a sensory code, where we communicate with the space (Troeger 2015, p. 36).

Table 4.1 Five systems of building classified by lifetime

Systems	Lifetime (year)	Explanation
Infrastructure	200–1000	"All outdoor public infrastructures stand longer than buildings. A city infrastructure may have a history of 1000 years; we have to be extremely careful about this when we design a building."
Load bearing structure, Staircase	100	"The load bearing structure, combined with staircases, and in relation to all the safety problems, can stand more than 100 years without any change (Unless an error occurred in design.)"
Façade Service core	50–60	"The façade and the main interior outlet piping system inside should last for 50–60 years. We do not frequently change façades in our culture because it is extremely expensive."
Functional layout	20	Interior partitions, utilities specific to each user territory
Interior	10	Ceiling, lighting, finishing

Source: Jia 2011, p. 6.

BE's architectural design has to address a comprehensive set of conditions and does so on precisely distinct levels to achieve a sustainable building with high quality and a manageable process. BEA architects work on the assumption that each building should be conceptually and technologically separated into five systems in accordance with the life cycle of materials, spatial and structural hierarchies, and social responsibility (i.e. who controls what) (Table 4.1). The building should be organized in such a manner that it does not mix these systems. This condition makes change easy and gives a great deal of decision flexibility when dealing with separate systems.

Structure and contents of BEA Project Books

Separating the systems in this manner aims to accommodate time and changes in the design. It also aims to extend the lifetime of major structures that are embodied with a large share of resources and energy. However, the purpose of this strategy is certainly not confined to its spatial significance. It is also about user control and economic management. The separate systems have a large capacity to meet the various criteria and demands of owners and users. With respect to BE's work, the separation of the five systems allows them to intensively focus on specific areas, while leaving other tasks for other people to deal with (Table 4.2).

Architectural design is a process of synthesis. Decisions are made on the basis of the comprehensiveness and precision of information. The contents

Table 4.2 Six chapters and primary subtitles of each project book

Chapter A. Management
A1. Basics **A2**. Contract Management **A3**. Organization Management; **A4**. Organization Management; **A5**. Project Description; **A6**. Area Diagram; **A7**. Project Book Title Sheets

Chapter B. Urban Design
B1. Basic Maps; **B2**. Building Codes; **B3**. Traffic and Infrastructure; **B4**. Outdoor Space; **B5**. Urban Structure; .... **B10**. Pictures and Visualization

Chapter C. Primary Structure and Safety
C1. Basic Plans; **C2**. User Requirements; **C3**. Primary Structural Plans; **C4**. Core Elements; **C5**. Safety and Fire Protection Concept; .... **C10**. Pictures and Visualizations

Chapter D. Building Envelope and Technology
D1. Basic Plans; **D2**. Climate; **D3**. Building Physics; **D4**. Building Envelop; **D5**. Façade Components; **D6**. HVAC; .... **D10**. Pictures and Visualization

Chapter E. Functions and Layout
E1. Basic Plans; **E2**. Specifications of Uses; **E3**. General Functional Plan; **E4**. Units; **E5**. Furniture Layout; .... **E10**. Pictures and Visualizations

Chapter F. Interior Surface and Finishes
F1. Material Concept; **F2**. Floors; **F3**. Walls; **F4**. Ceilings; **F5**. Interior Elements; **F6**. Core Area; .... **F10**. Pictures and Visualizations

of the project book intend to cover all the aspects of study, although different projects may emphasize certain aspects. For instance, interior design projects may include many pages of drawings in Chapter F. However, they are still related to the information on other chapters, such as Chapter C Primary Structure and Safety and Chapter A Cost Control. Decisions are also made upon the timing of decision makers. Clients may prefer to have strong presentations regarding functional arrangement, as discussed in Chapter E. Engineers have strong expertise in the thermal performance on envelope in Chapter D. A user may want to have customized design for his/her apartment fittings, as in the following case of the Metropolitan in Zurich; Chapter F will serve for his/her preference. Therefore, the chapters are independent and enable changes in different stages of decisions, for different projects.

The quality of design decisions responds to the quality and visualization of information and decisions. Information and design decisions must be properly presented. This condition is important because of the nature of architecture, where the form, atmosphere, and human comfort are consistently scrutinized by users and the public in the evaluation of buildings. BEA project books are equipped with detailed presentation standards, from line types, color codes to the layout of pages in A3 landscape. BEA architects believe that the project book is consistently an 'art piece' by itself at any stage of design and construction (see Figure 4.1).

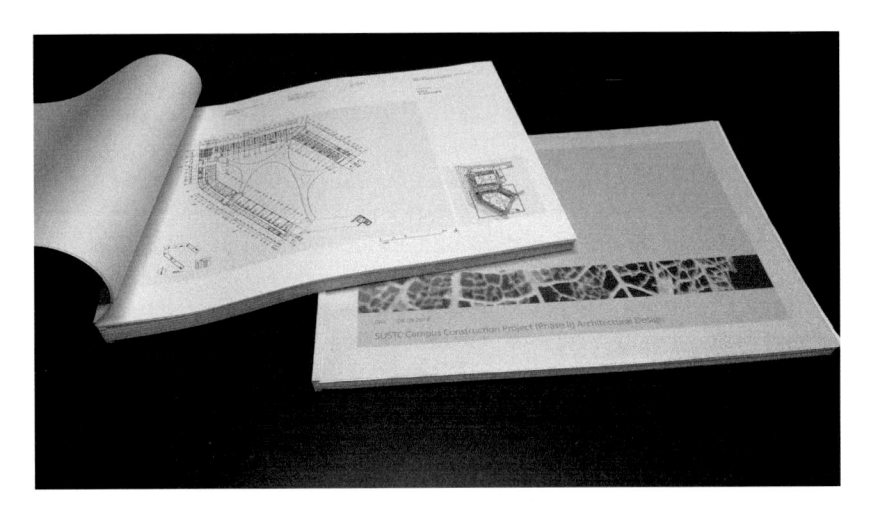

Figure 4.1
**Project book
of the
Engineering
School**

Two projects

Two projects serve as illustrations of the project book to explain the contents and management of the BEA design process – focused on an open process and sustainable design, rather than a project driven by function. The first project is an engineering school in Shenzhen, completed in August 2020 (see Figure 4.2). The illustrations are about the design process controlled and presented by the project book. The second is the Metropolitan, a high-rise housing project completed in Zurich in 2016 (see Figure 4.3). The illustrations about them are obtained from the final version of their project books.

Figure 4.2
**Engineering
school in
Shenzhen
2020**

Chapter A: Management

The question of architecture, as opposed to science, is not about the generalization of certain principles that can be applied uniformly everywhere. Architecture is consistently bound by the specific social, cultural, and technological conditions of a particular location. Eberle states that "Architecture is based on three things, namely, social and cultural understanding of our society, technology, and its background, including science, and an ability to make a formal decision"(Eberle 2003). BEA architects are dealing with an approach toward the building known as *Gestaltigkeit* or the ability to create a space or form of high tectonic quality, appropriate to and in keeping with the area. Each project intends to permit regional differences to play a decisive role in its design. In different regions prevailing structures, planning permission regulations, craftsmanship, and the building process itself are different. "We consistently try to identify the key problem, and then we find a direction to meet the problem on many levels, such as cultural and social levels" (Eberle 2003).

Considering that every project is unique for BEA architects, the background information and objectives of the project need to be clarified in Chapter A (Table 4.3). Whether a project is successful or not, good or bad, depends heavily on Chapter A because it manages three basic resources of any project: the people involved, the cost, and the schedule. The other chapters are controlled by Chapter A and but also have an impact on Chapter A. For

Table 4.3 Major content and structure of Chapter A Management

A1. Basics: Shows the history and intentions of the client. Basis for project processing in the individual Chapters A–F and the construction intentions. Chapter-based questionnaire of communication between the client and architect.

A2. Contract Management: Defining the contractual compliant performance phases. Setting up a performance description. A schedule of all the planning stages and the corresponding payment plan.

A3. Organization Management: To explain the project organization and project management on the part of the client and planners. Form and the quality objectives are defined. The internal organization chart and the corresponding contact list are important components of quality management.

A4. Organization Management: The phase-compliant identification of costs (cost-estimate) and a yield calculation are the elements of the cost chapter.

A5. Project Description: The construction and project description are based on the structure of the project book and information management. The information will be written and serve as the basis for each chapter.

A6. Area Diagram: An area calculation in accordance with the local building code is part of the construction input/submission to the approval procedures. Create a surface/volume calculation in accordance with the prescribed standards and identify the resulting figures.

A7. Contents of Project Book

instance, increasing costs of technical decisions on the façade in Chapter D will have immediate impact on the total cost of the project in Chapter A. Therefore, Chapter A has to have a framework to cover all the costs in the entire process of the project in detail. Chapter A is not only a management tool. Everyone involved needs to understand, negotiate, and achieve a common goal at the beginning of each project. The framework is also open in format, where any changes in the later stage of design or construction are immediately reflected in Chapter A. Thus, everybody is informed with the benefits and consequences of changing decisions on the three issues, namely, the people involved, the budget, and the schedule.

Chapter B: Urban Design

BEA buildings are "deeply rooted in the region, that is, their material resources, craftsmanship, and building regulations are based on the climate. All these factors play a decisive role in determining the generic nature of what is realized in a large extent" (Frampton 2003, p. 9). The intention is to permit regional differences to play a decisive role in their design. In different regions prevailing structures, planning permission regulations, craftsmanship, and the building process itself are different. "We consistently try to identify the key problem and then we find a direction to meet the problem on many levels, such as cultural and social" (Eberle 2003). For instance, BEA makes the distinction between an urban site and a naturally open site. In terms of an urban site that is already functioning well and contextually supplying an appropriate, useable vocabulary, they observe that creating something absolutely new is unnecessary. The objective is to maintain the existing structures and to reinterpret them. However, in an unbuilt context, where no suitable points of reference are found, a much more subtle set of instruments is used to arrive at a viable solution.

A good urban space has a human scale where the local community can associate with it; which encourages pedestrian movement; is attractive for people to gather; that protects from or is open to climate; and that has surrounding activities for people to engage with. The density of buildings and intensity of activities contribute to the shape and liveliness of a place (Jia and Li 2018). Chapter B (Table 4.4) is used as the first chapter because of the large and long-term impact of the building on the local community and surrounding; it is related to the upper level of decisions from the city, and the strong impact to the lower level of decisions on the buildings among all the technical chapters.

The Engineering School, which is situated at the boundaries of the northwest campus, follows the overall concept structure of the campus – "two-axis, three-corridor, and one-ring." The massing emphasizes the boundary on the northwest. It has two U-shaped courtyards, which have openings toward the landscape on the east and south, hosting outdoor activities for the campus. The sloping roof, which is lower at the east/south and higher at the west/north, fully reflects the consideration of the terrain characteristic of the site (see Figure 4.2). The special

Table 4.4 Major content and structure of Chapter B Urban Design

B1. Basic Maps: The basic plans are to be in three different projecting display levels and form the basis for the subsequent chapter topics. The three levels are city/town, district, and site/property.

B2. Building Codes: Map and text information on the legal basis in the three different scale levels. City-legal basis, legal basis of the district, and project-specific legal basis.

B3. Traffic and Infrastructure: Requirements of transport and infrastructure in three different scales. Technical infrastructure, transport development, transport links, and the networking of technical infrastructure on the property.

B4. Outdoor Space: The requirements of landscape architects will be in three differently defined scales. These requirements vary depending on the project size in the three (or fewer) pages represented. Description of special equipment and details of the lighting concept.

B5. Urban Structure: Information on urban and regional development. Analysis and information of building size, building heights, position on the site, and relationship to the environment (representation site level).

B10. Pictures and Visualization: Illustrations to the Urbanism Chapter.

features of the Metropolitan are emphasized by diagonally positioning the two towers, to give the neighborhood an urban square, and the surroundings a landmark that is visible from afar. The two towers defining a soft, green plaza in direct proximity to the first high-rise is an apt complement to the roadside environment. Their orientation underlines the quality of the planning, thereby optimizing the parameters of the urban setting and the arrangement determined by the building structures (see Figures 4.3, 4.4).

Figure 4.3
Metropolitan housing in Zurich 2016

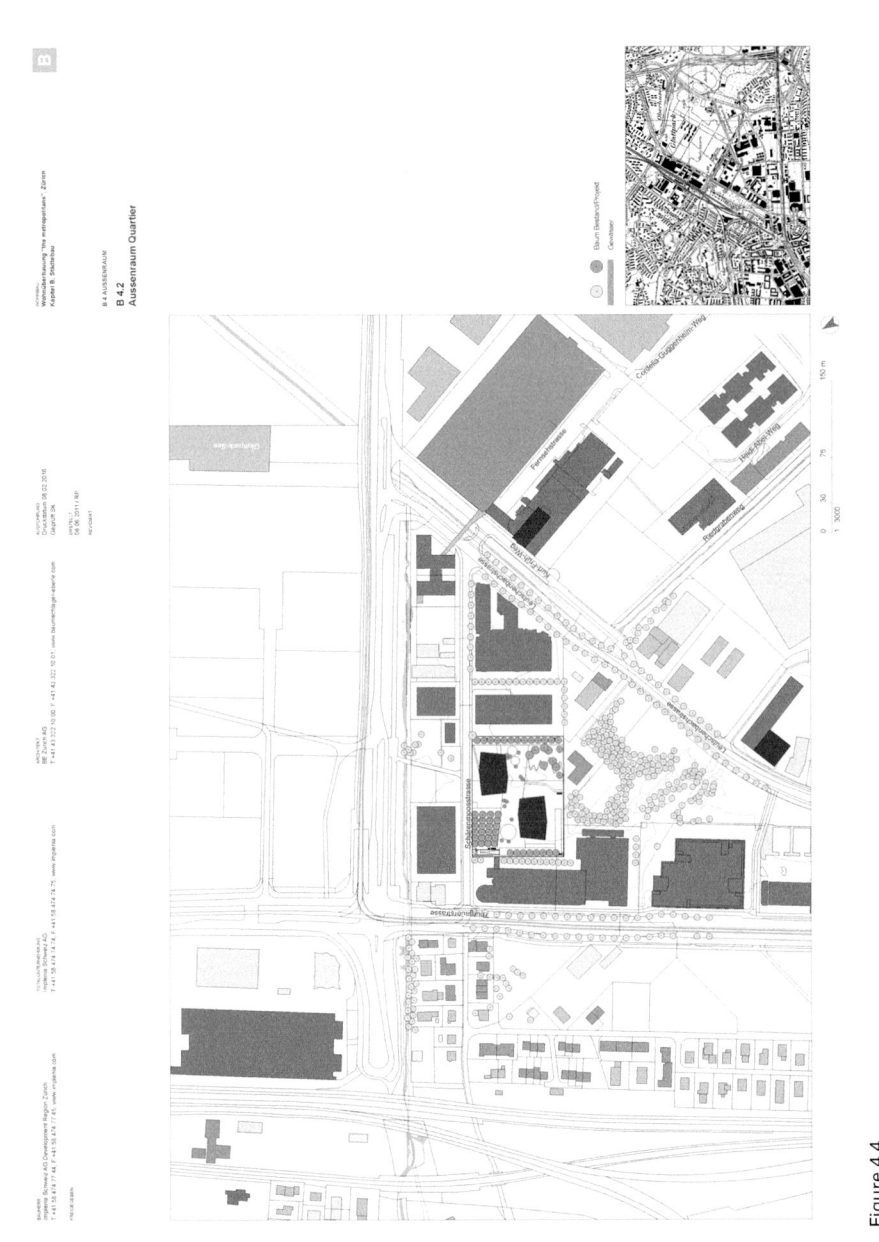

Figure 4.4
Site plan of metropolitan–urban context in project book

Chapter C: Primary Structure and Safety

The base building or support is the platform or "infrastructure" where variety and change of occupancy as well as public space for interaction among people in the lifetime of the building can occur. The quality of a base building includes but is not limited to architectural and tectonic qualities: permanency, adaptability, simplicity, public spaces, and energy saving service systems are also important. Among them, the architectural and technical quality and the design of public space require design skills partially borrowed from the traditional architectural discipline (Jia 2010). This is a separate chapter (Table 4.5) because "it will become easier for architects designing Supports to refocus on the traditional aspect of architecture; public space, building's tectonic qualities, spatial experience, façade, and definition of public space and urban character" (Kendall and Teicher 2000: 191). Technical issues, such as safety, are complicated enough that they cannot be decided by the clients and users.

Table 4.5 Major content and structure of Chapter C Primary Structure and Safety

C1. Basic Plans: Overview of floor plans and sections with all the supporting vertical and horizontal components. The plans form the basis for the next topic plans of Chapter C and the basis of Chapter D.

C2. User Requirements: Requirements of the client regarding building usage and the structural system are defined in drawing and text form, secured, and are the basis for project processing.

C3. Primary Structural Plans: Basic drawings for processing by the project engineer. Information on building the system in a structural plan and text form.

C4. Core Elements: Overview of the shell to create elements, such as cores, prefabricated concrete elements, and ramps. With type, detail, and position pages, the elements are shown in a detailed scale.

C5. Safety and Fire Protection Concept: Security concept for the project in plan and text form. Consultation with the client and the authorities. A plan based on the summary of sheets from Chapter E1.

....

C10. Pictures and Visualizations: Pictures and illustrations to Chapter C: Primary Structure and Safety

The concept of support or base building with respect to BEA architects includes the inner access (staircase, landing, and corridor) and the utilities (elevator core, kitchens, and bathrooms) in a building structure. The internal circulation is the internal public space presenting an image and identity of the collective living and working in the building. Managing significant changes or to allow user control for the service core in kitchens and bathrooms is difficult and expensive. The service core and positions of kitchen and bathrooms are fixed, although the sizes and layouts are variable.

The design of the Engineering School fully reflects the dignity, simplicity, and economic features of the university architecture. Nine departments are

found in the faculty. Each of them intends to accommodate research laboratories, administration spaces, and offices for professors with assistants in a
ratio based on their own preferences. However, a concrete program could
not be provided at the design stage. On the technical aspects, the research
laboratories are extremely different from one department to another. The
project adopted a base building design with capacity for variable department
and laboratory sizes, efficient floor plans, sufficient service cores for research
laboratories, and capacity for various room layouts (see Figure 4.5).

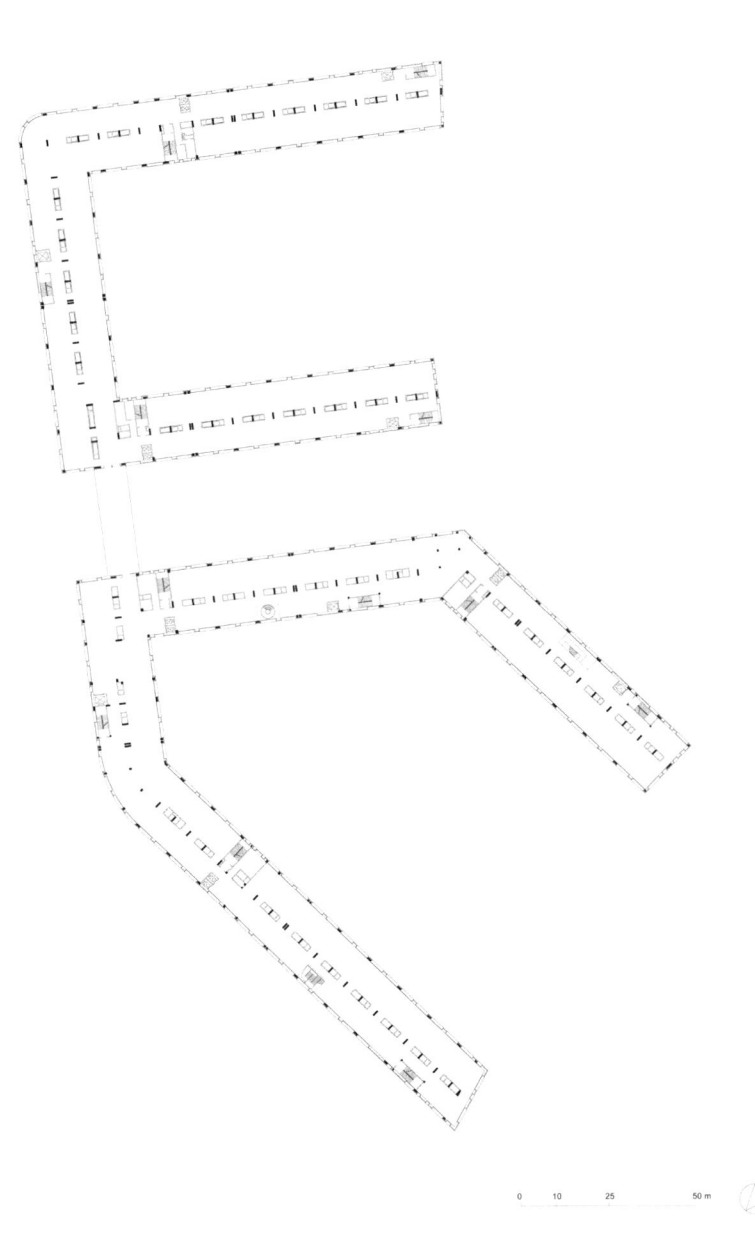

Figure 4.5
**Engineering
School –
primary
struc-
ture plan**

0   10   25   50 m

In the Metropolitan, the rooms are undivided between the structural elements. To omit or to add a room, one has to remove or insert a non-load-bearing partition wall. This process is a highly significant development with respect to ground-plan typologies: a fixed service zone and the possibility of adapting the living and working area to individual requirements are found. Extremely diverse domestic arrangements can be realized in such an apartment building. The individual is entirely responsible for deciding whether he or she wants to have any rooms at all or a number of rooms with different sizes. The locations of bathrooms and kitchens are fixed, while their layout and fittings varies from one apartment to another.

Chapter D: Building Envelope and Technology

BEA architects consider the façade of a building to be of particular importance because it is the part of the building that provides the key to saving energy, the complicated interrelationship between the exterior and the interior, the private and the public, and creates the crucial syntactical enrichment of the public outdoor space. The façade is expensive to build, with high embodied energy, is technically complicated, and is difficult to maintain. Therefore, the façade is treated as an independent chapter (Table 4.6). It is essentially part of the support or base building, representing the collective decision reflecting the community. It is not an area where individual or private needs dominate. However, BEA architects observe that it is important and crucial for the users to be able to operate and be in partial control of elements of the façade, that is, to adjust the lighting, ventilation, shading, and views. The outlook of the building changes in accordance with the actions and the wishes of the buildings' occupants. In BEA buildings the façade accommodates adjustable elements and constantly changes. Various technologies and materials have been applied, thereby resulting in intensifying this capacity for adjustment by users (Jia 2007).

Table 4.6 Major content and structure of Chapter D Building Envelope and Technology

D1. Basic Plans: Overview of floor plans and sections (possibly including façades) with all windows, exterior doors, gates, facade cladding, safeguards on the façade, sun protection, skylights, roof constructions, and roof linings.

D2. Climate: The relevant climate data in chart form with statements on the local annual averages. Define the standards of thermal/hygienic and visual/acoustical comfort.

D3. Building Physics: Optimizing the geometry of buildings and the facade, in cooperation with the building structure. Pages D 3.1 to D 3.3 must be regarded as a unit and serve as reference in building and optimizing the detection of certain energy goals.

D4. Building Envelope: Pages with plan, section, and front representation. Overview presentation of all significant views. Shadows to illustrate the plasticity and/or depth. Overview of façade and roof surfaces with an indication of the relevant structures.

D5. Façade Components: Overview of façade and roof elements, such as precast, window, doors, gates, sun protection, and fall protection. With type, detail and position pages, all the elements are shown in a detailed scale.

D6. HVAC: Water, electricity, heating, air-conditioning, and ventilation systems

....

D10. Pictures and Visualization: Illustrations to Chapter D Building Envelope and Building Services.

Chapter D provides a platform for deliberation on preferences for the façade design. In the case of the Engineering School, the university – the user – addresses the identity in appearance and also focused on views to the landscape from the windows of the building. The client – the construction department of the city – addresses the implementation of budget and safety. Considering that the budget was adjusted several times in the design process, approximately half of the meetings in the entire design process were about the façade. The façade was designed on the basis of the collective decision of the university. BEA architects provided technical services on the basis of the format of Chapter D. A consistent character of neutrality is typically maintained to insure a large capacity for variable internal use and subdivisions.

The apartments of the Metropolitan have outdoor spaces – loggias – fitted between the "internal façade" (climate envelope) and the external façade (see Figure 4.6). They extend from front to back or are positioned over a corner, and their attractiveness is enhanced by their extended share of the façade. The external facades of light concrete and the internal facades with their lustrous stucco surface enhance the inclination outline of the building. They provide a deepened perforated character on the façade. The appearance of structural figures on the façade constitutes an exemplary new part of the city on a macro-scale (see Figure 4.3). The stratification from the outside, the adjustable openings of the apartments, and their optimum orientation underline the quality of the design.

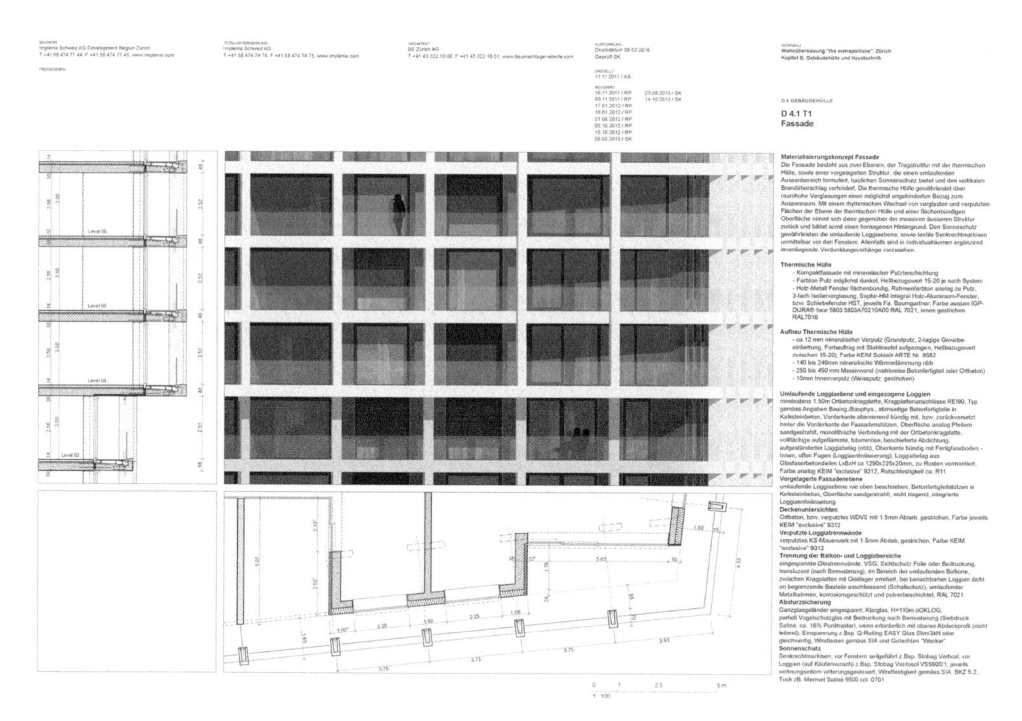

Figure 4.6
Metropolitan – façade study, a typical façade study page in the project book

Chapter E: Functions and Layout

This chapter is the second least important in the project book because the functions frequently change. However, making a separate chapter is important to provide sufficient study and proper presentation because it is related to the fundamentals of space efficiency, comforts of use, access, and capacity to accommodate different uses and layouts or floor plans. Chapter E (Table 4.7) is a criticism of the prevailing concept of "functionalism" in the 20th century and reinforces the concept and methodology of "levels." Functionalist thinking or "form-follows-function" produces low quality and short lifespan buildings because function changes faster than the buildings and has nothing to do with timeless quality of space. Design dominated by function does not provide a methodology of negotiation and capacity for changes. Although criticism on functionalism is not unique, a design methodology for replacing it is seldom as clear as the project book of BEA.

This chapter starts with E1. The basic plans and section are embedded in Chapters C and D. The decision made on these chapters provides control of functional layout and the possibilities of functions. Here, the size, location, and arrangement of functions need to be studied (E2). The dimensions of specific 'fixed' functions, such as auditorium, club house, and restrooms, need to be decided (E3). Spaces, such as rooms, need to be divided (E4). The quality of space needs to be defined (E5) and visualized (E6) for discussion and making decisions.

Table 4.7 Major content and structure of Chapter E Function and Layout

E1. Basic Plans: Overview of floor plans and sections with all interior walls, floor coverings (e.g., stairways), balustrades, handrails, paneling, interior doors, skylights, kitchen, bathroom furniture, and general equipment.

E2. Specifications of Uses: Target of the space and needs of the client or user. Schematic of the sequence of space or primary and secondary spatial relations caused by the use of properties and operations. Information by the client.

E3. General Functional plan: Overview of the uses defined as plan and section representation. Assignment of modules over the corresponding colored markings and legend. Statements of the relevant areas for rental and sale.

E4. Units: Classification of the use of units (e.g., department, wing, station, apartment) and color mapping of the individual units on colored markers and corresponding legend.

E5. Furniture Layout: Classification of the use of units (e.g., department, wing, station, apartment) and color mapping of the individual units on colored markers and corresponding legend.

...

E10. Pictures and Visualizations: Illustration to Chapter E Functions and Layout

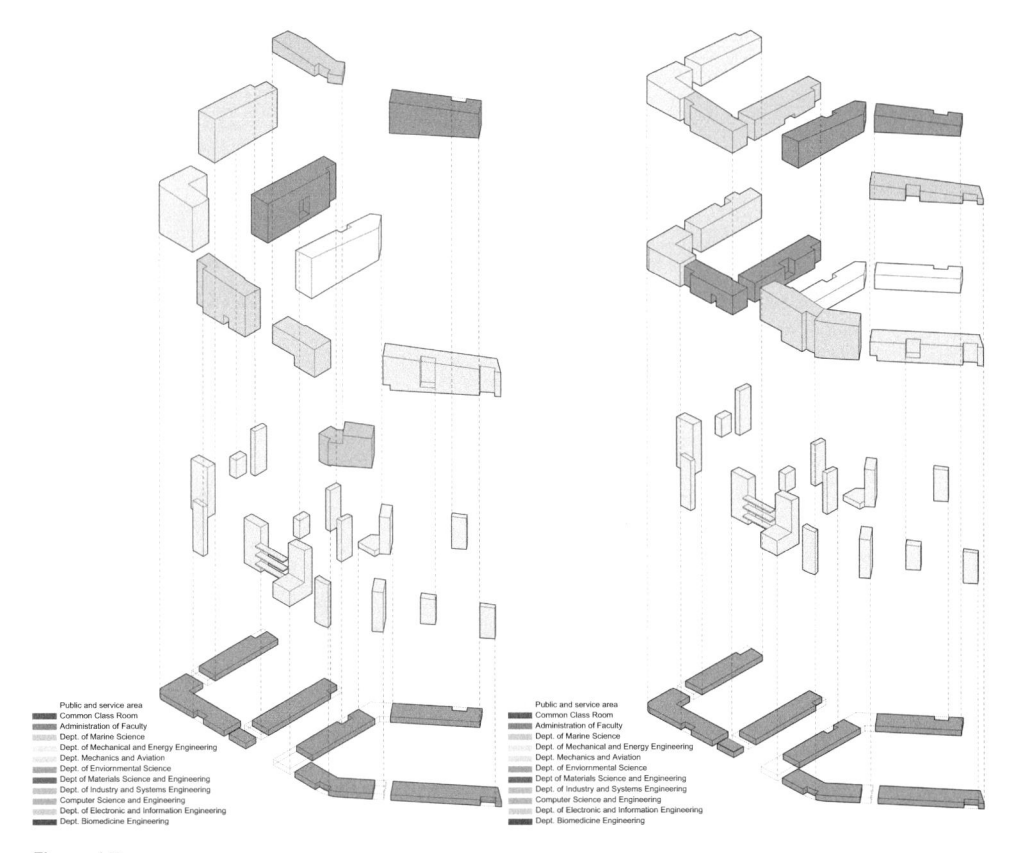

Figure 4.7
(a and b): Engineering school – changes of departmental locations from early proposal (a) to the final construction (b)

As a newly planned university, the engineering school is constantly changing in department composition, faculty members, budget, leadership, and requirements through the design and construction processes. These changes are ongoing. However, the design and construction processes operate smoothly. In the design process, the constant changes in requests raised by departments can be easily accommodated. (see Figures 4.7a, 4.7b; 4.8) Among the four projects conducted approximately at the same time on the university campus, the urban layout, structure, and general plan of the engineering school remain largely unchanged. The final project will be exactly the same as the initial competition project from five years ago. This is possible because of the strategic layout of the project book, where functional issues are independent. Through careful design of every functional requirement at the appropriate time (just before occupancy), the project fulfils highly diversified research laboratories of different departments and specialties and constant changes of the faculties and considers the quality of architectural space by the well elaborated indoor and outdoor spaces and green architecture strategies.

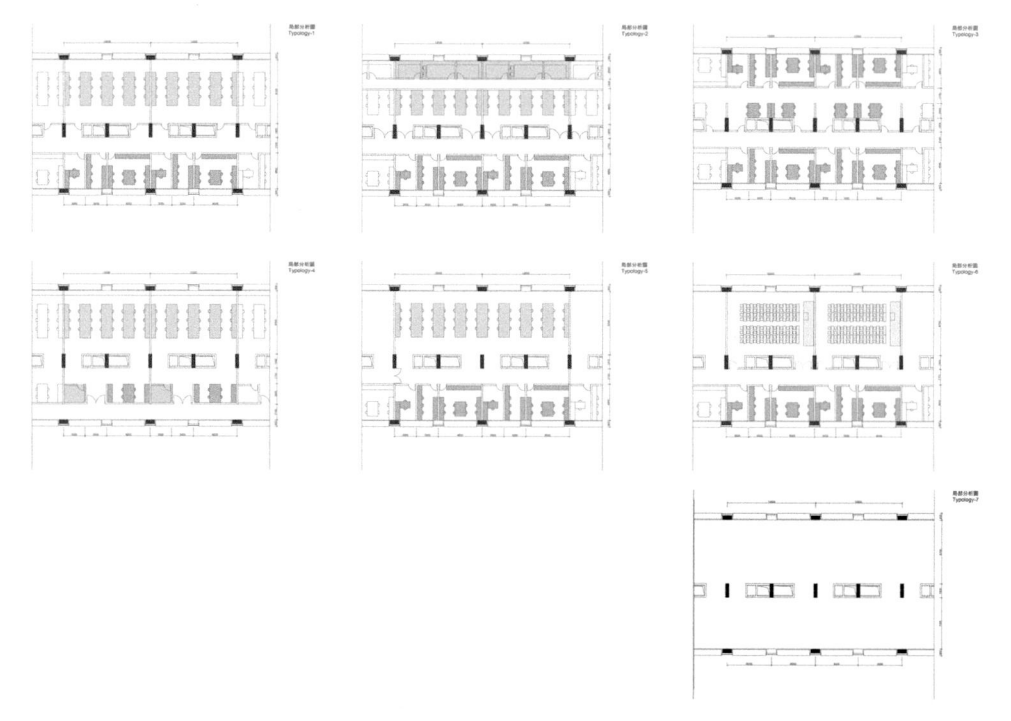

Figure 4.8
Engineering School – labs in different prototypes arranged by the departments of the school

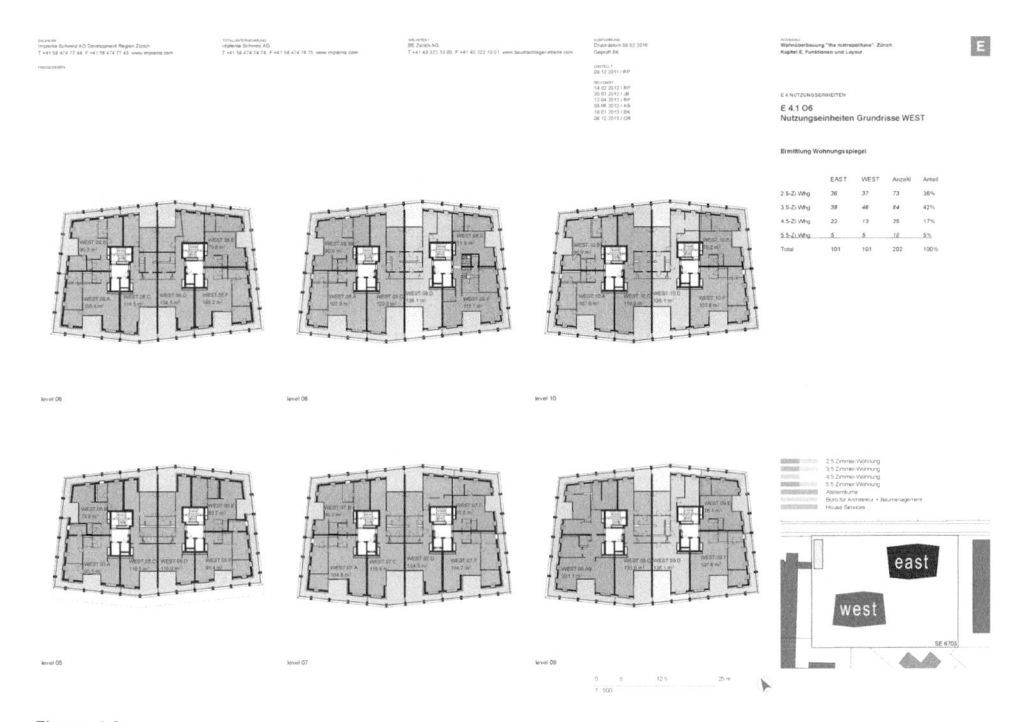

Figure 4.9
Metropolitan – floor plan and layout of apartments

The client of the Metropolitan recruited a salesman who bought a flat in the building. The flats in the entire building were sold through customization of the interior design in the negotiation among the residents, the salesman, and BEA architects. Chapter E and the 'sample' flat bought by the salesman functioned as a new marketing strategy targeting the high-end traveling residents – the project is located between Zurich and its airport city. The layout of every flat is unique on the basis of the negotiation on the size, price, location, and interior fittings.

Being different from the Engineering Department building as public property, the Metropolitan is private and sold by a new marketing strategy (see Figure 4.9). The constantly changing requirements and user-orientated decision-making process in the area of functional layout are the same in both projects, guided by Chapter E. Both projects are smoothly handled in administration with high architectural quality in urban space, structure, indoor and outdoor public areas, and finishes.

Chapter F Interior Surface and Finishes

Chapter F concerns the interior finishes. This is directly dependent on Chapter E, but can be called another decision level, since many choices are still available. Once Chapter E decisions are made, decisions can be made about interior surfaces and finishes.

Habraken mentioned a group of infill elements (decisions made by or for each individual occupancy and therefore not part of the Support or Base Building of Chapters C and D), including external wall elements of individual occupancies, internal partition elements, (raised) floor elements (if required), storage elements, doors, kitchen elements, and bathroom elements (1972, p. 63). Age van Randen provided four categories for the infill or fit-out:

1. The spatial layout of the dwelling and
2. The necessary elements, such as inner partition walls, frames, and doors.
3. Equipment found in the kitchen, sanitary fittings, and appliances.
4. The part of the installations (piping, wiring and ductwork) determined by the layout.

(1992, p. 82)

Interior fit-out has rapidly grown in the building industry. Product suppliers provide strong support in the quality of construction and intervene in architectural design decisions. The users have an important role in decision making. Making the interior as an independent chapter in the project book can support effective dialogue with clients, users, and suppliers in the design process. It is also a platform for the quality and budget control by understanding the texture, lighting, and atmosphere as the key area of control in design.

Table 4.8 Major content and structure of Chapter F Interior Surface and Finishes

F1. Material Concept: Concept for materialization and surfaces of floors, walls, ceiling, doors, and interior fitting elements with the help of reference materials or pictures. Additional descriptions of equipment, apparatus, and appliance finishes and styles.

F2. Floors: Assignment of sub floors and floor coverings on color diagrams. With detailed position drawings, the elements are shown and described in a detailed scale.

F3. Walls: Assignment of the wall and cladding systems on color diagrams. With detailed position drawings, the elements are shown and described in a detailed scale.

F4. Ceilings: Assignment of the ceiling systems and ceiling coverings on color diagrams. With detailed position drawings, the elements are shown and described in a detailed scale.

F5. Interior Elements: Assignment of the indoor extension elements (internal doors, railings, mounting elements, conveyors, etc.) with color diagrams. With detailed position drawings, the elements are shown and described in a detailed scale.

F6. Core Area

....

F10. Pictures and Visualizations: Illustrations to Chapter F Finishes and Carpentry

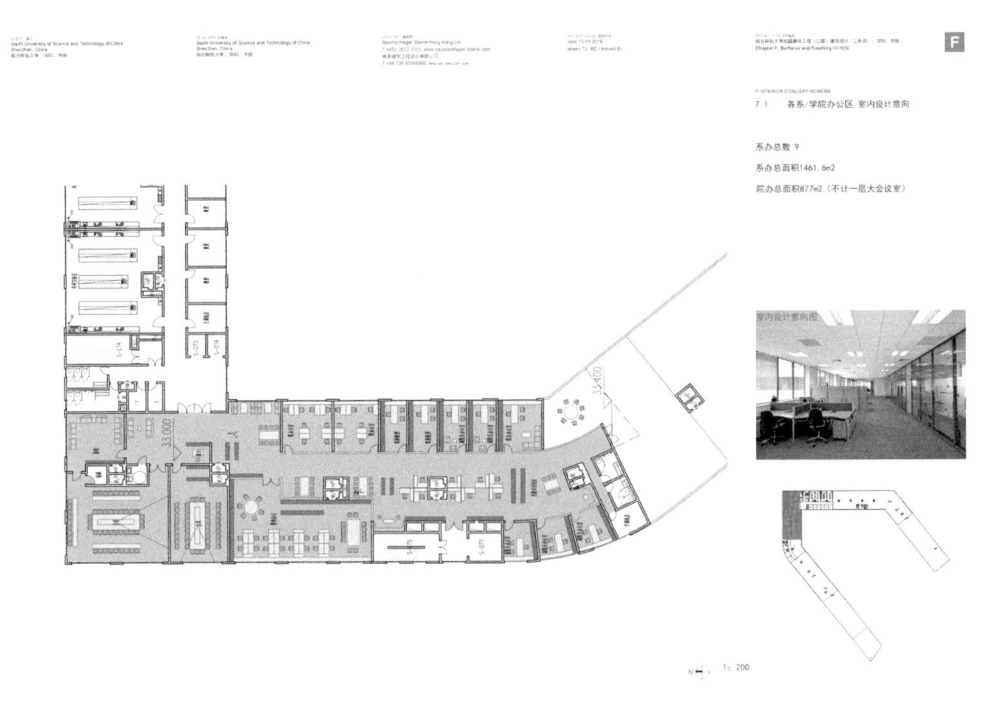

Figure 4.10
Engineering School – interior finishing of departmental offices in an extracted page from the project book

The interior design (that is, what is documented in Chapter F (Table 4.8)) of the Engineering School was conducted with two local interior design firms, in addition to BEA's design work. BEA's design covers the common areas of the school, the entrances, corridors, lounges, sanitary spaces, auditorium, faculty, and department administration offices. A special consultant was in charge of the technical arrangement and on the fittings of the laboratories in accordance with the specific requirements of departments laid out in Chapter E. The project book functioned as a platform of discussion among BEA architects, the departments, interior design consultants, and quality control instruments. It coordinated the various preferences of the eight departments.

A subsection "F10 Pictures and Visualization" is found at the end of every technical chapter (B–F). This section is important for BEA architects to present and control the design quality, especially for all the participants in decision making, including the clients and users, to build up a common understanding and effectively involve everyone in the process. The texture, utilities, lighting, craftsmanship, and overall interior atmosphere are precisely presented (see Figure 4.10). In the Metropolitan, the salesman's owned flat served as a showroom for the potential home buyers. They can visit and evaluate every detail of the finishes. They effectively communicated with the salesman and BEA architects for their own preference on the basis of Chapter F.

Summary and conclusions

Dynamic markets and client needs have caused fundamental changes in the service requirements in the construction and architecture fields. From specialized designers, architects have become general planning and consulting contractors in the building industry. In this context, BEA architects see themselves as a service enterprise that accords top priority to cooperation between architects and clients in a spirit of partnership. The perception of the client as a partner is based on the conviction that sustainable architecture is a team effort, with the long-term use and public significance of a building as the common denominator that cannot emerge from the autonomous creative action of an individual alone. Essentially, the BEA project book focuses on two issues:

1. Ensuring the optimum utility value of a building for the client, the users, and the general public in an effective design/negation process, and
2. Guaranteeing adherence to cost plans and time schedules while using the modern technical means and conditions of production.

In the process, the project book developed by BEA constitutes the basis for decision-making processes in design and construction in joint responsibility with the client and all people involved. It comprises all project information, from the first sketch to final planning, and serves as a strategic control instrument for all internal and external processes. The six chapters are coherent and open for independent intervention on the five spatial levels presented in the five technical chapters. In addition, it forms an efficient instrument of cost and quality control.

The project book outlines the planning issues by stages in a systematic manner. That is, the structure of the six chapters A through F corresponds to the logical sequence of project execution.

Chapter A introduces the general definition of objectives, the organizational basics, the historical and cultural background of the building site, the documentation of the targets, and the building's effective key indicators. These objectives serve as the basis of quality assurance. The systematic structure of all chapters puts clients and all the people involved in a position to understand the project and enable communication at any stage. BEA architects can conduct rapid and precise review of adherence to cost and quality targets and an overview of essential milestones.

Chapter B deals with questions of surroundings, urban planning, landscape, and outdoor space – the public domain. BEA clearly states that the quality of the architecture has a close relationship with the particular social, cultural, and technological backgrounds of the specific area where a building is situated. The decisions documented in this chapter have the largest and longest impact on the public and the community.

Chapter C focuses on primary structural issues and safety. It defines the building's infrastructure, assuring optimum conditions for capacity of variable and changing functions. This chapter is constrained by the decisions documented in Chapter B and provides an open intervention for the following chapters.

Chapter D focuses on the integral connection between the façade and technical service technology. It is an independent chapter because it addresses the importance of the façade that is both public and private. The technical (installation or mechanical, electrical and plumbing) systems become increasingly important because of rapid changes in the building industry. The efficiency of these systems have a strong impact on energy saving.

Chapter E discusses and documents the capacity of the "higher levels" (previous chapters) to accommodate various functions and proper arrangement where the clients and users have strong preferences. The functions together with user preferences rapidly change, as experience with these and other projects show. A separate chapter provides a negotiation platform at any time in the design process.

Chapter F is the last chapter addressing the quality of surface finishes and fittings that rapidly change during the life span of the architecture.

Creating a sustainable building design for BEA is about understanding, organizing, and optimizing the existing resources, which include all the people involved in the early stages of the design. The project book is a strong methodology of collaboration of all the people involved and quality control of the architecture. The project book itself is a "piece of art" that constantly involves and changes. BEA architects commonly hand over a copy to the clients and users after the project is completed for appreciation, memory, and interpretation.

References

Allen, S. (1999). *Points + Lines: Diagrams and Projects for the City*. New York: Princeton Architectural press.

Baumschlager Eberle Architekten (2020). *Office Profile 2020*.

Eberle, D. (2003). Notes of speech at University Hong Kong, 24 October, 2003. And Notes from keynote address to Open Building Conference in Hong Kong, 26 October 2003. Hong Kong: University of Hong Kong.

Frampton, K. (2003). Foreword. In L. Waechter-Böhm, ed., *Baumschlager & Eberle: Buildings and Projects 1996–2002*. Wien and New York: Springer, pp. 6–12.

Habraken, N.J. (1972). *Supports: An Alternative to Mass Housing*. Translated from the Dutch by B. Valkenburg. New York: Praeger Publishers.

Jia, B. (2007). Residential designs from Baumschlager & Eberle: An evaluation, *Open House International*, 32(3), pp. 7–15.

Jia, B. (2010). 'The qualities of the basics: Base building design. In A.J. Chica, P. Elguezabal, S. Meno and A. Amundarain, eds., *16th International Conference on Open and Sustainable Building: Proceedings of the International Conference*. Bilbao: Labein Tecnalia, pp. 90–98.

Jia, b. (2011). *Baumschlager Eberle* (in Chinese). Beijing: China Architecture and Building Press.

Jia, B. and Li, M. (2018). The quality and capacity of architecture in three social–spatial levels: An observation of design by BEA Hong Kong. In S. Kendall, ed., *Open Building for Resilient Cities* Conference. Los Angeles, CA: The Council on Open Building (U.S.), pp. 99–106.

Kendall, S. and Teicher, J. (2000). *Residential Open Building*. London and New York: E & FN Spon.

Randen, A. van. (1992) *Consumer Oriented Building: In Full Control of and Behind One's Front Door, Entangled Building*. Delft: Werkgroup OBOM.

Troeger, E. (2015) *Density & Atmosphere: On Factors Relating to Building Density in the European Cities*. Basel: Birkhaeuser Verlag GmbH.

Chapter 5

Open Building in Russia

Nadezhda Koreneva

Chapter overview

Over the past one hundred years, there have been many nation-wide, radical political turns and economic crises in Russia. These transformations have greatly influenced contemporary Russian spatial principles of urban development. Two phenomena are now evident, which show the emergence of the Open Building approach: the separation of design tasks into various levels of intervention corresponding to expected endurance and governance of decisions at each level (see Figure 5.1).

The first is "free plan apartments" (The Free Plan, Project Russia, 2001). This needs to be taken seriously for contemporary residential development. It operates at the level of a single building. The second, at the level of urban design, concerns "free plan neighborhoods" as an important phenomenon. Both have emerged in the post-industrial society during the establishment of capitalism in the country since the mid 1990s.

The "free plan apartment" is a trend to build empty apartment buildings without interior walls and equipment. Apartment buildings have mechanical systems shafts and designate basic wet zones in each unit of occupancy. On the one hand this approach is a good decision for organizing living units that can have variable layouts based on user preferences. On the other hand, it can be used to short-change buyers and future residents, because developers use this as a way to get excess profits. This chapter discusses the advantages, limitations and legal obstacles using real projects as illustrations.

The second is "free plan neighborhood" development, a concept at the level of the urban tissue, concerning new construction in existing neighborhoods – a kind of filling-in of space in existing urban areas. The definition of the concept, in contrast to foreign practice, is absent in the Urban Planning Code of the Russian Federation. This means there are no clear rules for its regulation. In any large city in Russia, we can find examples in which a new residential building is inserted into an established urban quarter. Such buildings usually do not fit well into the existing environment, creating discord with the surrounding buildings and impairing the quality of the living environment. This is happening because private property in Russia officially

DOI: 10.4324/9781003018339-6

Figure 5.1
A diagram
of the levels
of inter-
vention on
the Russian
residen-
tial envir-
onment.
Free plan
apartment,
free plan
neighbor-
hood, free
plan city

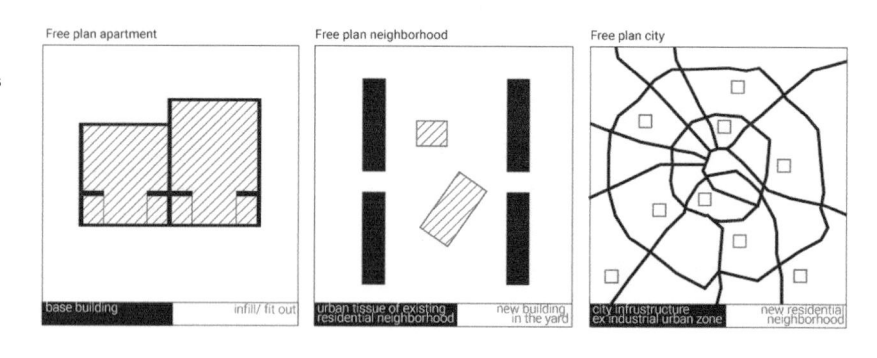

returned and the Soviet neighborhoods with large "no-mans-land" between the buildings were not ready for it. There was no clear separation between level of interventions and no shared responsibility and control. The process of land surveying and illegal invasion by the developers is still happening. The chapter describes examples of this phenomenon and suggests broad remedies.

At the city level, development strategies that relate to the Open Building approach can also be distinguished. Over the past ten years, there has been extensive development of new territories, a large-scale transformation of former industrial zones, and renovation of the old housing stock with a three-fold increase of density.

Such extensive development of territories contradicts the gradual historical and planned development of cities. The initiative for these changes often comes from governmental and powerful development business interests. Residents are also included in the decision-making process, but their force of influence is still very small, because the mechanism of participation of residents in the process of changing the city is more of a bureaucratic system than an instrument of real influence. The swiftness of the changes and the vagueness of decision-making mechanisms may be the result of a mixture of the Soviet and capitalist management systems of the city and the development of the country as a whole.

Introduction

One hundred years has passed since the revolution in Russia. Soviet history hindered the path to capitalization and formed prerequisites for the development of modern residential policy. Today, the tissue of the city and the living environment still depend too heavily on top-down, centralized political control. Gradual – and healthy – evolution of the development density of the city does not occur; rather, urban tissue has suffered ill-conceived surgical transformation, where the chief doctor is politics without a guiding vision or method.

The main generator of these changes was the abolition of private property in Russia in 1917. Officially, private property returned in 1994. Since then, responsibility of citizens ends at the door to their dwelling units. Private property is a basis of capitalist society and distribution of control and responsibility. The question of "what is shared," once the dominant concern of communist theory, is once again at the forefront, but without answers (Trudolyubov, 2015).

With the development of highway and rail transport, the boundaries of the cities began to grow. Since 2012, following the enactment of the Federation Council of Federal Assembly of the Russian Federation, the territory of Moscow has increased 2.5 times. Its borders came to include almost 150 thousand hectares (580 sq. miles) of the territory of the Moscow Region (Institute of General Plan of Moscow, n.d.). Giant micro-districts with chaotically arranged cheap prefabricated housing blocks proliferated. The main design principle of these districts was walking distance to the social infrastructure (schools, kindergartens, shops, etc.). Due to the "scientific and hygienic" norms of solar access promulgated by CIAM's Athens Charter, residential development areas acquired large empty spaces between buildings (CIAM Open Learn, 2001). All territories and dwelling units were owned by the state, and public courtyards had no clear boundaries. On this loose structure of "modern" city-planning came the construction boom in the 1990s. Developments that filled in the empty spaces were popular because the large empty spaces between buildings had no clear boundaries, resulting often in tall buildings suddenly appearing in the empty spaces (Krainyaya, 2011). Now the periphery of the city is built-up by high-rise residential buildings, mostly with uninspired architecture. Housing is designed according to outdated standards and the basic norms have not changed comprehensively since the time of the Soviet Union. While there is selective adjustment of specific design issues, they cannot fully meet modern challenges. So, the errors of modernism are repeated over and over.

But rethinking the positive and negative aspects of the centennial history of changes in tendencies in the construction and operation of the living environment is now possible. The global agenda has changed towards a concept of comprehensive urban block development, and the unit of residential quarters reduced in size. It is now possible to focus on the formation of residential environments during the time of capitalism beginning in Russia through the perspective of the Open Building approach. This is the time of the formation of market relations, the emergence of new players and the redistribution of tasks in the management and formation of residential architecture.

New Russian capitalism and new freedom in residential architecture

In modern Russia, capitalist relations are still being formed. Twenty-five years of capitalist relations is not enough and the institution of private property has not yet been clearly formed. But any crisis is a time of new opportunities. Therefore, thanks to a sharp change in the economic structure, new formats and mechanisms of interactions in the residential environment have appeared. New "products" have appeared in the real estate market. The end of the 1990s and the beginning of the 2000s was a time of the emergence of new values, new ways of life and as a result the beginning of new architecture in the residential sector. And most importantly, large-scale manifestations of principles close to the ideas of Open Building started to emerge. Architects had a new-found freedom and raised many questions. At that time, the concept of the middle class in society arose. In the early 2000s the construction of solid base buildings began, without the rigid standards of the prefabricated concrete products. It became possible to implement a wide range of architectural solutions. Housing began to be classified by price and quality: residential complexes were divided according to economy, comfort, business, premium and elite classes. Companies began to offer new housing standards, focusing on the new middle class. Quality and operational features became important.

Just in the segment of the middle and upper class a new phenomenon has formed that is close to the Open Building approach – the "free plan apartment." The term "free plan apartment" is not official. It has no legislative explanation so far. After perestroika, most people wanted special, individual decisions for their dwelling spaces. Architects could prove themselves at that moment precisely at the level of design. And consumers and occupants also needed to stand out, to become special and to exploit the opportunity to create "your own space." The design features of cast-in-place residential base buildings made it possible to design houses with clear span spaces with the capacity for a wide variety of free spaces inside each dwelling. In Soviet times, in the panel house building type, a narrow transverse span of the supporting structures was used, as a result of which spatial variability, while still marginally possible, was never considered in the design of the buildings' capacity. In fact, the concept of "capacity" did not exist.

The tendency to demolish the standard interior of the uniformly planned units built in Soviet times prompted developers, starting in the late 20th century, to build without any internal walls or finished floors. The structure of these apartment buildings includes fewer load-bearing walls and dwelling-unit-level engineering systems (heating/cooling, ventilation, piping). This phenomenon is very beneficial for developers, because the selling area of the apartment could get a little larger. Free layout is typical mainly for commercial ("market-rate") housing; in the sector of state-subsidized housing, the standard is the construction of all internal walls, standard bathrooms and kitchens, plus the cheapest finishes, wall coverings using standard wallpaper, etc. An important factor is compliance with the minimum quantitative indicators of the floor area of all rooms.

The lawlessness with land regulations and the new freedom spawned the development of micro-districts, often also illegal. This is another phenomenon that touches on the topic of Open Building and the challenges, and opportunities, of separation of design tasks.

The emergence of a market economy and the process of privatization of the state housing stock preceded the emergence of new participants in housing policy. New players are appearing on the market such as developers, marketers and management companies (see Figure 5.2). The market for an "infill industry" serving independent dwellings and the trends of designers' work has expanded but remains uncertain. Independent management companies also appeared. For example, it was after the housing and communal services reform in 2005 that a new Housing Code came into force in Russia, according to which the apartment owners themselves choose who will manage their building. There are two principal options with their own characteristics, when the households themselves perform management functions: choosing the most responsible and active people from among the occupants; or hiring an outside management company and paying them directly from fees collected from each household. In Soviet times to this day, there was an alternative to state ownership in the form of "housing cooperatives." Housing cooperatives are voluntary associations of residents with the aim of building and managing multi-story residential buildings. Members of the housing cooperatives by their own means participate in the construction, reconstruction and subsequent maintenance of their building (Gareev, 2015).

Free plan apartments

The free plan apartment phenomenon best illustrates the application of Open Building ideas at the building level. Developers build and sell buildings with dwelling units of fixed size without internal space-defining walls, flooring, dwelling-specific mechanical systems, fixtures and finishes; there are only load-bearing walls and columns, the exterior building skin, shared mechanical systems and rough structural floor slabs. The buyer of each dwelling unit conducts all subsequent work on the arrangement of the dwelling unit on their own. The main idea is that the initiative for planning the dwelling is completely given to the residents. The aspect of the distribution of tasks between the participants in the process is perfectly implemented: the architect and the developer work only with a serviced and enclosing structure, the "base building"; designers hired by residents make interior space, the infill (see Figure 5.3). The following is one example.

Tverskoy project
- Project location: 3 Tverskaya-Yamskaya str. 10, Moscow, Russia.
- Construction completed in 2010.
- Project design team: developer is Capital Group; support (base building) of the building with a façade design by Asadov architects; various designers hired by the owners of the units developed the infill designs.
- Number of dwelling units: 27 dwelling units of various sizes ranging from 157 m^2 to 262 m^2 (1690–2820 ft^2) (see Figure 5.4).

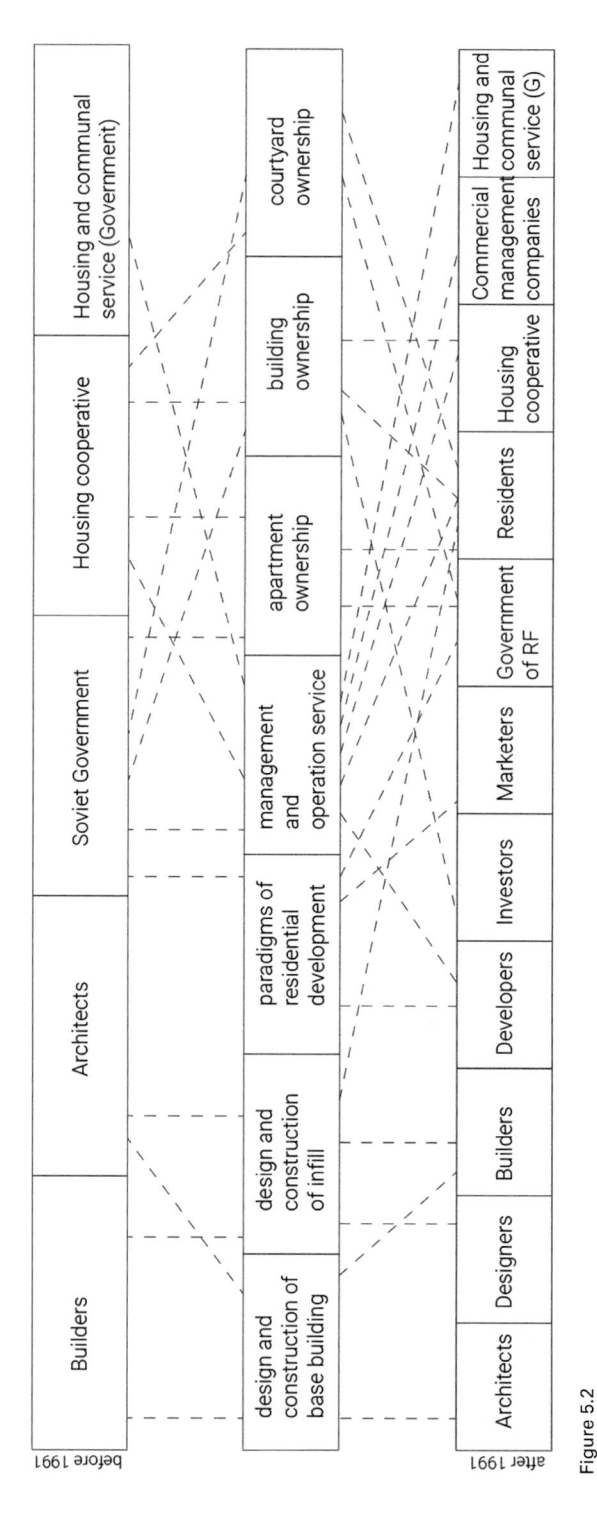

Figure 5.2
Scheme of the emergence of new participants in the housing development process and the structure of their interaction (before and after the return of private property law)

Figure 5.3
View of the "Tverskoy" project (Photo credit by the author)

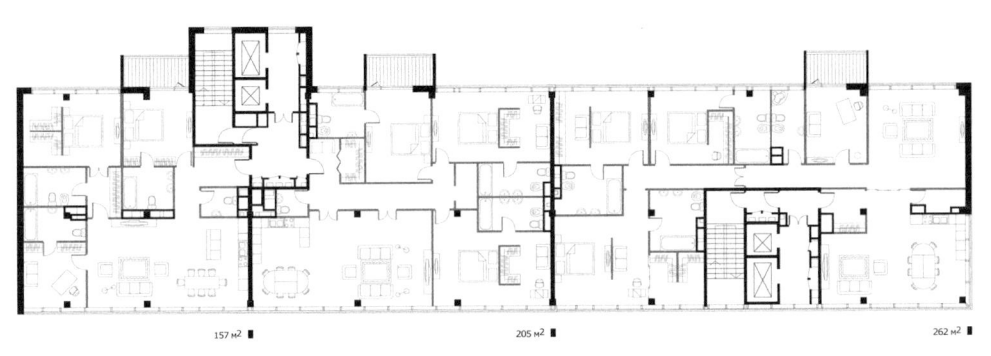

157 м² ∎   205 м² ∎   262 м² ∎

Figure 5.4
The example of layout of the free plan apartment residential building "Tverskoy" (Black walls are "base building;" light gray walls are "fit-out")

- Parking capacity: 65 cars.
- Area of the building site: 2000 m² (21528 ft²) and total floor area of the building: 8319.3 m² (89548 ft²).
- Project client is one of the largest Russian development companies: Capital Group (Moscow).
- New construction.
- Structure: monolithic concrete frame: bearing walls mainly between units and columns.
- Base building installation utilities: vertical shafts inside the dwellings; the fixed location of wet zones; vertical ventilation shafts, radiator piping inside apartment near front door.

Figure 5.5
Typical interior view of a Free plan apartment in the residential project. Note that the rough concrete slab is approximately 15 cm (6") below the entry door threshold)

- Infill system approach: clear separation between base building and infill. The developer sells a free layout and the buyer himself does all the finishing work.

The main problem in realizing a maximum of variable layout design is the inability, by law, to vary wet areas in apartments one above the other. That is, in fact, kitchens should be above the kitchens below, sanitary units above the bathrooms or corridors. Living rooms may not be below wet areas, kitchens and bathrooms. This legal restriction significantly limits the dwelling layouts. Most often apartments with a free layout are sold with potential allocation of interior walls of wet areas, the walls are laid out one brick high or one line on the floor (see Figure 5.5). There have been cases when in residential buildings with a free layout the first resident who gains official approval for the location of the kitchen and the bathrooms determines the legality of the other layouts of apartments associated with it vertically. According to the law, non-living spaces (kitchens, corridors, bathrooms, pantries) can be located only above other non-living areas (SP 54.13330.2016, 2016; SanPiN 1.2.2645-10, 2010). Therefore, it is forbidden to move the kitchen to the place of a larger living room, since in this case it will be above the living rooms of the neighbors below. This redevelopment can be legalized only when the apartment is on the first or second floor, and cellars or non-residential premises (offices, shops) are located under the kitchen.

Basically, the law on wet areas was adopted due to the difficulty of controlling leakage and sound isolation, which is rather strange compared to other countries and with the latest water and sound insulation technologies (Housing Code of the Russian Federation, 2004).

All redevelopment of unit layouts must be coordinated by a special agency of the city bureau of technical inventory (BTI). They keep records of the technical condition of real estate. Based on this information, various documents are issued that may be needed in real estate transactions (for example, when selling a dwelling unit, or registering ownership of real estate). They agree on everything according to the rules in accordance with the law. Therefore, if the reconstruction is done illegally, the owner must convert the plan to its original state for approval by the BTI service. In addition to the difficulties with the law, there is a disadvantage, due to the inadequacies of the infill company methods, in the fact that the building for the first five years turns into a large construction site with constant noise of builders and dust. In each apartment, fit-out construction can take from three months to a year or longer to complete. Common areas, as well as beautiful mirrored elevators, remain covered with cardboard and plywood for a long time to prevent damage by the constant handling of construction cargo and debris. Among other things, infill construction remains quite expensive. For example, for a dwelling with a total area of 40 square meters (400 sq. feet) in the suburbs of Moscow city, infill construction will cost from 20 to 30% of the cost of the empty apartment. Also, a negative consequence of this strategy were numerous court cases with developers to recalculate the value of the sales transaction. The cost of the apartment is determined based on the number of square meters of an empty unit and does not consider the potential surface area occupied by potential internal walls, whereas the cost of a finished apartment was determined as the sum of all the rooms. That is, there is at present a kind of additional payment for freedom of choice.

Positive experience:

1. Variable design opportunity.
2. Residents are active participants in the design process.
3. Infill industry market development potential.

Negative experience:

1. Free plan is not an official term.
2. Limited capacity for variation: according to the current Russian building code, wet zones in one unit in multi-story housing (bathrooms and kitchens) must be stacked above and below each other.
3. Long and expensive infill work.
4. The multi-story building turns into a large construction site.
5. Flexibility only on primary classes of housing.
6. Bureaucratic red tape to legitimize the layout.

Following is a brief explanation of the premises and consequences of implementing this approach as well as an explanation of reasons why success of the free plan apartment in contemporary practice is often deceptive.

Currently consumer preferences are divided. Part of the population prefers complete freedom in planning, and other buyers, on the other hand, prefer finished interiors, and possibly even furniture. The "white box" format is also very popular where all the walls are installed along with all the mechanical, electrical and plumbing systems for that dwelling, and everything is prepared for the finishing by occupants. Therefore, about five years ago, the tendency was to offer choices among three formats of proposals from developers. This diversification of the offerings in the real estate market helps developers to find more buyers.

Developers themselves design finishing options, from their own quality standards and materials used. Thus, an additional separate business is growing up. It is profitable for developers to do large-scale standardized design projects, and as a result, reduce the cost of infill constructions for residents.

For example, developers sell different housing in the same quarter with different finishing options. In one building without finishes, in another, a choice of finishes according to the developed standards in each dwelling unit. This scheme is used in order not to turn the building into a permanent construction site, which many residents understandably do not like. And whoever needs an individual layout design buys a dwelling unit in a neighboring building set up that way. This option is still popular in that it is possible to include the cost of infill construction in the price of the apartment, which means taking a mortgage for infill. That is, infill will be linked to construction costs at a mortgage rate of 6%, and not 12% as a consumer loan when infill is accounted for separately.

Free plan neighborhoods

With the beginning of new capitalist relations, housing policy at the urban level has also changed. Now, most of the land that once belonged to the state with all the built assets on it should have an owner. Industrial enterprises were privatized for reorganization by individuals and new companies, and dwelling units in residential buildings were privatized mainly by the occupants who then lived in them. Land with courtyard spaces, which were, in fact, communal property (ownership in common) of adjacent residential buildings, legally remained ownerless. The micro-district developments, which were then built up in most of the peripheral areas of Russian cities, had the structure of tall buildings with large spaces between them, often empty and un-cared for.

The definition of the concept of incremental, fine-grained urban densification of existing residential neighborhoods familiar to most historic cities in pre-modernist times, is absent in the current City Planning Code of the

the territory and apartments are state property

the territory is state property apartments are private property

the territory is household property apartments are private property

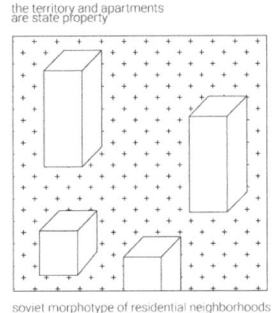 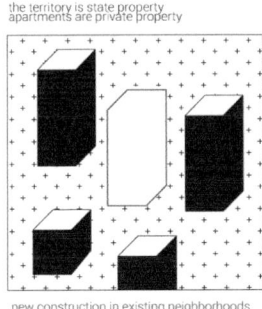 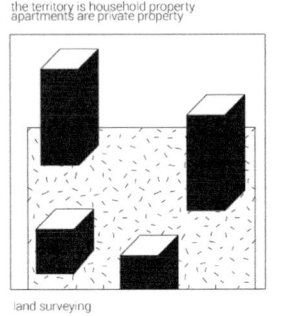

soviet morphotype of residential neighborhoods   new construction in existing neighborhoods   land surveying

Figure 5.6
Diagram of incremental urban densification of existing residential neighborhoods after return of private property law

Russian Federation. Incremental urban densification is clearly perceived negatively: the need for such development stems from the desire of the builder, investor and other local organizations to make a profit. In pre-modernist times, this development is the natural intensive development of the city, which is regulated by the local administration, local typologies and concepts of territory, and is considered as a component of smart growth of cities and efficient consumption of land and infrastructure capital, and the utilization and "reprogramming" of dispersed vacant places in the built-up territory.

In Russia, this phenomenon is negative and legislatively there is no provision for this (RBK Realty, 2013). Examples are often the cases of the construction of new high-rise apartment buildings between other tall buildings, mentioned above, destroying the in-between spaces as an established structure. A permanent component is residential building blocks of micro-districts, and "filling" in new development in it. It is about new construction which appeared after the return of the law of private property. At issue are distribution of responsibility and control, mechanisms of legal regulation of urban transformations, and the interaction of participants in the transformation of urban spaces of residential neighborhoods. This is an example of an urban conflict, where the influence of residents on the process is seen as local resistance, rather than participation in the design (see Figure 5.6).

Summarizing, we can give a brief positive and negative description of incremental urban densification development at this time.

Positive experience:

1. Use of existing urban infrastructure (roads, public places, etc.).
2. Bringing all necessary engineering communications to the territory (site).
3. Raising the tax base of local budgets.
4. Reduction of commuting; the growth of population mobility.
5. Increased opportunities for social interaction.
6. The possibility of improving the functional organization of the territory by filling the existing gaps in the area.

Figure 5.7
An example of new high-rise residential building, which caused discontent among residents of surrounding houses in the city of Yaroslavl, Russia (Lechenko, 2016). Existing urban tissue – existing neighborhood of five-story houses of the Soviet period. New 22-story residential development

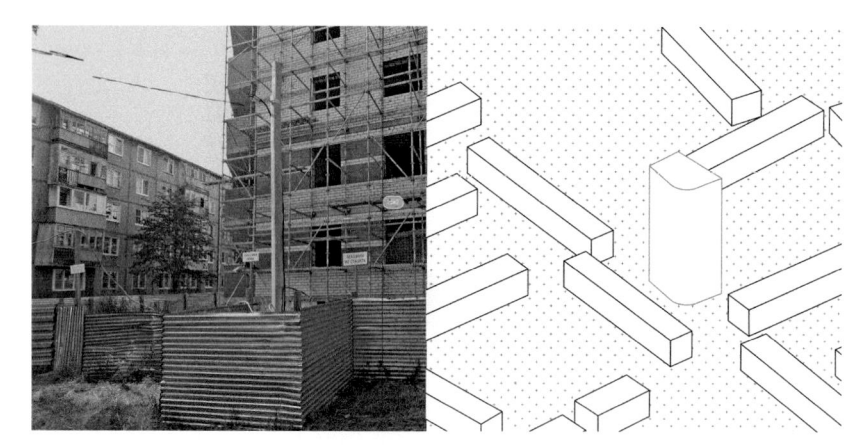

Negative experience:

1. The absence in the legislation of the Russian Federation of normative legal acts regulating densification development.
2. Negative protests of residents.
3. Unplanned reduction of open urban space.
4. Deterioration of the spatial qualities of the surrounding buildings
5. Possible decrease in market value of dwellings in surrounding buildings.
6. Breaking the structure of connectivity and permeability of space.
7. Broken grid of roads, urban structure.
8. Glut with the required number of parking spaces and, as a result, spontaneous illegal parking, which affects the quality of courtyards.
9. Chaotic zoning of public and private spaces.
10. Erasing the boundaries of responsibility and distribution of control and, as a result, environmental degradation.

Most recently (2018) all the land surrounding residential building projects has been surveyed. There are many cases when the land is registered only under the building construction site. All the difficulties with the appearance of alien built forms in the territory near the existing housing were only due to the fact that land ownership was not registered by the residents (see Figure 5.7). Officially the practice of irregular urban densification is over; the rules governing it are now established. All cities have their own strategy for changes, secured by related documents. At the city level the regulated document is the Land Use and Development Rules. For each site, the developer receives the Schemes of the Planning Organization of the Land, a document that regulates the rules and balance of the capacity indicators of the site. This document contains technical and economic indicators of the land plot, a restriction on density, a maximum building area, and a height limit of future construction. The site plan indicates the boundary of the permitted construction, the plan of the existing engineering infrastructure and their restricted areas. Also, for each city in Russia there are local standards for the provision of parking spaces, playgrounds, green fields, etc. for sports and so on. Nevertheless, the adjustment of the rules and construction conditions is often edited in favor of maximizing the profit of the developer. Participation of residents in the changes is very conditional.

Commercial real estate: a key to be official

A new alternative to residential housing development in Moscow is "commercial real estate." This means that buildings are constructed with "universal units" that can be used for either residential or commercial functions. The positive aspect of this development pattern is the rejection of the outdated design code of residential development and an opportunity to form a complex, multifunctional and comfortable environment of high density. But in fact, developers use this format as a legislative loophole, which allows them to increase the sales of apartments without providing social infrastructure (schools, kindergartens) and the required outdoor environment, and there is no regulation on acoustical isolation between apartments.

In this type of real estate there is no concept of fixed wet zones. Therefore, kitchens and bathrooms can be arranged as desired, which means you can make a truly free plan apartment. This gives a potential boost to the evolution of specialized infill companies delivering "everything behind your front door, per unit."

Moscow's "commercial apartments" are less expensive than equivalent strictly residential apartments, but there is no possibility for residents to obtain official residence permits – a necessity if households want to obtain services such as kindergartens or schools, which are a priority for residents with official residence permits attached to every person's official ID card.

There are cases when, by a court ruling, residents can legally equalize the status of commercial units for living units. The main criterion for transferring a unit to residential status is the two-hour daily interval during which sunlight must enter the living rooms. Accordingly, apartments with insufficient solar access, for example, with windows in the atrium of the house, today have no chance of becoming residential. In the future, the rules may change. Another important requirement is the availability of social infrastructure and parking spaces. More successful is the practice of the mass appeal of owners to the developer to transfer building of commercial real estate to residential status (Polidi et al., 2016).

Today mixed projects appear on the market more often, where some of the buildings are classic living units, and some are commercial units. The main difference is that commercial real estate has a more affordable price (approximately 20% less expensive), but it does not allow local residence permits, and has increased tax and utility bills. In the future, the rules may change, but for now this is the case.

Positive experience

1. Easy way for infill development, official flexibility.
2. Less expensive than residential real estate (10–20%).
3. Location in the existing infrastructure of the city.

Negative experience

1. Expensive monthly service fee, tax levy.
2. No official residence permits or access to free social infrastructure.
3. Neighbors can be both commercial organizations and residents.
4. High mortgage rates.
5. A tax rate higher than in residential apartments.

Free plan city: renovation and redevelopment programs in Moscow's residential development

At the level of city planning, Moscow has undergone major transformations of its residential development in the last ten years. All previously adopted strategic documents describing the rules for the development of the city are no longer relevant, but nevertheless valid and contrary to the new rules. That is, the urban development agenda, development trends, political and economic transformations, all change very quickly, and the new laws do not have time to change sequentially, as this is a complex and long bureaucratic process.

During the last ten years (2010–2020) redevelopment of industrial zones and complex integrated development on the territory where old buildings have been demolished is a contemporary trend of city planning strategy. The cities provide transport and utility infrastructure, enabling new development to occur. Thus, in the reactivated territories, functional mixing takes place. In the ex-industrial zones where people previously only worked, new residents now live and work, and exclusively living neighborhoods become places where people can live and work. The development intensity is being revised in favor of a threefold increase in density.

As an integrated development strategy, two ways are distinguished: Renovation and Redevelopment programs. Renovation means development of a new residential area in the place where the old Soviet-style five-story residential buildings will be demolished. It is a forced way of upgrading of decayed territory and densification of existing urban tissue (Mogzoev and Kuzmicheva, 2017; The official site of Moscow on Urban Policy and Construction). The Redevelopment program is a smart way of city transformation, where residential areas appear on the site of former industrial zones and the city becomes more permeable (Moscow RE:industrial 2018).

The Renovation program is a political election strategy and it is important to obtain the approval of the residents, which is extremely difficult, since the program has a number of possible negative consequences and citizens have protested. Now the grievances have subsided, and it will be possible to really evaluate the positive effect of this program in a few years. Urban density will increase, which means an increase in the burden on transport and social infrastructure. It is potentially harmful for the everyday environment of the urban tissue of the city.

This situation shows how political will can influence transformation of the tissue of the living environment, the imperfect management apparatus and the level of citizen interaction and control.

Of greatest interest from the point of view of the Open Building approach is the redevelopment of existing industrial zones in the city. Factories leave the existing urban fabric of cities, enabling the reorganization of these territories into multifunctional residential areas. The city structure and engineering infrastructure designed for industrial capacity is becoming a support for new multifunctional urban infill.

Positive characteristics:

1. Multi-level approach.
2. Considered solar access to inhabited spaces.
3. Optimized location of driveways and parking, closed private yards.
4. Hierarchy of public and private zones, a clear system of functional zoning.
5. Large volume of sold living space in developing neighborhood.

Negative characteristics:

1. Forced seizure of private property and disadvantageous compensation.
2. No gradual development – broken up historical development of everyday environment.
3. Significant excess of density and intensity of use of the territory.
4. Conflict of interest. The difficulty of making a compromise. It remains the decision-making lever for the authorities.

S.C.R.I.P.T.

What follows is an explanation of a current experience in the reorganization of existing residential urban spaces on the level of the urban tissue. The positive side of this approach is the possibility of organizing a new tissue structure that has a more graduated structure with division into quarters and clear zoning of public and private spaces. This structure has a clearer hierarchy of separation of spaces, which means clearer boundaries and rules for governance.

Currently, the profession of the architect is transforming, and a multifactorial design approach is becoming clearer. This is based on the understanding that a living environment is a process. Urbanization and transformation are the main challenges today. The role of space is significant, but equally important is the temporal factor. Design of the architectural environment and its scenarios should become a norm. The continual transformation of the living environment is the focus of the rest of this chapter.

A living environment is dynamic, not static. Urbanization and transformation are the challenges of our age. If we continue complying with the logic of the architectural slogans "Less Is More" of Mies van der Rohe (Cuito and Montes, 2002) and "Yes Is More" of Bjarke Ingels (Ingels, 2009), we can as well choose a new slogan for the modern age – "Process Is More." The role of space is important, but equally important is the time factor. Designing the scenarios for residential development including its architecture should become the norm.

The approach that the author's architectural firm propose and use in their residential urban block work is called S.C.R.I.P.T – programming codes for the development (over time) of residential environments. In this case the goal of the residential project is preparation of architectural, social and economic potential of the living environment. Therefore, the tool for spatial coherence and variability is the structure of the space and its future generated potential (capacity) (Habraken, 2005).

Strategy: S.C.R.I.P.T.

The approach that we have formulated and put to use in residential urban block projects is called S.C.R.I.P.T – programming codes for the progressive development of residential environments. The main principles of this strategy are:

S – Structure: general block structure, permeability and fine-grained block organization of the territory (LOT and PLOT concept), high density and middle-rise development, a complex hierarchy of public spaces.

C – Core: universal urban unit, adaptive capability of "UUU" to design a morphology of the residential tissue.

R – Rule: mechanism of interaction for "long-term" and "short-term" transformations.

I – Infill: typology of adaptable apartments.

P – Programming: scenarios of incremental development over time.

T – Transformation: the ability to transform yet preserve the original urban tissue.

The residential block project includes programming of the architectural, social and economic potential of the environment. The structure and generated space of the project is a tool for spatial capacity and adaptability. The strategy for programming of the living environment is an attempt to put into the project scenarios for its development. It is important to make a residential quarter with the capacity for self-adaptation to the challenge of the future.

Residential development in Russia is experiencing a time of change. The capitalist society has matured. Consequently, demands are different for the quality of residential environments. In parallel, the architectural profession is transforming, and a multifactorial design approach is becoming typical.

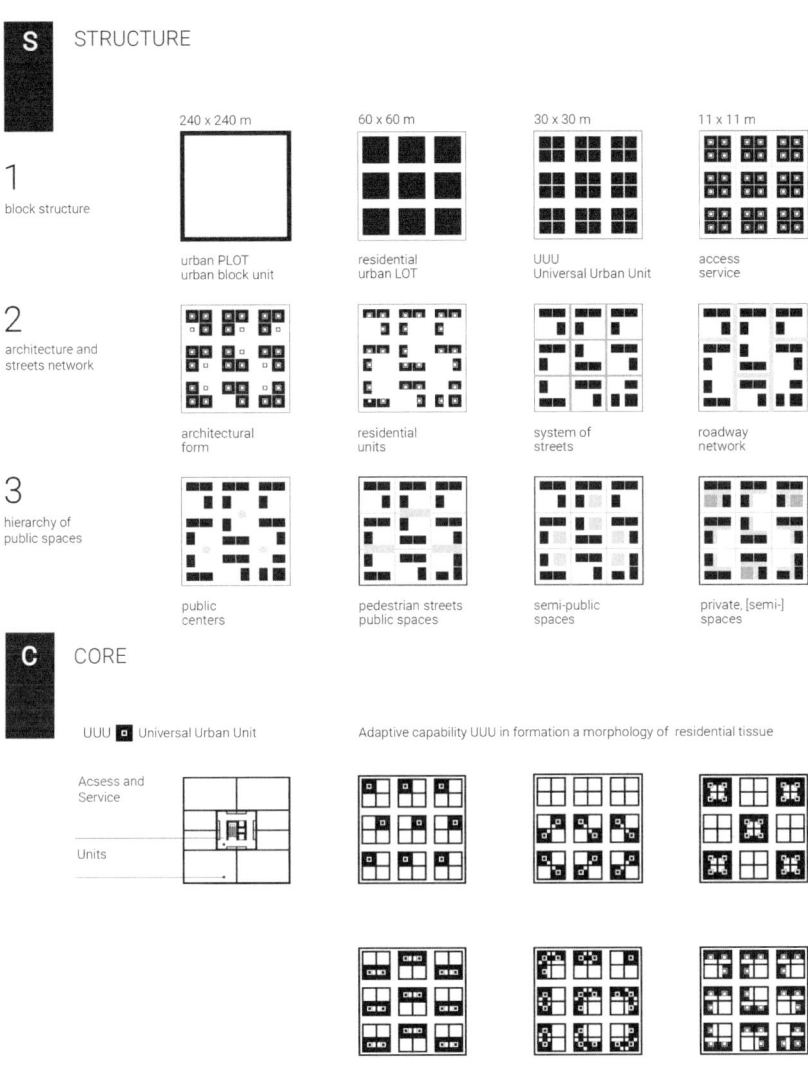

Figure 5.8
**Model of
project with
practical
applica-
tion of the
S.C.R.I.P.T.
approach**

S STRUCTURE

1
block structure

240 x 240 m
urban PLOT
urban block unit

60 x 60 m
residential
urban LOT

30 x 30 m
UUU
Universal Urban Unit

11 x 11 m
access
service

2
architecture and
streets network

architectural
form

residential
units

system of
streets

roadway
network

3
hierarchy of
public spaces

public
centers

pedestrian streets
public spaces

semi-public
spaces

private, [semi-]
spaces

C CORE

UUU ◼ Universal Urban Unit   Adaptive capability UUU in formation a morphology of residential tissue

Acsess and
Service

Units

Residential development and living environment have always been an indicator of any social, economic and political changes in Russia. Therefore,
the importance of sustainable adaptability of housing to the time factor is
increasing.

For the first time this approach was used in the residential area project
at the First Russian Youth Architectural Biennale. The project was awarded
a Silver Prize and generated substantial interest in the professional community (RBK Realty, 2017). Twenty-nine finalists were selected from 377
applications from many Russian cities that submitted their residential
block projects to the Biennale. The main goal of the competition was to
discover novel approaches to the development of residential environments
(see Figure 5.8).

Script: the approach and the strategy

S. Structure

The main challenge of the last decade for architects and urban planners in Russia was the focus on the residential unit structure. This happened due to the fact that over the last hundred years the district has grown so large that it has lost its former importance (Krainyaya, 2011).

For the developers of residential districts, the priority was the size of a residential district as a territorial unit.

For the Biennale, a project site was chosen with territory of 240 x 240 meters (787 ft. x 787 ft) designed as an urban plot (unit) of the larger district. The main planning solution was the division of these plots into nine residential units 60 x 60 meters (approx. 200 ft x 200 ft) (residential urban lots).

The connectivity and permeability typical for the capillary structure, which disappeared in the 20th century, has obvious advantages both at the city planning and at the architectural levels. The main architectural and city-planning principles of the residential structures in Russia, identified in the analysis, are the relatively high density (23000 m^2/ha) and low rise (4–6–8 floors) development, a complex hierarchy of public spaces, and the ability to transform and preserve the character of the initial tissue.

C. Core: unchangeable components constant layer

A universal urban unit (UUU) 30 x 30 m (approx. 100 ft x 100 ft) is an unchangeable, stationary component. In the center of the unit, there is a ladder-elevator shaft and a belt of engineering (mechanical) shafts. Possible unit modifications and combinations make it universal in the formation of the morphology of the urban tissue. The foundation and networks for the constructive engineering system are laid in each block, creating reserves and flexibility for further adaptive development (see Figure 5.9).

R. Rules

We propose a model or tool for decision making at the level of city planning based on distribution of responsibility and control in the management of urban transformation.

The core of the interactive regulation and a tool for managing transformations is the Script Lab (Bureau of Urban Transformations) – a center for research and design.

Short or rapid (in the range of 5–20 years or one generation) transformations concern changes in the articulation or distribution of private and public spaces, as well as the generation of internal dwelling unit spaces. A resident can make an application to the Script Lab and obtain professional answers to their changing needs in the form of ready-made variable adaptive solutions. The cataloging of variable solutions (menu system) and the centralized production of modular elements for interior spaces of a UUU and elements of

Figure 5.9
**Structure
and core
aspects**

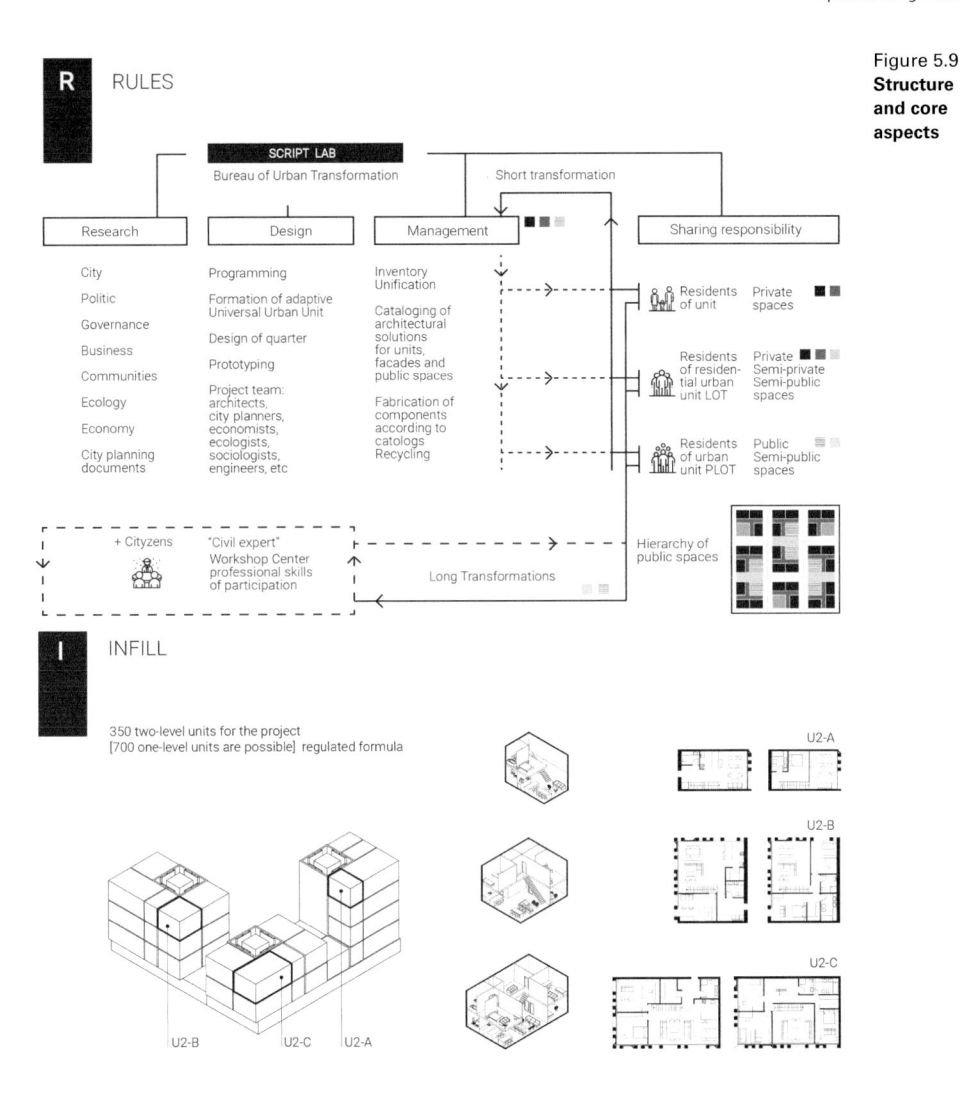

improvement are envisaged as a starting point, with eventual "open market" infill companies becoming available.

Long-term transformations refer to the level of public spaces, where a complex mechanism of interaction with different structures exist. For this purpose, we make a civil expert available within the Lab, providing qualified assistance in understanding the role and the boundaries of residents' responsibility in transformation of their residential quarter and a city.

I. Infill: filling – *variable components, generated space, free spaces*

The project of universal urban unit has three types of dwelling sizes. Each dwelling has an exterior utility systems service, which is located outside the

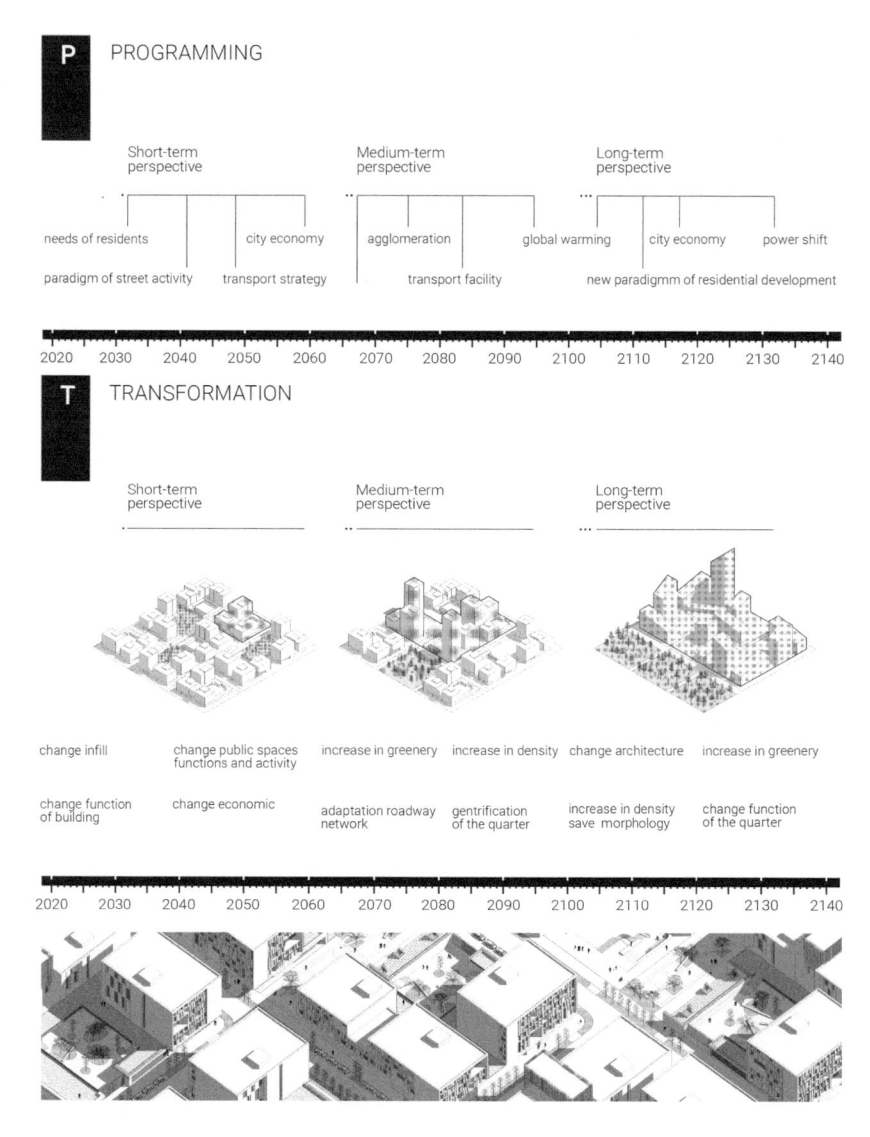

Figure 5.10
**Rules and
infill aspects**

dwelling and is located as part of the base building. Structurally, the living cell consists of two floors, but can be transformed into two single-story units. Since utility system services are external to units, a residential apartment has many scenarios of internal floor plan layout (see Figure 5.10).

P. Program

Programming of living environments is an attempt to lay into the project the scenario for its future development, based on the use of levels of intervention

Figure 5.11
Programming and trans- formation aspects

and consideration of change over time. We cannot predict the future, but after researching some previous paradigms of the organization of the residential environment and practices of strategic planning, we can build some hypotheses in programming the living environment. In this sentence, the hypotheses are rather conditional and abstract. It is crucial to make a residential quarter capable of self-adapting to the challenges of the future. Most important is the attempt to preserve the character of the urban tissue, even in the conditions of increasing density.

Three different time scales are considered:

1. Short-term perspective (5–10 years): changes at the level of a single unit, yard spaces and common areas.
2. Medium-term (buffer) (10–50 years): other changes that become a transitional scenario between the strategy of small and long-term changes.
3. Long-term perspective (100–200 years): changes in the tissue of urban environment and the effect of such changes on a living quarter, transformation hypotheses.

T. Transformation

Architectural solutions for the above scenarios. Cataloging adaptive product/ service solutions from the worldwide market based on smart interface standards.

In opposition to the traditional approach, we propose an architectural project with a scenario for changes in its residential structures. The importance of adaptive architectural and city-planning solutions in the creation of residential environments and the programming of scenarios for its future development are first in line (see Figure 5.11).

Conclusions

1. The Open Building approach is aimed at ensuring that architectural projects implemented according to its principles bring benefits to people, facilitates the possibility of adapting space to changing needs and reduces costs. Whether it's a change in the layout of independent dwellings or a reorganization of cities, Open Building is primarily a positive development and a blessing for people. In Russia, the use of these principles brings prosperity to developers, investors and individual players involved with profit. That is, the practice considered in this chapter is a positive result only in the architecture of the premium market. In social housing, the principles of Open Building are still impractical or burdensome for users, because there is no legislative basis for comprehensible implementation of processes aimed at planning for change and variety.

2. Russia has an Open Building approach. Its principles are manifested at all levels of development of the environment. But these principles are being implemented for the most part so far illegally, and not like in other countries, just because it's Russia. Now the ruling class still uses the Soviet system of government, and these are the principles of pressure and force. Proper regulation requires time and a complete change of the ruling generation. But the main thing is that Russian people have the interest to live in freedom and really want to change their environment, with supportive laws and rules.

3. The urban planning agenda is changing all the time and in recent years a vector has been set for the complexity and regularization of design decisions and design processes.

4. Mechanisms of legal regulation of city-planning processes are in the stage of formation. Due to the peculiarity of the pressure of political will in Russia, it is not possible to predict the time of transition to quality legal zoning. Reforming the system of city planning regulation is available only with the elimination of situation and location-based planning. In view of the recent transformations, the development of new design codes, excluding the federal and local building code and standards is relevant and timely. Forming a new environment is possible after a rejection of the current outdated regulatory system.

5. The process of the formation of capitalist relations was interrupted for 80 years. The border of the resident's responsibility still ends with the apartment door. Formation of laws on the Collective Ownership ('the commons') needs development in Russia.

6. Public hearings do not guarantee the prevention of urban errors. This is a political platform, where substantive and constructive discussions are rare. There is a need to improve the quality of participation, to train groups of people in a professional language in order to represent the interests of the public concerned. Residents could communicate with the authorities and developers at the same level and protect their interests at public hearings.

References

CIAM Open Learn (2001). Congres Internationaux d'Architecture Moderne. Available at: www.open.edu/openlearn/history-the-arts/history/heritage

Cuito, A. and Montes, C. (2002). *Mies van der Rohe*. London: Te Neues Pub Group.

Gareev, I.F. (2015). Housing cooperatives as an alternative housing funding scheme: Creative economy. *Housing Strategy*, 4, pp. 319–335.

Habraken, N.J. (2005). *Palladio's Children*. London and New York: Taylor & Francis.

Housing Code of the Russian Federation (2004). Chapter 4. Renewal and resetting of the premises in the multi-apartment housing.

Ingels, B. (2009). *Yes Is More: An Archicomic on Architectural Evolution*. Cologne: Tachen Publishers.

Institute of General Plan of Moscow (n.d.). History of Institute. Available at: https://genplanmos.ru/en/institute/history/

Krainyaya, N. (2011). About the block of the city, its past and future. *Architectural Newsletter AB*, 1, pp. 118–124.

Lechenko, E. (2016). *A Monster House Was Built Among the Five-Story Buildings in Bragino*. Available at: www.yar.kp.ru/daily/26618.5/3636042/

Mogzoev, A. and Kuzmicheva, K. (2017). Renovation of the housing stock of the city of Moscow. *Bulletin of Witte Moscow University*, 4(23), pp. 70–74.

Moscow RE:industrial. (2018). *Typology of Production Areas and Best Practices for Redevelopment*. Centeragency. RDNK. 192p.

Polidi, T., Baykova, T. and Igumenova, E. (2016). Development of the commercial real estate market as an example of ineffective urban policy. *Property Relations in Russia*, 4(175). Available at: https://cyberleninka.ru/article/n/razvitie-rynka-apartamentov-kak-primer-neeffektivnoy-gradostroitelnoy-politiki/viewer

RBK Realty. (2013). *How to Stop Construction in the Yard*. Available at: https://realty.rbc.ru/news/577d27959a7947a78ce92c02https://realty.rbc.ru/news/577d27959a7947a78ce92c02

RBK Realty. (2017). *The Country as One Quarter: The Best Young Architects of Russia*. Available at: https://realty.rbc.ru/news/59e4b5619a79476a4b8265b6

SanPiN 1.2.2645-10 (2010). Sanitary and epidemiological requirements for living conditions in residential buildings and premises, p. 3.8 Chief state sanitary doctor of the Russian federation. Resolution. Dated June 10, 2010 no. 64.

SP 54.13330.2016 (2016). Set of rules: Residential multi-apartment buildings (updated version SNiP 31-01-2003) p. 9.22.

The Free Plan; Russia's Shell-and-Core Apartment Buildings. (2001) (ed. Goldhoorn, B). Project Russia. A-Fond Publishers, Moscow and Amsterdam

The Official Site of Moscow on Urban Policy and Construction (n.d.). Available at: https://stroi.mos.ru/novaia-proghramma-rienovatsii-piatietazhiek

Trudolyubov, M. (2015). *The People Behind the Fence: Power, Property and Private Space in Russia*. Moscow: Novoe Izdatelstvo.

Chapter 6

Open Building in the global South

Amira Osman

Introduction

Several decades ago, the Open Building approach attracted substantial interest in so-called "developing countries." Investigations in slum upgrading, informal settlements and user participation could be found in various countries of the South, focused on residential architecture. This chapter reassess the role that this approach can offer in the global South by presenting a range of projects which have been conceptualized and built, most with no reference to Habraken's theories or Open Building as an approach to development. However, it is found that these projects are similar in several important ways: the idea of encouraging long-lasting residential architecture planned for change, enabling decision-makers to manage risk and uncertainty while accepting the distribution of control (and responsibility) across levels of intervention.

Some old texts on housing that dealt with contexts of informality and poverty were consulted and more recent examples of projects are offered as case studies in the three contexts of South America, South Asia and Africa. These projects are analyzed by considering to what extent design tasks are separated and technically "disentangled" and also to what extent the short- and long-term elements (physical and spatial) are assembled to ensure maximum capacity for adaptability with minimal social and technical disruption and conflict.

Self-built housing and informal settlement upgrades are perhaps the two concerns that most dominate conversations on housing in the global South. The concepts of participation and agency always feature strongly in these debates, as does the role of governments in housing processes. The failure of many formal interventions has meant that professionals and governments have tried to understand the prerequisites that could ensure the success of projects. Involvement of the users of residential developments and the beneficiaries of government subsidies in decision-making from the outset has been one factor that is considered important for community buy-in and instilling a long-term sense of ownership. While participation is important in

DOI: 10.4324/9781003018339-7

order to better understand a context and what interventions would thrive in unique conditions, it has also been used as an "excuse" to withhold delivery of essential services to communities desperate for professional services.

Kendall explains that

Ignorance of the (housing) types that grow well in [a specific context] soil mean that we (architects) will always be at a disadvantage if we try to make new interventions grow healthy roots in this particular soil. When we don't know these types, and try to make new ones, it's like a gardener being ignorant of the soil and the plant types that thrive in that soil, and who, trying to be creative and inventive, attempts to make new flowers never seen before. The chances that they will fail to take root are large!

(Kendall, 2015, p. 54, paraphrasing Habraken)

Community engagement is a mechanism for empowerment and increased agency. The spatial/physical has a profound impact on socio-cultural and economic conditions and allows for on-going participation rather than ineffective one-off participation at the start of a project (Osman, 2015, p. 13). Open Building is therefore a pragmatic mechanism for ensuring on-going participation through distributed control and increased agency.

In this chapter, the roles and responsibilities of governments, communities and individuals, and how synergy can be achieved between them, will be considered in the light of recent studies which show a massive increase in formal housing across Africa with minimal government intervention. This sheds light on the need to reconceptualize where government efforts and financing must be focused and draws attention to how housing may effectively be considered as continuation of public infrastructure into the fabric of buildings.

The Open Building approach allows for innovations by recognizing a hierarchical decision-making structure (like any infrastructure system) in the built environment, impacting design, technology, finance and procurement mechanisms. This chapter is premised on the belief that there is a need for new forms of governance and regulatory frameworks in the built environment disciplines that would allow for experimentation and testing of alternative forms of delivery. In this light, the Lutsinga Infrastructure House in South Africa is a possible mechanism which may be adapted for the countries of the global South to manage built environment projects in general, and residential projects in particular, considering unique socio-economic conditions as well as a large degree of informality in residential areas. To achieve the aims set out in this chapter, a proposal is presented to expand the mandate of the Lutsinga Infrastructure House beyond health and educational facilities to include residential developments.

The chapter concludes with a vision for housing practice transformation in the global South.

Background and definitions

This chapter presents examples of the Open Building approach that have been realized in countries in the global South in the recent past – and how these concepts may be applied in the future. It could perhaps be argued that these concepts, developed in the cold, north, highly industrialized, post-World War II Europe are not applicable to the very different socio-economic, climatic, cultural and religious conditions of the global South. Yet, there was a time when there was great interest in the concept of Open Building with regard to slum upgrading, informality and user participation in housing in countries currently considered to be a part of the broad category of the global South – an interest that this chapter revisits. These countries are generally accepted to be most of south Asia, central and south America, Africa, most of the Middle East and Oceana.

Some terms to describe these world regions are used interchange-ably: third world, developing, global South, emerging economies. The latter is a description that has come to define countries characterized by rapid economic growth and industrialization – many of them falling within the geographic region of the global South – and that are gaining prominence in the global market. It is a term that helps distinguish between these countries and so-called developing nations.

Brazil, Russia, India, China and South Africa are known as the BRICS countries, an acronym that may replace "emerging economies." As more developing countries transition into emerging economies, the category may have to be broadened to include more than these five countries. The relationship between these two types of economies and their respective impacts on built environment transformation is important when considering the relevance and application of Open Building, as economic conditions bring into the conversation the level of industrialization, skills (professional and non-professional alike), financing, regulation and traditional/modern methods of construction in these contexts. These factors differ from country to country across the global South which implies that the Open Building approach, like any methodical approach, should be adapted to suit the different circumstances. (*Editor's note: see Chapters 5, 9 and 13 for examples of developments toward Open Building in two of these BRICS countries.*)

For the purpose of this chapter, the term developing countries will be used to describe countries that are mostly reliant on agriculture, with a less developed industrial sector, poor infrastructure and a low GDP. These countries have a high incidence of informality; many of them are also experiencing high rates of growth and may be categorized as emerging economies; many of them fall within the geographic region of the "global South."

The socio-economic conditions of developing countries imply that built environment interventions and building production strategies need to be inclusive, broad based and at a scale that is accessible to a large portion of the population. These kinds of strategies are crucial for development projects to have real impact and to be truly embedded in their contexts. Indeed,

Schumacher believes that: "The primary causes of extreme poverty are immaterial. They lie in certain deficiencies in education, organization and discipline" (Schumacher, 1973, p. 164). Many of Schumacher's principles in his definitive work *Small is Beautiful* express the importance of how "everybody should produce something" as opposed to "a few people should produce [producing] a great deal" (Schumacher, 1973, p. 170). This is an ethos that is intrinsic to the concept of Open Building. Schumacher believed that this is the only condition that may bridge gaps in society and create growth. Development according to Schumacher, cannot be an "act" (Schumacher, 1973, p. 164); it is rather described as evolution and a process which cannot be comprehensively planned (ibid.).

Open Building for its part is about an attitude toward cultivating ordinary built environment that changes and transforms over time by the action of many parties. Open Building is a verb and not a noun; it is an act – or series of actions – over time in a built environment that is in constant, if slow, evolution and a building industry that allows for multiple small and large players across many levels. Development, according to Schumacher, is about ownership of the education, organization and discipline required to achieve progress by the whole society (ibid.). Open Building is about control of the decision-making process in the built environment and its distribution among professionals and ordinary citizens alike.

Indeed, Hamdi made parallels between the thinking of Turner, Habraken and Schumacher with regard to achieving a balance between order and choice, the government and the public, process and product (Hamdi, 1995, pp. 40–41). The Open Building approach is premised on a long history of engagement with these concepts and the applications in contexts of poverty and "social housing" was without a doubt integral to these early debates as reflected in older texts.

For the purpose of this chapter, Open Building is considered in terms of how it can support, and add substantively to the following:

- Income diversity
- Informal and formal development processes
- Upgrading
- Incremental development
- Participation by everyday citizens and professionals alike.

The basic principles of Open Building can be summarized as

> the way design decisions are separated [on levels of intervention (e.g. urban design separated from building design, or building design from fit-out, etc.)], how a building is "put together", how buildings are assembled in terms of long- and short- life components and how the interface between building components allows for disassembly, replacement and upgrading with no disruptions to other building systems or components.
> (Osman, 2015)

The chapter is premised on the belief that the concept of Open Building is timeless, and its principles are universal; they continue to relate to the state of the built environment globally and have special resonance for Africa and countries of the global South. Yet professions responsible for steering the building environment's continued development remain largely untransformed; there has been surprisingly little radical (vs. superficial) innovation in the field of housing since Habraken's *Supports* was first published in English in 1972. The principle of distributed decision-making articulated in that work offers a mechanism by which voices that may have been side-lined, excluded and unheard may regain decision-making roles. That book made an argument for abolishing social discrimination, suggesting that support structures (representing what is shared or common to all occupants) might be a part of government-funded infrastructure in which independent dwellings could be installed and change over time as social and economic conditions evolve and as technical standards rise. All of these concepts make great sense when considering the unique conditions in the global South. Therefore, for the purpose of this chapter, the definition of Open Building will focus on the following principles:

1. Separation between "supports" and "infill" – the relationship between what is shared and what can be independently decided per occupancy.
2. Disentanglement in design, technical infrastructure, construction and procurement.
3. Maximum capacity for adaptability of components of the built environment with a short lifespan, with minimum disruptions to those components of the built environment that have a longer life span and that, being shared, are more difficult to change.
4. System (process) development taking precedence over product design.

Applications of Open Building concepts in the global South have generally centered on the design of residential units that grow incrementally from one of two kinds of "starter (single family) house" (based on the CSIR, 2000, p. 104):

•   in the form of "core units" – usually a "wet core" – and/or the idea of a "minimum shelter" which is habitable from the outset as all the main components are there from the outset, usually to be expanded through self-help as a process in a defined "lot";
•   in the form of a "shell house" – usually to be subdivided – which is not habitable from the outset as it needs owner self-help action.

Self-help is here defined as a practice where "low-income groups solve their housing needs primarily through their own resources (both in terms of labor and finance)" (Zhang et al., 2003, p. 914). The most extreme form of self-help is "site and service schemes" where future residents use their own resources to build a house on a serviced plot of land from scratch, either using their own labor ("self-build") or employ the services of a local contractor or as Andrade-Narvaez (1981, pp. 14–15) states, where "the con-sumer and the producer are the same person". This was promoted by Turner (Turner, 2000) who argued that any formal strategy of housing delivery would be unaffordable for low-income residents. Hamdi also conceived of the idea of delivering "housing without houses." He writes that "cities of the poor are largely self-help cities – their growth is unplanned and usually follows lines of least resistance" (Hamdi, 1995, p. 5). Methods of delivery of housing have differed in different contexts and at different times, but the combination of sites and services schemes with some form of self-help has been predominant (ibid., p. 24). The approach adopted by the EMAD pro-ject (Expandable Minimum Ameriyah Dwelling) provided sites, security of tenure, basic infrastructure and a minimum shelter for immediate occupa-tion (Buwalda, 1980, p. 63).

While there are great benefits to self-help projects, historically, some have argued that government promotion of self-help "exploits labor" while others argued that it offered "self-helpers" great freedom as the process made housing more accessible and affordable; thus debates were polarized as to whether self-help was capitalist or socialist. Hamdi (1995, p. 25) and Andrade-Narvaez (1981, p. 15) believed that self-help is a "form of construc-tion [that] corresponds to the pre-capitalist forms of production" and that "the imposition of capitalism on pre-capitalist societies" as a major reason for the housing problem in Latin America (ibid.). By focusing on the house as an object in a market, as a commodity, the right to a house as a "container" (ibid.) for the family grouping that resides in it is denied.

Some argue that "sites and services" should be considered as a means of control – a method with a "hidden agenda" as claimed by Reza (Reza, 1986), perhaps romanticizing the idea of complete freedom. More recently, Boano and Vergara Perucich (Boano and Vergara Perucich 2016, pp. 62–63) have argued that incomplete houses to be finished by the residents (specifically, Elemental's "half-a-house" concept discussed later) are a "neoliberal method to produce social architecture," believing that this is a method to employ public funding towards the activation of capitalist real estate developments through providing land tenure and promoting entrepreneurialism – thus including the poor in banking systems. They see this as being very negative rather than as a form of empowerment; indeed, their position seems to reject the idea of self-help, arguing "Why doesn't the State provide affordable houses?" (ibid. p. 71). This position is problematic. The South African gov-ernment has had one of the most successful housing programs internation-ally in terms of the number of houses delivered – but this focus on housing numbers has led to sprawl, mono-functional housing environments and the perpetuation of segregation. Indeed, South Africa may be changing its focus from the delivery of subsidized housing units to site and services as it fails to reduce the housing backlog through its current housing program (Ensor, 2020). However, this approach would still not help in achieving compact, high-density, mixed-function and mixed-income neighborhoods aspired to in policy documents and urban visions.

Another housing project that has been influential in terms of shifting thinking and practice with regards to housing design and delivery approaches in developing contexts is the Previ Experimental Housing in Lima (1967). This well-known project aimed to achieve on-going growth as well as a rationalization of construction methods; it was premised on the belief that the homes would change over time (Salas and Lucas, 2012, p. 9). The project questioned the concept of housing as a finished product and aimed to design a structured process which allowed for growth over time. The project had three components with opportunities for some parts of the development to be conceptualized and built by well-known architectural firms, some parts which involved renovations to existing building and others aiming to facilitate low-cost, self-built housing.

Some of the innovations that emerged from this experiment are around "rationalized" versus "industrialized" systems and the idea of "technological families" (ibid., p. 11). These principles led to the improvement of processes towards the production of compatible elements in small, labor-intensive, equipment-light production plants (some located on-site) (ibid., p. 14). While the intention was to implement an "intermediate approach" bringing together imported industrialization as local traditions in construction, it is shown that 40 years later the new technologies had not taken root in that context (ibid.). When it comes to housing, it seems that past lessons are never learned according to Dickinson (Dickinson, 2020) who explains how a project with similar intentions went very wrong in New Orleans. "Make It Right" was intended to provide 150 homes designed by well-known architects after Hurricane Katrina; by focusing on the individual (detached) residential units and emphasizing the identity of the individual designers, it does not seem that projects such as the Previ housing were re-visited. Why would this have been important? Despite some of the failures of Previ, some principles that emerge in that project are:

1. The projects are diverse and with diverse project teams.
2. There is a level of disentanglement implied and decision-making is spread between the various stakeholders.
3. The project aims for future adaptability with minimum disruption.
4. The project approach implies a focus on process.

It is based on perceived positive principles discussed above that the case studies for this chapter have been selected.

Introduction to the case studies

This chapter has consulted old texts on informality, poverty, self-built housing and informal settlement upgrades – the two concerns that most dominate conversations on housing in the global South from an architectural viewpoint. However, the chapter adds a different Open Building perspective on the role of governments and communities and how synergy can be achieved for maximum efficiency. This is considered in the light of recent studies which show a massive increase in formal housing across Africa (and the global South generally) with minimal government intervention. This reality sheds light on the need to rethink where government efforts in housing finance and delivery must be focused. The argument presented is premised on an understanding of housing as an extension of the principles of infrastructure into the fabric of buildings, rather than just the utilities running along or under the streets or road networks weaving communities together.

Towards these aims, and to reinforce some of these principles, select case studies are presented. Several older projects are showcased as well as more recent examples of projects in the three contexts of South America, South Asia and Africa. The role that the Open Building approach can offer in the global South is demonstrated in this selection of projects which have, with only a few exceptions, been conceptualized and built with no reference to Habraken's theories or Open Building as a concept – yet they exhibit the principles of Open Building in one or another way; they are based on the idea of encouraging long-lasting residential architecture planned for change, enabling decision-makers to manage risk and uncertainty while accepting the distribution of control (and responsibility) across levels of intervention. These projects are analyzed by considering to what extent design tasks have been separated, to what extent they are "disentangled" in construction methods and to what extent the short- and long-term components are assembled to ensure minimum disruptions and maximum potential for adaptability.

The case studies are analyzed using the following criteria:

- To what extent they are "disentangled" (technically and in terms of decision-making) in the manner that they are designed and constructed.
- To what extent the short- and long-term elements (physical and spatial) are assembled to ensure minimum disruptions when change occurs, and maximum capacity for adaptability.
- The use of capacity analysis as an implicit part of the design/development process.

"Legacy" case study projects

Projects of The Uam-X Housing Workshop by Jorge Andrade in Mexico

These projects are significant because the architects' reference to Habraken and the link to Open Building has been deliberate. Professors and researchers from the Autonomous University Metropolitan developed the Housing Workshop (TAVI) in the 1970s which has been an important initiative promoting alternatives for the design, financing and construction of housing in Mexico. The work of TAVI was presented at the 2016 Venice Biennale and published in *Archdaily* (*Archdaily*, 2016). All the information on the project is from this *Archdaily* article on the Biennale where Jorge Andrade and Andrea Martín Chávez presented two housing schemes:

1. The Cohuatlán housing project (Figure 6.1), built in the Guerrero neighborhood of Mexico City in 1978, and the Xacalli complex, begun in 1998. Cohuatlán was a pioneering work in Mexico in more ways than one. It is one of the first housing cooperatives in the country and was funded from different public institutions and implemented through a joint venture. It was the first time, in Latin America, that a SUPPORT project was implemented.

Figure 6.1
The Cohuatlán housing project is the first built experiment in Latin America that implemented Habraken's theories (photo credit Onnis Luque)

2. The Xacalli complex (Figure 6.2) is made up of houses which have evolved incrementally. Its inhabitants – and initial promoters – were people affected by the 1985 earthquake in Mexico City. The arrangement of the houses defines spaces with different levels of local organization: families, immediate neighbors and the whole in general.

Information on Xacalli is also published by the architect on a dedicated website (Andrade, n.d.). Its evolution continued for many years (1986–2003). The architect described the process of appropriation and occupation of urban land through a progressive housing project developed under the control and direction of its own organized inhabitants. The Xacalli housing complex comprises 50 houses which developed incrementally. The Xacalli civic association emerged in 1986, after the earthquake of September 1985. An important design decision was to include patios which are shared by groups of five to ten dwellings. This helped facilitate their maintenance, control and use.

The plan of the complex is based on spatial levels of territoriality and ownership. Space is allocated for possible expansion. The initial "starter" unit is two floors with a living area of 68.80 m² (740 ft²). The second stage is a

Figure 6.2
**Xacalli
external
view
(*Archdaily*,
2016) (photo
credit Onnis
Luque)**

vertical extension on the upper level of 24.50 m^2 (264 ft^2). This brings the unit to 93.30 m^2 (1004 ft^2) and the final and third stage is the addition of two rooms bringing the total final area to 118.40 m^2 (1275 ft^2). Gabled roofs were used to help in rainwater management but also to serve two important functions. The first is to collect stormwater; the second is to help restrict the vertical growth of houses to no more than two floors. The inhabitants are in charge of the growth of their own dwelling units (Andrade, n.d.).

Chile's Elemental and the "half a house" experiment, 2004

Aravena has designed numerous noteworthy projects with various programs in various contexts – however, he is mostly known for his significant contribution towards rethinking housing for the poor in well located city sites through a partnership (a "do-tank") known as Elemental. Could Aravena's approach be considered Open Building? The process delivers "part of the house." Yet, the house is not separated into Open Building levels. Aravena asks "which part should one construct?" which implies an engagement with the concept of a support. Aravena also asks "how can one set the rules of the game" which implies a positive concern with allowing maximum user control within set parameters.

The multiple sources of finance used for the construction are not used to deliver different components of the project based on long and short life elements. Rather the funding has been used to deliver buildings that are to a great extent conventional. The Elemental experiments grapple with the concept of "capacity" – but they have not investigated the idea of mixed income, mixed functions or mixed typologies within the same development. Many aspects of the projects are rooted in similar conceptual underpinnings as Open Building; however, a deeper engagement with its core principles would have added much value to an already valuable experiment. The attempt to balance

Figure 6.3
Quinta Monroy project by Elemental, www.archdaily.com/797779/half-a-house-builds-a-whole-community-elementals-controversial-social-housing (Linelle Visage)

Figure 6.4
Quinta Monroy after resident additions, www.phaidon.com/agenda/architecture/articles/2016/january/14/why-2016s-pritzker-winner-makes-half-built-houses/ (Linelle Visage)

between uniformity and variety/individual agency in the built environment is an aspect that has great resonance with the Open Building approach, as is the attempt to involve many decision-makers in the design and construction process (see Figure 6.3, 6.4).

Incremental housing demands a different approach to finance, design and implementation. International precedents demonstrate that initial developments intended as incremental projects have evolved into fully functioning urban settlements, integrated within city contexts – and most importantly, these settlements continue to evolve as the built environment is in constant change and never static. This is an important principle which needs to guide the planning for housing and human settlements.

The Elemental approach is rooted in a long history of engagement with the topic of adaptation and change of residential units as well as user participation in the decision-making. Elemental have therefore made a significant contribution towards translating the principles into implemented projects.

The incremental/evolutionary nature of the Elemental designs allow for increased user involvement through the lifetime of the building. The options of unit growth are quite defined (probably due to the nature of the sites and the higher densities achieved) and do not allow for multiple growth paths or options. The internal layout variation is quite limited because of the small size of the spaces and the urban settings also pose some constraints externally.

There is an awareness that the primary structure needs to have a strong urban presence and needs to be of a high quality and robust nature. In Arevena's Milano experiment it becomes evident that the architect's approach implies that much of the building expenditure goes towards the structure and roof. With the Anto Fagasa project, the Elemental website states:

> The housing unit is defined by structural 3 floor high partition walls. All complex items (firewall, facilities, circulation and structure) are associated to the wall. This system generates a triple height interior void, in which families can do spatial modifications.
>
> (Elemental, n.d.)

Aravena also asks "how can one set the rules of the game" which implies a positive concern with allowing maximum user control within set parameters – thus ensuring that individual actions do not infringe on the collective good. However, it is not explicitly stated that many times users are unknown and that the physical structures would have to allow for unknown clients and needs.

While some Open Building practitioners state that the architectural configuration should allow you to "be the boss behind your own front door" (acknowledgement to Karel Dekker of the Netherlands), in the Elemental case, the façades are also open to adaptation and construction by the residents, not from a library of choices determined by the architect but completely open to occupant preferences from readily available building materials.

The multiple sources of finance used for the construction are not used to deliver different components (or Open Building levels) of the project based on long and short life elements and the ownership model has not allowed for different forms of ownership (perhaps split into one agency owning the "supports" while the users own the "infill"). Rather the funding has been "put into one pot" as it were – to deliver buildings that are to a great extent "conventional" in that there is no strict system separation between the built environment levels – in Open Building terminology.

The Elemental residential experiments grapple with the concept of "capacity" – perhaps to excess in the case of the "Make it Right" house they developed for New Orleans which has a massive porch for future expansion by the residents. But no explicit capacity analysis was conducted. But apparently, they have not investigated the idea of mixed income, mixed functions or mixed typologies within the same development.

The work of Elemental and Aravena is most significant. It has brought aspects neglected in mainstream architectural debates to the forefront and while many of the projects are repetitive in solution there is no doubt that there were diverse and unique processes behind each project solution and the repetitive structures are devised in such a way to allow for a degree of variation in the long term.

- Date of construction: various.
- Architect: Elemental, Alejandro Arevena.
- Size: various.
- Public/Private developer: public with resident finance of additions.

Degree of "disentanglement"	Intentional design and construction features that allow for change over time	Methods of decision-making in the design and the construction of the building
• Materials • Details • Connections • When decisions are made	• Is there a distinction made between short- and long-term building materials and components? • Are the building elements (physical and spatial) assembled in such a manner so as to ensure minimum disruptions if changes are made? The projects in most cases clearly distinguish between long- and short-term elements, with the long-term elements being delivered upfront in the form of a "half a house" The way that the houses are delivered does imply a large degree of adaptability potential with minimum disruptions – the urban form becomes a strong permanent component in the Quinta Monroy project	• How were design decisions made? • Who participated? • How was the building constructed? • Were small and big construction companies involved? There is a level of disentanglement as parts of the buildings are delivered by one group of decision-makers and other parts evolving over time as input by the residents/ users Again, while having a distinct architectural character, the project is mostly known and became famous because of its focus on process rather than because of its form

I talked to Aravena about Habraken and Open Building a few years ago (he was not that famous then) and asked him if he was aware about them. He agreed that Habraken's concepts are in his work but he never followed them. It was a little bit strange, in my point of view, but I understood he was trying to create some new concept or theory as a unique idea. The most important thing for me are the following two:

1) Aravena also said, at that time, that his professional life has changed after he read Hermano de Soto's book about informal economy and property rights. The Peruvian economist believes that social housing is a product, which must be inserted into the formal economy in order to give the same economic status for the poor. Aravena has worked on this view: social housing as a "commodity." He gave an interview to a Brazilian journalist saying that architects must provide the medium class DNA for the poor in favelas. A disaster!!! I am strongly against this idea. On the contrary, poor people do not have social, economic and political conditions to be considered as middle class who need properties (they need other much more important things!). I work with the perspective that social housing must be built as a collaborative process between the State, architects and people (self-builders) but not only about the design.

2) It is urgently necessary to understand what happened in Chile after Aravena's social housing schemes have been built. Mostly these environments are a mess! As social housing is understood by him as a product to be delivered, there is no permanent social program there. Social housing is not a design problem even if design improvements are VERY important and necessary all over the world (especially Latin America and Mexico). Due to the design, Aravena probably deserves an award. He brought up an important debate. But if we broadly consider the social housing issue, as Habraken has written about – housing as a process – Aravena's proposal leads us to a much more profound debate. (*From private correspondence with the author and editor with Professor Denise Morado, Departamento de Projetos, Programa de Pós-Graduação em Arquitetura e Urbanismo (NPGAU), Belo Horizonte – Brazil.*)

"New" case study projects: applications of Open Building in Brazil

Fidalga Building

The architects of the Fidalga Building (2011), Andrade Morttin Arquitetos Associados, aimed to integrate the building into its context. Located in a vibrant neighborhood of São Paolo, Brazil, the building has publicly accessible spaces on the street level. With regard to the individual dwelling units, these are "designed as open spaces that offer complete freedom of occupation to accommodate the lifestyle of each owner. With double height, each unit has several vertical pipe shafts, strategically located, allowing to relocate every internal room." The glass and wood panels on the façade were intended to express this freedom by giving the building a sense of lightness (Figure 6.5).

Figure 6.5
**Fidalga
Building,
São Paolo,
external view
showing the
distinct glass
and wooden
panels
(*Archdaily*,
2011)**

The floor plan (Archdaily 2011) has been used to test to what extent the building has the capacity for change with minimal disruptions to the overall functioning of the building or other dwellings within the building (Figure 6.6). The seven floor plans are each different. We have produced diagrams showing where the common services and vertical circulation cores are located, elements that may be considered part of the Support, and how these allow for different configurations at each floor level. It can be seen from the diagrams that there is a degree of "looseness" to the planning that allows for adaptation.

Some of the adaptable features appear to be more of an aesthetic form of expression rather than being a deliberate and studied attempt to ensure a separation of design decision-making levels. While the project has been designed with a degree of capacity for change, the shape of the building is limiting in some ways.

A summary follows:

- Place: São Paolo, Brazil.
- Date of construction: 2011.
- Architect: Andrade Morettin Arquitetos Associades.
- Size: 3775 m².
- Public/Private developer: private.

Existing Structure

Outdoor Space

Additional Walls and Space

Staircase

Lift

Wet Services

Existing Exterior Walls

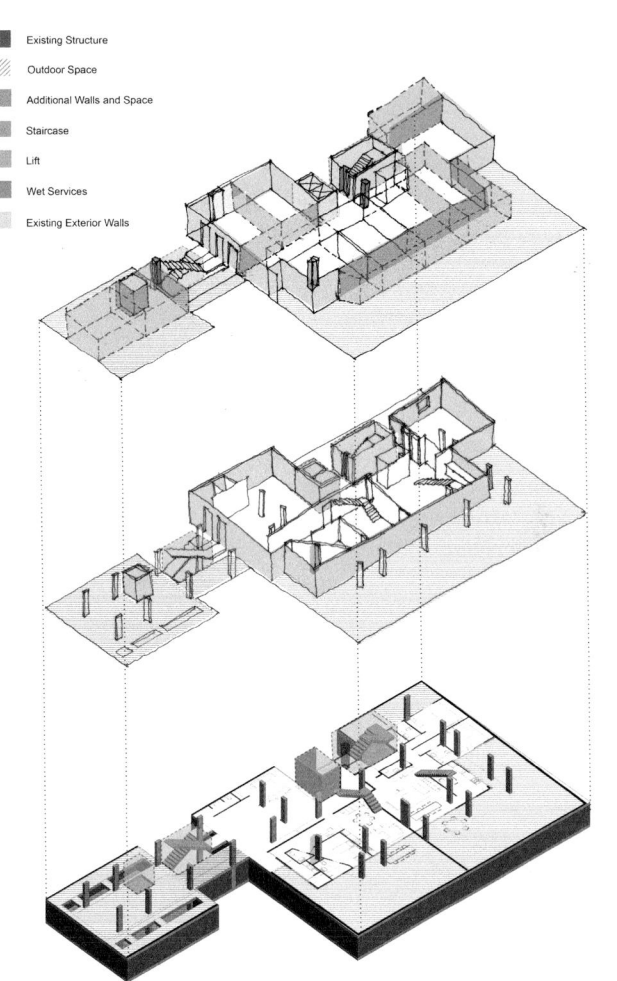

Figure 6.6
**Analysis of
the Fidalga
first floor
plan – analyt-
ical diagram
(Tebogo
Ramatlo)**

Degree of "disentanglement"	Intentional design and construction features that allow for change over time	Methods of decision-making in the design and the construction of the building
• Materials • Details • Connections • When decisions are made	• Is there a distinction made between short- and long-term building materials and components? • Are the building elements (physical and spatial) assembled in such a manner so as to ensure minimum disruptions if changes are made?	• How were design decisions made? • Who participated? • How was the building constructed? • Were small and big construction companies involved?
There is a limited degree of "disentanglement": technically, the materiality and detailing of the building implies that some degree of adaptation is possible; with regards to the decision-making, the strategic location of service shafts theoretically allows the inhabitants to adjust the spaces – thus participating in the decision-making – with minimal disruptions to the rest of the building	The building has clearly been designed, constructed and detailed with a view to achieve a level of change and adaptability While the short and long term elements (physical and spatial) do not seem to have been considered in an intentional manner, the building certainly has some qualities that allow for on-going change – the architects did not set out to achieve a multi-level decision-making process and some of the feature have therefore become more cosmetic that functional	This is not evident from the limited information on the internet.

Pop Madalena Building

The same architects of the Felgado Building (2015), Andrade Morttin Arquitetos Associados, continued with similar explorations at the Pop Madalena Building, also in a São Paolo neighborhood. The architects distinguish between the building elements: "the prevailing structural element in the constructed volume is the slab, the horizontal plane that constitutes the main composition matrix when stacked." Within this matrix, they have used "industrialized materials and components to build the vertical enclosure system. Glass, different kinds of thermoacoustic metallic tiles, and galvanized wire guard-rails, among others, are part of this repertoire" (*Archdaily*, 2015).

Figure 6.7
External view, Pop Madalena Building, São Paolo (*Archdaily*, 2015)

The main tower has seven floors of apartments units, with different sizes and allowing for variable floor plans which may be combined to adjust the area of apartments. What the architects refer to as an "exploded volume" aims to create "a connected, coherent architecture" and "voids and gaps ... provide some permeability and help create scale adjustments to each particular situation" (*Archdaily*, 2015; Figure 6.7).

The range of units in the buildings vary greatly from 55 to 250 m² (592–2690 ft²) designed in such a way that they could be combined and subdivided. The plans of the building have been analyzed to demonstrate their capacity for change. Similar to the Fidalga, the capacity for change is somewhat limited by the shape of the building and the location of the services and vertical circulation nodes.

While the capacity of the spaces has been established, with some slight adjustments, the capacity could have been enhanced. The project may be summarized as follows:

- Place: São Paolo.
- Date of construction: 2015.
- Architect: Andrade Morettin Arquitetos Associades.
- Size: 7682 m².
- Public/Private developer: private.

Degree of "disentanglement"	Intentional design and construction features that allow for change over time	Methods of decision-making in the design and the construction of the building
• Materials • Details • Connections • When decisions are made	• Is there a distinction made between short- and long-term building materials and components? • Are the building elements (physical and spatial) assembled in such a manner so as to ensure minimum disruptions if changes are made?	• How were design decisions made? • Who participated? • How was the building constructed? • Were small and big construction companies involved?
While there is no deliberate intent by the architects to detail the building with a view to "disentangled" levels, some decisions are inherently supportive of technical disentanglement and some of the decision-making is distributed and involves the future residents of the project	Again, no clear Open Building intentions are demonstrated in the design, construction or detailing, yet the "connected and coherent architecture" coupled with flexible plans and the permeability achieved allows for a degree of adaptability that distinguishes this project from other conventional methods of design and construction A clear distinction is made between different building components as demonstrated in the selection of material, how they are used and how they are visually disconnected – this allows for a degree of physical and spatial flexibility and minimum disruption if adaptations are implemented – thus ensuring the permanence of a long-term structure and the changeable components within it	This is not evident from the limited information on the internet.

Simpatia Street Housing

Another São Paolo example is the Simpatia Street Housing by Alvaro Puntoni, João Sodré, Jonathan Davies (Gruposop):

> The apartments are actually empty spaces, open plans where residents can adapt the ambiences according to their needs and desires ... They are organized in two opposing blocks, Simpatia and Medeiros, with differentiated conformations and views, but both offer multiple forms

of occupation, according to their users' life needs. This diversity is expressed by the randomness of the openings of the north and south faces that mark the uniqueness of each apartment. On the east and west façades, glass planes in the full extension of the units mark the presence of the edifice in the urban landscape, flooding the environment with the internal light of the units.

(*Archdaily*, 2011a)

The concept of "Convivial Spaces," as described by the architects, is reminiscent of the expression used by some Open Building thinkers: "lovable buildings" which implies buildings and environments that resonate with many people over many years. These building have "capacity" in the sense that they adapt to the needs of residents over time (Figure 6.8):

The vertical circulation block (stairs and lifts) between the two apartments opens onto balconies facing the inner void as spatial continuity of the forecourt. At each unit it enlarges and offers a gentle space to enter them. It is a space for encounter and coexistence.

(*Archdaily*, 2011a)

The architects also adopt an approach which they have termed "urban kindness":

On the lower courtyard the pool is dropped onto the ground, bordering the garden along Medeiros de Albuquerque Street. Once again, a

Figure 6.8
Simpatia, external view
(***Archdaily***, **2011a**)

relationship with the canopy of trees is established. Under this structure, with access on the basement, a laundry room opens onto the garden. Finally, along the street the edifice offers to the city – through the setbacks of border closure – a bench, a tree and a small square to the city: sincere "urban kindness."

(*Archdaily*, 2011a)

While the capacity aspects of the plans have been established, with some slight adjustments, the adaptability potential could have been enhanced. The idea of lightness again pervades the project and the services are kept to the perimeter of the building which opens up the floor plans for different configurations. The project may be summarized as follows:

- Place: São Paolo.
- Date of construction: 2011.
- Architect: Alvaro Puntoni, Joao Sodre, Jonathan Davis.
- Size: 3000 m².
- Public/Private developer: private.

Degree of "disentanglement"	Intentional design and construction features that allow for change over time	Methods of decision-making in the design and the construction of the building
• Materials • Details • Connections • When decisions are made	• Is there a distinction made between short- and long-term building materials and components? • Are the building elements (physical and spatial) assembled in such a manner so as to ensure minimum disruptions if changes are made?	• How were design decisions made? • Who participated? • How was the building constructed? • Were small and big construction companies involved?
This project seems to adopt many of the values shared by Open Building thinkers – though the terminology may be different The building components demonstrate a level of disentanglement and decision-making is therefore inherently distributed – these principles are made evident in the visual language of the building	The design, construction and detailing is not explicitly based on Open Building but does demonstrate an understanding for some Open Building principles The manner in which the building has been conceptualized no doubt allows for a degree of physical and spatial flexibility as a distinction between long- and short-term components	This is not evident from the limited information on the internet.

The residences at the Future Africa Campus in Pretoria, South Africa

The architect of this project has developed an approach to building materials, construction and detailing that relates to the context and socio-economic conditions of South Africa (Eksteen, 2019). The project, built in 2018, focuses on "making" with a view to ease of implementation, installation, assembly and disassembly as well as the creation of structures with high "capacity." Based on their website (Future Africa, n.d.), the design of the Future Africa campus at the University of Pretoria has been an integrative process learning from the collective knowledge and experience of manifold contributors, as collated by the Future Africa Management Team and articulated by Earth World team of architectural experts: "The architecture of the campus should play an active role in shaping minds, as much as it does in shaping environments." One of the main project intentions was to combat the exodus of African academics (Eksteen, 2020).

The new approach to the design of the buildings and gardens is intended to facilitate a new generation of scientists in Africa through a remodeled Doctoral program: "This new approach was based on new methods of learning and teaching, revolving around a lifestyle rather than a lecture hall." The website continues to describe how:

> The brief required for a number of programs to be accommodated on the campus, including a dining hall, a conference center, research commons and 300 living units, with varying scales, ranging from single bedrooms, to family units. A further requirement was to keep further expansions in mind from the beginning.
>
> (Earthworld Architects, n.d.)

A framework for change at campus or urban tissue level can be observed which allows for change to happen separately from the design of the individual buildings. However, this evolved intuitively rather than methodically or intentionally. The linear east-west structure of the building is interspersed by communal areas and routes that cut through the building in the north-south direction. This makes the building appear as separate components that may at some time, in the future, be adapted independently of each other; this may allow for adaptation and changes to be implemented at different time by different architects (see Figure 6.9).

The concept is based on what the architects refer to as "Afri-Tech," combining high-level design processes with local resources and skills. Existing design and construction processes, common in the region, were challenged. With regard to the housing component, in order to minimize time on site, as well as to rethink how traditional materials are employed, the 300 housing units are off-site prefabricated precast concrete and assembled on-site, with services and fittings having already been installed. Each living unit is constructed from a series of precast concrete modules, allowing for

Figure 6.9
Africa Campus, the communal areas as distinct components allowing for different interpretations/ adaptations (photo credit: Earthworld)

COMMUNAL AREAS_

Figure 6.10
Housing units as disentangled "boxes"

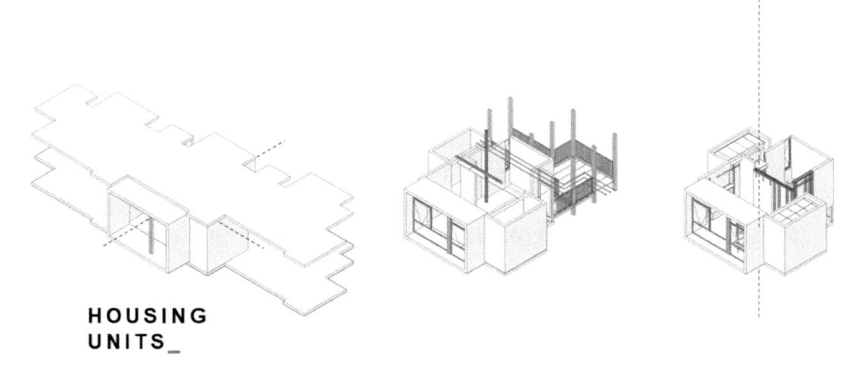

HOUSING UNITS_

variations in composition and size. This approach improves quality control and challenges traditional uses for precast concrete as a construction material (ibid.; Figure 6.10) .

The project architects challenge the traditional construction process which sees many involved: "from sourcing, to manufacturing, to retail, eventually reaching site through contractors. Shortening this value chain would drastically reduce cost and time; dealing directly with manufacturers also allows for greater understanding of construction materials and improving quality control." The architects therefore aimed to establish inter-disciplinary partnerships with designers and manufacturers. As one example, flat-pack, structural timber portal frames were developed to carry the communal facilities in the development. The resultant segments were easily transported in small trucks, could be handled by one or two people and assembled in a few hours. The whole process intended to reduce the need for water, shuttering and heavy machinery (ibid.)

While no mention is made by the architects of Open Building, it is obvious that many Open Building principles have been adopted. Design decisions were clearly separated according to long-term and short-term components. There is an intentional separation between different components of the building where some components are permanent, and others are considered to be more temporary or changeable. The housing units are designed as "disentangled" and separate components where the structure, partitioning and services are distinct from each other. The furniture is conventionally designed so that it is not attached permanently to the structure. The architect set out to make these distinctions evident in the detailing and visual language of the building – which implies a degree of disentanglement. The architect has said that he aims to challenge what he calls "slavery" in the construction industry and advocates a community-based process through "meaningful making" which gives unskilled labor value within a project. He also believes in adopting a different role for architects where there are both pre- and post-interactions with the building and the site (Eksteen, 2020).

The developments' siting allows for minimum disruption of the features of the site and capturing the views, and sunlight, from the north. Every few meters, external, shaded staircases are introduced. The structural and spatial elements are visible and also distinct. The non-structural elements such as the wooden purlins and polycarbonate roof sheeting are used to create protection to the walkways, with concrete slabs over the stairs (ibid.).

The exposed, disentangled components of the building, the building process and the resultant systems have rendered this a valuable experiment in Open Building – while never referencing Open Building. The façades have distinct elements of concrete, steel and glass sections. The steel frames allow for projecting "boxes" which house some of the communal areas which are grouped rather than distributed throughout the building to allow for maximum engagement and interaction. These glass boxes have concrete floors and project from the main façades in the internal courtyards. The building is layered horizontally, with a concrete wall separating the residential spaces from the walkways.

The use of materials and the detailing is unique in that the different materials and components are clearly distinct from each other yet work together to create a harmonious whole. The logic of the structure ensures distinct partitioning, façade systems, furniture and residential units; these distinct components and the method and sequence of assembly allow for a level of disentanglement. As an example, furniture is unattached to the structure or the partitions. The residential sections of the project are now starting to be personalized by their new inhabitants. The furniture systems are designed for maximum flexibility and the spatial arrangement is intended to encourage impromptu gatherings, meetings and collective cooking and eating in indoor and outdoor spaces on several levels and intervals. These communal spaces are dispersed throughout the building. The architect set out to "break up the building" into distinct sections, materials and components. Indeed, he claims it became complex to the extent that he "couldn't draw it." It was better presented as a sequence based on how decisions were made (Eksteen, 2020).

The residences at the Future Africa Campus fulfil several of the requirements of Open Building. The building offers lessons in Open Building in its final product, in its process of design and construction as well as in its conceptual underpinning.

- Place: Pretoria, South Africa.
- Date of construction: 2018.
- Architect: Earthworld Architects.
- Size: 300 units.
- Public/Private developer: public.

Degree of "disentanglement"	Intentional design and construction features that allow for change over time	Methods of decision-making in the design and the construction of the building
• Materials • Details • Connections • When decisions are made	• Is there a distinction made between short- and long-term building materials and components? • Are the building elements (physical and spatial) assembled in such a manner so as to ensure minimum disruptions if changes are made?	• How were design decisions made? • Who participated? • How was the building constructed? • Were small and big construction companies involved?
The project does differentiate between long- and short-term elements and this is made evident in the architecture	The building was designed with a view to achieving maximum adaptability with minimum disruptions (this may be more evident in the other components of the campus and not just in the residences?) While the final "product" has a very distinct architectural character, it is still evident in the texts about the project and in communications with the project architect, that there was a strong focus on "process" and that this was not an "object-driven" process	There is a level of disentanglement achieved and the project has allowed for the involvement of different people, with different skills, to be involved at a later stage in the construction process – thus not all decisions were made from the outset and it became a process that emerged and involved others. Prefabricated building elements are manufactured by a network of small suppliers. Components are transported to the site with small trucks, can be carried by two people and installed within hours.

Urban Think Tank's Empower Shack in South Africa

The Empower Shack, Khayelitsha, Cape Town, South Africa is a project led by Alfredo Brillembourg and Hubert Klumpner of Urban Think Tank which started in 2013 and is ongoing at the time of writing (2020). The NGO Ikhayalami, BT Section Site C (the client) Development Committee, City of Cape Town local architect, Design Space Africa, are all involved and there are various local and international supporters, sponsors and collaborators. The project has gained some recognition and was long listed in 2018 for a Royal Institute of British Architects Prize (van Niekerk, 2018).

> Ikhayalami understands the need for poor households to upgrade their dwellings incrementally, often beginning with improvements and extensions to existing informal structures. This certainly does not mean that iKhayalami believes that a better shack is the end of this incremental process. Nothing demonstrates this better than our widely acclaimed "Empower Shack" project that we have implemented along with *Urban Think Tank.* In this project we have built forty formal homes where shacks once stood, with the formal structures incorporating many community design principles. In 2019 we built 20 of these. Another 32 units will still be constructed.
>
> (Ikhayalami, 2019, p. 4)

The Ikhayalami 2019 report states that the Empower Shack project is "an urbanization scheme that combines incremental housing upgrade with a safer urban environment that offers its inhabitants new economic and social possibilities" (Ikhayalami, 2019, p. 9). Seventy-two existing single-story shacks have been upgraded to double-story housing units through "structured community workshops, enumerations, affordability assessments and microfinance contracts" (Ikhayalami, 2019, p.9). The organization acted as the interface between the community and the government – with an intention to affect a policy shift and renewed thinking with regard to tenure security and higher density alternatives for low cost housing (Ikhayalami, 2019, p. 9).

The project offers a solution to informal settlement upgrading by suggesting a methodology for distribution of space and delivery of basic services in combination with house unit upgrades and the creation of new economic and social opportunities. It thus ventures into micro-financing, renewable energy, water management and skills training, demonstrating an understanding for the complex ecosystem that ultimately helps generate a viable residential environment.

The principles of the design process are extracted from their website below (Empower Shack, n.d.):

* The design decision-making process has included community workshops (a structured methodology of negotiation has been set up), enumerations, affordability assessments and microfinance contracts as

well as an exploration towards densification through changing the typology from single story detached shacks into attached double-story units.

- The project team argues that densification offers more efficient land-use to infrastructure ratios and guarantees that all current occupants of the site will find a home in the redevelopment and no relocations would have to take place (see Figure 6.11).

- The proposed increased density also generates opportunities for cross-financing and additional rental and sales stock that add wealth to the settlement. By integrating with existing municipal planning frameworks, the newly configured settlement offers new plot sizes and a more rational allocation of public space.

- Digital planning tools have been developed to synthesize user inputs and preferences with micro-finance obligations and municipal planning frameworks.

- "Preferential planning: computational planning synthesis allows layout scenarios to be generated from individual location and cluster preferences."

- With regards to neighbor preferences, "Households are surveyed to determine optimal neighbor allocations. Computational analysis determines best case positioning and clustering."

- The building units are priced to meet meaningful financial contributions from recipients by designing generous but robust living spaces and service cores that meet building code obligations through fit-for-purpose bridge contracts.

- The design is based on a "core and shell" system, where the core service infrastructure with upgradable unit shell gives access to immediate increase in habitat quality while allowing for incremental development.

- The long-term goals are to influence a new direction in housing policy and offer much needed diversity and access to housing for the gap market.

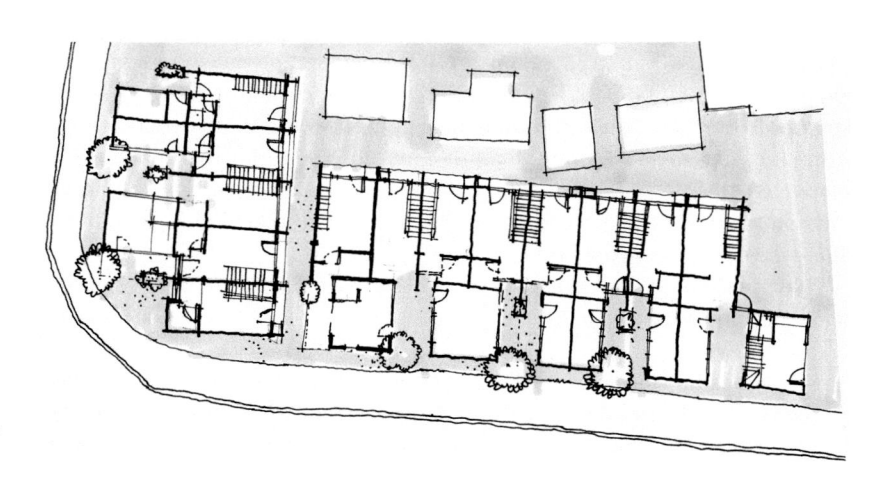

Figure 6.11
**Empower
Shack
site plan
(drawing by
author)**

Figure 6.12
Empower Shack 3 external view (Urban Think Tank Instagram Post) (Linelle Visage)

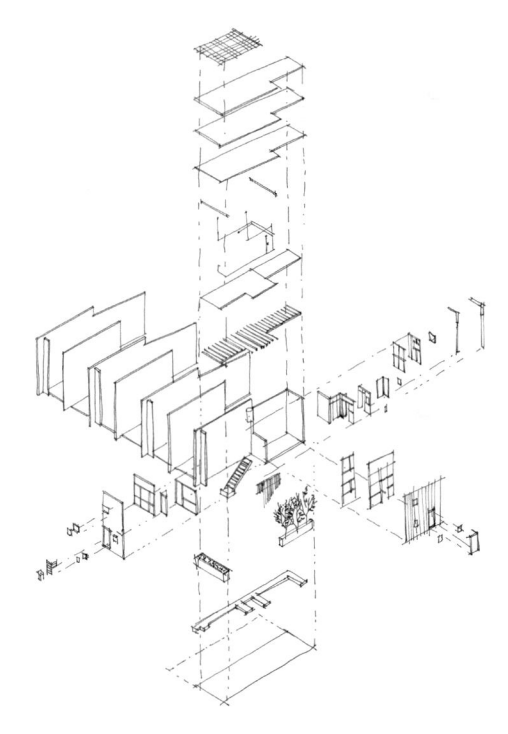

Figure 6.13
Empower Shack "core and shell" (http://u-tt.com/project/empower-shack/) (Linelle Visage)

The structure is a simple composition of corrugated sheeting, plywood and hollow core bricks (see Figures 6.12, 6.13). It presents some aspects of Open Building thinking as follows:

1. While it is focused on the provision of an adaptable "shell," it does seem to demonstrate a levels distinction between short- and long-term elements in the design; the residents are able to personalize their internal space.

2. There is some distribution of decision-making and disentanglement in process.
3. There are clear architectural qualities to the final product, yet the "shell" structure seems to allow for adaptation with minimal disruptions.
4. This is also a project that, while having distinct architectural character, seems to imply that it focuses on process more than being product- or object-driven.

Architecture labeled as "humanitarian" and based on experts from the North operating in the global South is cause for much contention. However, an analysis of this case study reveals that there may be parallels with Open Building thinking and the development of tools and a system that explores the relationship between urban design and the site of an individual project.

- Place: Khayelitsha, Cape Town.
- Date of construction: 2013 – ongoing.
- Architect: Alfredo Brillembourg & Hubert Klumpner of Urban Think Tank.
- Size: 72 shacks upgraded according to the 2019 Ikhayalami report.
- Public/Private developer: led by the NGO Ikhayalami and funded by various local and international supporters, sponsors and collaborators.

Degree of "disentanglement"	Intentional design and construction features that allow for change over time	Methods of decision-making in the design and the construction of the building
• Materials • Details • Connections • When decisions are made	• Is there a distinction made between short- and long-term building materials and components? • Are the building elements (physical and spatial) assembled in such a manner so as to ensure minimum disruptions if changes are made?	• How were design decisions made? • Who participated? • How was the building constructed? • Were small and big construction companies involved?
	While it is focused on the provision of an adaptable "shell," it does seem to demonstrate a level of distinction between short- and long-term elements in the design; the residents are able to personalize their internal space. There are clear architectural qualities to the final product, yet the "shell" structure seems to allow for adaptation with minimal disruptions	This is also a project that, while having distinct architectural character, seems to imply that it focuses on process more than being product- or object-driven

Is Open Building a solution in the residential sector in the global South?

Housing shortages are often a cause for protest in the global South, leading to contentious political discussions about the role of government in providing housing. Governments try to address these issues through various strategies, either by focusing on building houses or by trying to provide housing opportunities through sites and services schemes, upgrading of informal settlement, etc.

Determining the exact size of the housing backlog is difficult because the demand is dynamic and constantly changing. With the pressure governments face with intensifying unhappiness and community unrest, governments sometimes feel compelled to abandon long-term plans and visions, resorting to immediate interventions such as land allocation and mass-low-cost housing schemes in undesirable locations. This means that governments run the risk of deviating from designing lasting, sustainable solutions. The result is "rows upon rows of 'one-size-fits all' houses located at the periphery of cities, far from work opportunities and services" (Osman, 2017).

The more vocal unhappy residents are, the more governments are pressured into providing mass housing in conventional ways: focusing on the house unit and the numbers delivered (products) rather than on the process and on new thinking. Sometimes policy is also not clear on what the right to adequate housing translates into in terms of actual projects on site.

I have previously argued that models of delivery cannot continue to depend on governments alone. Governments should rather see their role as facilitators of a diverse and multifaceted process ensuring the involvement of many players. By changing the process, different types of housing products and housing delivery methods would be generated. These new models would be less reliant on subsidies. More diverse and complex funding sources and models would necessarily come into play. Where subsidies are essential, there will be a shift from individual subsidies and products to collective models of housing (Osman, 2017).

In this new vision, low-cost and affordable housing becomes an integral part of all city developments in well located, mixed income, mixed function, mixed community settings. There will be shifts from ownership and more focus on rental options. Private developers would be supported to operate in the field. Delivery of housing will be quick and efficient with minimal bureaucracy and delay. The social as well as the technical aspects of housing will be considered in conceptualizing this new model of delivery (Osman, 2017).

These principles may be achieved if policymakers, planners and designers adopt Open Building principles in the development of housing strategies. Such strategies will also be a mechanism to think of housing as infrastructure. A conventional understanding of infrastructure makes reference to public buildings and amenities, transport structures and roads, service lines for water, sanitation and electricity – yet the definition can be broadened. The National Development Plan in South Africa (National Planning Commission,

2012) differentiates between hard infrastructure and soft infrastructure. One can also differentiate between the hardware and the software of the environment by bringing "people" into decision-making roles around the "built environment." The Open Building approach – understanding built environment as hierarchically structured – requires that we view the built environment as operating on different levels requiring careful management of the relationships between the agents that operate at those levels as well as the need to "disentangle" those levels to allow for a degree of permanence without restricting the necessity for constant transformation.

By approaching housing as residential infrastructure, finance and procurement strategies would be adjusted accordingly. Open Building "base buildings" would be considered a part of neighborhood infrastructure – in the same way that roads and service lines are considered a part of the neighborhood infrastructure and are accessible and used by all, irrespective of income level or social status. This "open" approach allows for distributed decision-making in the design, funding and delivery of built environments. This way of conceptualizing the built environment and an "open" approach would acknowledge the coexistence of formal and informal systems and the disparity in terms of infrastructure in different parts of the country and within cities.

Housing as infrastructure implies that the delivery of housing is a crucial driver for economic development and poverty reduction through job creation activities – not as a mere provision of products (houses) that depletes state resources. It also implies that effective implementation mechanisms in housing delivery would encourage public/private partnerships and facilitate ease of management and maintenance of the housing stock being delivered. It implies that we think of the delivery of housing in the same way that we would consider any other infrastructure project as in services, roads or bridges.

The size of Africa's urban population nearly doubled in 20 years from 237 million in 1995 to 472 million in 2015. Africa's urban population is expected to almost double again between 2015 and 2035, according to the African Economic Outlook (African Development Bank, 2016). The widening infrastructure gaps are presented as both a challenge and a great opportunity for investment and large-scale developments; unlocking infrastructure backlogs and managing integrated supply chains can transform the economic performance of a country as well as achieve more equitable development by ensuring affordability and accessibility. Housing needs to be considered as one of those infrastructure opportunities and not as an isolated demand-driven, unitary-product-focused sector.

To achieve these aims, and to rethink housing as part of a broader concept of infrastructure, we need forms of governance and regulatory frameworks that allow for experimentation and testing of alternative forms of delivery through pilot projects. This needs to be balanced with a parallel activity of delivery actions that can be scaled up to have real impact. The latter activity would adopt approaches tested out in the former. These new forms of governance and frameworks will allow for efficient construction of residential infrastructure, the development of networks of suppliers to those industries and the entities engaged in operating and maintaining this new infrastructure.

The delivery of residential infrastructure could thus become a tool to create job training opportunities for low-skilled people, encourage private investment, lower the cost of doing business, promote spatial inclusivity, and could be established with a view to strong backward linkages to supplier industries. By seeing residential development in this way, funding would be better rationalized. Subsidies would be used in the delivery of long-term, robust and high-quality base buildings in which multiple interpretations and local-level activities may play out – in a dynamic, ever-changing way without disrupting the character and stability that an environment also demands.

Mechanisms and tools for managing the built environment in the global South

In South Africa, the state has committed substantial funding to public infra-structure to address backlogs. In Gauteng Province alone (containing both Johannesburg and Pretoria), from 2013 to 2016, an investment of R30 billion ($1.8 billion) was made in infrastructure with R42 billion ($2.5 billion) being planned for the next three years. This focus has led the Gauteng Department of Infrastructure Development (GDID) to initiate the Lutsinga Infrastructure House, described as a "project nerve center" which "uses technology to track developments in the planning, design and construction" of all infrastructure projects.

> The Lutsinga Infrastructure House comprises five operating systems, including an immovable property monitoring system, a project man-agement system, an e-maintenance system, an expanded public works monitoring system and an infrastructure monitoring system … the infrastructure monitoring system was particularly important as it would provide the GDID with a concrete figure in terms of the impact projects were having on macroeconomic variables, such as its contributions to economic growth, employment and the socioeconomic impact of these projects on Gauteng residents.
>
> (Solomons, 2016)

This facility demonstrates that while a national infrastructure plan needs to be centrally driven and monitored, this also needs to be aligned with localized project management systems. If this operates efficiently, and if its mandate is extended, it will allow for the creation of conditions for embra-cing smaller-scale, dispersed projects and project packages that are more accessible to smaller firms and new entrants.

Today, the Lutsinga Infrastructure House is based in Gauteng Province and is managed in five-year periods where the infrastructure funding pipeline has projects of about 60 billion rands ($3.935 billion). Lutsinga, which reports to the Treasury and is owned by the Gauteng Department of Infrastructure Development (GDID), is a technology hub and an infrastructure delivery management system and a project management system which aims towards integration and standardization of processes and the implementation of the government's Infrastructure Delivery Management System (IDMS).

Lutsinga so far does not include the delivery of housing in its operations. The delivery of Health and Educational infrastructure is, however, included in the projects that Lutsinga oversees. The Lutsinga hub aims to eliminate silos and create platforms whereby different entities of delivery are not operating in isolation. The inclusion of housing as part of infrastructure, and thus including it in these systems and not as a separate stream of delivery could be an important contribution. Housing, after all, includes all the services, amenities and entities that support it and lead to its success.

The Lutsinga Infrastructure House in South Africa is an interesting case study for countries of the global South in terms of a mechanism for management of built environment projects – especially considering unique socio-economic conditions as well as a large degree of informality in residential areas. Other countries have experimented with similar tools.

> In Rio de Janeiro, a control center has been built to make responses to emergencies quicker and more effective. The center links normally discrete groups of information such as CCTV, weather information and reports of crime, and proved very effective last year when a building unexpectedly collapsed in downtown Rio. The control center quickly had gas and electric companies close off supply to the area, temporarily closed the subway, evacuated the area, closed the roads, alerted the emergency services and informed local hospitals. It also informed citizens of what to do via Twitter and Facebook.
>
> (Stott, 2013)

While these examples focus on the use of technology, it is also important to explore community-based, context-relevant and effective tools in countries of the global South. Community networks and community leaders could serve as vital sources of information. If set up well, with good community buy-in, these networks could become key partners for housing funding and delivery agencies. This is especially important in a context such as South Africa where protests around housing and service delivery are notoriously frequent. Communities taking government agencies to court is also a part of the South African housing landscape – and many significant rulings have been made supporting communities. However, these ruling have not necessarily changed the lives of people on the ground, nor have they led to the creation of good partnerships between communities and local governments;

on the contrary, this seems to have increased animosity and conflict rather than initiated change.

By using both high tech and low tech methods of data collection and communication, the agencies tasked with funding and delivering housing may be able to keep a closer eye on community need and unrest and unhappiness may be addressed before it explodes, as it has several times over the last few years. Real and authentic partnerships are needed between communities and local government – with an important role for mediating agencies.

A vision for housing delivery in the global South[1]

I do not remember who once wrote: "As far as housing is concerned, the whole world has remained underdeveloped." Housing thinking seems to transform and advance and has been doing so at least since the 1960s, yet housing practice and funding seem to be trapped in old ways of top-down decision-making and housing as a professional product rather than housing as a process. Despite key writings and theories that have been in circulation since the 1960s, there also seems to be confusion about how effectively and efficiently housing delivery can actually occur. While participation and user control of housing processes is often accepted as vital to the success of housing projects, the tools to achieve this have remain flawed. While housing is seen as a process, rather than a product, the methods of design and delivery that accommodate both stability and change, the formal and informal, and that can embrace complexity, the unknown and the unexpected have yet to evolve to achieve that vision.

We need systems and processes that ensure that the role of government in housing remains that of facilitator, where decision-making and control is distributed and where distinct and separate levels of the built environment help structure decisions at different levels. We need to know how to design/ plan for an unknown future and unknown clients, or clients with dynamic and constantly changing needs. We need the skills to design with distributed control in the built environment (who makes which decisions, when). An understanding of cities, infrastructure and the built environment in terms of levels will help. Systems and connections (disentanglement – making changes to one system of a city without disrupting others as in any well-functioning infrastructure system) and mediation between individuals and the collective in the built environment (through balancing individual and collective aspirations) are all crucial to a sustainable built environment.

We need to facilitate inclusive transformation through the promotion of a system that is inherently participative (I do not mean the "sit around the table and talk" type of participation – though that too is important). This alternative participative process is achieved through new professional guidelines and skills, new systems, methods and technologies, new forms of engagement, and most importantly, through the potential to replicate interventions at scale to achieve maximum impact.

I propose a system that self-regulates, increases resilience and reduces professional control at some levels – allowing for informality at others. This system is designed only as much as is needed and the processes of emergence are allowed to take over (Hamdi, 2004).

In this vision, government-funded structures that are beautiful, robust and long lasting are provided (Habraken, 1999). These are not alien structures. They have emerged from the urban field – like indigenous trees, they have grown from the soil of the context (Kendall in Osman, 2015). Their visual language, materiality and scale have roots and are familiar to the people of that context; everyone understands them intuitively and grasps how the structures are designed and constructed. They have a scale and interface with the public realm that is highly inclusive and inclusionary, and they relate to the finer grain of existing urban fabric, implying a relationship with the streets that encourages variety of commercial activity.

The imagery – in terms of architectural character, infrastructure, massing and materiality – is innovative and varies from place to place, yet in each context it is a language that is known and embraced – and will emerge over many years. These are structures that are sensitive to climate and context. These structures, and roads and the public spaces that support them, are an expression of the collective aspirations of particular communities. They therefore have a unique identity and are creative and imaginative – but are also conventional in the best sense. Within these structures, individuals, social housing institutions, government agencies and the private sector carve out space, design and sell or rent to develop housing stock within it. Government reserves space for fully funded homes for those unable to co-fund.

This is not a place where one can declare "my house is my castle." No home is identifiable as an isolated, independent object; homes merge and disappear in the collective and streets and public space take precedence over individual space in terms of the functions and activities they "hold." Yet also, the streets and public space sometimes defer to the buildings when they need to – in a manner evident in old medinas and medieval city centers. People acting on space and buildings and pedestrians are prioritized.

These structures also accommodate other functions that are needed to support residents of an area – educational, healthcare, commercial, etc. Different agents lease parts of these structures while owning the infill. Perhaps they could even be designed to allow for a degree of incrementality and slow evolution.

In this scenario, and following in the example of vernacular contexts, architecture and planning are not distinct disciplines – architecture is now merged with town planning (Turan, 1990). In this context everyone is king or queen behind their own front door.[2] These spaces – behind the front door – are an expression of individual aspirations. They are related to financial capabilities, needs and the preferences of the occupants; if the individuals or families want to make changes to their spaces, they may do so without disrupting the overall structure or their neighbors; conflict is therefore minimized.

These structures – let us call them residential infrastructure – are funded by governments as are roads, utilities and public spaces in between; government only supports what is shared. There are no individual subsidies – everything funded by government is for the use of everyone. Similar to a road serving everyone – we do not say you earn x per month so use "that" road – this residential infrastructure serves everyone.[3]

Multiple funding mechanisms and funding sources are used to fund different components of these structures. Small, multi-skilled teams provide quick infill services for these structures at various price points – allowing for the evolution of small construction enterprises (Kendall, 2006). Large structures are designed and built in such a way that they are constructed by small construction companies; all building components are easy to transport in a small truck, every building component can be carried by two people, can be easily installed and allows for skills transfer.[4]

The density allows for small businesses to flourish (Dewar and Uytenbogaardt, 1991). Small interventions leading to small actions are acknowledged as having immense catalytic and transformational potential. As these small activities are vital for the survival of vital communities, the design of spaces and buildings to accommodate these activities and all levels of economic activity are embraced.

As this environment evolves – and it is premised on evolution and inclusion, collaboration and learning – so does the society hosting it evolve. Everybody is involved – everyone is a decision-maker at some level of the environment – everybody is a producer – everybody produces something (Schumacher, 1973). A dynamic situation is created, and growth is enhanced. To achieve this vision, financial, management and procurement systems are aligned with the separate design intentions.

Conclusion: expanding the understanding of infrastructure in the global South

This chapter has presented several case studies. Parallels have been drawn with Open Building thinking and practice; lessons have been extracted for contexts in the global South. The chapter concludes by presenting some management systems in the built environment and argues for the inclusion of housing delivery as part of infrastructure systems as well as the creation of diverse forms of management, including community-based management systems. Alternative forms of governance will allow for efficient construction of residential architecture when it is considered as infrastructure; this will also allow for the development of networks of suppliers to those industries and the entities engaged in operating and maintaining this new infrastructure. Infrastructure investment in the global South is crucially important because it creates job training for low-skilled people, encourages private investment, lowers the cost of doing business, promotes spatial inclusivity, and has strong backward linkages to supplier industries.

A conventional understanding of infrastructure makes reference to public buildings and amenities, transport structures and roads, service lines for water, sanitation and electricity – yet the definition can be broadened to include Open Building as an approach to the delivery of infrastructure delivery at city, neighborhood, building and fit-out levels. The need for viewing the built environment at hierarchical levels-of-intervention requires careful management of the relationships between the agents that operate at those levels as well as the need to "disentangle" those levels to allow for a degree of permanence without restricting the necessity for constant transformation and innovation. This approach offers a way to rethink infrastructure finance and procurement strategies.

The concept of "base buildings" is introduced as a new kind of infrastructure. These would be considered a part of neighborhoods in the same way that roads and service lines are considered a part of the neighborhood infrastructure accessible and used by all, irrespective of income level or social status. This "open" approach allows for distributed decision-making in the manner in which the built environment is designed, funded and delivered.

A unique characteristic in the global South that might be addressed by using this "open" approach to the built environment is that it would allow for the acknowledgment of the coexistence of formal and informal systems and the disparity in terms of infrastructure-thinking (e.g. levels thinking) in diverse countries and within the unique conditions of different cities.

Notes

1 This is an adaptation of a talk presented at the plenary session for the Southern Africa City Studies Conference. 2020. Urban Research Agendas 2020 and Beyond and published at http://amiraosman.co.za/2020/09/01/what-does-transformation-look-like/
2 Acknowledging the Dutch architect Karel Dekkler in personal conversation.
3 Stephen Kendall in personal conversation.
4 Andre Eksteen in personal conversation on the Africa Campus, University of Pretoria.

References

African Development Bank (AfDB) (2016). OECD Development Centre and the United Nations Development Programme (UNDP). African Economic Outlook (AEO) 2016 (15th edition), Special theme: Sustainable Cities and Structural Transformation, pp. 146–147.

Andrade-Narvaez, J. (1981). Dwelling transformations Santa Ursula, Mexico City, Massachusetts Institute of Technology, Master of Architecture dissertation.

Andrade-Narvaez, J. (n.d.). Xacalli, available at https://pdfslide.tips/documents/conjunto-habitacional-xacalli-ac-ciudad-de-tavixocuammxproyectos construidosproyectoconstruido.html, accessed 03.09.2020.

Archdaily. (2011). Fidalga Building by Andrade Morettin Arquitetos Associados, in *Archdaily*, available at www.archdaily.com/518179/fidalga-building-andrade-morettin-arquitetos-associados?ad_source=search&ad_medium=search_result_all, accessed 31.07.2020.

Archdaily. (2011a). Simpatia Street Housing by Gruposp, in *Archdaily*, available at www.archdaily.com/160951/simpatia-street-housing-gruposp-arquitetos?ad_source=search&ad_medium=search_result_allhttps://www.archdaily.com/160951/simpatia-street-housing-gruposp-arquitetos?ad_source=search&ad_medium=search_result_all, 31.07.2020.

Archdaily. (2015). Pop Madalena Building by Andrade Morettin Arquitetos Associados, in *Archdaily*, available at www.archdaily.com/866957/pop-madalena-building-andrade-morettin-arquitetos-associados?ad_source=search&ad_medium=search_result_all, accessed 31.07.2020.

Archdaily. (2016). The projects of the UAM-X Housing Workshop present at the 2016 Venice Biennale, available at www.archdaily.mx/mx/795606/conoce-los-proyectos-del-taller-de-vivienda-de-la-uam-x-presentes-en-la-bienal-de-venecia-2016, accessed 03.09.2020.

Boano, C. and Vergara Perucich, F. (2016). Half-happy architecture. *Viceversa*, 4, pp. 58–81.

Buwalda, J. (1980). Expandable Minimum Ameriyah Dwelling (EMAD); Proposals for low cost housing in New Ameriyah City. *Open House*, 5(2)

Council for Scientific and Industrial Research (CSIR). (2000). *Housing Is Not about Houses: The Boutek Experience*, Editor: Schlotfeldt. Pretoria: CSIR Division of Building and Construction Technology.

Dewar, D. and Uytenbogaardt, R.S. (1991). *South African Cities: A Manifesto for Change*. Cape Town: Urban Problems Unit, University of Cape Town.

Dickinson, D. (2020). "Make It Right" Goes Wrong in New Orleans, in *ArchDaily*, November 1, available at www.archdaily.com/950523/make-it-right-goes-wrong-in-new-orleans, accessed 17.01.2020.

Earthworld Architects. (n.d.). Future Africa Innovation Campus (2017), available at www.ewarch.co.za/post/3096/futureafrica/, accessed 14.02.2020.

Eksteen, A. (2019). Personal Communication, Project Architect for Africa Campus. Pretoria: University of Pretoria, Earthworld Architects.

Eksteen, A. (2020). Democratising the Building Industry: The role of a circular economy in a new approach to making. A talk delivered at the Tshwane University of Technology, 2nd A_DRIC/[A3] Mini-Conference, available at https://tutarchitecture.co.za/2020/05/2nd_a_dric-mini-conference/, accessed 03.01.2021.

Elemental. (n.d.). Elemental, available at www.elementalchile.cl, accessed 03.01.2021.

Empower Shack. (n.d.). Empower Shack, available at http://u-tt.com/project/empower-shack/, accessed 14.02.2020.

Ensor, L. (2020). State will give land not houses, says Lindiwe Sisulu, in *Business Day*, 16 November, available at www.businesslive.co.za/bd/national/2020-11-16-state-will-give-land-not-houses-says-lindiwe-sisulu/, accessed 17.01.2021.

Future Africa. (n.d.). Future Africa Campus Design, available at www.futureafrica.science/index.php/campus/future-africa-design, accessed 14.02.2020.

Habraken, J. (1999) (first published in English in 1961). *Supports: An Alternative to Mass Housing*. London: Urban International Press.

Hamdi, N. (1995). *Housing without Houses: Participation, Flexibility, Enablement*. London: Practical Action Publishing, Intermediate Technology Publications.

Hamdi, N. (2004). *Small Change: About the Art of Practice and the Limits of Planning in Cities*. New York.

Ikhayalami (2019). Ikhayalami Development Service, Annual Report 2019.

Kendall, S. (2006). *Homework: A New American Townhouse*, Victoria: Trafford.

Kendall in Osman, A. (ed.), (2015). UJ_UNIT2 2015, Architecture and Agency, FADA, University of Johannesburg.

National Planning Commission (2012). *National Development Plan 2030: Our Future – Make It Work*. National Development Plan 2030, available at www.gov.za/sites/default/files/gcis_document/201409/ndp-2030-our-future-make-it-workr.pdf, accessed 30.07.2020.

Osman, A. (2015). Open Building versus Architecture or Open Building as Architecture? UJ UNIT2 2015, available at http://uj-unit2.co.za/open-building-versus-architecture-or-open-building-as-architecture/, accessed at 14.02.2020.

Osman, A. (2017). South Africa urgently needs to rethink its approach to housing, in *The Conversation*, June 4, available at https://theconversation.com/south-africa-urgently-needs-to-rethink-its-approach-to-housing-78628, accessed 27.07.2020.

Reza, A. (1986). In Memories to the Future, Building from Spontaneity: Reconsidering Occidental Theories and Third World Realities. Master's dissertation, Massachusetts Institute of Technology.

Salas, J., and Lucas, P. (2012). The validity of Previ, Lima, Peru: Forty years on. *Open House International*, 37(1), pp. 6–15.

Schumacher, E.F. (1973). *Small Is Beautiful: Economics as If People Mattered*. London: Abacus.

Solomons, I. (2016). GDID opens infrastructure projects monitoring centre, in *Engineering News*, May 25, available at www.engineeringnews.co.za/article/gdid-opens-infrastructure-projects-monitoring-centre-2016-05-25/rep_id:4136, accessed 30.08.2017.

Stott, R. (2013). Without architects, smart cities just aren't smart, in *Archdaily*, available at www.archdaily.com/353281/without-architects-smart-cities-just-aren-t-smart/?fbclid=IwAR01uJy4OYIJ1WxzC3ogyA5Il1zfGI_saNLORbpoKq2qLr_FZfM00Sj-eZs, accessed 27.06.2019.

Turan, M. (ed.) (1990). *Vernacular Architecture*. Aldershot, UK and Brookfield, VT: Avebury, Gower Publishing Group.

Turner, J.F.C. (2000). *Housing by People: Towards Autonomy in Building Environments (Ideas in Progress)*. London: Marion Boyars.

van Niekerk, G. (2018). Khayelitsha Shack nominated for Royal Institute of British Architects prize, in *Huffington Post*, January 2, available at www.huffingtonpost.co.uk/2018/01/02/khayelitsha-shack-nominated-for-royal-institute-of-british-architects-prize_a_23321300/?ncid=other_saredirect_m2afnz7mbfm&guccounter=1, accessed 31.07.2020.

Zhang, L., Zhao, S.X.B. and Tian, J.P. (2003). Self-help in housing and Chengzhongcun in China's Urbanisation. *International Journal of Urban and Regional Research*, 27(4), pp. 912–937.

Part 2

The policy environment for residential Open Building

The adoption of central government policies and guidelines providing incentives and standards for widespread implementation of residential Open Building has been a significant turning point in the first decades of the 21st century. Further, the application of Open Building principles is a key to the regeneration of the existing building stock, whether through adoption by government or by public/private enterprises. This part of the book reviews several such propositions and policies, in Europe, Japan, China and Korea. The results are still being assessed, but the evidence is that building industry traditions have a strong immunity to central governmental policies.

DOI: 10.4324/9781003018339-8

Chapter 7

The future of Open Building resides in the existing stock[1]

Frank Bijdendijk

A new focus

Architects, builders, clients, financiers and governments, in short, the real estate sector, must adjust to a new paradigm. New construction is no longer representative; instead, the sustainable use of the existing built environment is the norm. Across the whole of Europe new construction is becoming less and less necessary to meet expansion needs. Those needs are being increasingly met through renovation and transformation of unused existing buildings.

The data in Figure 7.1 shows the number of applications for building permits – measured in 'useful floor area' – in the European Union between 2005 and 2014, decreasing by 63.6%. These permits were related to both new construction and transformation of existing buildings. However, the vast majority were new construction. This period includes of course the largest economic crisis, starting in 2008, since the Second World War. But these ten years make it unequivocally clear that Europe can continue with significantly less new build than in previous years. It seems very unlikely that the level of construction output will return quickly to the level it was before the crisis.

This same crisis has not only caused grave damage in our sector, but often unnoticed structural problems have been revealed, such as the impotence of the supply-orientated thinking and the belief in linear growth that has dominated the real estate sector since World War II. Because, firstly, the war damage and the subsequent reconstruction created a large production of new buildings, and thereafter Europe experienced almost continuous economic growth and demographic change, the latter of which was reflected in a strong growth in population. The demand seemed limitless and suppliers dominated the market. Everything was sold or leased. All of a sudden, however, the demand showed its power by simply disappearing. Economic growth stagnated and the ageing population went hand in hand with declining birth rates. Population decline is apparent in a number of European countries.

Figure 7.2 shows that in Europe the number of births has now become equal to the number of deaths. It is expected that both trends will continue

DOI: 10.4324/9781003018339-9

Figure 7.1
**Building
permits:
annual data**

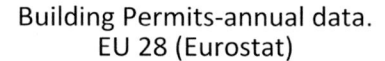

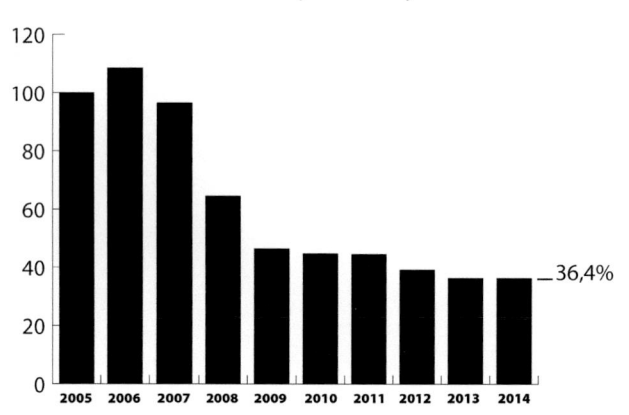

Figure 7.1
**Building
permits:
annual data**

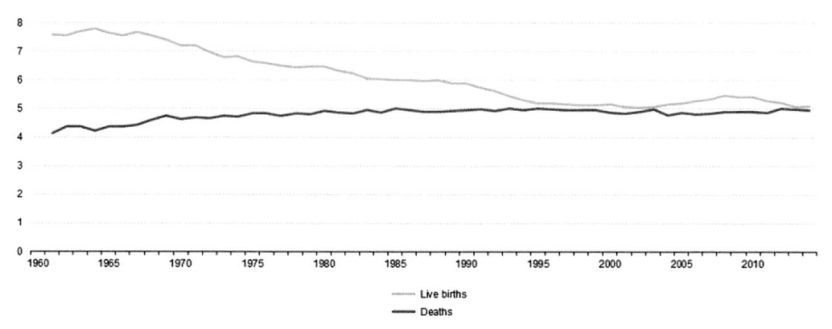

Figure 7.2
**Births and
Deaths
1961–2014
(EU-28,
EUROSTAT)**

and that the number of deaths will exceed the number of births. This is accompanied by a substantial increase in the ageing population.

Figure 7.3 makes it clear that population growth in Europe is presently exclusively the result of immigration and is no longer due to natural population growth.

From Figures 7.4 and 7.5, it is possible to see that in Europe during the 20 years prior to 2014 there was already a considerable ageing in the population, and this will continue to increase in the projection to 2080.

Conclusions are obvious. The population growth rate will decline and with it the need for expansion of building stock. The decrease in the number of planning applications will probably turn out to be not just a crisis phenomenon, but more structural in nature. But an equally important factor is that the demographics will greatly change, and thus the nature of the provision of building stock. These two observations point in the direction of a consistency in size but also a change in building stock in terms of function.

These particular problems of the crisis give us something to think about, but there are many other considerations that incite much more focus on the

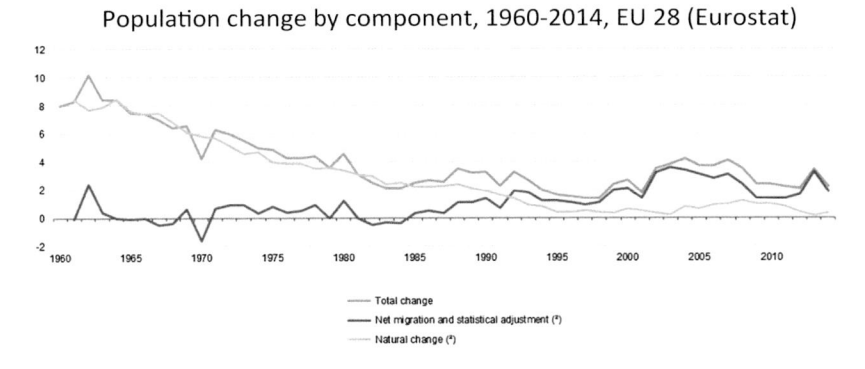

Figure 7.3
**Population
change by
component,
1960–2014
(EU-28,
EUROSTAT)**

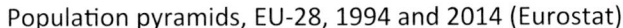

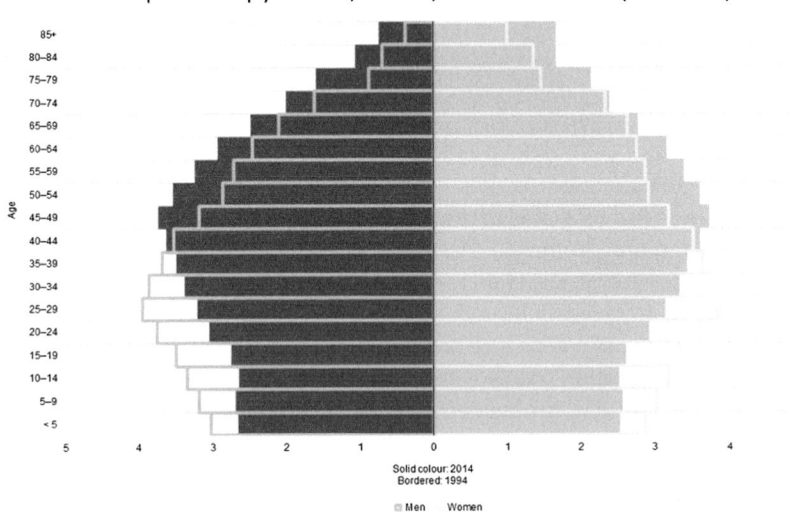

Figure 7.4
**Population
pyramids
1994–
2014(EU-28,
EUROSTAT)**

existing built environment. These are considerations that always existed but have had too little attention under the influence of the persistent demand for more and more of the same.

The first consideration is the special significance that the existing built environment has for people. People get attached to their homes, their living environment, their workplace. That represents great emotional value.

A second consideration which is related directly to the first is the enormous economic value represented by everything that is built. In my homeland, the Netherlands, this comes to about 2000 to 2500 billion Euros ($2427–$3033 billion). If we conveniently assume that the value per capita of the building stock in our part of Europe is roughly equal to that in the Netherlands, then we come out at EU 28 on a value of about € 60,000 billion ($72,800 billion). That is more than three times the gross national product in those same countries. The preservation of that value is off course extremely relevant.

Figure 7.5
**Population
pyramids,
2014–2080
(EU-28,
EUROSTAT)**

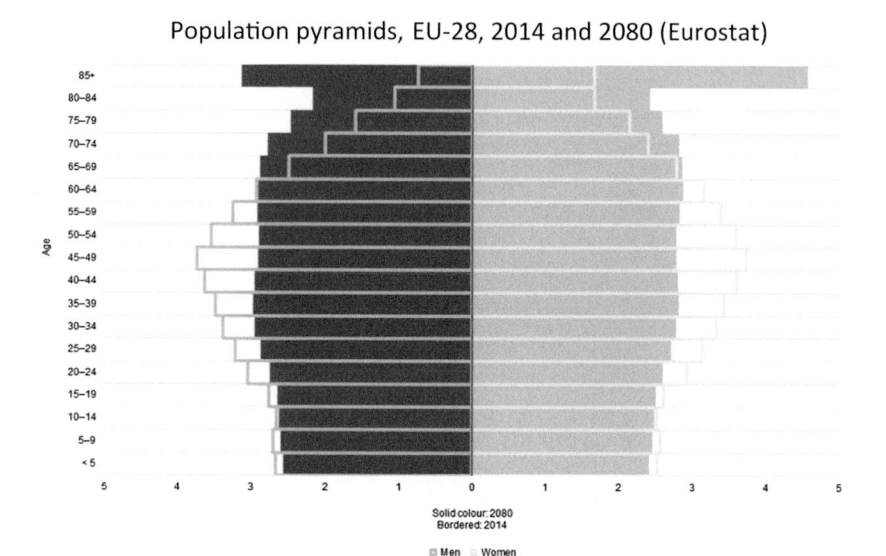

Figure 7.5 Population pyramids, EU-28, 2014 and 2080 (Eurostat)

A third consideration follows on from the observation that 99% of all housing needs can be met with the present existing housing stock. New construction is required for only a maximum of 1% of housing needs.

And the fourth consideration is formed by the huge money flows that go into the stock, on one side from the exploitation of the real estate and on the other side, the conservation and adaptation thereof.

In short, the existing built environment is both socially and economically enormously important. The key for value preservation socially as well as economically lies in the sustainable use of that stock. People make buildings for people. Real estate in use has value, unused real estate is worthless.

People and real estate

When it comes to sustainable use of the existing built environment, then it is most important to consider its users first, the people for whom it is made, the people from which demands come, those that have been in the subordinate position for a long time. What do those people want from the built environment and how can this be accommodated in their housing needs in the long term? What interaction is there between people and real estate?

People make real estate, but it differs in three respects from all other human products. Namely: it is larger than a human being, it lasts longer than a human being and it is fixed at one spot.

Buildings are larger than a person, they have an inside and an outside, one can enter, and one can go out. Inside they fulfil a function for people and outside they have a certain public character. Buildings were already there when you were born and will still be there when you die. Buildings have users and owners. Users change, owners change but the buildings remain. Buildings are seemingly immobile. Altogether those features inspire confidence, people identify and connect with them. The built environment is, as it were, of a higher order, just like a landscape, a beach or a centuries-old forest. To connect oneself (in Latin *religere*) with something higher is something that is everlasting, of all time and of all people. That is deep within us and is not a whim or a fad. That is why it is so important. The built environment represents for many people an emotional value, because it is easy to make an emotional connection with it. This is obvious in residents who consider their property as part of their lives. We see it also in the reactions of people in their work environments. And we see it walking with people through a city or town and watching their reaction to the public spaces between buildings. There are places where everyone says: 'Let's sit here and have a beer' and other places where they say: 'Let's move on and not sit down.' The built environment does something to us. There is undeniably a special interaction.

Emotional value in real estate translates into economic value. And as we are able to have a positive influence on that emotion then added value is created in the course of trade. The art is to keep that value forever. How can we do that? That is one of the key questions, because the economic value of the existing built environment is so large. If we consider Europe as a company that we might call Europe Limited, the calculated value of approximately €60,000 billion is relevant to the balance of the 'Europe Limited.' Since 2008, 10% to 20% of the value was lost, which corresponds to €6,000 to 12,000 billion. And this is relevant to the profit and loss account of the 'Europe Limited.' Compare this to the size of the European emergency fund, which contains only approximately €1,000 billion.

Real estate moves along

The place-relatedness of existing real estate is a given. Once it is there it is not manageable anymore. The (outward) appearance can be influenced just as its function (within) can. To determine how this influence directs itself we must consider the needs of people. And we must of course focus on those needs that may play a role in that particular interaction. What is going on with these people? What is going on in our society? What picture can we use to explain this?

In Europe following the years after World War II there existed the idea of the manufactured society. The idea was based on the assumption that people could be divided into groups with a collective or shared identity. The thinking was that if the Government could fulfil collective needs then the citizens would be satisfied; and the Government was able to fulfil this task because of the targeted research methods used to figure it all out. In that way the Government could 'make' society. The idea then was that all people were the same, equal on a high level. This interpreted into something like this: all people are married and have two children. All men work out of the home,

Figure 7.6
**Bijlmermeer
in the 1970s**

BIJLMERMEER

**Demolition
in 1998**

Figure 7.7
**The demo-
lition of
Bijlmermeer
in 1998**

they step into their car and go to their work in the morning and then drive back home in the evening. All women stay in the kitchen and do housework. All children play outside. And what are the needs of these people? A large flat in a green location with a parking garage of course!

And so, for example, in the Netherlands, the Bijlmermeer was developed as an expansion area of Amsterdam: 13,500 spacious flats in a green location. They were completed in the late 1960s and by the late 1990s they had been largely demolished (Figures 7.6 and 7.7).

Within the whole of Europe, we find countless examples of these sorts of mono-functional modernist and failed residential areas (Figures 7.8–7.12), too many to mention. It is apparent that the concept had rested on a huge fallacy. This is definitely the case – it was the fallacy of the manufactured society that was greatly based on the assumption that all people were equal and wanted the same, and moreover this equality was viewed as one of a permanent character.

But in the last century during the early 1990s, at just about the same time that the demolition of the Bijlmermeer started, we suddenly came to the understanding in the whole of Europe that this old social image did not exist in reality. Not all people were equal! No, on the contrary, no two people were alike (Figure 7.13 – 7.15).

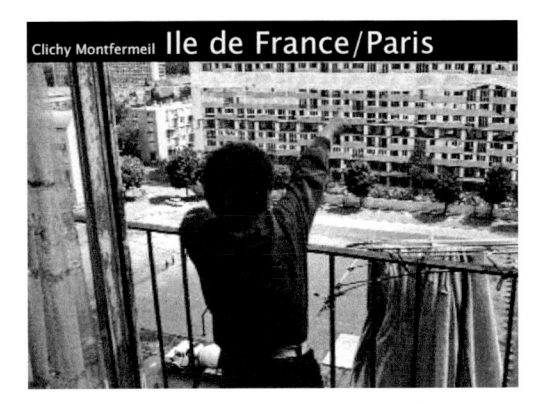

Figure 7.8
Paris

Figure 7.9
Marseille

Figure 7.10
**Dublin,
Ireland**

We now live in a highly individualized society. An emancipated society in which people in general are well educated and well informed, a society in which people themselves know what is good for them and are no longer prescribed to by others. And finally, a very dynamic society within which the

Figure 7.11
Berlin

Berlin (Germany)

Figure 7.12
Madrid

Madrid (Spain)

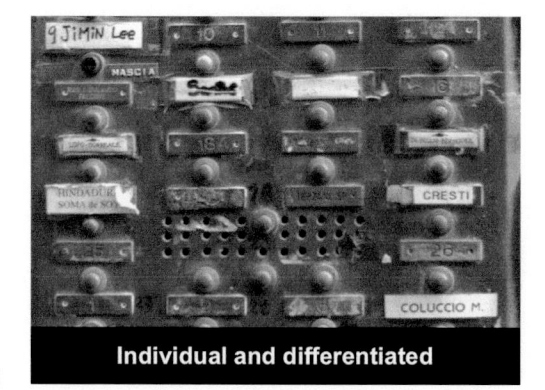

Figure 7.13
**Individual
and
differentiated**

Individual and differentiated

highly individualized needs can change on a daily basis. And the driving force behind the latter is formed by the technological developments that follow in an ever-increasing rate and have an enormous impact on our daily lives. Think of the new shopping and the new way of working for example. And in addition, there is a second important influence as we have just seen, namely that

Figure 7.14
Self-aware

Self-aware

Dynamic and open to change

Figure 7.15
**Dynamic
and open
to change**

of a strong demographic change in Europe. That highly individualized, strong dynamic need associated with people who do know what is good for them, stands diametrically opposed to the malleable society in which Government and hierarchical governance structures promulgated and set definite patterns.

How can change be accommodated in real estate?

In the last period in which we saw our needs actually being met in new construction, adaptability of the built environment was not a subject that received a lot of attention. Now that new construction is needed much less and that we are experiencing a lot of problems in the existing stock, its adaptability is suddenly a main topic. Traditionally, real estate and the ownership thereof is tied to land and land ownership and that makes everything that is connected to it an integral part of it too. According to regulation, this is also applicable to additions made afterwards. Of course, there are some (temporary) exceptions to this rule. But the question is whether these structures in a society that is becoming more dynamic can offer enough space.

The question is: 'How can we ensure that the existing stock can continue to accommodate the ever faster changing housing needs?'

LOCATION	1000 years
OUTSIDE	100 years
INSIDE	10 years.

Here the distinction between interior, exterior and location can help us, because they do not need to change at the same rate. We can work with different wavelengths. Indeed, that is also in line with social reality. The interior then serves the users' functions, which should, as we have seen, change more quickly. As real estate has the quality of being able to easily adjust to new usage requirements then this should satisfy the user and strengthen his bond with that real estate. The economic value of it is then improved. The exterior has a kind of dual function. On one hand it must allow for use within and on the other hand it represents a certain appearance which people can easily identify with. The changing pace of the exterior is therefore much slower than that of the interior. The wavelength is therefore a lot bigger. The last is true 'a fortiori' of the location and location characteristics. From there the wavelength of the change event is larger and the required capacity for change even smaller. The location in that respect is in collusion with the exterior of the buildings. We see therefore that those different paces of change connect to the human requirements. Interestingly enough this matches closely to the economic possibilities, because at a large wavelength deep investment of a large size is required, which is not easy to attain. The opposite is true for the parts with a small wavelength. That should be very inexpensive to change.

And so, we come to the answers to the questions that we have set ourselves around the interaction between people and the built environment. That interaction is always based on the human needs which have to do on the one hand with the direct use and on the other hand with the emotional bond. And therefore, the interaction involves driving forces and different wavelengths for the interior, exterior and location successively. And with this the simultaneous control over these form important challenges in the promotion of sustainable use of the existing built environment. How do we deal with real estate so that it is able to respond with different wavelengths? How do we **regulate control** over the interior, exterior and location? How do we **divide the responsibilities** between the user, owner, stakeholders and governments? And, by extension **how do we deal with existing laws and regulations** to accommodate the new developments that are opening up so strongly.

Open Building has the answer
Here we come to the area of Open Building. Open Building is about these different rates of change. Open Building is also based on the influence of the user on these changes. Open Building is not just technical or architectural

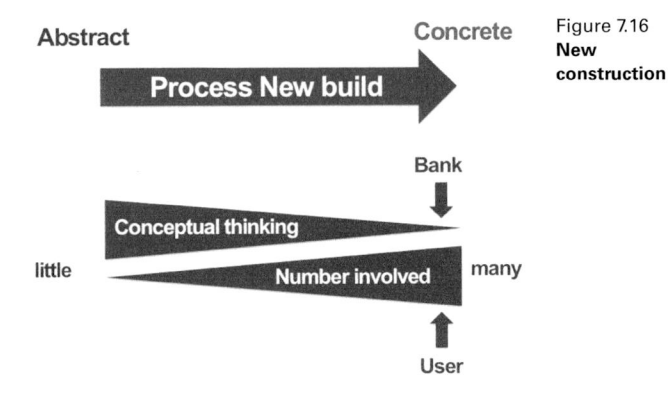

Figure 7.16
New construction

thinking but above all it is a way of thinking that is based on user influence with room for individual discretion and responsibility.

We will come back to this. But before we do that, for a better understanding, it is useful to firstly look a little deeper into the characteristics of the work process and the characteristics of the business/revenue models for the renovation and transformation of the existing stock compared to new construction.

The work process: a comparison

New construction

What are we able to show in a very simplified form with regard to a typical new construction process? That begins always with the client, the one giving the commission. She has a plot to build upon and asks, 'what do I wish to build there?' Then an overall program of requirements is formulated. She then considers how that program should be structured. She will consult an architect equipped with sketch paper and markers. Together they will start outlining the plan. An idea develops which both are enthusiastic about. The client asks the architect to develop the idea further. By the following meeting the architect has a sketch ready. To move forward, advice from other specialists is now necessary – this would be experts in structural and mechanical engineering. Step by step the building becomes more concrete and precisely detailed and more specialists are taken on board. Eventually more and more experts are involved in this process of the steadily increasing materialization of the building. So, around the time of tendering, the client arranges its external financing. In the next step after completion, the user finally appears.

So new construction has been described as a process that begins on a high level of abstraction, with few involved and ends on a very concrete level with many involved: a process involving initially investment, and then exploitation, comprising firstly designing, then building and then using.

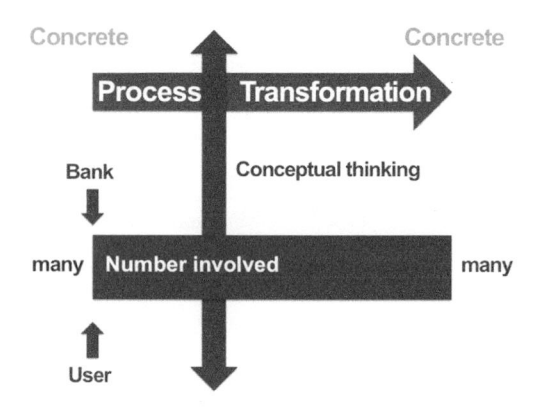

Figure 7.17
**Renovation/
transform-
ation**

Renovation and transformation

In renovation and transformation, the process begins where the process of new construction ends. There is an existing reality, existing financing and an existing use. The owner of the building is not happy with the property. This can be for different reasons. For example, because the energy consumption of the building is too high; because the leasing of the building is difficult; because the building does not meet user requirements; because the building has come into a downward spiral etc. The owner will therefore improve the existing property by renovation or transformation. That decision is condu-cive to investing. But now we start with an existing building and we have from the beginning all the disciplines necessary for a new construction pro-ject on the table in the course of the investment process, because we can only reinvest if we have the specific mapping of the existing building. For that reason, all the experts are necessary. Furthermore, the building has already been financed and thus the investor is also at the table. And in gen-eral, the building is already in use and therefore the users are already at the table too, in one way or another. And finally, the building is situated in an environment where third parties have vested interests and who want to be part of the decision-making. Conclusion: the number of those involved and the stakeholders is very large from the very beginning. And with all these stakeholders and experts, the owner has to go through a process that leads to a better exploitation of the building via a new concept. And with residen-tial buildings it is also not uncommon that realization of a new concept takes place in normal circumstances – when the building is in use.

So described, renovation and transformation is a process that starts with a very real building and many people involved and also ends with a very real building and many people involved. During this process, all of these stakeholders should participate at a high abstract level in the design and the decision-making on new concepts for the existing building.

In summary, if we compare these two processes we come up with the following: the process of new construction begins abstractedly with few people and ends concretely with many people, while renovation and transformation both begins and ends on a totally 'concrete' level and with many people involved. Such a process is much more complicated than that of new construction. This suggests, therefore very high demands on the design of the process and the way it is managed.

The business model, a comparison

New construction

In new construction the focus is on development costs.

What can we show in a very simplified form with the business model of new construction? The business model is, as we will show, primarily focused on controlling the building cost. By this we mean the total investment required for the creation of a new building. The reasoning is as follows:

In general, for building projects there are four types of clients: project developers, housing corporations, private and institutional investors. In the years before the crisis (2008) the project developers, the institutional investors and the corporations in Europe were dominant. Because of the total construction volume, they took about 80 to 90% for their own accounting. Let us then delve into the revenue models and financial control by these three.

We begin with project developers. Project developers and their financiers state one thing clearly: never build first and then sell. That is too risky. The adage is: sell first and then build. In this way project development is much less capital intensive and much less risky. Only with an initial investment on a land option plus preliminary design, can a developer create a sales brochure. With residential real estate the buyer would pay in instalments after sale (on paper), the project developer was assured of his sales price and he had immediately a significant part of his risk removed.

Also, outside of residential building the guiding principle is this: pre-leasing of shops to large retail chains or of offices to large office users, followed by pre-sale to an investor. With the pre-lease contract in the bag the developers can then find end-investors quite easily. Also, the financing of shops and offices goes by this principle. The consequence of the principle is threefold. The number of developers has increased enormously because the necessary equity was reduced. The product becomes less interesting because only stereotype products in this manner could be financed and sold. And finally, this was the method that determined the business model of the developer. And this is exactly what we want in this regard.

The developer naturally wants to optimize his performance. And if the sales price established is fixed, the only means to increase profits is by controlling – read as lowering – the development costs. Thereupon is based the business model of the project developer. That is why in Europe there is an enormous number of building cost specialists. Each project manager feels at home with this. Apart from the fact that this may in itself lead to impoverishment of the product, this control principle is deeply contrary to the essence of real estate. That is because it is focused on short-term interests, while real estate is made for the long term. It is in that long term that users, owners and end-investors have more interest. But in this system of separation of initiative and exploitation there is little space for those interests and few influencing possibilities.

Now we go to investors and corporations as the commissioning party. As far as these buildings constructed for sale are concerned, they apply the same principles as the project developers. But strangely enough, they used control of building costs as the predominant mechanism in the development and realization of new rental properties that they exploited themselves. That can be outlined as follows.

Residential rents show that development costs may only be in part secured from the present value of the rental income. This is true for the social (subsidized) sector though also to some extent in the commercial sector because of the crisis. The secured part of the initial investment was named 'profitable' and the unsecured part 'non-profitable.' The latter is of course not financed externally. This security should either come from equity or from Government subsidies. In many European countries, however, these were lifted after the crisis. Now in a good selling market there is a reasonable chance in due time to recoup the unprofitable investment from the sales profit. But nonetheless, there is almost no investor or housing corporation looking to hedge the initial losses on the exploitation from their own equity. Therefore, the landlords were obliged to be strong on the building costs. No one thought this strange, because that met with a tradition of decades of widespread conventions in construction. Yet still the caveat applies that investors and housing corporations especially as owners should have a focus on the exploitation and sustainable quality. It is certainly not the case that this was missing. But the financial management of investments has dominated the short-term interests.

Increasingly similar considerations apply to the commercial lessor. During the crisis it appeared to be more difficult also in the free market to apply a cost-effective rent for the leasing of high-quality buildings.

In summary: cutting back on building costs within the main categories of clients has always been the major financial instrument of their investments. Thereupon was based the business model of the clients for new construction. That's a fairly simple business model focused on the short term and widely established. And there are in Europe a lot of experts in this field.

Renovation and transformation

In renovation and transformation, the focus is on exploitation or extracting value.

Renovation and transformation go hand in hand with existing real estate. It is therefore inevitable that the exploitation of the real estate is central in the business model of the owner, who is almost always the initiator. Here initiative and exploitation are not separated and that leads to different financial management than with new construction projects. Naturally the cost of

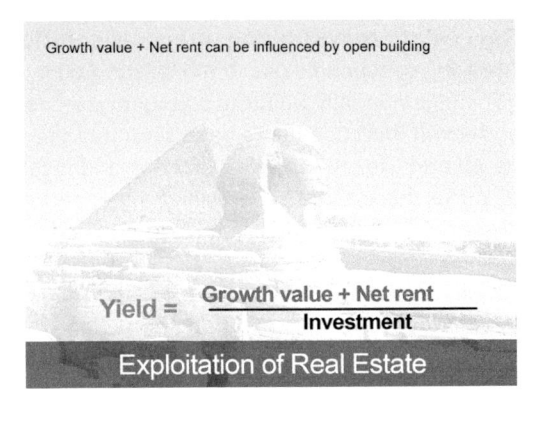

Figures 7.18
and 7.19
**Exploitation
of real estate**

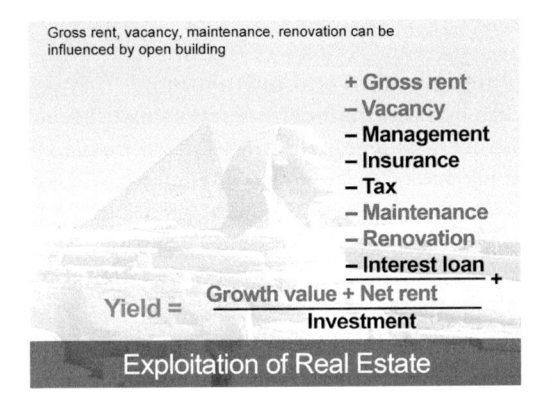

Figure 7.19

additional building investments is important, and it is clear they must be managed just as with new construction. But here more factors play a role. For example, the question of how high the capital value of the existing real estate in the reinvestment project can or must be, in other words: how much has been offset? (See Figures 7.18, 7.19.)

We have to also consider the question, which knobs can we turn to change the existing unprofitable exploitation to a profitable one? Not only is the number of knobs huge, but there are many interrelated ones in between. It may be wise not to minimize the additional investing but to increase it in order to obtain a better exploitation. Examples are extra investing to reduce energy costs, reduction in maintenance costs or reduction in leasing risk or in improvement of future rents of the property, or in improving the future development worth of the property. The amount of possibilities and combinations is vast and there are many cross-connections. Applying Open Building principles can influence all of them. This exploitation focuses on financial management in the long term and thus fully meets the essence of real estate. But this management regarding future cash flows is more complex and uncertain than the established management of one-off building costs. In Europe there are, therefore, very few experts in this field.

Real estate moves along: practical solutions

Applying sustainable use to the existing built environment will only succeed if it can continually adapt to changing user requirements without too much additional investment. We have seen that the wavelength of the change can be different for the interior, exterior and location. It is obviously important to make these three time frames independent of each other, so that they do not hinder each other in their mutually different change processes. These are the precise principles of the Open Building approach. That separation should take shape both technically and materially and in terms of management. What technical conditions do we encounter, what framework of rules and regulations and what in terms of the financial aspect? And how can we deal with them and constantly move with them in order to accommodate the existing built environment?

Materialization and technique

Let's start with the most concrete aspect, the materialization plus technique and the control thereof. Here, the principle of Open Building comes to the rescue. In his book *De dragers en de mensen, het einde van de massawoningbouw* (1961) first translated into English under the title *Supports, an Alternative to Mass Housing* (Praeger, 1972), John Habraken laid out the basic principles. It made a distinction between support (or base building), infill and urban fabric. These concepts we explain briefly as follows. The infill or fit-out represents layout and amenities, which change rapidly and over which the user should have control. The support or base building means foundations, roof, supporting structure, access, main utilities and all or most of the façade. These change slowly and form the solid framework for quick installation and easy customization of the infill. The control over the base building lies with the investor as owner and long-term investor. This can also be a housing corporation. The urban fabric represents the location as well as the fixed location characteristics such as public space, the property's footprint and sometimes the building height too. These in turn form the solid framework wherein the base buildings can be adapted. And control over it and ownership thereof is generally by a public body, usually local Government. So, we see that in that system there is a hierarchy between the three levels. In every case the higher level with the larger wavelength forms the regulating and physical framework within which the lower level with a smaller wavelength can move. That lower level cannot step outside the rules and physical framework.

Base building

If we apply this approach to existing buildings, it means we need to make a technical and material separation between base building and fit-out. If the base building is not designed to accommodate many fit-outs, then it is the primary concern to increase the capacity of the base building as much as possible. The accommodation capacity of the base building depends from the start on the carrying capacity of foundations, vertical loadbearing structures (walls and columns) and horizontals (floors and beams). A question here is thus: can the load-bearing capacity be increased if it is not enough? The accommodation capacity of the base building depends, secondly, also on the free space it offers. This refers to the height between the top and the bottom of the fixed-bearing floors. This headroom in post-war houses is usually no more than 2.5 m (8'6"). Consequently, this strongly limits the possibilities to use it for other functions. Base buildings of schools and offices with head-room of 3 m (9'9") and more and industrial buildings are more suitable in this respect. The accommodation capacity of the base building depends, thirdly, also on the possibilities for partitioning. And this in turn depends to a large extent on the size of the spans and of the spacing of the support points or walls, which carry the vertical loads on the foundations. Fourthly and finally, the accommodation capacity of the base building depends on its accessi-bility thereof; accessibility for users as well as for facilities such as gas, water, sewage, electricity, air, data traffic etc. In low-rise buildings this leads to the maximization of the potential number of access possibilities from the public area, for people and for pipes and cables. With higher building this has far greater consequences. Then we must ask the following questions: how do we improve the horizontal and the vertical access for people and utilities, and how do we get these two systems together?

Fit-Out

If the accommodation capacity of the base building complies, then we come to the fit-out. Here we should not only consider layout, floor and ceiling finishes, but also lighting, heating, ventilation, water, sewer and connections for data traffic and placement of a meter cupboard (for gas, water and elec-tric meters). In short everything necessary to make a building ready for use. In this, fit-out is thus the requirement that it is independent of the base building; it can easily and cheaply be adapted to the constantly changing user requirements or functional changes. On that matter, the product supply industry already has many answers ready.

Within the sphere of installations there are prefabricated components that can be put together like a kind of model construction system. The same applies for components that are used for architectural elements and partitions, floors and ceilings. These systems usually have a lot in common in that they can be reused elsewhere after disassembly. This offers the potential for lease or rental of these components, where the user pays only for the use and the supplier takes back his high-quality products after the term of use has expired, for reuse or recycling. In this case, the knife cuts both ways: scarce resources are not lost, and the user is not stuck in a situation without an alter-native. That possibility is extremely good to have.

But for the sake of clarity: it is quite possible to make such a separation of the base building with traditional construction methods. Interior walls for example can still be cemented with all types of bricks or blocks or with the well-known metal studs and gypsum boards, or even wooden elements. The disadvantage is that the residual value is low unless the subsequent user can continue to use these constructions in their entirety.

In the area of partitioning components, the construction industry is changing rapidly. We can still expect many innovations; these could come from unexpected sources, for example from the furniture manufacturing industry. Finally, we see in this respect that within our current legal frameworks it is not the legal ownership but the economic ownership of the fit-out that can be transferred to the user as occupants of the base building surface. And the occupant may be given the option to sell the fit-out to the next occupant through a so-called 'substitution,' a transaction that occurs often in the retail and in the hospitality sector.

Rules and regulations

It seems technically and materialistically that it would be quite easy to find solutions to the problem of buildings that 'move along.' However, accommodating user preferences is not just a technical problem. Existing laws and regulations should not stand in the way, one of which – control and/or ownership of the installations – we have touched upon already. But within this area the problems loom. The multiplicity of restrictive regulations is huge. And again, most are not primarily meant to provide freedom of use but based upon very different principles. They were mostly formed in the post-war years when construction of new mono-functional buildings set the tone. Furthermore, these regulations are enforced by independently operating bodies. That has led to regulations and the application of these regulations that do not fit the dynamic the real estate market demands. Let us consider at a glance what can actually lie in the way.

- Firstly, we have to look at the ownership rights in the real estate sector. This is based on the principle that everything above and below a piece of land and that associated with it is the property of the landowner; within the real estate sector, this also applies to everything attached to it. So, at first glance it might seem that it is difficult to reconcile full ownership over the fit-out to the inhabitant. We could determine juridical constructions that solve this problem in part. But for an adequate and universally usable legal separation of ownership of base building and fit-out, many legislative changes are necessary.
- Secondly, we have to consider environmental law (or regional planning). This gives local Government the ability to determine the use of land. An exhaustive list of permitted uses can therefore stand in the way of allowing a much-needed use for the land in question. It would be better to have a list of things which are *not* possible so that there is unlimited space for everything else. That is much wiser in a dynamic society, in which no one knows what will happen or what the requirements are in the market.

- Thirdly we have to consider the building codes and regulations. One of the most pressing questions that may arise from the application of the regulations is what is the standard that applies to renovations? Are they the same standards as in the current new construction or are they the same standards that prevailed in the initial development of the real estate? The latter seems more reasonable than the first, because existing buildings undergoing renovation or transformation and having to adapt to new build standards are often unenforceable.
- A fourth category of regulations that we have to consider are shaped by the legislation that covers gas, water, electricity as well as the connection requirements of utility companies. The legislation and connection requirements give the utility companies a kind of monopoly position. And there might be in terms of user control significant complications making it very costly.

The degree to which all of these regulations work prohibitively is not only an objective truth as a direct result of the content of the rules themselves, but also depends to a large extent on the smoothness with which they are applied. And that is a subjective truth, because with good will it is also evident that within the current legislation, regulations and local ordinances a lot is still possible. But if this good will is lacking, there are countless opportunities to greatly reduce user-control. Even on that point there is still a lot to do. On the one hand we need to work on raising awareness on the enforcement of regulations, on the other hand we have to work hard to be convincing and put forward convincing arguments.

Finance and financing

Flexible use of existing real estate does not always fit within the traditional financial parameters. This is especially the case in change of use, which costs not only additional investment resources but also often just leads to a new acceptable return when the first existing value is written off. That problem is often apparent with vacant offices, shops and industrial buildings. Investors have long been reluctant to implement these write-offs in the hope of an improvement in the market. And curiously enough, the commonly used valuation methods on write-offs also stood in the way, because these methods often came out from the fictional assumption that the real estate within a certain time (e.g., two years) will be entirely rented. In such a case the methods were not appreciated by the reality, so writing-off was unnecessary. Large write-offs suddenly also raised questions. And therefore, most investors opted for gradual change despite the fact that the real and current market value was now much lower than that of the book value.

This can create barriers to redevelopment. This was especially true in the early years of the economic crisis (2008–2010). But meanwhile investors have accepted the new reality. In completely vacant office areas, for example, residual values of around €200/m² floor space are already taken into account. Some talk of offices as having m²-price equal to that of the floor covering.

If the write-off is accepted, the problem is whether as a result there is additional investing that has an appreciation that is higher than the investment. The appreciation depends of course on the rental possibilities, the rental price level and the expected rent price development after transformation. The problem is then to finance that investment if the necessary equity is missing. Here we can come up against the ingrained approaches of the banks. They are used to finance only after rental. They finance then on the basis of guaranteed cash flow. This can be quite difficult at the present time because the traditional markets fail, and buildings need to be specifically made suitable for variable and changing use. The demand for such capacity is a feature of the market of today and tomorrow. That means a new vision is needed for the financier who was accustomed to single-tenant contracts for five to ten years. For it is precisely small-scale rental to changing users and rental contracts with short terms that have a future. It seems controversial, but in this market, it is wise to offer leases for workspaces that can be cancelled on a monthly basis, the same as with living spaces. That is totally against tradition, but by opening the back door like this we may stop the resistance at the front door. This new way of thinking in the world of real estate financing must be accepted.

If the financier goes into this, then they finance not guaranteed cash flow but a market-conforming building. Guaranteed cash flow and market-conforming buildings have two entirely different magnitudes. In the latter case, other criteria are taken into account, such as location, capacity for variety and change, and the appearance of the building. Unlike the signed leases of reputable parties, they are far more difficult to put across to the back office. But there are clear signs of a change in forward thinking financiers and where they are going to take this.

Stakeholders in the supply-chain: towards a new form of cooperation

We have shown the process of renovating and transforming existing real estate to happen on a very precise level with many experts and stakeholders involved from the start. Restricted by a system of legislation and financial tools mainly equipped for new construction projects makes for a highly complex working process. But there is another complicating factor and that's the fragmented nature of the supply-chain and its customs that maintain the status quo.

Evolution of cooperation in the builders' supply-chain

Ever since the Renaissance, an increasing separation and disaggregation of activities has characterized the development of the builders' supply-chain.

The first step was the distinction between design and its implementation. With industrialization came new and modern building materials: glass, steel, cement and later reinforced concrete. Because there was no widespread experience for applying these new materials and because fabricating them was very costly there was a growing need for construction calculations, safety and financial efficiency being the main criteria. Construction engineering became its own professional discipline. When technological advancement allowed for large-scale application of sanitary systems and distribution of electricity and drinking water, mechanical engineers became involved, followed by physicists concerned with daylight, heat and sound insulation etc. By this time DIY (do-it-yourself) building traditions could no longer be blindly trusted, and the design of the built environment became the domain of professionals, its construction brokered by many parties. On top of this we've seen a growing sense of responsibility with governments creating a diverse body of legislation concerning technical and even aesthetic qualities of the built environment.

With the actors of the built environment (clients, designers, contractors and governments at all levels) becoming more and more independent, wide-ranging specialization became viable, resulting in the ongoing disaggregation of the production process that generates our buildings. Today one often needs dozens of different parties involved, professionals or institutions – individuals or companies for the creation of a building or even a single building product. This makes organizing and managing the building process a complicated and often tedious endeavor. But it also leads to a very narrow focus of every individual stakeholder in the supply-chain, protecting self-interest over the interest of the resulting product outcome. And lastly, this disaggregated and specialized body of experts completely alienates the end-user of a building from its many creators.

The idea of the architect as master builder being able not only to adequately design a building according to a given program of requirements, but also to be able to understand to some extent all relating disciplines and techniques became very popular during the previous century. When building techniques were still relatively straightforward (e.g. masonry or timber) all was well with this idea. Today, however, our technical advancements have offered us so many possibilities that it's a phantasy for a single professional to oversee all important interdependencies, let alone understand all aspects of the building process in detail.

On top of this, creating a building is project-based. Every building has its own location, design, planning, budget and type of building system. This means that for every new building a new specific collaboration must be established, and all of its members are in permanent transit from one project to the next. This only further increases all of the negative effects of the disaggregated nature of the industry.

Another hallmark of the building process complicates matters further: the process of selection for building partners often being a call for tender or bid proposals. This competitive system of negotiation for price results in a collaboration that has by definition a conflict of interest. Within the contracting business the benefits of this system of open competition is often used as an argument for maintaining it. Whether or not its drawbacks are preponderant remains the question.

Drawbacks of a tradition

The many parties involved in the building process are very dependent on one another. One professional produces information on which others depend. One manufacturers' product has to fit or is even composed by that of other producers. Contractors depend on drawings and descriptions by various designers. Designers need to trust and understand the mindset of the contractors to know what to draw (and what not).

In such an interdependent system mutual trust, respect and reciprocity is of utmost importance. It would benefit from a state non-belligerence, but the competitive system of tenders prior to actual collaboration often makes a participant enter a project with a sense of tension.

Distrust and competition are hallmarks of a tender process. It's hard to turn a relation founded on competitive tension into a harmonious collaboration. With a competitive attitude often come all sorts of precautions for price escalations, ways to shirk responsibility and a habit of blaming mistakes on other parties involved.

The end-result is negatively affected by this reality, often resulting in failure costs or even construction mistakes. And while these inefficiencies burden all participants in the process, it's the client risking the most. It's the client that has plans and contracts drawn up at their own expense and risk that, by definition, cannot be flawless. And there is no fool-proof legal solution to completely exclude this risk, although the business of legal council is doing well by making us believe otherwise.

Even the often-recurring blame that the building sector is a hulking industry incapable of radical innovation can be explained by this system of distrust. Innovation is the result of experiments and experimenting means making mistakes. Mistakes can only be productive in an atmosphere of trust and respect which are surely lacking more often than not in our current building sector. Also, margins are often too slim to experiment outside of actual production like we see in the car- or high-tech industry for example.

Surely, we should be able to see the error in our usual way of doing things. But is the industry able to change? In the supply-chain, from manufacturer – broker – subcontractor – contractor – client – end-user, every link makes a profit subsequently raising the price of a product. An average manufacturer that dares to bypass this chain with some innovative product is excluded from trading his other products. Only market outsiders dare to undertake such a thing. Also, many parties and individuals involved derive their sense of self-worth from the game that comes with trade. It's hard to let go of such a deep-rooted culture so the industry maintains a deadlock on itself, making a breakthrough seem near impossible.

Process renewal is essential

We have seen some improvements in the past decades but always on the level of a product, hardly ever on the conceptual level of a building as a whole. Examples of such products being boilers, roof coverings, prefabricated façade elements, a range of innovative ways to supply energy, and more. All of these products have one thing in common: reflecting the segregated/disaggregated nature of the sector. They were all developed by one company, under one brand, often in competition. To bring about innovation based on collaboration, a change in culture is necessary.

When it comes to renovation and transformation of real estate, this culture change is absolutely vital because, as we have seen, the number of professionals and stakeholders involved is daunting. Competitive tendering or bidding is only possible with limitations because the end-user, financial stakeholders and third parties with vested interests are often a given, as are, to some extent, designers and suppliers involved with the building already realized.

Combined with the urgency of finite resources, with circularity becoming an inescapable necessity, all professionals involved should not only design and construct a building but also consider how their creation might be disassembled in the future without the loss of valuable resources. For example: the possibility of the original manufacturer retaking components leads to a very different role for these companies, making the process of building even more complicated both technically and financially, and in turn rendering the traditional purchasing by tender and based on short-term price competition completely obsolete. Renovation and transformation have an even bigger challenge: the reuse of traditional building components in existing buildings. These renovation developments are still in their infancy but are unavoidable.

Ongoing technological advancements, scarcity of resources and changing roles result in innovative building products and methods, but these can only be applied adequately when the building process or rather its culture can be restructured. For inspiration on alternative models we should look beyond the edges of the conventional building industry. Other industrial chains of production might prove suitable for inspiration.

The question is: what traits can we adopt, remembering that buildings are not cars or computer chips that are mass-manufactured and stockpiled. Buildings have more contextual preconditions and last much longer and are as such not fit for stockpile production. Traits we *can* incorporate are the way relations of stakeholders are structured based on a different interaction, a base of trust and cutting-edge technological tools.

A new collaboration, a new set of rules

Given the complexity of renovating and transforming existing real estate, an inversion of the traditional process is obvious. So, it makes sense to start, before anything elsc, with the forming of a collaboration. And with collaboration come rules. The basis should be trust and transparency. Business interests should not be ignored but margins and profits should be openly discussed beforehand. If someone makes a judgment error during these initial agreements an opportunity to recuperate should be found together.

There should be a willingness to learn and openly share knowledge, because all parties involved work on the basis that success means continuity. As such, mistakes are welcomed as learning opportunities rather than harshly sanctioned. Except for one mistake: the abuse of the mutual trust. Such an error should be punishable by exclusion without any form of compensation.

Conclusions

- New construction will decrease.
- Demographics and technological developments lead to large dynamics in housing needs.
- These must be accommodated in the existing stock.
- The existing stock must become flexible.
- This is the terrain of 'Open Building.'
- Urban fabric, base building and fit-out have different rates of change.
- Rules and regulation must be adjusted.
- Work processes in construction and business models on investing require a new approach.
- There is a tremendous opportunity for integrated product/service companies.

The future of Open Building is open transformation and resides in the existing stock.

Note

1 Editor's note: this chapter is drawn from a lecture by the same title, presented by the author at The Future of Open Building Conference, hosted by the ETH Zurich in September 2015.

Chapter 8

Japan's Act Concerning the Promotion of Long-Life Quality Housing

Kazunobu Minami

History of research and development in the housebuilding industry in Japan

The average number of years of residential buildings in Japan before rebuilding used to be almost 30 years vs. 66 years in the US and 80 years in the UK (A Quick Look at Housing in Japan, 2018). There are various reasons for the short lifespan of Japanese housing. Fires following the Great Kanto Earthquake that struck the Tokyo area in 1923 caused a huge loss of building stock, so only a small number of old pre-war houses remain in the Tokyo Metropolitan area. We had a shortage of more than four million housing units in Japan after the Second World War in the mid 1940s. Many public housing units were built then, but the quality was low and needed to be rebuilt once Japan began to enjoy economic growth. That resulted in the statistically short life of Japanese housing. The rapid economic growth that followed the Second World War enabled the Japanese society to afford to live in larger houses with modern facilities.

In the 1970s, the total number of dwelling units in Japan began to exceed the number of households, changing the aim of research and development from supplying a large number of homes to improving their quality and meeting diverse residential needs. At the time, many dwellings did not fully satisfy residential and daily life needs due to the change of the family structure and lifestyles. The durability of interior finishes and equipment (fit-out) was shorter than the durability of the buildings themselves; the failure to perform appropriate maintenance became a social problem as well.

To overcome the challenges facing housing supply, the Ministry of Construction started the KEP (Kodan Experimental Housing Project) in 1973, and also the Century Housing System (CHS) in 1981 following KEP (Figure 8.1).

The KEP program developed and adopted a movable partitioning system and movable storage system enabling the residents to change their positions by themselves. Many dwellings for family use are smaller than 90 m^2 (900 ft^2), requiring that they be occupied skillfully or remodeled to keep up with

DOI: 10.4324/9781003018339-10

Figure 8.1
Some key initiatives in the research and development in Japanese housing since 1970

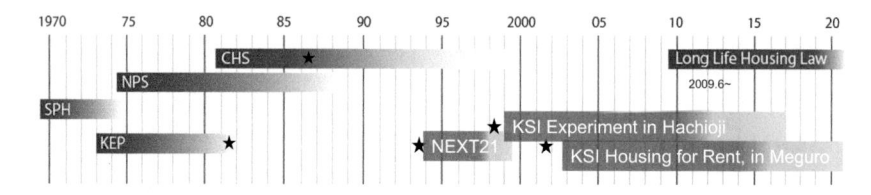

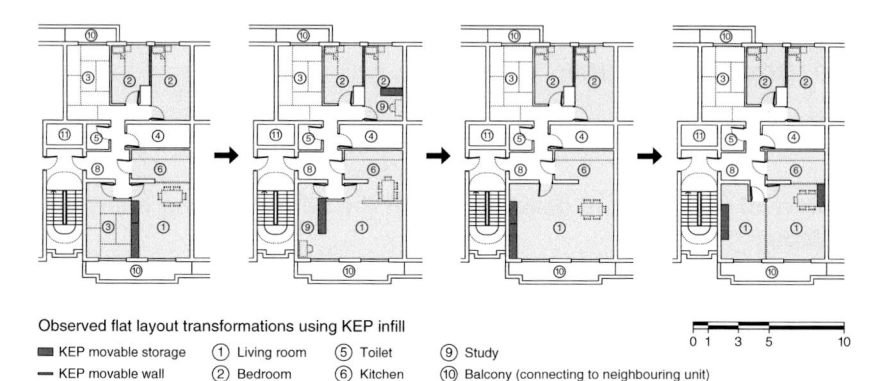

Observed flat layout transformations using KEP infill

Figure 8.2
KEP renovation in time

■ KEP movable storage ① Living room ⑤ Toilet ⑨ Study
— KEP movable wall ② Bedroom ⑥ Kitchen ⑩ Balcony (connecting to neighbouring unit)
③ Tatami room ⑦ Study ⑪ Pipe shaft
④ Bathroom ⑧ Entrance

the growth of the children. We have conducted research on the outcomes of the movable infill system to examine whether the attempted adaptability has worked in the 30 years after people started living there. We found that the KEP housing with adaptable infill (fit-out) has worked to adjust to the changes of family size and lifestyle. As children grew, and mostly at the time when children left home, many families used the KEP system to adjust the room arrangements to fit to their changed ways of life. We may be able to say that the KEP system has worked very well, as it was planned 33 years ago (Figure 8.2).

The Ministry of Construction's Century Housing System (CHS) Guidebook (*Century Housing System Guidebook*, 1997), stipulated the following guidelines as basic standards for CHS certification of housing receiving government loans.

1. Base buildings have long-term durability.
2. To maintain them after construction, inspections must be easy to carry out.
3. The floor plan, interior finishes and equipment (fit-out) are replaceable.
4. The interior finishes and walls of the dwelling can be repaired, renewed, replaced, or moved easily without impacting other parts.
5. Building drawings are provided to appropriately inform residents of the characteristics of CHS housing.
6. The above can be done for a long period of time.

Service lifetimes were set for each component and the mutual impacts were studied to set anticipated lifetimes: Component Type 04: 3 to 6 years, Type 08: 6 to 12 years, Type 15: 12 to 25 years, Type 30: 25 to 50 years, and Type 60: 50 to 100 years. The interface details of each component were designed so as not to damage the long-lasting building elements when shorter lifespan elements are moved or replaced.

An important milestone is NEXT21 (Osaka Gas Co., 2019; SD25, 1994), an on-going experimental multi-family housing project built by the Osaka Gas Company in 1993 (see Figure 8.3). The goal is to demonstrate new concepts of multi-family housing that incorporate sustainable design methods, design for change, and advanced technologies expected to be used in the near future. This structure is a kind of three-dimensional urban design with no dead-end interior corridors, giving it a real sense of a city neighborhood. It consists of one underground floor, and six floors above ground level. It is made up of the skeleton (base building), infill (fit-out) and the cladding. The design concept focuses on what the highly individualized lifestyle is expected to be in the 21st century and also looks into issues relating to high-density urban housing and how to conserve resources in building operations and maintenance. The building is an environmentally friendly building incorporating various energy and resource conserving design strategies and building systems.

Figure 8.3
NEXT21

In keeping with the Open Building principle of separating design tasks, one team of architects designed the skeleton, another team designed the cladding "system," and another 13 architects designed the original 18 units, each using the cladding system according to the design of each dwelling. Subsequently, other architects have been engaged to redesign dwellings, which involved reconfiguring the cladding accordingly as required to correspond to the reconfigured floor plans of the dwellings.

This structural system and utility pathways running under exterior walkways both offer the capacity to reconfigure dwelling units and to change functions from residential to commercial, etc. The cladding system is assembled from a series of multiple independent subsystems which can be removed, moved and reinstalled from inside the building. This type of decomposition of the building subsystems makes the building flexible from a technical point of view, where components like the mechanical equipment can be easily replaced, and the reuse of each individual unit is incorporated into its design, to respond to changes in lifestyle and occupancy patterns.

The only fixed part of the building is its structural skeleton which is made up of columns and beams of cast-in-place concrete, the stairs and elevators, and the pathways for mechanical systems to reach each independent unit of occupancy. The concrete structure is clad with metal panels to protect it from wind, rain and other elements which might cause corrosion. This, together with other measures, gives the building a lifespan of more than 100 years.

The Act Concerning the Promotion of Long-Life Quality Housing

Present-day Japan faces three problems: (1) people cannot enjoy the feeling of wealth they desire as members of a mature society, (2) the falling birth rate and aging of society are increasingly presenting a welfare burden, and (3) global environmental problems and waste problems are becoming increasingly severe. To overcome these problems, a general consensus has emerged that we must transform society from its existing state, a consumption society which builds and demolishes, into a stock society which builds good objects and takes scrupulous care of them to preserve them for long periods of time. The goal of extending the lifespan of housing is part of a larger effort to overcome these 3 problems.

To extend the useful life of housing, a consensus developed in Japan requiring that houses should be constructed that have excellent quality and durability, and that are easy to manage and maintain. At the same time, it became clear that it was necessary to promote systematic inspections and repairs, and to allow smooth changes in interior décors and facilities in accordance with the evolving lives of the inhabitants. It was also increasingly clear that the society should assist the secondary market of existing houses by development of an accurate housing maintenance information system, such as records of how dwellings were built, maintained and managed, and improving information service methods on performance and quality of existing housing.

Out of these new understandings, the new law called "The Act Concerning the Promotion of Long-Life Quality Housing" was promulgated on December 5, 2008 and came into force on June 4, 2009. This was the core legislation relating to creation of systems for the approval of plans pertaining to the construction and maintenance of "Long-Life Quality Housing," which is defined as superior housing with features of long-term use in good condition. The concept of this law was presented by former Prime Minister Yasuo Fukuda in 2007. The Government started the pilot projects in 2009 by subsidizing the private sectors' R&D to make housing in Japan have longer-use lives. The new law aims to supply long-life housing in Japan from now on, in addition to using the existing houses much longer.

The total number of units of Long-Life Quality Housing approved in Japan since its establishment in 2009 is 1,132,284 at the end of March 2020 (MLIT, 2020a). Most of them are detached houses. Only 21,880 dwelling units were condominium units in multi-family buildings. In recent years, approximately 100,000 units of all kinds have been certified annually (11% of all housing starts: 25% of single-family homes and 0.1% of multi-family homes, almost no certification of rental housing). As not many condominium developers think that the recognition of long-life housing has much to do with sales promotion, applications for condominiums under the new law have been very few. On the other hand, developers of detached houses have taken great advantage of the recognition as long-life housing and have utilized it for their advertising and sales promotion. The technical guidelines which require that the common equipment piping in condominiums can be maintained without entering the unit make the number of applications for condominiums very small. This requirement for condominiums, however, was recently revised to increase application of the new law.

The Ministry of Land, Infrastructure, Transport and Tourism (MLIT) studied their ten years implementation of the Act Concerning the Promotion of Long-Life Quality Housing and disclosed the result of their review in July 2020 (MLIT, 2020b). MLIT recognizes the small number of approved apartment units and will improve the approval process by simplifying the requirements for the fit-out of each unit and those for the base building. The author thinks the reason for the small number of approved dwelling units has been affected by the condominium sales market in general in large cities in Japan. The condominium developers have enjoyed the market in which they can easily sell the units without effort. They do not have to complete the many pages of application documents to get approval under the new law. In contrast, the developers for the detached houses have needed to add value for their customers to sell houses, in most cases located in medium and small cities and villages in Japan.

Technical guidelines of the new law

The technical guidelines of the 2008 law explain the technical details required for extending the lifespan of housing. There are nine chapters in the technical guidelines, and an appendix. The basic idea of these technical guidelines was based on the Century Housing System, discussed above.

Chapter 1.　Durability of the materials; measures to prevent deterioration;

Chapter 2.　Structural design; earthquake resistance

Chapter 3.　Ease of maintenance and renewal

- Measures should be taken so that the maintenance (cleaning, inspection, repair and update) of the interior finishing and facilities which have shorter lifespans than the building structures can be carried out easily.
- The building should be designed so that private piping and common piping are easily maintained (see Figure 8.4).
- The building should be designed so that common drainage pipes are easily maintained. It shall be possible to maintain common piping of condominium apartments without entering private parts of dwellings. However, if it is difficult to design the common (base building) pipe shaft so that it is directly accessible from common or public space, it is possible to substitute that rule by establishing formal agreements with residents that allow maintenance staff to enter dwelling units in the case of maintenance or repair work (see Figure 5a and 5b).

Chapter 4.　Adaptability

- Measures should be taken which permit the modification of room layouts according to changes in the lifestyle of the occupants. In order to be able

The requirements for piping space in a private condominium dwelling

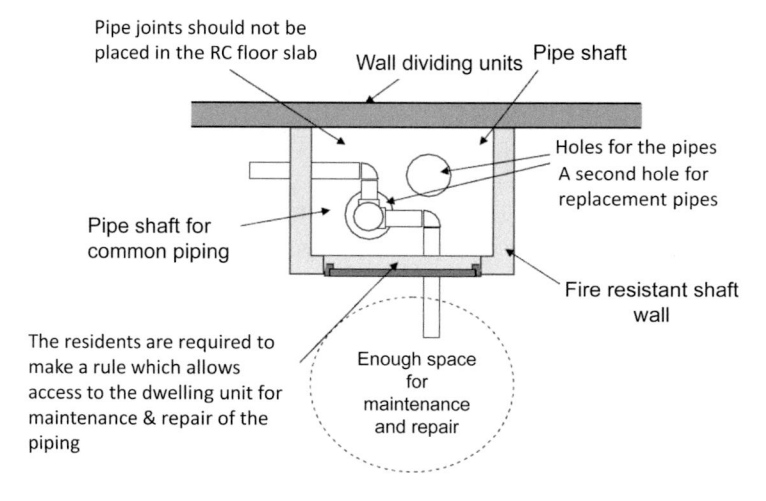

Figure 8.4
The requirements for piping space in a private condominium dwelling

Figure 8.5
Movable kitchen system

to modify the layout of a dwelling, the floor slabs of a condominium must ensure at least a vertical clear distance of 2,650 mm (8.7 ft).

Chapter 5.   Universal design for the elderly and handicapped
Chapter 6.   Energy efficiency; energy conservation
Chapter 7.   Floor space for each unit
Chapter 8.   Living environment
Chapter 9.   Long-term maintenance planning

- Elements necessary for structural resistance
- Parts which prevent the infiltration of rainwater, and
- Water supply and water drainage systems.

The inspection details and periods for the above items must be contained in the maintenance plans. Inspections must be performed at least once every ten years.

Appendix: documentation and house records

Clients can apply for tax reductions and can receive subsidies by designing and building houses or condominium projects which comply with the new law and technical guidelines. Specific incentive measures have been implemented. When a person has purchased or constructed and occupied long-life-span superior housing, the person is exempt from income tax, receiving an income tax exemption. The fixed asset tax is reduced by 50% for two years longer than in the case of ordinary housing which is five years for a dwelling unit.

The government at first attempted to establish the technical guidelines that require the base building piping space to be placed facing along common corridors because they understood why this would benefit the long-term adaptability of the large residential buildings, but the large developers which have a strong political power pointed out that the new guideline may reduce their design freedom and reduce the sales prices. They thus required the alternative, which is a rule that will allow maintenance staff to enter each dwelling unit in case of maintenance and repair. The political power of the developers is strong, increasing the difficulties of implementing the Open Building approach. But specialists and government officials are trying to reach the goals of Open Building implementation even if it takes time.

Recent technical developments for the future of housing in Japan

Research and development continue to improve the adaptability of multi-family dwellings and enable residents to continue living in their homes for a longer period of time. Efforts continue to be made to prolong their useful lifetimes by considering environmental and resource problems and economic efficiency. Several key developments are outlined below.

Relocatable kitchen and movable partitions

A number of recent technical innovations show the potential for even greater capacity for change in both the new and existing housing stock. In 2016, Mitsui Real Estate sold apartments in Akabane-nishi in Tokyo, in which storage units dividing rooms can be installed and moved by residents in the same manner as furniture. Although bathrooms are fixed, the remaining space is free for the residents to plan. The idea of the movable partition and storage is basically the same as the KEP infill system. The ceiling inside the room is flat and no columns or beams protrude into the rooms, so the movable storage walls can be installed anywhere without limitations. The entire dwelling unit has a double or raised floor and double or dropped ceiling. The height of the double floor is 130 millimeters (5.2") and the double ceiling is from 120 to 140 millimeters (4.75–5.5") thick. This space is used to install equipment, wiring and piping. The kitchens can be relocated to any of seven optional positions including in the center of the apartment by preinstalling the gray water pipes under the raised floor. The wheels under the kitchen units allow them to be relocated in seven alternative places in the room. There are three conduits under the floor to connect piping and wiring. The cook top exhaust hood on the counter draws away cooking smells and returns cleaned air back to the apartments. The author visited the units and found some of the families move the movable storage walls once in a while to easily make a temporary bedroom for their guests (see Figure 8.5).

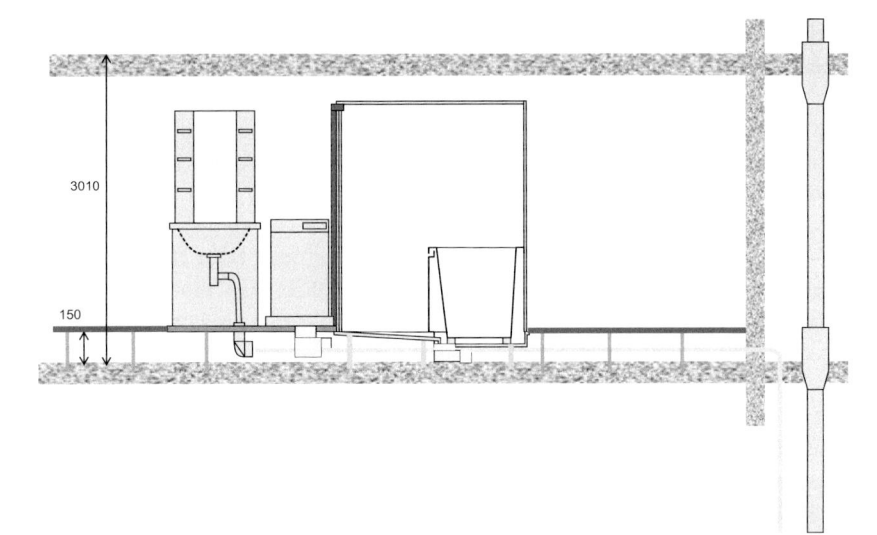

Figure 8.6
Diagram of zero-slope drainage system

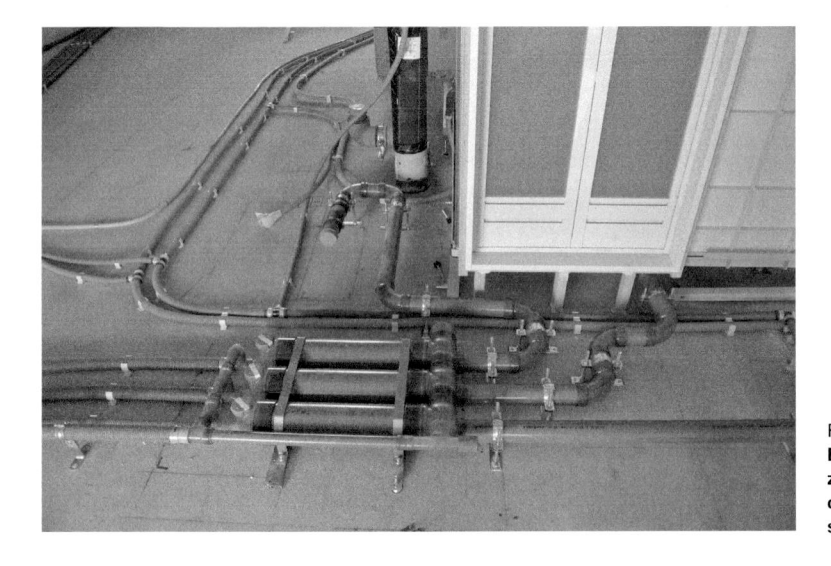

Figure 8.7
Example of zero-slope drainage system

Zero slope gray water drainage pipe

Three companies – Nomura Real Estate, the Haseko Corporation and Bridgestone – have developed a zero-slope grey-water drainage system to permit flexible positioning of apartment kitchens and have already sold an apartment in Mitaka, Tokyo in March 2018 followed by several different types of projects. The three companies have continued their R&D and applied their newly developed zero-slope drainage for the bathrooms and washing machines in the new apartment for the workers of Bridgestone company in

Totsuka, Kanagawa prefecture which was finished in March 2019. In the zero-slope siphonic drainage system, grey-water pipes run horizontally, allowing a much greater range of locations for bathrooms and kitchens. Traditional drainage pipes are larger in diameter and require slopes, taking more sub-floor space and restricting spaces for kitchens and bathrooms to be located close to vertical pipe shafts. This system does not apply to black-water or toilet drainage (Figures 8.6, 8.7).

The vertical clear space between floor slabs of each floor of the project referred to is 3020 mm (9'9") which is a bit higher than that of ordinary Haseko housing which is 2970 or 2920 mm (9'3"–9'7"). The inside diameter of the zero slope pipes is about 20 mm (3/4") and pipes are installed under the raised floor whose free space is about 150 mm (6"). The finished floor is thus 200 mm (8") above the structural floor slab which is 200 mm (8") thick. The raised floor system (one of many on the market) is made of low-cost material such as plywood panels supported by adjustable steel posts and hard rubber "feet." The rubber feet absorb the sound and vibration. In contrast to the gray-water pipes which could be located freely in a unit, the black-water (sewage) pipe is located at a fixed place in the middle of a unit. In their early stage of R&D, three companies used the kitchen garbage grinder to manage kitchen waste but now they do not use this. Instead they use a filter to separate kitchen wastes.

Developers tend to reduce the height of apartment ceilings to minimize the cost of construction. Also, there are regulations to control the maximum height of buildings in residential areas. From this point of view, reducing the height of apartments by only 50 mm (2") is important for the developers.

In Japan, we have a large number of old housing units which need to be cleared out and renovated. Almost all of them have limited floor heights. This new technology enables layout of pipes to be freely deployed, helping us to renovate those existing apartments.

The Urban Renaissance Agency (UR) owns more than 700,000 units of housing needing refurbishment. They are therefore exploring many experiments for renewal of this housing stock. They deployed an infill refurbishing test project called "Rakuinkyo" in existing condominiums for home-based care for the elderly residents. In recent years, UR worked together with IKEA and MUJI to refurbish some units. The attempts to invite new residents to old housing with less skilled labor works are now an important topic for their research. (See Chapter 11 for further discussion on this topic.)

Strategy for future technical developments and innovation for the building industry

The construction industry in Japan is currently facing a severe shortage of skilled workers, and thus improving productivity is a pressing issue. So far, the construction and housing industry in Japan has been improving productivity through innovative refinements to construction methods, in both reinforced concrete as well as conventional wooden structures. The construction industry, which has overcome numerous ordeals, including oil shocks and the collapse of Japan's bubble economy, will likely overcome this shortage of workers to a great extent through application of robotics, IT (Information Technology) and AI (Artificial Intelligence).

Robotic systems for pulling and lifting construction materials have already been introduced in order to reduce the burden of on-site operations on aging workers as well as to improve productivity. Tests have also been conducted on tasking robotic systems with cleaning operations so that workers can focus exclusively on on-site operations during the day. In the near future, it may be possible for workers to commence operations from first thing in the morning thanks to robotic systems conducting cleaning operations at night.

The efforts of individual companies and on-site initiatives alone will be insufficient for achieving significant improvements in productivity, however. It is vital for the industry to engage the issue collectively. When personnel related to the construction industry were interviewed, personnel in both Design Divisions and Construction Divisions said that, although the in-house inspections, client inspections and government inspections conducted at each stage throughout the construction process are necessary in ensuring construction quality, these inspections are a major time burden. In order to make inspection operations more advanced and streamlined, future developments may be in areas such as laser-based measurements, image recognition technology-based inspections, drone-based layout inspections and photography for construction records. Attaching RFIDs (Radio Frequency Identifiers) to construction materials and architectural parts will likely accelerate on-site confirmation and provide greater accuracy and may also facilitate confirmation of concealed areas.

Government agencies also likely need to examine ways to streamline various inspection operations for the purpose of improving the productivity of the industry as a whole. For example, in the future, the ratio of existing structures that undergo repair will increase, which means that forming databases and disclosing information on previous building approvals so that clients and designers can clearly determine whether to make use of an existing structure or to rebuild during the initial stages of operational planning will likely lead to smoother project progression and increased productivity.

Utilization of BIM (Building Information Modeling) is expected to improve productivity. Initiatives are progressing with regard to building approvals that utilize BIM, such as standardizing expressions used in drawings and specifications for applications. In the near future, in addition to ensuring consistency between design drawings and application drawings, automatic confirmation will also be conducted for both stand-alone and group regulations relating to various types of area calculations, physical dividers to prevent the spread of fires, fire prevention equipment, measurements of evacuation distances, etc. And this is likely to greatly reduce the amount of time necessary for building approvals and for receiving consent from fire departments. Eventually, legal compliance will be automatically checked starting from the basic design stage, and this will likely eliminate the need to redo operations.

With regard to factory-produced housing or major subsystems, application of type certification and manufacturer certification systems will streamline building approvals and also simplify on-site inspections. In the field of factory-produced housing, which has been increasingly componentized for some time already, unique CAD systems have been introduced for design, production and construction, so engaging in building approvals that utilize BIM based on these systems will likely be easier than for other general structures. This may also serve as a basis for entire infill or fit-out product services and the companies delivering these services to be granted certification.

So far, growth of the Japanese economy has been supported by initiatives in which industry, academia and the government are in close cooperation. In terms of technology, further developing the housing and construction industries in Japan, which are already highly advanced, will require not only technological development and technological innovations but also restructuring of social systems to produce new value. It is clear that, in the future as well, the key to promoting social system reforms and technological innovations in an integrated and effective way will be cooperation between government sectors in charge of policy and private sectors in charge of research and technological development – in other words, the promotion of open innovation in cooperation between industry, academia, various levels of government and civil society entities as well.

Conclusions

Technological developments in the construction and housing industries in Japan during the 1970s and 1980s were promoted through participation by major companies in national technology development projects under government leadership, and these produced results. However, in terms of technological development currently in progress, it is necessary to cooperate with start-up companies in fields other than the construction industry that possess advanced technologies, including IT and robotics. In particular, it is necessary to proceed in a different way than before, including in relation to the state of government subsidies for research and development, etc. In addition, in regard to the ideal state of construction production in the future, it would be preferable to construct a vision, and research and development initiatives, that can be shared by society as a whole.

The concept of Open Building, which preserves a building stock by designing it to adapt to change, is at the heart of housing solutions for

Japan's future. Promoting longevity is one way to reduce the future burden on a declining workforce. But, aligned with this, Japan also needs to compensate for its coming labor shortage by developing techniques so that fewer construction skills are required for those new buildings that do need to be constructed and renovated. The author thinks it is becoming more important to design and construct buildings which require less skilled labor. The configuration of structural elements must be simple. It is not easy to develop robots that can work at construction sites, so simple structures which robots can work with would be welcome. At the same time, the infill (fit-out) of those buildings needs to be simple like furniture, easy to install on site, and easy to replace, including by residents. The concept of Open Building, which focuses on adaptability with time, will play an important role for housing in Japan's future.

Acknowledgments

The author would like to express deep gratitude to all of the researchers who provided advice regarding the writing of this chapter.

References

A Quick Look at Housing in Japan (2018). The Building Center of Japan, June 2018.

Century Housing System Guidebook (1997). Century Housing System Promotion Council, March 1997.

Ministry of Land, Infrastructure, Transport and Tourism (MLIT) (2020a). Available at: www.mlit.go.jp/report/press/house04_hh_000945.html (accessed July 8, 2020).

Ministry of Land, Infrastructure, Transport and Tourism (MLIT) (2020b). Available at: www.mlit.go.jp/jutakukentiku/house/jutakukentiku_house_tk4_000168.html (accessed October 10, 2020).

Osaka Gas Co., NEXT21 (2019). Available at: www.osakagas.co.jp/company/efforts/next21/ (Accessed December 27, 2019).

SD25 (1994). Special issue NEXT21, Tokyo: Kajima Institute Publishing Company (in Japanese).

The work of John Habraken and the SAR design methods. *Toshi-Jutaku*, September 1972, pp. 8–52. Kajima Institute Publishing Co. Ltd., Tokyo.

Other sources

Minami, Kazunobu (2019). Innovative technologies for sustainable and adaptable housing. *Proceedings: Constructing Smart Cities*, June 17–20, 2019, International Council for Research and Innovation in Building and Construction (CIB) World Building Congress 2019, Hong Kong Polytechnic University.

Minami, Kazunobu (2017). Japanese innovation in adaptable homes. In A. Lifschutz, ed., *Loose-Fit Architecture: Designing Buildings for Change AD*, pp. 38–45. Oxford: John Wiley & Sons.

NEXT21 (2005). All about the NEXT21 project: Ex-knowledge. (in Japanese)

Osaka Gas Co. (2017). Future report experiment with and verify the neo-futuristic residential complex: What is NEXT21? (in English). October 2017.

Skeleton Infill (S/I) (2005). *Housing: Data File of Architectural Design and Detail 101*. Kenchiku Shiryo Kenkyusya (in Japanese).

Chapter 9

Research, development and implementation of long-life sustainable housing in China

Liu Dongwei and Wu Zhichao

Future sustainable housing in China

The concept of sustainable development appeared in the middle and late 20th century after human beings witnessed the negative consequences of the industrial revolution and the transformation of the market economy. These included the impact of these forces on global population, resources and environment, and the severe damage and threat to the natural environment on which human life depends for its survival. In the 21st century, building a sustainable society has become a general trend, having both technical and socio-political dimensions. In this regard, the development and construction pattern of housing, one of the vital factors of a sustainable society, puts forward not only new requirements for current construction concepts and construction technology, but higher goals for the means of construction and the full life cycle of buildings. This has completely changed the mode of traditional industry thinking as well as design, production and construction patterns (Qing and Qiuyuan, 2008). Currently, China's housing construction and real estate industry are facing several transformation and development issues that need to be addressed urgently in light of these new forces.

The crisis in urban and rural living environments and sustainable housing

With rapidly accelerating urbanization, the environmental problems caused by large-scale construction and over-development of housing are becoming increasingly evident. Hindered by the long-term traditional production mode, China's construction industry gives rise to high energy consumption, high pollution and high waste, destroying the harmonious relationship between man and nature. The analysis and research on the full life cycle of architecture show that their energy consumption and environmental impact are manifested on the one hand in the process of production and construction, and on the other hand in use and maintenance. Such decades-long impacts have severely affected the living environment of urban and rural areas at the

DOI: 10.4324/9781003018339-11

level of entire communities, as well as residential buildings and individual residences. This has become a bottleneck restricting the sustainable development of China's construction industry and social economy.

Demolition and rebuilding of real estate development and the service life of housing

The design service life of ordinary buildings and housing in China is 50 years, but the average service life of actual housing is only 30–40 years. This is far lower than that of developed countries. The short-lived housing is related to social and economic reasons such as ideology and short-term interests, as well as reasons of construction and living such as inadequate structural safety and poor quality, an aging building stock, changes of use and user preferences, and poor maintenance. Current cycles of demolition and rebuilding produces an annual loss of wealth of nearly RMB1 trillion ($154 billion). Therefore, prolonging the service life of buildings may not only solve the existing housing problems and future housing development in our country, but realize the transformation of construction from resource consumption to asset sustainability.

Construction technology, industrialization, housing design and construction quality

At present, China's construction industry is dominated by traditional production and construction methods. These have brought about a number of problems. These include a low level of factory-based production and industrialization, expensive construction methods, insufficient technological innovation, shortage of skilled workers, hidden dangers in construction safety and quality, etc. Why? The relevant design and construction systems for harnessing the power of industrial production methods in support of modern construction have not yet been fully established in China. This has resulted in a low degree of integration of production and construction technology, and a shortage of quality control technology, as well as shortages in the production and supply of advanced building components. In this regard, housing construction should focus on innovation in construction and production methods and the upgrading of the construction industry generally, to reduce dependence on and overcome the constraints of traditional ways of working. This will be the basis for a needed shift from traditional manual "construction" to harnessing modern industry "manufacturing" in new ways, in the modernization of the construction industry.

Supply, quality and long-term maintenance and renewal of housing

Currently, housing products in China leave much to be desired, such as low performance, environmental, economic and safety performance standards and poor durability.[1] In terms of daily living, housing is plagued by peeling walls, toilet water leakage and smells, poor sound insulation, poor indoor air quality, insufficient storage space and inconvenience for the elderly. Due to outdated design and construction thinking and technical means, housing can hardly be transformed to meet the future needs upon completion, which is not conducive to the maintenance and renewal of equipment and the various installations (pipes, wires and ducts). As the real estate industry in China is entering the era of incremental building stock reactivation, we should review housing supply methods from the perspective of sustainable development and construction. This will enable us to build housing that serves as long-term assets for society and as long-term values for residents leading to a future-oriented living environment.

Building standards and construction research of long-life sustainable housing

In light of the development of international sustainable construction methods and new concepts of housing technology, the theories of "Open Building"[2] represented by European countries and Skeleton and Infill Housing ("SI")[3] represented by Japan, have evolved continuously (see other chapters in this book), and their design methods, building systems and technical practices have also made great progress (Hideichi and Shinichi, 2006). Based on the current social and economic development requirements and the need for modernization of the construction industry in China and building on the theory and practice of Open Building and SI housing, efforts are urgently needed to explore these new construction supply models in the Chinese context. This needs to be undertaken with the background of the modernization of the construction industry, "green" and sustainable construction systems, and the promotion of research and development in housing systems integration. We expect the results will boost the transformation and upgrading of the production and construction methods of China's construction industry and speed the transformation of housing construction methods.

Establishment and development of long-life sustainable housing

In 2010, at the China–Japan Long-life Sustainable Housing International Summit Forum, the China Real Estate Association launched the *Initiative to Build Long-life Sustainable Housing* for the whole society. On May 18, 2012, the China Real Estate Association and the Japan–China Association for Building and Housing Industry jointly signed the Letter of Intent for Cooperation in the Construction of China–Japan Housing Demonstration Projects. Both sides reached an agreement to promote further exchanges and cooperation in the development of demonstration projects between China and Japan. They proposed to build a new type of "Chinese Long-life Sustainable Housing" featuring long life, high quality, and low energy consumption. The means to achieve this goal was to harness the power of industrial production in the support of new methods of construction. The China Institute of Building

Standard Design & Research of China Construction Technology Consulting (CCTC) was entrusted to conduct organizational and management research, technology research and development, and to design and implement demonstration projects. A number of contracts were agreed to, to carry out the first series of demonstration projects. In 2014, the first long-life sustainable housing demonstration project, Greenland · Nanxiang William Mansion, was completed. It attracted wide acclaim from the whole industry and society. The second series of demonstration projects were completed in 2015 and the third in 2017. By the end of 2019, the total construction area of the national demonstration projects has reached over 1 million m² (10.8 million ft²) (Tables 9.1 and 9.2). Long-life sustainable housing has led the transformation and upgrading of China's contemporary new housing construction methods with new concepts, new models, new standards and new systems. These advances are helping to solve the bottleneck of China's urban and rural living environment construction and realize the future-oriented green and sustainable development construction by breaking through the barriers of China's long-standing traditional production and construction methods (Figure 9.1) (LIU, 2018).

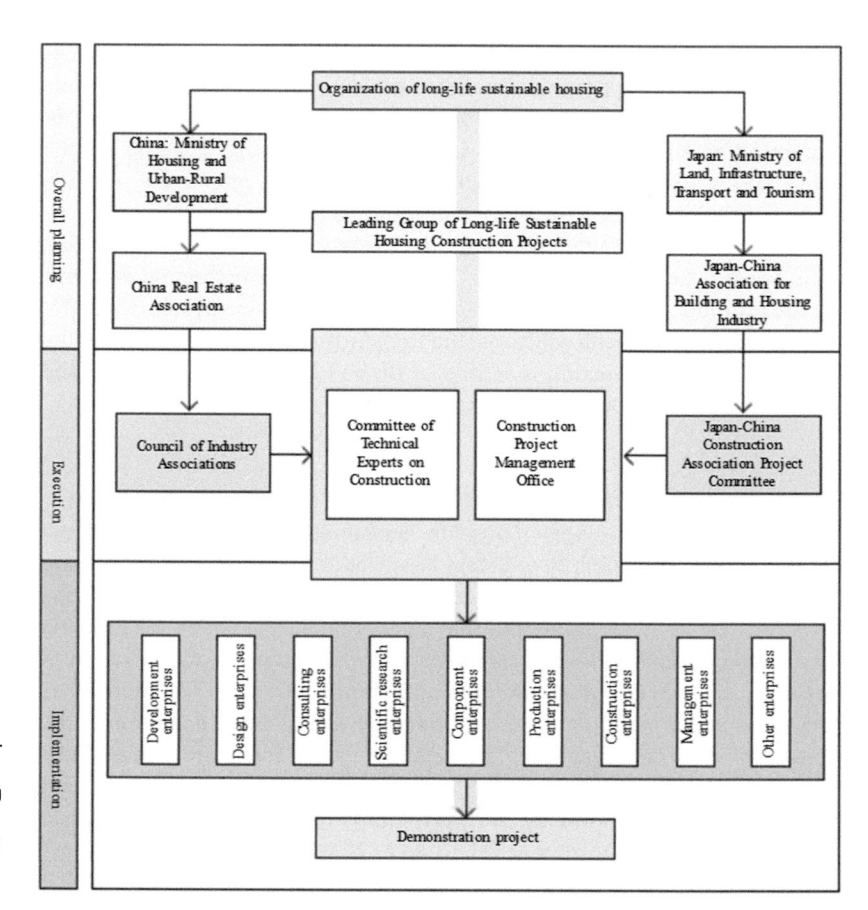

Figure 9.1 Implementation and management mechanism of China's long-life sustainable housing demonstration projects (drawing by the author)

Theories, methods and construction models of long-life sustainable housing

Based on international sustainable building theories, housing design and construction methods, the Open Building approach uniquely brings building problems into a broader social, economic and living environment system. It does so through recognition of a hierarchical organization of built environment, represented by, for example, the idea that the 500-year urban fabric sets the stage for 100-year buildings, and buildings set the stage for the 30-year infill or fit-out systems for independent dwellings (Kendall and Teicher, 2000). Tasks are separated according to life-cycle patterns, rather than being consolidated or unified.

Advances in Japan's building construction and its general building methods in the last 30 years have led the world's building industrialization. There, a series of experiments were implemented, starting with the KEP system,[4] which solved the problems of housing industrialization technology and residential adaptability with the idea of rationalization of construction production. This was followed by NPS,[5] which is characterized by a standard design system, providing residents with a different set of general housing designs; CHS,[6] a basic achievement of sustainable housing based on variable life-cycle of building elements; and KSI, a symbolic achievement of sustainable housing in Japan (Urban Renaissance Agency, 2005).[7] On this basis, Japan carried out a range of sustainable housing construction projects at the end of the 20th century, such as "environment-symbiotic housing" and "resource recycling housing." The Japanese government put forward the concept of "200-year housing,"[8] enacted it in a law in 2008 and began implementing it in 2009, offering incentives for construction of long-life housing[9] based on the SI housing system (Technical Explanation of the Long-term Good Housing Accreditation Benchmark, 2008). (Editor's note: These are discussed in more detail in Chapter 8).

China's long-life sustainable housing is based on the green and sustainable concept and methods of Open Building and SI housing as developed over many years in Japan. It focuses on China's construction status and housing supply mode and proposes a new housing construction and product supply method for the future. New projects will be carried out to achieve long life, excellent quality, low carbon footprint of buildings and living environments with long-term value at less cost now and in the future (see Figure 9.2) (Liu, 2015).

Figure 9.2
Construction method and housing system of long-life sustainable housing (drawing by the author)

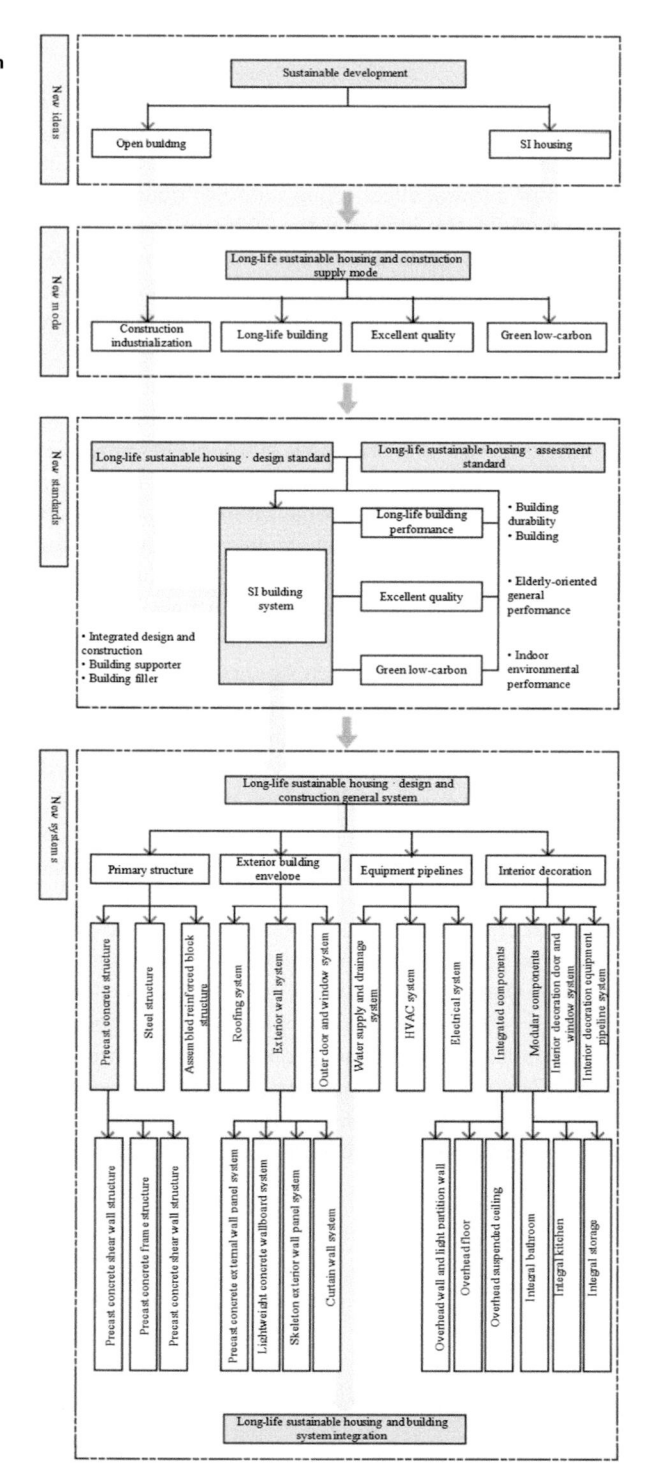

Design and assessment standard of long-life sustainable housing

After a 10-year period of development of long-life sustainable housing, the Design and Assessment Standard for Long-life Sustainable Housing (hereinafter referred to as the "Standard") was implemented on August 1, 2018. The Standard, led by the China Association for Engineering Construction Standardization and China Real Estate Association, was prepared by the China Institute of Building Standard Design & Research. It identifies 60 steps in the building industry supply chain. The Standard defines the basic concept of long-life sustainable housing and lays out the needed design and assessment standards. This will guide the research and development, practice, design and construction of long-life sustainable housing in China in the future (Figure 9.3).

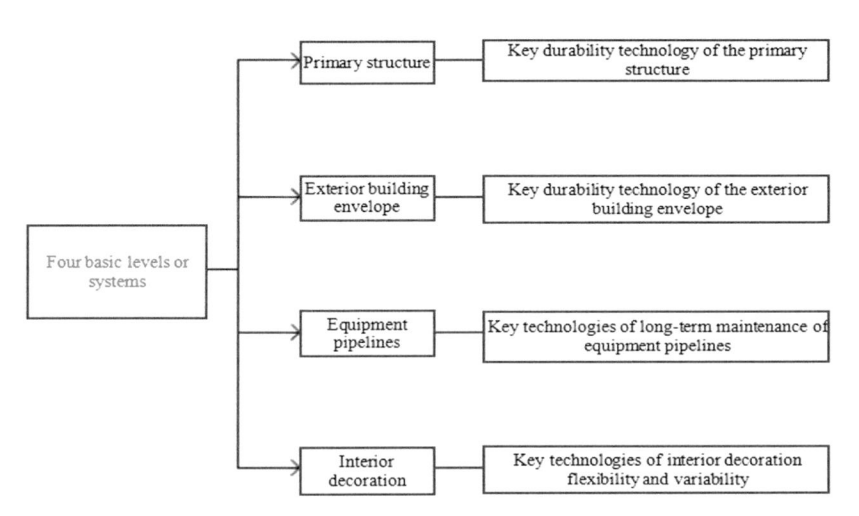

Figure 9.3
Four basic system levels of long-life building design and construction (drawing by the author)

Guided by S/I and Open Building methods, the coordination of the design and construction of the primary structure, exterior building envelope, installation pathways and interior decoration (infill) is being realized (see Figure 9.4). This is also reflected in the coordination of architectural, structural, MEP (mechanical, electrical and plumbing) and interior fit-out specialists; as well as the whole process of overall planning, design, production, construction, operation and maintenance.

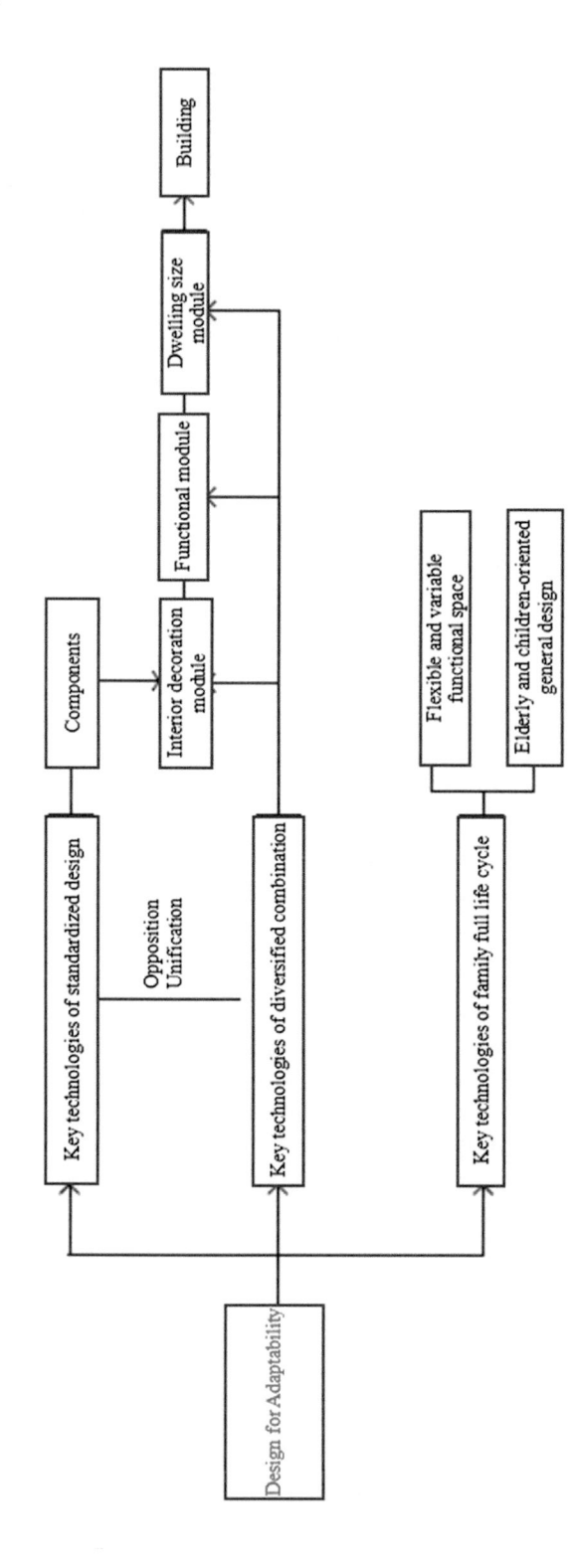

Figure 9.4
Design for adaptability (drawing by the author)

Building systems, design and construction of long-life sustainable housing

Design for durability and long-term adaptation

Long-life sustainable housing puts forward two distinct but complementary goals: the extended physical life and the functional life of buildings. The former is aimed at the primary structure of buildings (common to all inhabitants), while the latter focuses on whether the functional use of buildings meets the changing residential occupancy needs. This suggests two separate design tasks. The technical strategy is to reasonably prolong the physical life of each system while facilitating changing functions and layouts of units in future use. Especially for the durability of the primary structure, efforts should be made to maintain the strength of the building structure to prolong its service life. As for the research and development of key technology for durability of the exterior building envelope, thermal insulation performance should be improved to ensure energy conservation of indoor cooling and heating through passive technologies (see Figure 9.5, Table 9.1).

The adaptability of long-life sustainable housing means that the primary structure remains unchanged but offers the capacity for a variety of interior layouts to meet the changing needs of diverse family structures and lifestyles (see Table 9.2). This approach includes standardization of key façade technologies. The approach adopts standardized components for the interior equipment, installations and decoration. On this basis, different combinations are made to form diversified finished dwellings. In light of the possibility of changes of future residents, the research and development of elderly and children-oriented dwelling sizes are being carried out.

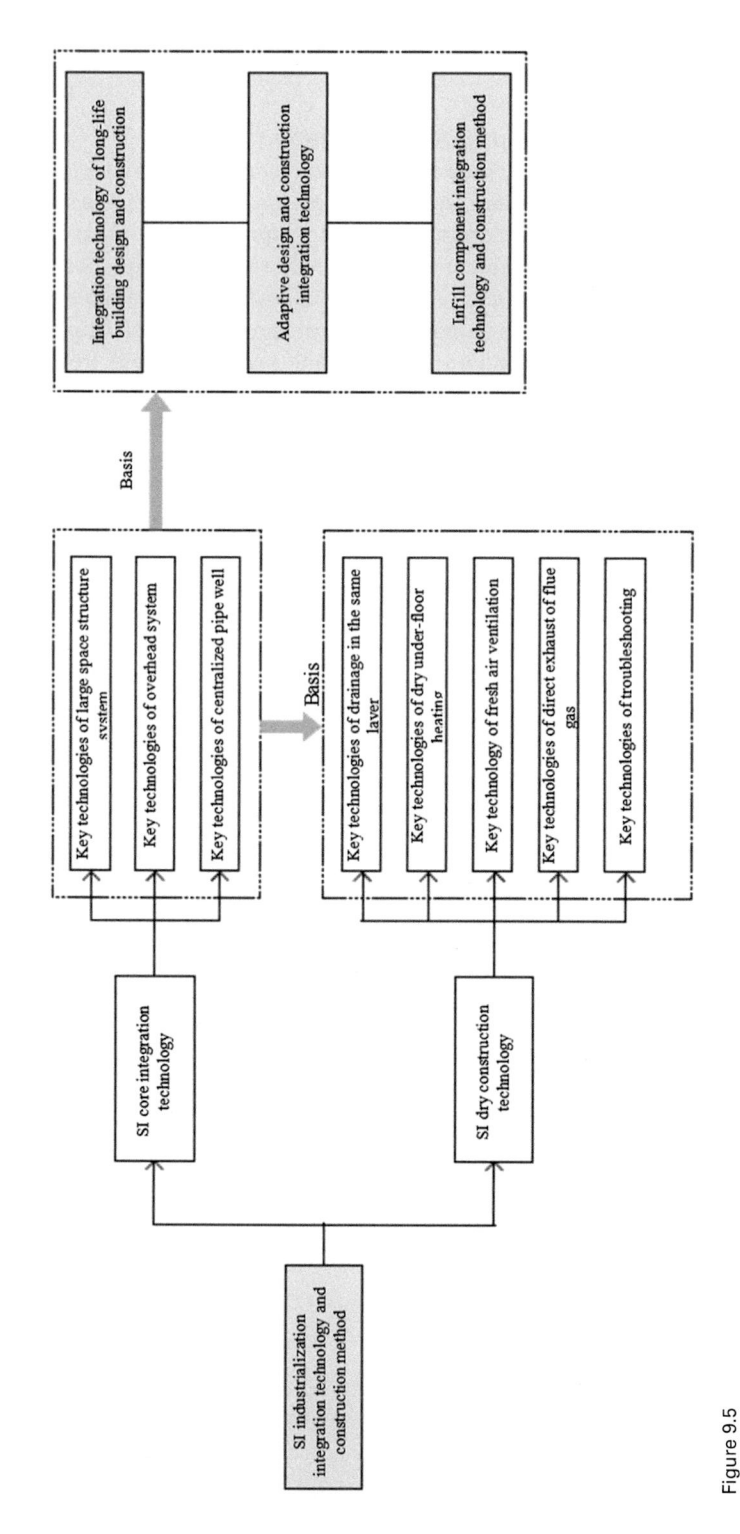

Figure 9.5
SI Industrialization integration system and construction technology (drawing by the author)

Table 9.1 Development, exchange and practice of related research of long-life sustainable housing

Establishment and development	Scientific research	Technical exchange	Demonstration project
The 11th Five-Year Plans for Economic and Social Development (2006–2010) Establishment and Exploration of Long-life Sustainable Housing	• 2006 National 11th Five-Year Science and Technology Support Program Topic, Key Technologies of Green Building Life Cycle Design: Yashi Alloy Apartment Demonstration Project • China–Japan Cooperation Technology Integration System • 2008 Ministry of Housing and Construction "China–Japan JICA Housing Cooperation Research" 20th Anniversary Japan SI Technology Research, International Sustainable Housing Research • LC (Lifecycle Housing System) Industrialized Housing System	• 2006 2nd China–Japan Housing Technology Exchange Meeting (Kunshan, China) • 2008 3rd China–Japan Housing Technology Exchange Meeting (Tokyo, Japan) 2008 China–Japan Technology Integrated Housing • The 8th China International Housing Industry Expo 2009: Theme Demonstration Exhibition "Tomorrow's Housing No.1": Sustainable Living Concept of "Long-life Sustainable ·Housing" – Beijing · Yashi Alloy Apartment as Prototype • The 1st China Real Estate Science Development Forum: Improving Housing Quality and Service Life	2006 China–Japan cooperation Beijing·Yashi Alloy Apartment Technology Integration Project
	• The Ministry of Housing and Construction prepared the Technical Guideline for Construction of China-Skeleton-Infill Housing in 2010 • Design Specification for Prefabricated Housing (industrial standard) was approved (i.e. Standard for Design of Assembled Housing JGJ/T398-2017)	• The 2010 China–Japan Long-life Sustainable Housing Summit Forum (Hangzhou, China) put forward the initiative of "Building Long-life Sustainable Housing" • The 9th China International Housing Industry Expo: Theme Demonstration Exhibition "Tomorrow's Housing No.2"	2010 China–Japan cooperation Beijing Summit Photosynthetic Grove Technology Integration Project
The 12th Five-Year Plans for Economic and Social Development (2011–2015) Research and Development and Practice of Long-life Sustainable Housing	2011 National 12th Five-Year Science and Technology Support Program Project, Research and Demonstration of Key Technologies of Industrial Design and Construction of Security Housing • The Ministry of Housing and Construction published the Excellent Public Rental Housing Design Schemes • China–Japan Cooperation in Standardization and Components Research and Development of Public Rental Housing • The Public Rental Housing Industrialization Practice was published	• The 10th China International Housing Industry Expo 2011 • Research on the Trend of China's Housing Design and Technology	2011

(continued)

Table 9.1 Cont.

Establishment and development	Scientific research	Technical exchange	Demonstration project
	• The Research on China's Long-life Sustainable Housing Assessment Index System was published in 2012 • The issue of housing industrialization in the Architectural Journal was published • Residential Buildings for the Elderly Atlas (national standard) • Research and Development of Elderly-Oriented Components	• 2012 China–Japan Housing Industry Conference: China Real Estate Association and Japan–China Association for Building and Housing Industry jointly signed the Letter of Intent for Cooperation in the Construction of China–Japan Housing Demonstration Projects, and the first batch of long-life sustainable housing demonstration projects was signed. • China Forum on Sustainable Living and Housing Industrialization Technology Development (Beijing, China): Housing Construction and Quality Assurance • Research on Housing Industrialization in Japan, South Korea, Singapore, Taiwan and Hong Kong	2012 1st series: Shanghai • Greenland Shanghai Greenland Nanxiang William Mansion
	• The Ministry of Housing and Construction launched the Research on Modernized Architecture and Component Technology System of Construction Industry in 2013 • The CBS launched the Research on China's Long-life Sustainable Housing Technology System	• 2013 China Sustainable Living and Housing Industrialization Technology Forum (Beijing, China): Long-life and Elderly-Oriented Building • National Conference of the Ministry of Housing and Construction on the Construction of Affordable Housing	2013 1st series Zhejiang · Baoye Zhejiang Baoye Xinqiao Romance
	• The Research on Construction and Development of Green Affordable Housing-Research Report on Promoting Green Building Construction and Industrialization Practice of National Affordable Housing was published in2014 • The issue of housing interior decoration industrialization in the Architectural Journal was published • The Ministry of Housing and Construction issued the Green Guidelines for Public Housing • Shandong Province proposed to build long-life sustainable housing in the Opinions on Vigorously Promoting New Urbanization • The series SI Housing and Housing Construction Model was published	• The 6th China Real Estate Science Development Forum in 2014 (Tianjin, China): International Open Building • The 6th China–Japan Housing Technology Exchange Meeting (Shanghai, China) • Sino-European Seminar on Building Energy Efficiency Policies and Strategies: Standardization and Industrialization of Affordable Housing • The 13th China International Housing Industry Expo: "Tomorrow's Housing" First Interior Decoration Industrialization Show House-Shanghai Greenland Long-life Sustainable Housing as Prototype	2014 1st series Jiangsu • New City Jiangsu New City Dijing Residence

Table 9.1 Cont.

Establishment and development	Scientific research	Technical exchange	Demonstration project
	• Research on Open Building and Sustainable Housing in Europe and America • The 2nd China–US Real Estate Summit Forum (USA) • The Ministry of Housing and Construction issued the National Building Standard Design System for Modernization of Construction Industry in 2015. • Nine series of atlas including Design Examples of Prefabricated Concrete Structure Residential Buildings-Shear Wall Structure (National Standard), were released	• The 7th China Real Estate Science Development Forum 2015 (Tianjin, China): China Long-life Sustainable Housing Industry Alliance was established and the 2nd batch of long-life sustainable housing demonstration project was signed • China Open Building Keynote Speech at Zurich Open Building International Conference • China–Japan Fabricated Concrete Building Technology Exchange Meeting (Shanghai, China) • The 11th International Conference on Green and Energy-efficient Building: Interior Decoration Industrialization Show House	2015 2nd series Shandong • Luneng Shandong Luneng Lingxiucheng Park Shijia Beijing • Zarsion Beijing Fengkejian Zarsion Beijing • Strong Beijing Strong Qingtang Bay
The 13th Five-Year Plans for Economic and Social Development (2015–2020) Diversified Development of Long-life Sustainable Housing	• 2016 Long-life Sustainable Housing Project Selected as Science and Technology Innovation-Driven Assistance Engineering Demonstration Project of China Association for Science and Technology • The Ministry of Housing and Construction prepared the Outline for the Modernization of the Construction Industry • Shokoi Cuncao Learning and Knowledge Garden Project: Research and Development of SI System for Existing Buildings • The Prefabricated Architecture was published. • 2017 Long-life Sustainable Housing Project Selected as Science and Technology Innovation-Driven Assistance Engineering Demonstration Project of China Association for Science and Technology • Beijing Urban Master Plan (2016–2035) clearly states that the long-life sustainable housing standard will be established and promoted on a pilot basis by 2020, and the long-life sustainable housing standard will be fully implemented for new housing by 2035.	• The 8th China Real Estate Science Development Forum 2016 and 3rd China–US Real Estate Summit Forum (Changzhou, China): New Construction • International Forum on Open Building Development and Practice (Beijing, China) • The 7th China–Japan Housing Technology Exchange Meeting • The 1st International Forum on Industrialization Technology of Existing Residential Renovation (Beijing, China): Urban Renaissance Agency JSrelief • Research on Sustainable Housing in Northern Europe • The 9th China Real Estate Science Development Forum 2017 (Chengdu, China): The 3rd batch of long-life sustainable housing demonstration project was signed • The 15th China–Japan–Korea International Conference on Housing (Tokyo, Japan): Industrialized Construction System of Existing Buildings in Shokoi Cuncao Learning and Knowledge Garden • The 4th China–US Real Estate Summit Forum (USA)	2016 2nd series Shandong • Haier Shandong Haier Century Residence Tianjin • Real Estate Tianjin Real Estate Shengting Mingjing Garden

(*continued*)

Table 9.1 Cont.

Establishment and development	Scientific research	Technical exchange	Demonstration project

	• Standard for Design of Assembled Housing (industrial standard, JGJ/T398-2017) was released.
	• The Architectural Design Information Collection (3rd Edition)-Industrial Housing was published.
	• Industrial Design of Housing Interior Decoration-Integral Storage (national standard design, 17J509-1) was released
	• Comparative Study of International Sustainable Housing
		• The 18th National Congress of the Communist Party of China "Marching Ahead of Time" Large-scale Achievement Exhibition: Beijing Strong Qingtang Bay Public Rental Housing Selected
		• Innovation Achievements Exhibition of Central Enterprises: China Construction Technology Consulting (CCTC) proposed to build building featuring long-life building, industrial construction, green and low-carbon, and excellent quality; "Green · Technology · Livable" Show House
		• Interior decoration industrialization show house joined the Build Tech Asia in Singapore
			2017
			2nd series
			Beijing • Modernland
			Beijing Modernland
			  Xishan Shangpin Bay
			  Residence MOMA
			3rd batch
			Henan • Bi Yuan
			Henan Bi Yuan Rongfu

	• Design and Assessment Standard for Long-life Sustainable Houmsing (association standard, TCECS-CREA513-2018) was released in 2018 • Long-life Sustainable Housing-Research and Practice of Future-oriented Green and Sustainable Housing Construction in China was published • Graphic of the Standard for Design of Assembled Housing (national standard, 18J820) was released • Standard of Sustainable Residential Areas (association standard, T/CECS-CREA377-2018) was issued • Technical Standard for Residential Interior Assembly Decoration Engineering of Shanghai (DG/TJ08-2254-2018) was issued • Technical Regulations for Interior Assembled Decoration Engineering of Residential Buildings in Beijing (DB11T1553-2018) • The Architectural Discipline Development Report of the Architectural Society of China was published: Research on the Development Strategy of Architectural Industrialization	• The 10th China Real Estate Science Development Forum 2018 (Dalian, China): Release Ceremony of the Research and Practice Achievements of Long-life Sustainable Housing • China Real Estate Excellence Supply Chain Management Innovation Conference: Release of Long-life Sustainable Housing Components Supply and Acquisition Platform • The 9th China Living Environment Summit Forum (Jinjiang, China): Study on Green and Sustainable Housing • The 16th China–Japan–Korea International Conference on Housing: Future-oriented Sustainable Housing (Nanjing, China) • Hong Kong Open Building International Conference	2018 3rd series Beijing • Chengjian Beijing Chengjian Chaoqing Zhizhu

Table 9.1 Cont.

Establishment and development	Scientific research	Technical exchange	Demonstration project
	• 2019 Technical Standard for Prefabricated Interior Decoration (industry standard) (Draft for Approval) • The Code for Design of Urban Apartment Buildings (association standard) was launched • The Henan Provincial Commission of Housing and Urban-Rural Development launched the Henan Province Long-life Sustainable Housing Engineering Technical Standard • Regulations on the Implementation of Long-life Sustainable Housing Indicators in Beijing Housing Construction Plan (2020-2035) • Beijing Municipal Commission of Housing and Urban–Rural Development launched Research on Long-life Sustainable Housing Standards for Security Housing in 2020	• The 11th China Real Estate Science Development Forum 2019 (Shanghai, China): Green, Healthy, Smart and Livable • The 18th China International Housing Industry and Construction Industrialization Products and Equipment Expo: China Tomorrow's Housing 2019 Exhibition Area, Healthy and Smart Future Housing New Design Exhibition Area • The 2nd Forum on Win–Win Cross-Strait Cooperation in the Health Industry for the Aged (Taiwan)	2019 Declaration Xi'an • Jintai Xi'an Jintai Project 2020 Declaration Chongqing • Heyi Chongqing Heyi Project

Table 9.2 Technical strengths and durability of primary structure and exterior building envelope

	Items	Ordinary housing	Durability technology	Long-life sustainable housing
Primary structure	Thickness of concrete protective layer over steel reinforcing	15mm	Enhance the protection of the primary structure	Increased by 40%
	Concrete strength	C30	Increase compression resistance	C40
	Maximum chloride ion content in concrete	0.3%	Improve wear resistance	0.06%
Exterior building envelope	External shading	Rarely set	Increase thermal insulation performance of windows	Aluminum alloy roller shutter
	Balcony guardrail	Steel art	Improve corrosion resistance and durability	Aluminum alloy
	Insulation layer	Heat transfer coefficient of single insulation layer 1.2	Enhance thermal insulation performance of walls	Heat transfer coefficient of inner and outer double insulation layer 1.08

Note: The statistical data comes from Shanghai Greenland Long-life Sustainable Housing Demonstration Project; the heat transfer coefficient of thermal insulation layer is 1.2, which is the standard for the Shanghai area.

SI industrialization and interior decoration components for long-life sustainable housing

Both long-life technology and adaptive technology are based on the separation of design tasks basic to SI housing (support and infill), creating conditions for technical innovation through the coordination of large structural systems + infill systems + strategically placed pipe shafts. The SI housing principles are used as the method for coordinating the whole construction industry supply chain, thereby enhancing continuity, the development of the whole life cycle and the housing production and construction process and optimizing resources (Figures 9.6 and 9.7).

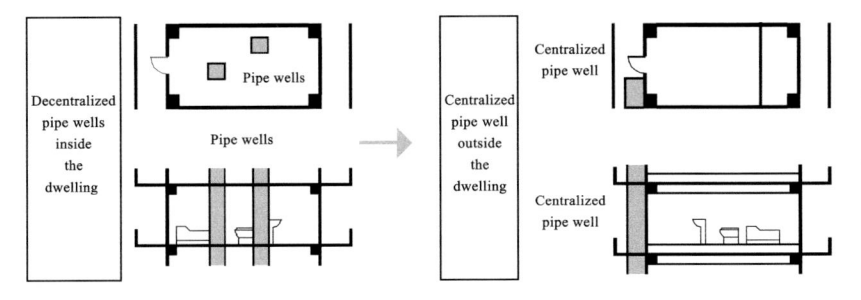

Figure 9.6
Centralized pipe shaft outside the dwelling (drawing by the author)

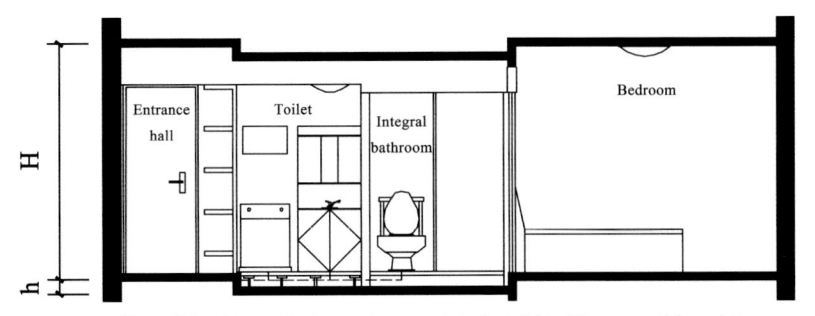

Figure 9.7
"Same floor" drainage (drawing by the author)

Note: H is subject to design requirements; h is the height of the recessed floor slab.

Same floor drainage mode-raised floor

The assembly technology of interior decoration components and the dry construction method of assembly include the key technologies of well-coordinated modular components. Compared with the decade-long or century-long service life of the primary structure, infill components see shorter replacement periods. Thus, their maintenance and replacement cannot affect the safety of the building structure. Furthermore, systematic assembly methods for interior decoration work may realize the fast and convenient replacement of components and enable daily inspection, maintenance and repair as well as long-term maintenance and repair (Figures 9.8–9.10).

Figure 9.8
**Under-floor
heating
system
(drawing by
the author)**

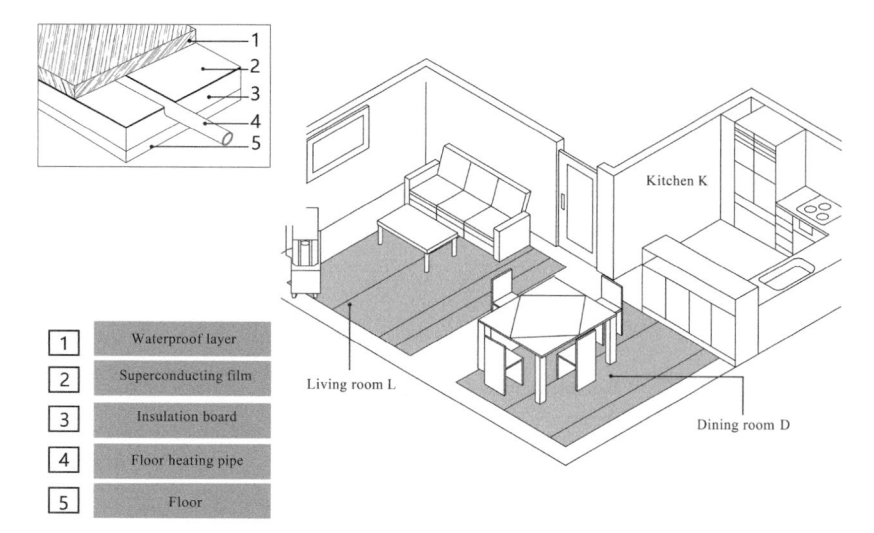

1	Waterproof layer
2	Superconducting film
3	Insulation board
4	Floor heating pipe
5	Floor

Figure 9.9
**Direct flue
gas dis-
charge
(drawing by
the author)**

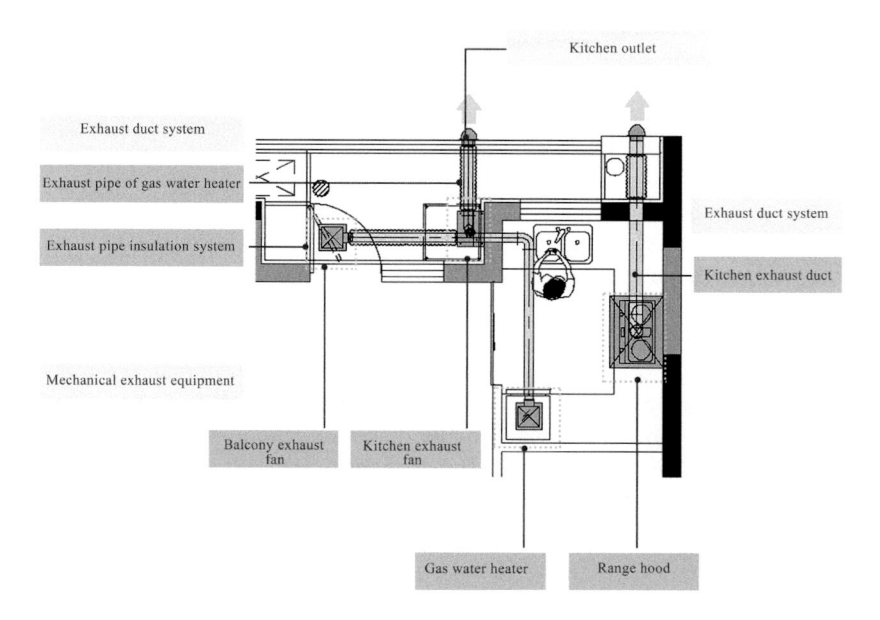

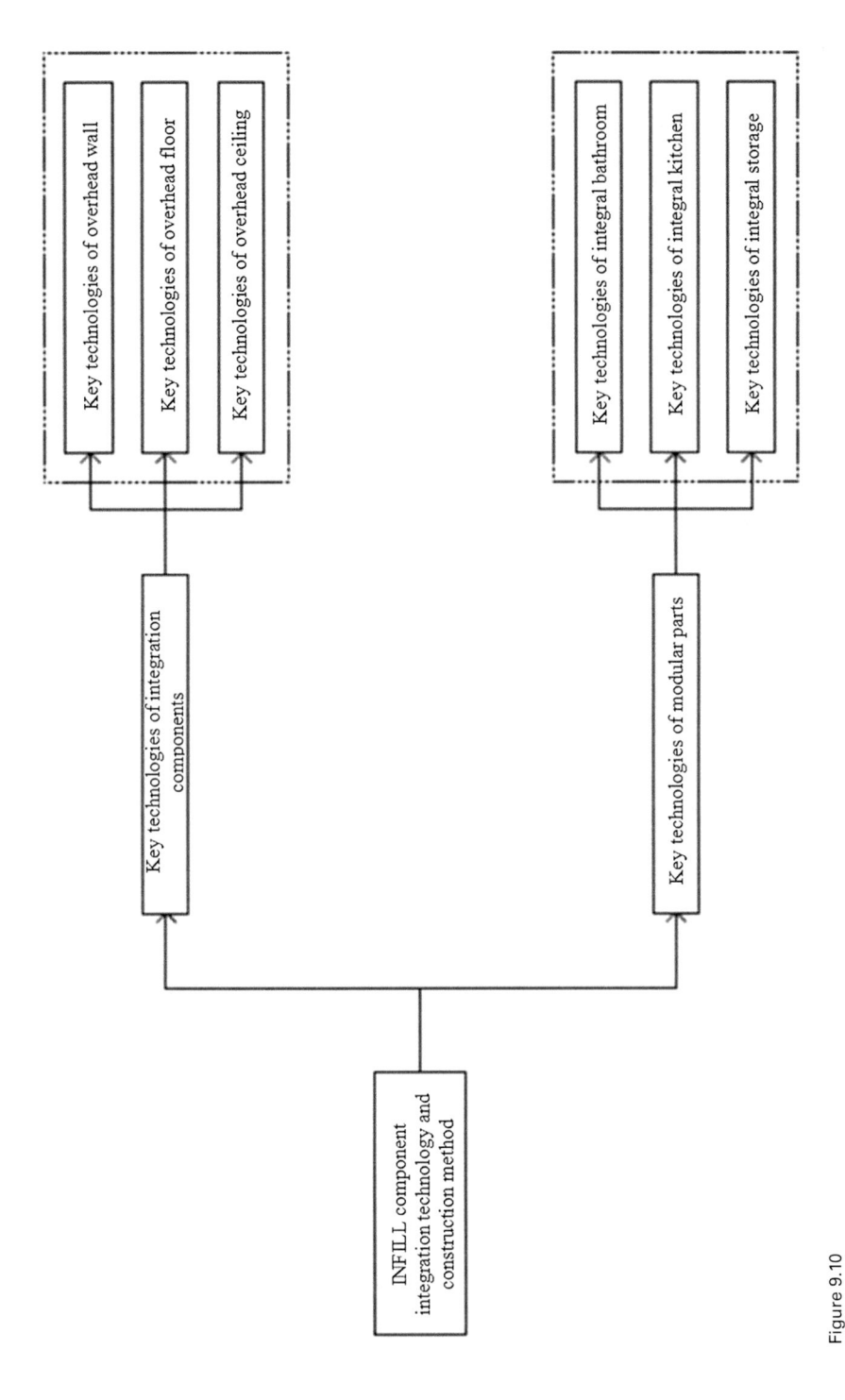

Figure 9.10
Interior decoration component assembly technology and construction method (drawing by the author)

The significance of long-life sustainable housing demonstration projects to innovation in the building industry

Overall solutions and innovative practices of the demonstration project

After a decade of development, our demonstration projects have adopted new ideas, new methods, new standards, new systems and technical innovations to build housing under the green and sustainable construction mode. These developments are central to promoting, transforming and upgrading the new housing production mode in the modernization of China's construction industry.

The research and practical results of the long-life sustainable housing demonstration projects include the following aspects based on the international Open Building and SI housing theories. The projects:

1. explored the green and sustainable mode of housing construction.
2. employed new housing construction and supply methods to realize long-term performance and value of the full life cycle of building, harnessing the power of industrialization, and high quality and low-carbon products.
3. established the sustainable housing system and top-level design principles, leading the new direction of housing construction in China.
4. supported by research and development of new building systems, provided an overall technical solution to meet the needs of future living environments.
5. used construction technology innovation in component prefabrication to improve the housing quality and living performance.
6. implemented technologies such as 'assembly-based interior decoration' and dry construction methods.
7. applied integrated information management technologies such as housing operation, maintenance and renovation performance.
8. explored management and quality assurance technology in the industry supply chain links such as design, production, construction, operation and maintenance in the whole construction and long-term renewal process.

Industry supply chain and technology promotion of demonstration projects

The long-life sustainable housing demonstration projects bring together domestic and foreign partners. These include architectural design companies, scientific research institutes, development enterprises, related building component and construction enterprises. Their work was to carry out interdisciplinary and cross-industry collaborative practice, promote the transformation and popularization of science and technology, and realize the comprehensive connection of industrial supply chains. The Long-life Sustainable Housing Industry Alliance takes leading real estate and brand leaders, including Greenland Group, Baoye Group, Future Land, Luneng Group, Tianjin Real Estate Group, Haier Real Estate Group, Zarsion Group, Strong, MOMA, Bi Yuan Group and Beijing Urban Construction Group, as the main entities for implementation. It is doing this in part using a series of "experience halls" and "show houses" as technical exchange windows (Figures 9.11–9.14).

Figure 9.11
Light gauge steel joist system for overhead ceiling (Shandong Luneng Long-life Sustainable Housing Demonstration Project) (photo by the author)

Figure 9.12
Piping separation in overhead ceiling (Shanghai Greenland Long-life Sustainable Housing Demonstration Project) (photo by the author)

Figure 9.13-1, 9.13-2 **Modular sanitary fixtures (Beijing Fengkejian Long-life Sustainable Housing Demonstration Project) (photos by the author)**

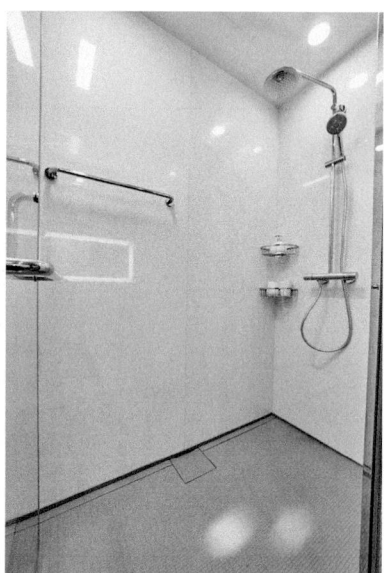

Figure 9.14 **Modular kitchen (Beijing Fengkejian Long-life Sustainable Housing Demonstration Project (photo by the author)**

Significance and value of demonstration projects to society, industry and the market

According to the national green development concept and strategy, efforts are now focused on several objectives:

1. To meet the people's demand from "having a house to live in" to "living in a good house."
2. Improve the quality level along the entire supply chain.
3. Reduce the negative impact on resources and on the environment.
4. Accelerate the transformation to a sustainable housing development model of practice.
5. Build high quality housing with long life, with green and low carbon characteristics, by harnessing industrial, scientific and technological innovation (Sun, 2018).

Long-life sustainable housing has explored a new housing construction and development path that conforms to the development of the times and pursues transformation. From a social point of view, the construction and promotion of long-life sustainable housing demonstration projects will boost upgrading of China's housing from resource consumption to asset sustainability, thereby enhancing social harmony, environmental protection and the sustainable development of the housing industry. From the perspective of the industry, the construction of long-life sustainable housing featuring good performance and energy and resource conservation is an urgent need for the transformation and upgrading of the industry and the improvement of housing quality (Liu, 2010). From the perspective of future demand, long-life sustainable housing, as a new type of building supply practice, is not only an innovative achievement in promoting housing construction under the background of social and economic transformation and modernization of the construction industry, but an excellent social asset left for future generations (Figure 9.15).

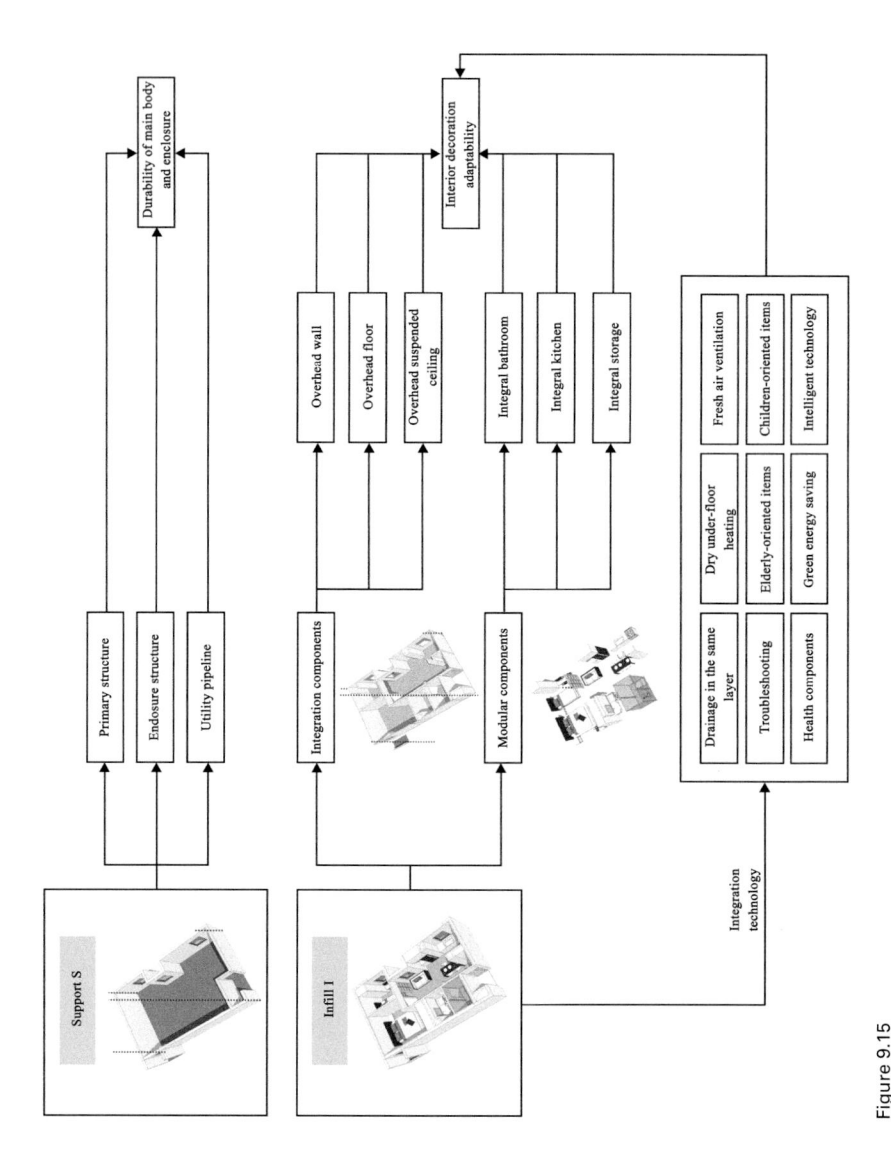

Figure 9.15
Technical solution for overall industrialization of long-life sustainable housing (Shandong Luneng Long-life Sustainable Housing Demonstration Project) (drawing by the author)

Sources

Figures and tables in this paper are made or compiled by the authors based on the research results and data of the research office where the authors work.

Notes

1 The Technical Standard for Performance Assessment of Residential Buildings (GB/T50362-2005) stipulates that housing performance is divided into five aspects: applicability performance, environmental performance, economic performance, safety performance and durability performance.
2 The Open Building approach is based on the architectural theory and method of Stitching Architecture Research (SAR) of the Netherlands in the 1960s. It is divided into three decision – making levels: urban tissue, base building and infill, which correspond to the public (society), collective (group) and private (individual) respectively. Its implementation separates the design of the base building (or support) from the design of the fit-out (or infill). As a systematic architectural methodology, the Open Building approach assures that large housing projects can last a long time while also responding to changing user and technical requirements.
3 SI housing is the important result of many years of research by Japan's Housing Development Plan for Creating Life Value (1994–2000). This large-scale technological research and development involving 40 companies started from the basic viewpoint of environmental resources and socio-economic sustainability and stressed that housing should reflect the characteristics of the times and society and should be durable. Also, such research and development aim to simultaneously improve the asset value and use value of housing. SI housing refers to the approach to housing construction in which the support S (skeleton) and the fit-out I (infill) of the housing are completely separated, which embodies the basic concept of long-life housing.
4 Kodan Experimental Housing Project (KEP) is a "housing supply system formed by open components" produced by factories developed by Japan Housing Corporation (1973–1981). It aims to realize the rationalization of housing interior and exterior component production and render flexible and variable living space through the combination of system components.
5 New Plan System (NPS) is collectively referred to as the "Public Housing Design Plan Standard" in Japan. It is a new series based on KEP that can adapt to diverse designs. NPS replaced Standard of Public Housing (SPH), which was adjusted by the PC construction method in 1970. Comparatively speaking, SPH is a standardized design for dwelling size, while NPS is a standard design system, providing residents with a different set of general housing designs.
6 Century Housing System (CHS) is based on a three-year in-depth study by Japan's Ministry of Construction (now the Ministry of Land, Infrastructure, Transport and Tourism) since 1980, forming a new housing construction system, including the whole process of design and construction, production supply, maintenance and management, etc., to continuously provide residents with a comfortable living life. Later, the Japanese government launched the Long-life Sustainable Housing Construction System Accreditation Cause and formulated the Long-life Sustainable Housing Construction System Accreditation Benchmark.
7 KSI (Kikou SI, institutional SI housing) is a kind of sustainable housing developed by Japan Urban Renaissance Agency since 1998.
8 "200-year housing" is one of the key policies mentioned by Japanese Prime Minister Yasuo Fukuda in his policy address in May 2007. It has established the

strategic goal of "reducing environmental load, reducing housing expenditure and building high-quality housing." To this end, Japan has set up a "200-year Housing Committee." In July 2008, the 34th Summit Group of Eight Summit was held in Japan. At the meeting, Japanese representatives first put forward the concept of "200-year housing" to demonstrate their unique concept of sustainable development.

9 Long-term Good Housing is based on the Promotion Law of Long-term Good Housing Popularization passed by the plenary session of the Upper House of the Japanese Parliament in 2008 and formally implemented in 2009. This measure aims to popularize "200-year housing." According to this law, the Ministry of Land, Infrastructure, Transport and Tourism has formulated the Long-term Good Housing Accreditation Benchmark. (Editor's note: this is discussed also in Chapter 8.)

References

Hideichi, M. and Shinichi, T. (2006). *21st Century Housing Model*. Trans. Chen Bin, Fan Yue. Beijing: China Machine Press.

Kendall, S. and Teicher, J. (2000). *Residential Open Building*. London: E&FN Spon.

Liu, D. (2018). *Long-life Sustainable Housing-Research and Practice of Future-oriented Green and Sustainable Housing Construction in China*. Beijing: China Architecture & Building Press.

Liu, D. (2015). *SI Housing and Housing Construction Mode · System · Technology ·Diagram*. Beijing: China Architecture & Building Press.

Liu, Z. (2010). Implement the scientific outlook on development and build China's long-life sustainable housing. *Housing Industry*, 5, pp. 15–16.

Qing, J. and Qiuyuan, X. (2008). *Sustainable Housing Construction*. Trans. Chen Bin. Beijing: China Machine Press.

Sun, Y. (2018). *Long-life Sustainable Housing-Brand Practice of High-quality Housing in China's New Era*. Beijing: China Architecture Design & Research Group.

Technical Explanation of the Long-term Good Housing Accreditation Benchmark. (2008). Kyoto: General Corporation Housing Assessment Association.

Urban Renaissance Agency (2005). *KSI-Kikou Skeleton and Infill Housing*. Yokohama: Urban Renaissance Agency.

Xiangzai, U. (1983). *General System of Architectural Industrialization*. Trans. Yao Guohua. Shanghai: Shanghai Scientific & Technical Publishers.

Chapter 10

Korea's 100-year housing program

Soo-am Kim and Hyeonjeong Yang

Background to housing supply in Korea

The Korean government has pursued a mass housing policy in its multifamily housing supply, accounting for almost 75% of all housing units, in order to solve the problems of a housing shortage. As a result, although the general building technology has developed over the years, the current housing process has generated a number of problems. These problems include lack of diversity to meet resident's diverse needs; absence of any concept of resource conservation to meet urgent global environmental issues, and methods of construction that do not consider maintenance. As a result, the housing stock is rapidly aging. Demolition and rebuilding are required in only 30–40 years following initial construction. A new paradigm for housing design and construction is needed.

Given this background, Korea's national government research unit has been conducting research for 20 years on new design methods and building technology for apartment buildings and long-life housing. Based on these studies, the government implemented a housing performance indicator system in 2006. Despite this, the performance measures such as durability, variability, and ease of maintenance did not improve. At that time, 100-year housing research and mock-up housing were constructed, and the results were provided to the private sector. However, the construction costs were 10–20% higher than the conventional approach. In order to solve this problem, a long-life housing (100-year) certification system was implemented in 2014, and research was conducted to reduce construction costs and to verify the technology and the delivery system. At the same time, a pilot project was built based on the results of the research, with completion expected in 2019. This chapter describes the background, technology development, projects, and institutions involved in the mission of 100-year housing in Korea.

Background to the promotion of long-life housing

The background to the promotion of long-life housing in Korea is best explained by considering both international and domestic factors.

DOI: 10.4324/9781003018339-12

International factors

In the latter years of the 20th century, a global consensus began to emerge on the need for sustainable architecture to preserve the global environment. In Korea, to comply with this global direction, it has been necessary to find solutions for energy and resource saving in the building sector. As an idea to save resources, a *Reduce-Reuse-Recycle* approach was pursued and the need for long-life buildings was recognized.

Domestic factors

The domestic factors can be divided into social factors and technical factors. A solution to the short lifespan of multi-family housing was desired, a problem which was caused by a relationship between social and technical factors. The housing supply rate exceeded 100% in 2008, and it was then recognized that there was a need to improve housing performance at the national level.

There is a tendency for people to prefer demolition of existing buildings and construction of new ones (often called 'reconstruction'), over mainten- ance of the existing building stock because of a social trend to prefer new houses. Homeowners also think they can have a bigger house and increase their property value with less investment through the process of scrapping and constructing new buildings. Multi-family housing is dominant in Korea, accounting for 76.4% of total housing (rental apartments comprise approxi- mately 61.4% of total housing as of 2018). However, a critical view of multi- family housing began to emerge in relation to the waste of resources and the massive discharge of construction waste due to reconstruction.

In terms of technical factors, Korean multi-family housing faces the following problems in design, construction and maintenance.

- First, the lifespan of multi-family housing in Korea is too short compared to that of advanced countries (about 1/3–1/2 compared to Europe and the United States).
- Second, the standardized spatial configuration of multi-family housing does not meet the diverse and changing requirements in residents' needs. Unlike other countries, Korean multi-family housing uses a bearing wall structure, not a problem in itself except that capacity for variation and change are not considered in the structural design.
- Third, the facilities deteriorate in a short period of time after their com- pletion because design and construction are implemented without consideration of maintenance, which leads to the premature deterior- ation of housing. Wet construction – dominant in on-site construction – embeds short lifespan installations (piping, electrical conduits, etc.) in the reinforced concrete structure. In particular, drainage piping for toilets and bathroom bathtubs and showers are placed below the concrete slabs in the ceiling spaces of lower dwelling units and receive limited maintenance.

- Finally, insufficient separation between common and dwelling-specific installations is a key contributor to early deterioration.

Current status of the Korean housing market and long-life building practices

In the Korean housing market, an average of about 529,000 housing units have been built per year for 20 years since 2000, producing a housing supply rate of 104.2% in 2018. However, it is still a builder's market, in which about 100% of new housing is sold. As such, there is little interest in improving housing performance and lifespan.

Some private construction companies have adopted a system of installing drywall/metal stud partitions between children's rooms, and between the living room and adjacent rooms, so that occupants can alter the number or sizes of rooms. The system is called a "flexible apartment." Bearing walls are used dominantly in this building type, but the area of the dwelling where drywall partitions can be used has a slightly longer span without columns or bearing walls. Since 2010, the column & flat plate method and the frame structure method have been used in SH (Seoul Housing and Communities Corporation) housing and LH (Korea Land & Housing Corporation) pilot housing, but the consideration for drying and maintenance of the infill is insufficient. In addition, it does not meet long-life housing standards (explained further below).

Since the late 1990s, national and public research institutes have been performing research on "flexible" housing, long-life housing, and housing components. The Korea Institute of Civil Engineering and Building Technology (KICT) performed two experimental long-life housing projects, one from 1997 to 2000, and another from 2003 to 2007. With support from the Korea Agency for Infrastructure Technology Advancement (KAIA) under the Ministry of Land, Infrastructure and Transport (MOLIT), a research program called "Technology Development for Long-life" (Technology Development for Long-life Housing with Durability and Flexibility) was undertaken from 2005 to 2010. The purposes of these studies included the design of standard models for long-life housing, structural durability and structuring methods, the development of interior components and "dry" joints, maintenance, and the promotion of long-life housing. Mock-up houses were also built to propose the possibility of distribution of long-life housing into the market.

Infill companies participated in the research and development of long-life housing, led by the above institutes, but commercialization has largely been unsuccessful. Partition wall parts are not used on the construction sites, but drywall/metal stud partitions are installed at some sites. ALC blocks (Aerated Lightweight Concrete), concrete blocks and panels are used in toilets, bathrooms, and kitchens, etc. where water is used. As a ceiling material, a lightweight steel ceiling frame and gypsum board is usually used.

For toilets and bathrooms, a company successfully developed, commercialized, and constructed an on-slab piping system, the use of which is gradually increasing[1] (Figure 10.14).

In terms of Ondol (a floor heating system), which is so characteristic of Korean residential culture, a lightweight dry Ondol system was developed and is being used, but there are limitations to its expansion due to its high cost[2] (Figure 10.15). A "wet" version of the Ondol floor heating system is lower cost but suffers from having heating pipes buried in the concrete with poor maintenance results.

The Ministry of Land, Infrastructure and Transport (MOLIT) recognized the necessity of responding to the demand for the systematic management of housing in order to meet the various housing needs of the people in the future, and to prepare countermeasures to Korea's short housing lifespan in comparison to the advanced countries. Therefore, in consideration of social and economic conditions, the Ministry attempted to find mid- to long-term management strategies and improvement plans for the systematic management of existing houses and improvement of construction standards to support the long life of new housing.

Accordingly, "A study on mid- to long-term management strategies according to the life cycle of multi-family housing (2012–2013)" was conducted and the "Study on a long-life housing certification system" was initiated as part of a construction standard study for new housing. Based on the research results, opinions from the housing construction industry were collected and some of the housing laws were revised in December 2014 to launch the system, which became effective on December 25, 2014. The long-life housing certification system expands and develops the three performance items (durability, flexibility, and maintainability) related to long-life under the "Housing Performance Rating Indication System," and has been institutionalized since 2006. By establishing construction standards and certification systems for long-life houses, the basic foundation to promote long-life housing was prepared at the national level. An opinion was proposed that technology development and demonstration should be conducted at the same time as well as the system to commercialize long-life housing. As a result, the related planning and research was conducted. Based on this work, a study called the "Development of a supply model for cost-saving long-life housing and building a demonstration complex" was conducted from September 2014 to December 2019. A third national R&D effort was underway as this was being written (2021) focused on various business models and improvements in institutional processes, with detailed research to be undertaken through 2023.

Long-life housing certification system

The long-life housing certification system was launched on the following background. First, since the lifespan of multi-family housing in Korea was about one-third to half of that of the advanced European countries and the United States, it was necessary to solve the problems of resources waste and high social cost.

Second, the current design of multi-family housing made it difficult to respond to the diversification and change of residents' needs, and as the buildings are becoming larger and built higher, a new construction standard was needed to systematically manage this.

Because these two problems cannot be resolved autonomously in the housing market, the long-life housing standards and legal grounds for a certification system were prepared, and detailed regulations were established to promote its expansion and adoption.

Outline of long-life housing certification system

In the Housing Act, long-life housing is defined as follows. A "long-life house" is defined as "a house that has sufficient structural durability to be maintained and managed for a long period of time and has excellent flexibility (capacity) that allows for the easy change of its internal layout according to the residents' needs."

The long-life housing certification system consists of regulations, rules, and notices (standards for construction and certification of long-lived houses) on housing construction standards, based on Article 2 (Definition) and Article 38 (Construction standards and certification systems for long-life housing, etc.) of the Housing Act. It is delegated to local ordinances, and incentives are given for housing with a grade of excellent or higher.

The priority target of the long-life housing certification system is not individual houses but multi-family housing complexes. It is segmented into obligatory and voluntary targets; complexes with 1000 units or more are obligated, while for those with less than 1000 units the targets are voluntary. A certification is obtained based on the project approval design documents by complying with the certification criteria.

Four certification grades (Normal, Good, Excellent, and Outstanding) are defined, and complexes with more than 1000 units must meet the lowest general grade. An incentive is given for projects which achieve the Excellent and Outstanding grades as a means of promotion.

The scope of long-life housing certification performance is limited to durability, flexibility, and maintainability (individual dwelling and common areas). These performance ratings are the lowest grade among the performances defined in the housing performance rating system when building multi-family housing projects. Currently, housing construction companies do not consider them important when they sell housing; even residents who are familiar with typical housing do not consider them a priority. However, in recent years, the importance of these factors has been increasing due to residents' changed housing needs as well as the national direction of maintaining a long-life housing level. Other important performance areas related to long-life

Figure 10.1
**Long-life
housing
certifica-
tion system**

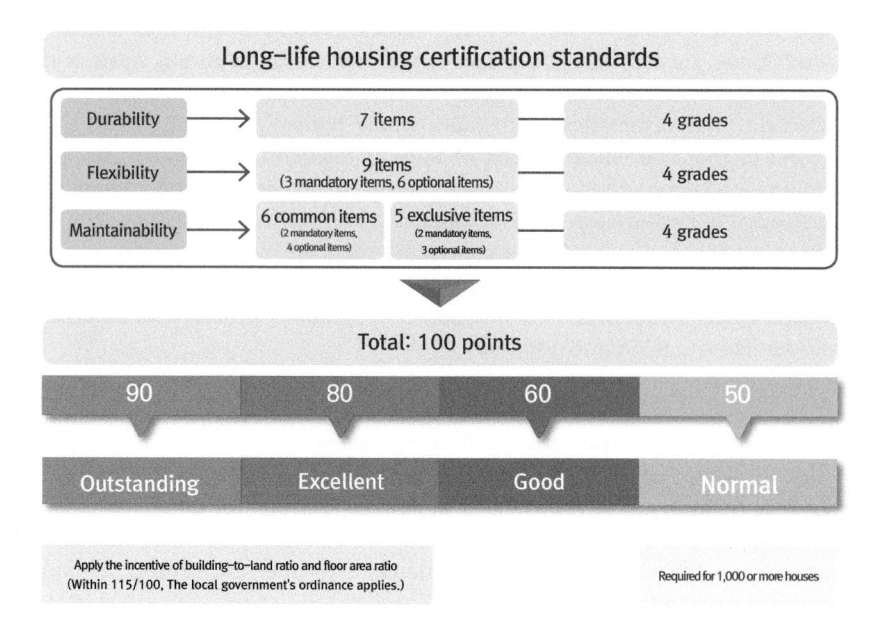

housing include safety, energy saving, and barrier-free performance, etc. of buildings. The safety performance of a building is recognized as sufficient according to the standards of building regulations; energy saving performance and barrier-free performance are already covered under the national zero energy certification and barrier-free certification system, as well as the building standards.

The long-life housing certification system defines three areas of performance: durability, flexibility, and maintainability. These are explained below and in Figure 10.1. There are four grades of Normal, Good, Excellent, and Outstanding, which are assigned depending on the sum of scores for each performance area. The maximum score is 100 and defined as the following: 50–59 points out of 100 is Normal, 60–79 points is Good, 80–89 points is Excellent, and 90–100 points is Outstanding. Large complexes with 1,000 units or more must achieve a general grade (50–59 points) or higher; building coverage ratio and restrictions on floor area ratio can be relaxed up to 115/100 if they receive an Excellent or Outstanding grade, as defined in the local government ordinance.

The areas of long-life housing certification are divided into durability, flexibility, and maintainability; maintainability is further divided into exclusive (individual dwelling) space and common space. In addition, the certification items for each area consist of mandatory items that must be applied and optional items that can be applied depending on technology level and conditions. Each of these certification items is divided into four grades, and the total score of each area is determined based on the sum of acquired grade points. But in terms of durability, the lowest grade score is given if the grade is different for each certification item. Evaluation is based on the project approval design document.

Durability

Durability is evaluated based on reinforcing steel cover thickness and concrete quality. While it is based on the specified grade criteria, the lowest grade is given if the grade is different for each item while meeting the grade of 4. As reinforced concrete housing is the most common type of Korean multi-family housing, only reinforced concrete structures are defined.

Flexibility

For flexibility, whether the flexibility method of separating support and infill designs can be applied or not is evaluated. This is based on the sum of scores of required and optional items when the required items are satisfied. The flexibility evaluation items are divided into support and infill. The evaluation focus is the ease of flexibility within the unit, and infill aims at dry installation methods and components.

For the support, the structure type (mandatory; the length ratio of bearing walls and columns within household) and floor height are evaluated; columns are preferred.

For infill, the interior wall materials and construction method within the units (mandatory; the ratio of drywall out of total internal wall length, the construction method of flexibility), the piping method (on floor piping in the bathroom and toilet), and the space flexibility (dry or raised floor), flexibility of wet zone (freedom to move bathroom, toilet, and kitchen), and the flexibility of exterior wall and industrialization method (industrialized product of exterior wall and replacement method) are evaluated.

Maintainability

Maintainability is divided into exclusive (individual dwelling) area and common area and is evaluated according to the sum of the required and optional items when the required items are satisfied.

For the exclusive (dwelling) area, there is an evaluation of ease of repair and inspection (securing independence between common facility piping and exclusive facility piping, and design that supports easy repair and replacement of piping and wiring are evaluated; mandatory and optional items include no pipes or wires buried in a structure and dry Ondol) and the horizontal separation plan for one unit (when a unit is divided, the space and facility plan are evaluated).

For the common part, the ease of repair and inspection (two items from the common piping arrangement plan in a common space and the installation of an inspection door in a common piping space are evaluated as mandatory items; two items from the piping arrangement without interference in a piping space and the piping structure allowing assembly are evaluated as optional items) and the acceptability of future changes and energy source changes (securing extra 20% margin for piping space, installing piping space) are evaluated.

Demonstration of long-life housing: 100-year housing project

Overview of national R&D project

The 100-year housing research project pertains to the "Development of a Supply Model for Cost-Saving Long-Life Housing and Building a Demonstration Complex," and is the first project regarding long-life housing in Korea.

The research purpose is to verify the methods and technologies of reducing construction costs. The approach to doing this is through the development and construction of a supply model based on the certification system. The goal has in addition the goal of expanding the spread of long-life housing by rationalizing certification standards and systems.

Long-life housing is characterized as having high durability, flexibility, and maintainability for 100 years of occupancy. This goal is possible because it is easy to replace or change infill elements while maintaining support performance for a long time. Long-life housing has the advantages of allowing a resident to freely change the layout according to the resident's life cycle or the change of residents, while maintaining durability. Furthermore, it can maintain its performance through easy monitoring of deteriorating infill performance. Long-life housing gives significant socio-economic effects such as resource saving, carbon dioxide and construction waste reduction at a national level. It also has the advantage of reducing the social burden of customized housing and housing costs, and finally enabling aging in place.

However, as housing performance improves, construction costs also increase. Moreover, provisioning becomes challenging because of some new technologies. This was the reason why long-life housing was not actually accepted in the housing market even though research institutes led the development of technology. Accordingly, there was a need to prepare a provisioning plan by conducting a research project to develop a cost-saving supply model and to verify technology, cost, and systems at the national level.

Therefore, it was necessary to demonstrate through supply chain modeling that development and construction can reduce construction costs while maintaining the concept and performance level of a long-life building. That is, it was necessary to demonstrate that the construction cost of a long-life building is close to that of conventional housing. A research project was conducted with the condition that the cost level of a cost-saving long-life building with a "good" grade was close to that of conventional housing. In addition, the technology and cost of the "excellent" and "outstanding" grade-level housing were also demonstrated.

In this project, the concept of cost-saving long-life housing was defined as housing where support and infill can be separated with 100-year durability but its construction cost level is close to that of conventional housing (bearing wall type structure) when it has a good grade from the long-life certification system.

The research period was from September 2014 to December 2019. The research was divided into three steps.

- The first step was the detail design for the development and construction of a long-life housing supply model with cost savings.
- The second step was the construction of a long-life project.
- The third step was the consideration of a future direction through analysis and evaluation.

KICT (Korea Institute of Civil Engineering and Building Technology) led the research group. Infill manufacturers, academia, design offices, and construction companies participated in the research and construction with substantial contribution from SH (Seoul Housing and Communities Corporation) and LH (Korea Land & Housing Corporation).

Plan design of long-life housing supply model

The concept and direction of the plan design is as follows:

- First, the area of an independent dwelling unit is $59m^2$ with four bays and 3LDK (Living, Dining, Kitchen), which is the most widely constructed area for public and private housing in Korea.
- Second, the performance target for each grade that can realize the performance of long-life housing certification system, and a floor plan, are planned. The performance level of three grades (good, excellent, and outstanding) that will be applied to the demonstration construction is planned for the same plan type.
- Third, the support part and infill part are separated in the plan. The support part includes the structure and common installations (piping, wiring, ventilations ducts, facade, etc.) and the infill part includes installations specific to each dwelling unit and other interior elements. Common facilities are placed in common areas and exclusive (dwelling) installations are placed inside the legal boundary of each dwelling area.
- Fourth, to reduce the cost of the structure, the following are planned: a simplified plan shape, the module of the upper and lower floors adjusted with a column structure, the simplified arrangement of columns, and the efficient use of basement floor, reduction of floor height, and rationalization of infill design.
- Fifth, variation is considered as a plan layout by taking into account the changes in life cycle and diversification of lifestyles.

- Sixth, the changes in location or size of wet zones such as toilets, bathrooms, and kitchens are considered, and installation wiring and piping are separated from the structure to allow their easy inspection and replacement.
- Seventh, the interior wall and ceiling systems use "dry" methods of assembly and the modular coordination design, joint detail, and installation methods are considered for ease of construction, movement, installation, and removal.

Performance target of model plan

The "normal" grade, which is the lowest grade among the four grades of the certification system, is slightly higher than the grade currently under construction. Therefore, the normal grade is excluded from this research project as it is the mandatory minimum requirement under the Housing Act for complexes with 1000 or more units. In this project, only the good, excellent, and outstanding grades were considered and the performance target of the plan model per grade is as follows:

Good

This has the basic durability, flexibility, and maintainability that long-life housing should have.

In this project, the good grade uses the column and flat plate structure. The durability is the same strength (24 MPa) as the cover thickness of conventional housing.

The plan has a fixed wet zone when remodeling occurs in the future, but it has a variation where the size and number of other rooms can be changed. It also has the image of a house that allows maintenance of piping and wiring. The common piping is placed in a common (support) part and the infill piping and wiring equipment are separated from the structure. The toilet system adopts on or above – slab piping, enabling maintenance by an individual household from within their space. The boundary wall between units is a reinforced concrete bearing wall.

Excellent

This has high durability, improved spatial flexibility, and excellent maintainability compared with a good grade.

In this project, the excellent grade was a frame structure, which increased the concrete cover thickness (10 mm increase) and strength (24 MPa→27 MPa). Compared with the good grade, the interior (infill) walls are dry and there are no columns inside, so kitchens can be moved. The variety and ease of change are improved, so one unit can be divided into two households. The ease of maintenance and replacement of pipes was improved and vertical pipes that can be easily assembled were used. There is also a spare space for facility shaft available for future piping changes.

Outstanding

In addition to the excellent grade, the capability of moving a wet zone was expanded and a space plan and facility change plan were implemented to increase the ease of infill change (capacity). Ease of installation and dis-assembly of the joining method of partition walls was secured. The use of adjustment bolts in a dry wall and the easy de-mountability and installation of a joint between the floor and ceiling were implemented.

Flexibility scenario of long-life housing

The plan of a long-life demonstration housing unit is 59 m^2 (635 ft^2) and its basic type (standard type) consists of 3LDK (3 bedrooms, a living room, a kitchen, and dining room), 2 toilets, and other subsidiary spaces. This assumes a household of two parents and two children. The plan was considered to have at least four different variations according to changes in life or family composition. In addition, this plan enables other variations or free space.

Extended living room type

Even if a family has only one child or two young children, a large living room can be made by removing the walls of a room adjacent to the living room if their lifestyle is mainly based on the living room.

Merged bedroom type (2 rooms into 1 room)

Two small bedrooms can be merged into one large bedroom. Two small rooms can be merged and used either as the master bedroom or a large room for children's extended activities.

South-facing kitchen and dining room type

In Korea, kitchens are usually located in the back/north, but the kitchen and dining room can be rearranged to the front/south to be used as a spacious living room/dining room/kitchen. At this time, the original kitchen can be changed to a basic room. As basic equipment was installed during construction for kitchen movement, rearrangement is allowable with minimal changes.

Partial rent type

This is a housing type that is only available in Korea. Two small bedrooms are merged into a studio and can be rented with an adjacent toilet. There is

Figure 10.2
**Plan vari-
ation for
flexibility
scenario
of long-life
housing**

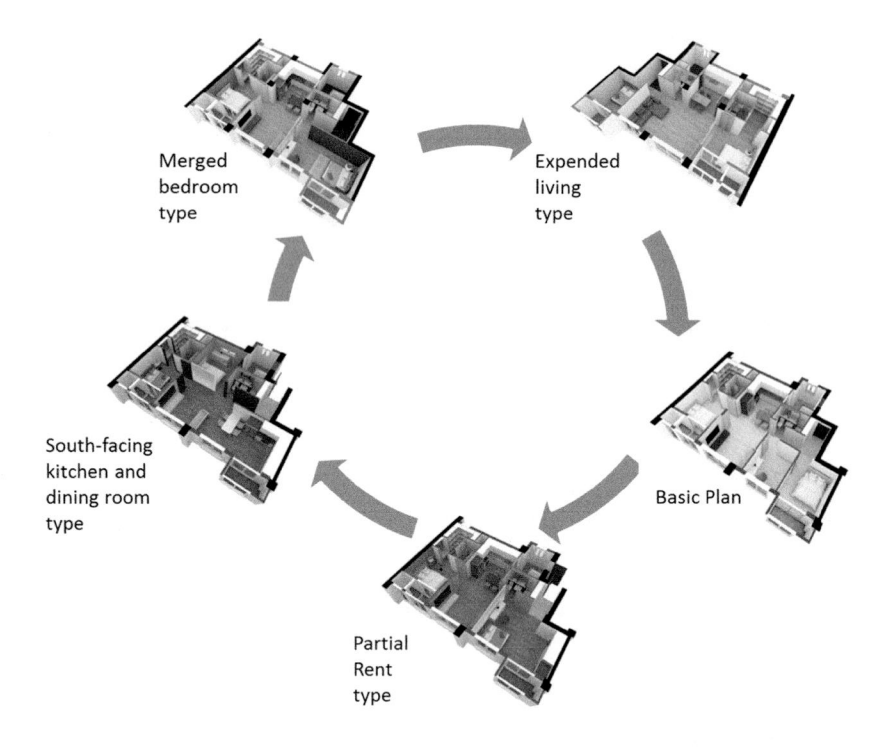

Merged
bedroom
type

Expended
living
type

South-facing
kitchen and
dining room
type

Basic Plan

Partial
Rent
type

no ownership change. It is constructed so that a separate entrance can be made to public space and spare facilities and spaces are prepared in an adjacent utility shaft so that a kitchen can be constructed in the rental space. It is possible to provide a low-cost and safe residential space for the increasing number of single or two-person households, and lessors can earn rental income by leasing the remaining space (see Figure 10.2).

Technology for long-life housing
Economics and three basic performance priorities, i.e. durability, variability, and maintainability, were considered for the technologies applied to long-life demonstration housing.

Support technology
1. Durability improvement. A reinforced concrete structure usually consists of the cover thickness of reinforcement and concrete quality. The flat plate structure, where the good grade is applied, is slightly more reinforced (concrete strength 24 MPa) than that of general multi-family housing in Korea. The frame structure with an excellent or outstanding grade has a cover thickness reinforced by a 10 mm (.4 in) increase compared with the good grade and its specified concrete strength was reinforced to 27 MPa.

Its slump, unit binder weight, and water-binder ratio were increased to help secure durability of 100 years.

2. Adoption of column-type structure. The structure of Korean multi-family housing is usually the bearing wall structure, but the column-type structure system is applied in this project. In the flat plate structure, the columns are located inside a dwelling unit. However, in the frame structure, the columns are placed outside of a unit, in a long span configuration. In addition, to efficiently utilize the underground space while reducing the amount of underground construction, the span and size of columns were determined in consideration of the passage and size of vehicle parking in underground garages.

A minimum required floor height was secured to reduce cost; the floor height of the frame structure is 3000 mm (9.8 ft) while that of the flat plate structure is 2800 mm (9.2 ft). The ceiling height is set to 2300 mm (7.55 ft).

3. Separation of structure and utility installations. In conventional housing, there is no design concept considering the difference in the lifespan of parts and materials, so it is common to bury facilities in structures or Ondol floors. Because this shortens the housing lifespan, the basic concept with long-life housings is a design that considers the inspection, maintenance, and the replacement of installation facilities through the separation of building structure and facilities by considering their respective differences in lifespans. If it is unavoidable, double piping and wiring were allowed to be applied in building structures or Ondol floors. In particular, the Ondol is commonly applied to all housing in Korea, so the dry Ondol floor system was developed (see Figure 10.15). However, as its cost is 3 to 5 times higher than that of a conventional wet system, the Ondol was applied only to some units in the demonstration housings.

4. Arrangement of common piping in the common (support) part, installation of inspection door, separation of common piping and exclusive (dwelling unit) piping. In conventional Korean multi-family housing, the layout of common facilities and exclusive (dwelling unit) facilities is not divided but entangled. In this project, both common facilities and supplies are placed in a common area to separate them from exclusive (dwelling unit) piping. However, with respect to the sewage and drainage pipe shaft for toilets and bathrooms, the conventional method was used because of the characteristics of the separated location of two toilets in Korean housing (generally, two toilets are used in dwellings over 60 m^2 (646 ft^2) as well as the cost increase due to the increase in floor height as a result of installing raised floors.

For the common piping space, 20% of the pipe shaft area was prepared by considering the expansion and change of facilities associated with future space changes. An inspection door (larger than 600mm x 1,500mm) (2ft x 5ft) was installed to allow inspection of common piping, and sufficient clearance between pipes was secured. Additionally, pipes that can be disassembled were installed to ensure ease of maintenance for vertical piping,

5. Securing degree of freedom for space arrangement. By adopting the column structure, the degree of freedom of space was secured which is incomparable to conventional housing with a bearing wall structure. In conventional housing, bearing walls are used to separate rooms. Accordingly, there is either limited or no variability between two rooms or a room adjacent to the living room. However, long-life housing supports the variability of a room and living room as well as the limited location change of kitchen and toilet in a unit.

Infill technology

1. Dry wall and construction method. There are two types of interior walls. ALC (Autoclaved Lightweight Concrete) blocks were used for the toilet walls (wet zone where water is used) and drywall on metal stud partitions were used where there is no water use (bedrooms and living area). The drywall partitions consist of steel studs + sound insulation material + 2-ply gypsum board (100 mm or 4 in).

   There are three types of partition installation methods.

   - The first type is installed between two floor slabs; it is strongly fixed in place. It can be disassembled and re-installed during remodeling, but some damage may occur to the Ondol floor and ceiling.
   - The second type is the floor-to-ceiling support method and the ease of disassembly is high due to its high variability. Even if the walls are removed, there is no damage to the ceiling and floor.
   - The third type is a movable wall that can be installed and disassembled. This was installed only in some exhibition spaces. Several types of technologies were developed in this project and a movable wall was developed even before this project. However, it was not commercialized and was only applied to mock-up housing. This is type is to be developed in Korea in the future.

   The three systems were sufficiently verified through the tests such as sound insulation, safety, and support in the laboratory and mock-up test, but the movable lightweight wall was not adopted by the company in the 110 rental demonstration housing units.

2. Ceiling system. The Korean ceiling system is a suspension-type dry system that uses steel hangers, carrying channels, and two layers of gypsum board. The dry system installed between two slabs used this method. However, a system that receives the compression of wooden base material was adopted as the ceiling system applied to the dry wall installed on the floor and ceiling. The movable lightweight partition wall system that is partially used is the same ceiling system. This is because the wall system is a system supported by compressive force.

3. Floor heating system – Ondol. Ondol is a unique Korean floor heating system. The wet floor Ondol system is used for all housing. The Ondol layer is 110 mm (4.3 inches) thick. In this project, the layer consists of a cushioning material 30 mm (1.2 in), two layers of PE film, lightweight aerated concrete 40 mm (1.5 in), hot water pipes, cement mortar 40 mm (1.5 in), and floor finishing material. This configuration is the most inexpensive general Ondol heating system. For heating in Korea, district heating and individual gas boilers are used. The district heating method was used in this project. The hot water Ondol coils are zoned per room and distributed by a distributor control valve system.

    This scheme was applied to 110 rental housing units. The dry system was applied to 4 of 6 housing units. The configuration of the dry system is shown in Figure 10.15.

4. Toilet system. The toilet system in Korea usually uses an under-slab piping system and has a similar size and arrangement of sanitary equipment. In addition, there is a floor drain for floor cleaning and its floor level is 50 mm–80 mm (2 in–3 in) below the threshold by cutting the upper part of a slab. This is for use of "indoor shoes." The bathroom door opens into the toilet. These facts cause issues related to noise and maintenance and cause the locations of toilets to be fixed. In Korea, there are now two types of on- or above-slab piping systems: the on-slab floor system and the wall piping system. In this project, the on-slab wall-type piping system was used (see Figure 10.14), and a sliding door was installed without slab cutting. A floor drain was installed and could be used by the resident without being disturbed even when wearing indoor shoes. In addition, the threshold height is about 20 mm (.8 in) which enables barrier-free accessibility.

5. Kitchen system. A standard system was used for the kitchen, but the kitchen location was moved in one unit to prepare for any future kitchen location change. The kitchen located in the north was moved to the south and all the facilities required for the kitchen were connected to the facility piping and wiring in a spare piping shaft. This effort was an attempt to respond to changes in residents' needs ten years after the rental period was finished.

6. No embedding of piping and wiring into structure. In principle, piping and wiring for individual dwellings should not be embedded into a (support) structure. If this is unavoidable for a structure or Ondol layer, double piping (pipe sleeves) was allowed. Double piping was applied to exclusive water supply piping and electrical and communication wiring even if they were not embedded.

Cladding

A lightweight exterior wall that was produced in a factory was installed and applied to one unit of the demonstration housing. The expected exterior wall constructability and performance were then tested.

Figure 10.3
**Demons-
tration
project**

Long-life demonstration housing project

Overview of demonstration housing (Figure 10.3)

- Location: Gaon Village Complex 9, 183 Dajeongbuk-ro, Sejong Special Self-Governing City, Republic of Korea.
- Architect: HAEMA Architects + Long Life Housing Research Center.
- Owner: Korea Land & Housing Corporation.
- Housing Units: 116 units out of total 1,080 units.
- Unit Area: 59 m² (635 ft²).
- Support structure: reinforced concrete frame structure (column & beam) one building, column & flat plate structure one building.
- Story height: frame structure (3,000 mm) (9.84 ft), column & flat plate structure (2,800 mm) (9.2 ft).
- Infill: dry wall/metal stud walls, dry ceiling, on-slab wall piping toilet/ bathroom, dry-type Ondol (4 units).

Outline of the project

The long-life demonstration project had a dwelling unit area of 59 m² (635 ft²). This is because the most dominant area of recently constructed multi-family housing in Korea is 59 m²–84 m² (635–904 ft²). The project is a rental complex in which the units will be sold to their occupants after ten years of renting. It has 116 units in two buildings out of a total 1080 units in 13 buildings. Other buildings in the same complex comprise conventional multi-family housing with a bearing wall structure.

The project consists of two buildings with a total of 116 units. One building has 58 units of the frame structure consisting of 28 units with an excellent grade and 30 units with an outstanding grade, one building with column and flat plate structure, and 58 units with a good grade.

Out of 116 units, 110 units were rented, but the remaining six units are used as research and display units (demonstration units); 110 units have the same layout, but three different levels of technologies were applied per grade (supply model). The plan variation and infill technology were applied to six units (three per building). The variation of the supply model was applied to four out of the six units and a new technology based on two concept proposals that were awarded through an ideas contest was applied to the remaining two units. For the next five years, they will be used as display units while promoting long-life housing technology to housing companies, residents, and the general public. This housing will be converted to sale after ten years of rent. Therefore, it is meaningful that this illustrates an example of space variation according to a resident's needs at the time of conversion.

Three supply model grades

The durability criterion reinforces the thickness of the reinforced concrete and improves the quality of the concrete to make a strong and durable structure which is the basic condition of a building with a 100-year lifespan.

The flexibility criterion improves the dwelling unit capacity by using the column-type structure. In addition, the drywall partition and the movable light-wall facilitate the jointing assembly of the wall/floor/ceiling so that it can be changed in five ways according to the residents' lifestyle. Toilets are equipped with an on-slab wall-type piping system and the relocation of kitchen and toilets is facilitated through the provision of spare pipe shafts. We have planned a spared pipe shaft so that two families can separate some area of one unit.

Regarding maintainability, the private/common Piping Shaft can be separated and maintained. In the common pipe shaft, inspection doors are provided for easy inspection and repair, and piping and wiring are prohibited from being embedded in the structure. In addition, double piping (pipe sleeves) and dry wall which allow for easy repair and replacement of piping and wiring are applied.

Outstanding grade units

The following is a model designed to meet the requirements of an outstanding grade. In consideration of various lifestyles, the plan adopted a 4-bay-type structure capable of modifications into several different types. See Figure 10.4.

For an outstanding grade, plan variation is higher than that of an excellent grade, and the individual performance grade along with the level of infill are higher. Therefore, the cost is also increased. Compared with ordinary buildings, construction costs will rise by more than 6%.

Figure 10.4
Specification of out-standing grade units

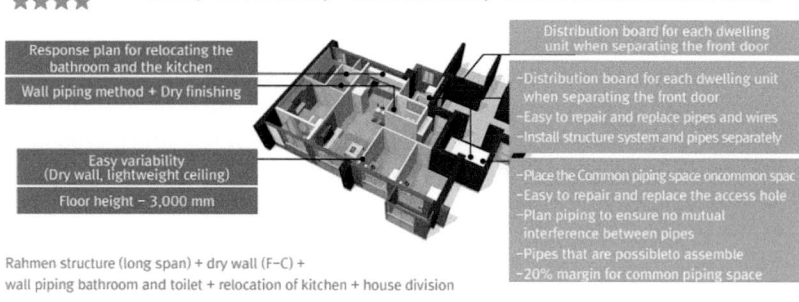

Outstanding ▶ Housing responsive to future changes that enables free space planning and house division with light construction work and prepares against demand increase in the future

★★★★ Durability – Grade 2 / Flexibility – Grade 1 / maintainability – Grade 1 for exclusive and Grade 1 for common

Response plan for relocating the bathroom and the kitchen
Wall piping method + Dry finishing
Easy variability (Dry wall, lightweight ceiling)
Floor height – 3,000 mm

Distribution board for each dwelling unit when separating the front door
–Distribution board for each dwelling unit when separating the front door
–Easy to repair and replace pipes and wires
–Install structure system and pipes separately
–Place the Common piping space oncommon spac
–Easy to repair and replace the access hole
–Plan piping to ensure no mutual interference between pipes
–Pipes that are possibleto assemble
–20% margin for common piping space

Rahmen structure (long span) + dry wall (F–C) + wall piping bathroom and toilet + relocation of kitchen + house division

Figure 10.5
Specification of excellent grade units

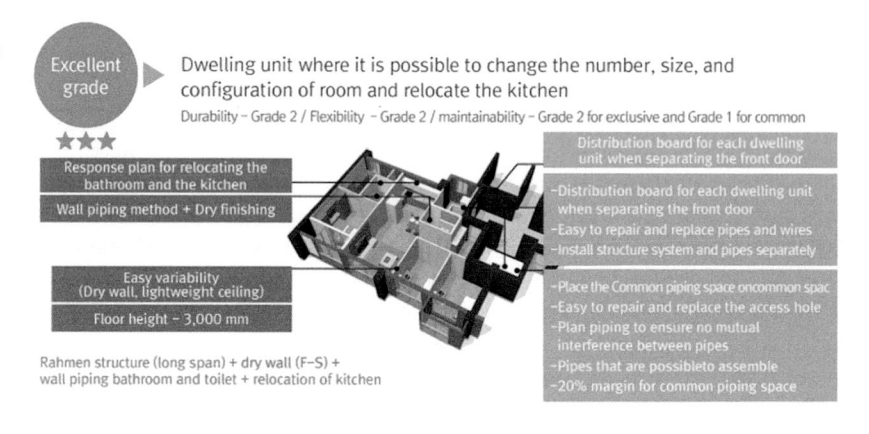

Excellent grade ▶ Dwelling unit where it is possible to change the number, size, and configuration of room and relocate the kitchen

★★★ Durability – Grade 2 / Flexibility – Grade 2 / maintainability – Grade 2 for exclusive and Grade 1 for common

Response plan for relocating the bathroom and the kitchen
Wall piping method + Dry finishing
Easy variability (Dry wall, lightweight ceiling)
Floor height – 3,000 mm

Distribution board for each dwelling unit when separating the front door
–Distribution board for each dwelling unit when separating the front door
–Easy to repair and replace pipes and wires
–Install structure system and pipes separately
–Place the Common piping space oncommon spac
–Easy to repair and replace the access hole
–Plan piping to ensure no mutual interference between pipes
–Pipes that are possibleto assemble
–20% margin for common piping space

Rahmen structure (long span) + dry wall (F–S) + wall piping bathroom and toilet + relocation of kitchen

Excellent grade units

An excellent grade has more advanced technology than a good grade, and individual performance grade is higher. For example, an excellent grade is more flexible because there are no columns inside the unit. We planned an independent entrance and facilities to allow a partial rental unit as described above. See Figure 10.5.

Good grade units

The following is the model designed to meet the requirements of good quality. In order to reduce the cost, the columns are arranged inside the unit, but some degree of plan change is possible. Considering the ease of main-tenance, the common facilities are placed in the common part and only the drainage pipe space is located "on slab" in the unit. The horizontal pipe was a double sleeve pipe, etc. (see Figure 10.6).

Figure 10.6
**Specification
of good
grade units**

Six units for display

Out of six display dwelling units, four units have the basic floor plan of the demonstration dwelling and are reconfigured as the variation type. Two units are built by technically reinterpreting two ideas awarded from an idea contest focusing on life in the year 2030. The basic type consists of four bays located toward the south side, and 3LDK+2Bath (see Figures 10.7-1 and 10.7-2).

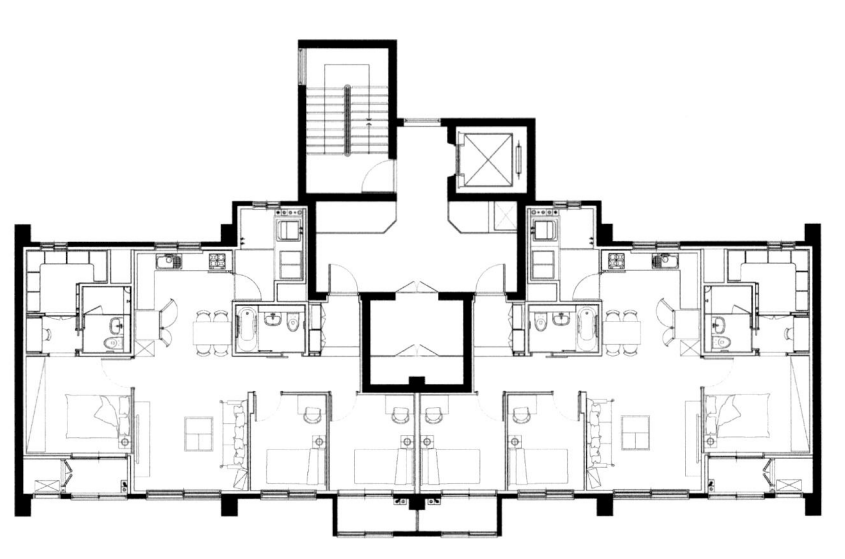

Figure 10.7-1
**Frame struc-
ture type
with basic
floor plan**

Figure 10.7-2
Column struc- ture type with basic floor plan

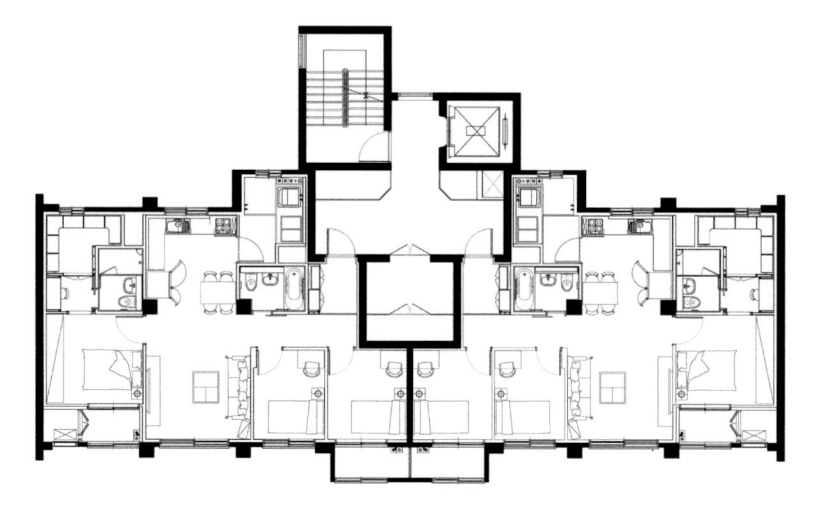

1. *Extended living room type*. From the basic type, the dry wall partition between the adjacent bedroom and living room was removed and converted into a large living room. The floor at the disassembled wall and the finishing of the ceiling are changed and some of the electrical facilities and wirings were removed and rearranged. This responds to the needs for a larger living room and was changed from a 3LDK to a 2LDK space (see Figure 10.8).

Figure 10.8
Plan of extended living room type

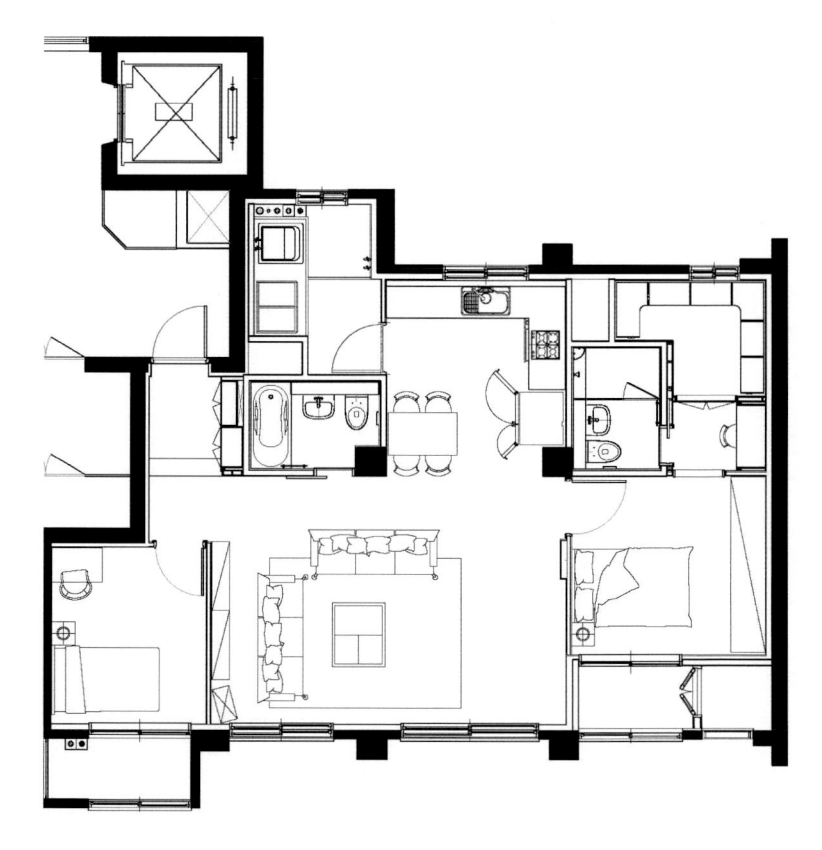

2. *Merged bedroom type*. From the basic type, the drywall partition between two bedrooms was removed, the demolished part of the ceiling and floor was refinished, the door of Bedroom 3 was removed, and a wall was ultimately installed to make a large bedroom. This type was converted from a 3LDK to a 2LDK space to respond to the lifestyle change requiring a large bedroom (see Figure 10.9).

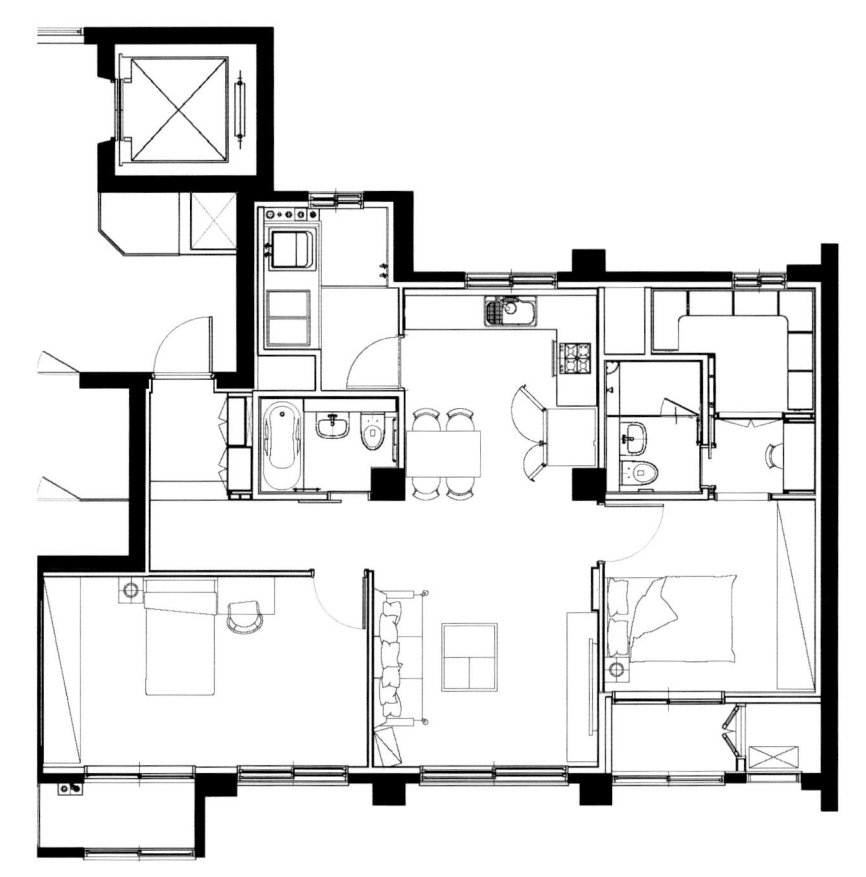

Figure 10.9
Plan of merged bedroom

3. *South kitchen type*. From the basic type, the kitchen located in the north was moved to the location of Bedroom 3 in the south, Bedrooms 2 and 3 were demolished, and the kitchen was changed to a bedroom for space reconfiguration. Due to the space layout change, the location of lighting, utility installations, and electrical switches in Bedrooms 2 and 3 were removed and relocated. Accordingly, the new kitchen used facilities previously installed in the common piping for water supply, drainage, and ventilation. Although this is a 2LDK layout, the living room, dining room, and kitchen have an open space in the south, leading to an atmosphere of a spacious indoor space (see Figure 10.10).

Figure 10.10
**Plan south
kitchen type**

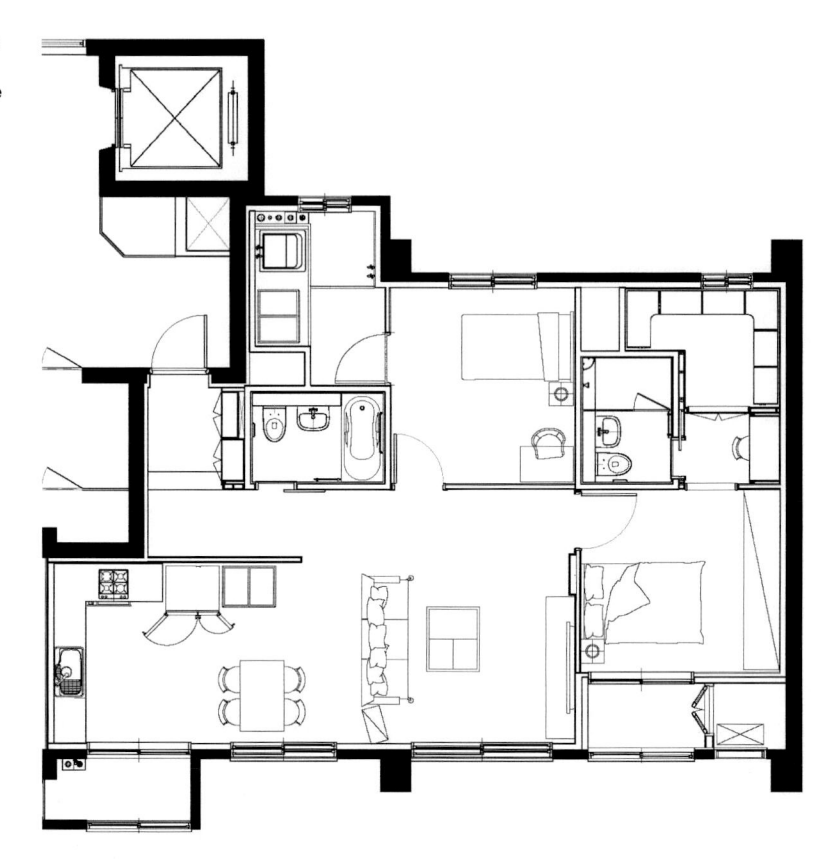

4. Partial rent type. This is a unique housing type only available in Korea, to our understanding. If a large space is not required from the basic type after children become independent, some space can be rented out to earn rental income. The space that is rented out should be equipped with a separate entrance door, toilet, kitchen, and necessary facilities (individual meters for water supply & drainage, and electricity).

In this project, the basic type was designed by considering the separation of the two entrances, kitchen, and toilet to allow part of the space to be rented out, allowing for easy separation.

The entrance of the rental space was installed in the area that was previously used as a multipurpose (utility) room in the basic type. The performance of the wall between the living room and Bedroom 2 was reinforced to maintain its performance as a separating wall between two households.

The tenant used the entrance and family toilet of the basic type as they were, having merged Bedrooms 2 and 3 of the basic type, and made a kitchen in the former location of Bedroom 3 to form a studio-type space.

Therefore, the configuration of space and facilities included the demolition of Bedrooms 2 and 3 in the basic type and re-arrangement of facilities according to the function of the space. The kitchen has the same configuration as the south-side kitchen (see Figures 10.11-1, 10.11-2).

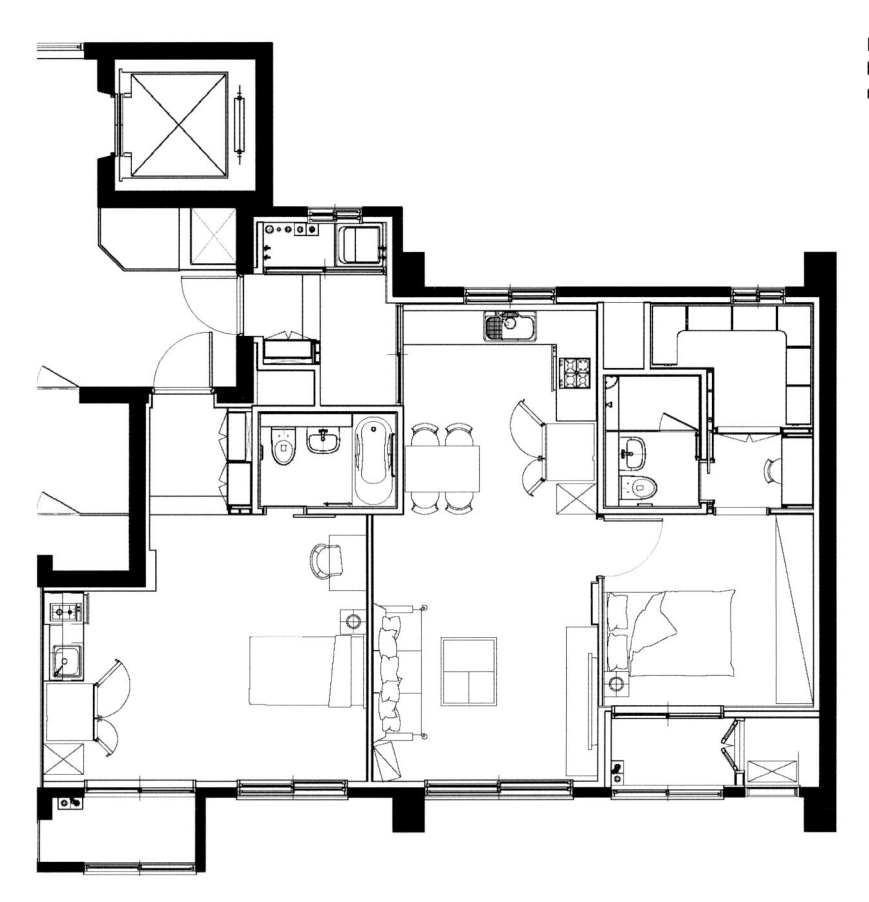

Figure 10.11-1
**Plan partial
rental type**

Figure 10.11-2
**Picture of
the dem-
onstration
unit (land-
lord unit)**

5. *Housing growing together for the year 2030 type*. From the basic type, one bedroom, two toilets, and a kitchen were maintained, and the remaining space was opened so that it could be changed as required. As a model for a telecommuter, it was configured to use a movable infill wall (folding wall, sliding wall, etc.) that can easily switch from a workspace into a rest space and vice versa (see Figure 10.12).

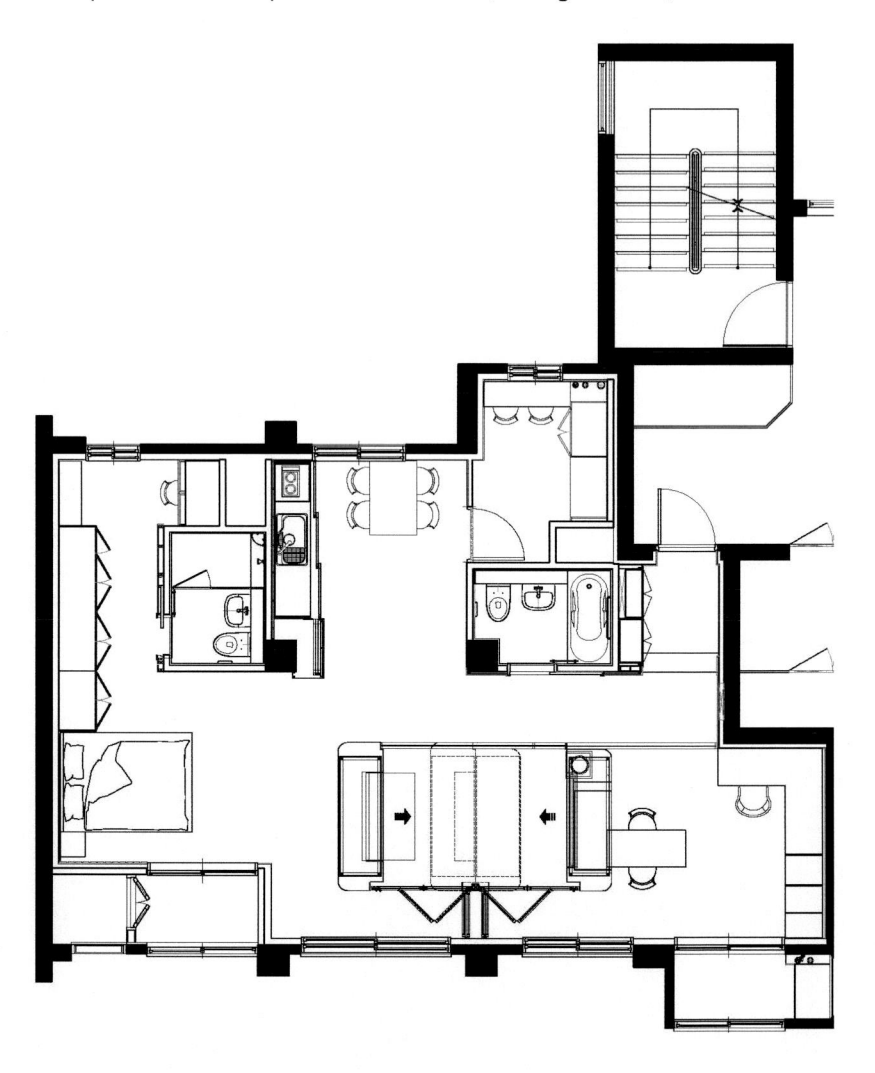

Figure 10.12
Plan

6. Living nomad type. From the basic type, the location of Bedroom 1 and the two toilets were fixed, and the kitchen was moved to the south. However, the other spaces excluding the toilet were planned as an open space without fixed partition walls to secure a free space. It is possible to freely divide and separate the space according to the change in life patterns. Therefore, it is possible to organize a space that can be changed

at any time such as a separate space when privacy is required, a guest room that can be used when hosting guests, and a spacious living room. The walls of two different systems were used to enable a change in the spatial configuration by using the combination of a hinged wall and a sliding storage-type moving wall. The hinged partition wall was installed between the room that was converted from a kitchen in the basic type and Bedroom 1 to facilitate partitioning if required. The sliding storage-type mobile wall is located between the living room and the combination of Bedrooms 2 and 3 in the basic type to accommodate partitioning if required (see Figures 10.13-1, 10.13-2).

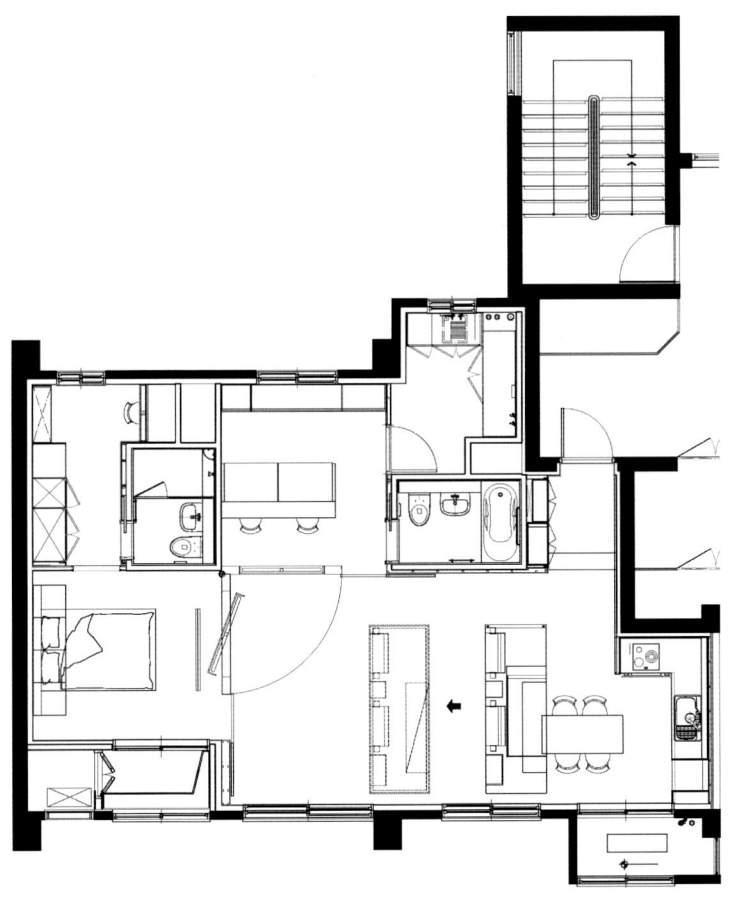

Figure 10.13-1
**Plan living
nomad type**

Figure 10.13-2
**Picture of the
living nomad
type demon-
stration unit**

Figure 10.13-2
Picture of the living nomad type demonstration unit

Residential building types

There are two residential buildings. One has a flat plate structure and the other has a frame structure. One floor of each building consists of four units, with two units sharing an elevator and stair (see Figures 7.1 and 7.2).

Results of long-life housing project and future directions

This chapter described the background, certification system, and projects of long-life housing in Korea. The long-life demonstration housing research was finished in December 2019 and the rent-out was completed. The current demonstration housing is occupied by residents, and six display units are used to promote and educate on the technological achievements. The results obtained from the long-life housing demonstration project are summarized as follows:

- First, the model development and demonstration housing of long-life housing was the first attempt in Korea to build demonstration housing based on the long-life housing certification system. In a situation where only the normal grade of long-life housing was acquired in the housing market, demonstration housing with good, excellent, and outstanding grades were constructed. People who were interested in long-life housing such as public and private construction company employees, public officials, general citizens, and students, visited the demonstration projects. These projects will be reference cases for long-life housing in the future.
- Second, an estimated 10%–20% cost increase with long-life housing was expected compared to conventional housing in the housing market. However, the experimental results showed that the cost of housing

with a good grade increased by less than 3%, and the cost of excellent and outstanding grades increased by less than 6%. There is a positive response in the housing market and some public sectors agencies are considering its adoption.

- Third, there are still many areas for improvement for long-life housing technology. However, it has been demonstrated that the construction of long-life housing is possible with the current technology. The positive evaluation includes the design technique for change of structural design, the ease of utility installation maintenance, and the variable responsiveness through the relocation of kitchen facilities in connection with space reorganization. Some INFILL technology, such as drywall partitions and on-slab piping-type toilet systems, are increasingly being applied to conventional housing. The application of dry Ondol systems is also increasing. In particular, the switch to the use of column structures and the application of the on-slab piping method will become popular in the near future as they have been proven to be effective in reducing inter-floor noise (see Figures 10.14, 10.15).

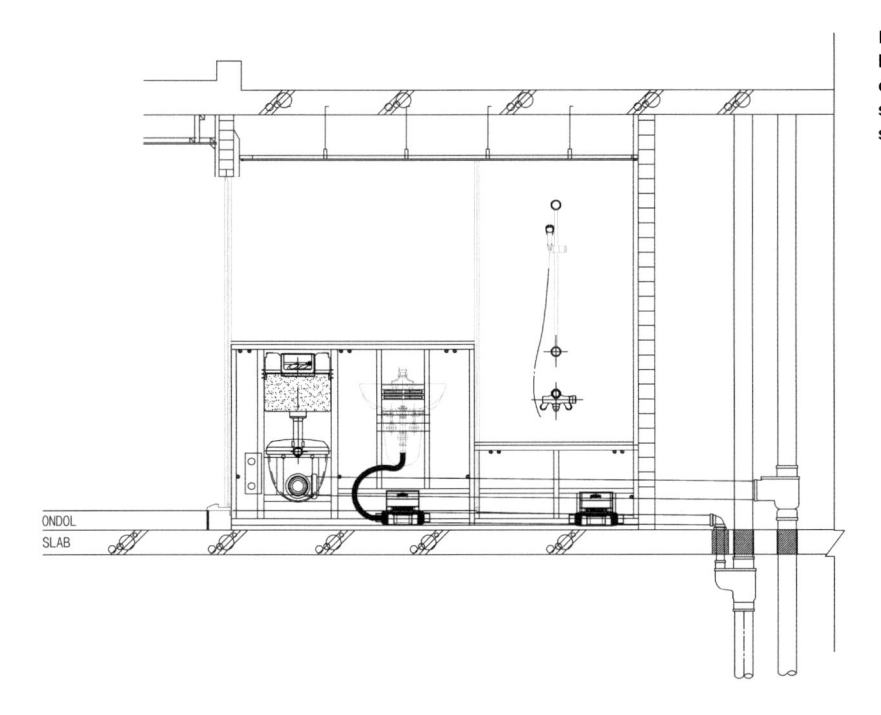

Figure 10.14
Drawing of an "On-slab piping system"

Figure 10.15
**Dry Ondol
floor heating
system**

Conclusions

In Korea, there were few alternatives to removing the industry's negative response to what were believed to be higher construction costs for long-life housing, thus blocking widespread conversion to long-life housing as a general mode of practice. To remove this negative impression, national level R&D was conducted, and demonstration projects (two buildings in an apartment complex) based on the study were built in September 2019. The study was completed in December 2019. Because the comprehensive results were presented in February 2020, the actual impact on the market at the time of this report (October 2020) is not significant, but the foundation for expanded implementation was made, a consensus between government–suppliers–consumers was formed and the potential benefits of long-life housing were verified.

The reasons why the supply of long-life houses has not been expanded in Korea up to now are as follows:

- First, the long-life housing certification system became effective, but it is limited to a normal grade. From 2015 to December 2019, 673 complexes have been certified, but only one complex has acquired a "good" grade.

  The level of excellent and outstanding grades is much higher than that of general housing projects, and there is an incentive of alleviating the coverage ratio and floor area ratio, but they are not working in the market. This also means the incentive is not working as an incentive for long-life housing construction because there are various certification systems in Korea. Continuous system improvement is necessary for this.

- Second, one of the obstacles for moving toward long-life housing is the structural system. In Seoul, 35-floor multi-family housing projects are still being constructed with a bearing wall structure and switching to a column type is difficult because the bearing wall structure is the most economical and familiar system. The bearing wall structure type was introduced in the 1980s and has been widely used and architects and builders are familiar with this design. This is also acting as an obstacle to the development of infill systems.
- Third, although the recognition about long-life housing in the market has improved compared to the beginning of this study, there is not sufficient availability of industrially produced components or systems. Recently, some infill parts and materials have been developed, but there is limited variety, and the development of an infill industry is slow. That is because there are fewer applications than standard business practices which everyone understands.

Promising situations are emerging

- First, the implementation of the long-life housing certification system and a pilot project helped the industry and general public understand the concept of long-life housing and its benefits.
- Second, even after the demonstration project was completed, private companies and public sector entities are visiting the pilot project, and their interest is gradually increasing.

  A public sector entity, LH (Korea Land & Housing Corporation), has been conducting two pilot projects since last year, and some housing corporations under local governments are planning pilot projects. The SH (Seoul Housing and Communities Corporation) in Seoul is switching the structural type to the column type. Some top-class private construction companies are also reviewing long-life housings.
- Third, some infill companies are also expanding their application in general housing construction based on the experience of participating in demonstration projects.
- Fourth, the Ministry of Land, Infrastructure and Transport is also interested in revising the standards for long-life housing and its development.

In conclusion, long-life housing in Korea is still in the beginning stage. The government is leading system reorganization and making long-life housing a priority, and the interest in long-life housing is gradually increasing mainly in the public sector. When discussing the direction of future housing by taking into account the changes in life after recent COVID-19, the necessity of long-life housing was confirmed once again. In the private sector, quick change may be difficult because they are familiar with the conventional way of thinking and working in the field, but they are also gradually pursuing long-life housing in their own way. Because the private companies also agree on the future direction for long-life housing, it is expected there will be a gradual change.

Additional sources

1. www.kaia.re.kr/portal/main.do
2. www.kict.re.kr/index.es?sid=a

Notes

1 Skysystem Co. Ltd., www.ospsystem.co.kr/kr/index.php; ChungWan Co. Ltd., www.chungwan.co/kr; Watos Co. Ltd., www.watos.com/index.php
2 Dadam Solution Co. Ltd., www.dadamsolution.com

Part 3

Developments toward a fit-out industry
The key to residential Open Building

The Open Building approach was initially formulated with two goals: first, to reintroduce the user as a decision-making agent in the housing process; and second, to harness the power of industrial production in the housing process by clearly distinguishing each dwelling unit as an independent design task, thus liberating it to become a consumer-oriented product/service.

This part of the book lays out the principles of an infill industry and reviews developments in Japan, largely focused on the renovation of existing building stock that may be the best indicator of the future potential of an infill industry; and in China, where several companies have moved into the infill market with apparent prospects for long-term success. Chapter 14 ends with an abbreviated history of efforts to bring infill to the market and offers some reasons why this path has been and remains difficult.

> Sustainability demands an increased hierarchical depth that allows each dwelling unit to adapt individually over time. This is not only advantageous for the inhabitants, but allows renovation whenever a single unit needs it, which, of course, is the case with any freestanding suburban house. In other words, the autonomous dwelling should be considered the living cell in the environmental organism, and its autonomy is an essential requirement for keeping existing stock up to date. Environmental sustainability demands that every dwelling can be renovated, improved, accept new technology or follow new cultural priorities in direct relation to what the market has made available.
>
> (Habraken, 2017, Back to the future, *AD*, 05/vol. 87/2017)

Chapter 11

Infill systems
A new industry

John Habraken

Editors' note:
This series of diagrams and accompanying narrative was presented at the CIB W104 Open Building Implementation Conference in Taiwan in 1994, and also published in the **Open House International** issue *Infill/Fit-Out Systems: Toward a Residential Infill Industry* (Stephen Kendall, guest editor), vol. 26, no. 3, 2001.

In his typically lucid way, John Habraken conveys through a series of diagrams the essence of what an infill industry can mean to the future of a regenerative residential building stock. It is important to retell this story, because we remain trapped by a culture and an obsolete paradigm that runs deep in the design and construction sectors. It is a worldwide problem. This paradigm is producing a building stock that's more expensive every year, can't contribute to the urgent need to move toward a circular economy, and is unable to adjust to changing demands and what people really want. Infill systems will make buildings cost less, as Chapters 13 and 14 point out in the case of the Chinese Infill company reported on there.

DOI: 10.4324/9781003018339-14

INFILL SYSTEMS, A NEW INDUSTRY

Figure 11.1

Infill systems represent a new industry, different from the traditional building construction industry. To understand infill systems, it is necessary to explain that they operate on a different level. The following slides will explain the concept of levels

Figure 11.2

The familiar model of the urban environment gives us a street with houses. There are two levels of action. One is the street and the other is the house-lot with the house

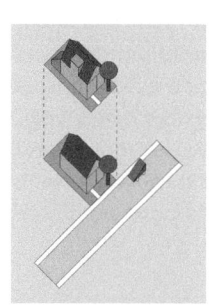

Figure 11.3

The house can change independently from the street. Over time all houses will change, but the street is more permanent

Figure 11.4

The house is related to the occupants: the household. The changes to the house are in response to their needs. The street is related to the community. A single household cannot make the street change. A higher authority, representing the community, must change the street

Figure 11.5
In the same way, the house and the street are produced by different professionals. The street is designed by urban designers and is built by contractors specializing in civil works. The house is built by a building contractor and designed by an architect. Thus, different professionals operate on the different levels

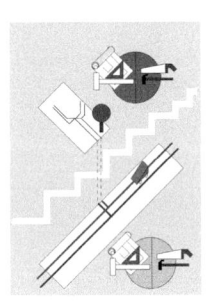

Figure 11.6
Pipes for utilities and sewage are particularly important. Their organization follows the same division of levels. There are pipes on the street level that serve the individual houses. The houses have their own distribution of pipes that is different for each house. The pipes in the house may change independently from those in the street. The contractors who install the pipes in the houses are not the same as those who install the pipes in the street

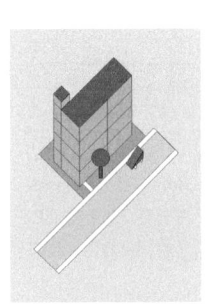

Figure 11.7
Instead of the house, consider the large apartment building built on the same street

Figure 11.8
Here we have the same division of levels. The apartment building is designed and built by the professionals who do buildings. The streets are designed and built by professionals who do urban design and build infrastructures

Figure 11.9
But if we look at the occupants the situation is different compared to the single house. The occupants of the apartment building are a community. The street is built for a community as well, albeit a different community. Where is the individual household?

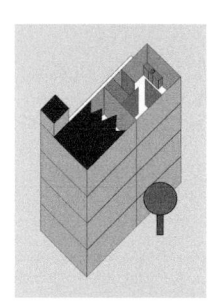

Figure 11.10
When we look inside the apartment building, we see the individual households. They have their own space in the building. But what parts relate to them and what parts relate to the community of the apartment building?

Figure 11.11
When we make that separation, we can take out the partitioning and all the equipment for bathroom and kitchen as well as heating and ventilation. This is the infill package of the apartment building: it constitutes a level of its own. The elements that belong to the single apartment make an 'infill package' or just 'infill.' The remainder of the building is called the 'base building' or 'support'

Figure 11.12
The infill package is related to the individual household. The 'support' or 'base building' is related to the community of households. The distinction that we see here is similar to the distinction between the street and the single house. But the physical elements are different

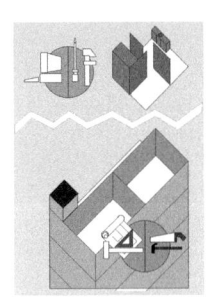

Figure 11.13
The level of the infill is the basis for the new industry that is the subject of these images. The base building or support is built by the same contractors who also build the individual house: they make buildings. The base building or support is also designed by the architect who works for the owner of the building. But the infill package becomes the product of a special industry that produces and installs infill packages. It is designed by interior designers or specialized architects who work for the owners of the infill

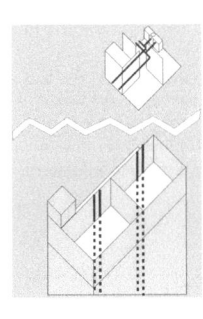

Figure 11.14
Here too we must give attention to the ducts, cables and pipes. They too are divided on the level of the support and the level of the infill. Each infill package has its own set of ducts, cables and pipes, distributed in its own way and installed as part of the total infill. The apartment building has the ducts, cables and pipes that serve the community in the building. They connect to the individual infill packages. The ducts in the base building are designed and installed by professionals who are not the same as those who install the ducts, cables and pipes in the infill system. The ducts and pipes in the infill system are different in nature and technology from those that go into buildings

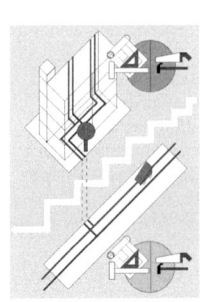

Figure 11.15
We now can see three levels: first the level of the street, supporting the level of the base building. Each has its own designers and installation companies

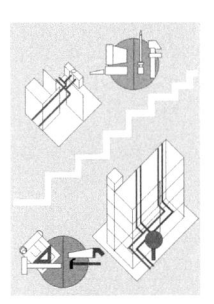

Figure 11.16
Next is the level of the building as distinct from the level of the infill just as the level of the street is distinct from the level of the building

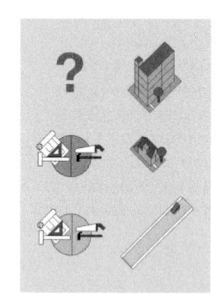

Figure 11.17
We now can understand the reason for the new infill industry. Traditionally we have two levels of industry: the level of the streets, and the level of the building. Today the large apartment building is built just as the single house. That creates a problem because the independent household no longer has a level of its own

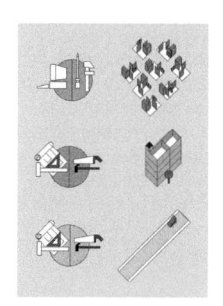

Figure 11.18
The infill industry corrects this situation. It recognizes the household as an independent agent in the built environment. An independent infill industry follows different principles of production and distribution compared to the traditional building industry. It has its own components, its own designers, and its own installers. It allows for new technology and new logistics

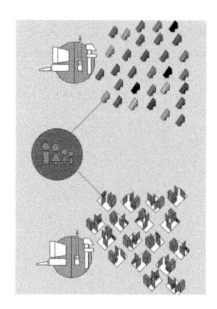

Figure 11.19
The new infill industry relates to the building industry as the car relates to the street. The infill industry serves the individual user. The individual household now can choose an infill package like it can choose a car. The new infill industry will become as important as the car industry. The price of a simple infill package is similar to the price of a car

Chapter 12

How housing renovation is meeting the challenge of oversupply of dwelling units in Japan

Yoshiro Morita and Yongsun Kim

Introduction

Japan met a tipping point in the housing sector in 2009, when the annual number of housing starts fell below the level of one million units which had been maintained for more than 40 years. Japan had long enjoyed economic profits from new housing construction. However, as a result of lack of consideration of the total building stock, the Japanese housing market is now over-built, and is faced with a high vacancy rate of 13.6% (8.46 million units). This mismatch of supply and demand is causing significant realignments in all parts of the housing sector, as well as new opportunities. Shuichi Matsumura (2020) points out some of these new opportunities in his book *Open Architecture for the People*, in which he refers to the stock of empty buildings in Japan as a 'spatial resource,' opening the way for an entirely new way of thinking about how everyday life can find fulfillment and 'personal entertainment' whether by experts or non-experts, rather than simply another kind of business that is strictly the domain of professionals. He looks forward to a time when Japan will become a society that 'plays' with the stock of buildings (Sato et al., 2017).

It is in this context that this chapter presents several cases of innovations in housing renovation that remain in the professional sphere, in both the public and private housing markets.

Figure 12.1 compares the loss of the housing stock since the 1950s in Japan and the USA, indicating how residential buildings in Japan have been demolished after a short lifespan. Figure 12.2 shows that vacant dwelling units are mainly seen in old rental multifamily buildings which have lost their competitive edge in the market.

DOI: 10.4324/9781003018339-15

Figure 12.1 Comparative loss of housing stock since the 1950s in Japan and USA (Morita Yoshiro, Maeshima Ayako, Robert Schmidt III)

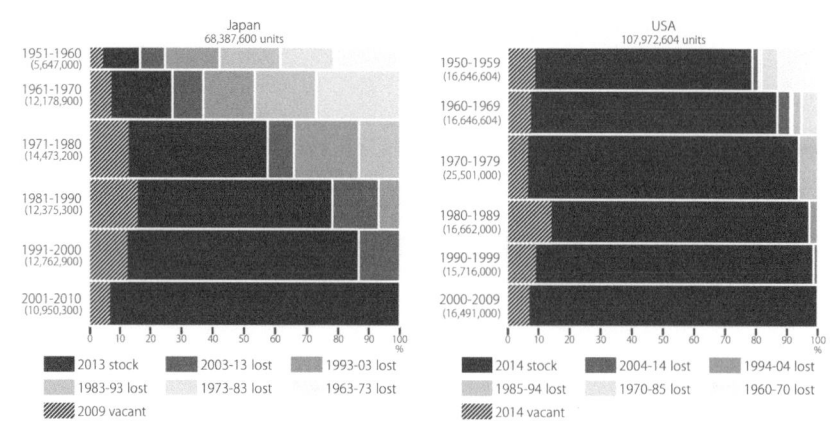

Figure 12.2 Loss of housing stock since the 1950s by year of construction, structure, building type, and ownership (Morita Yoshiro, Maeshima Ayako, Robert Schmidt III)

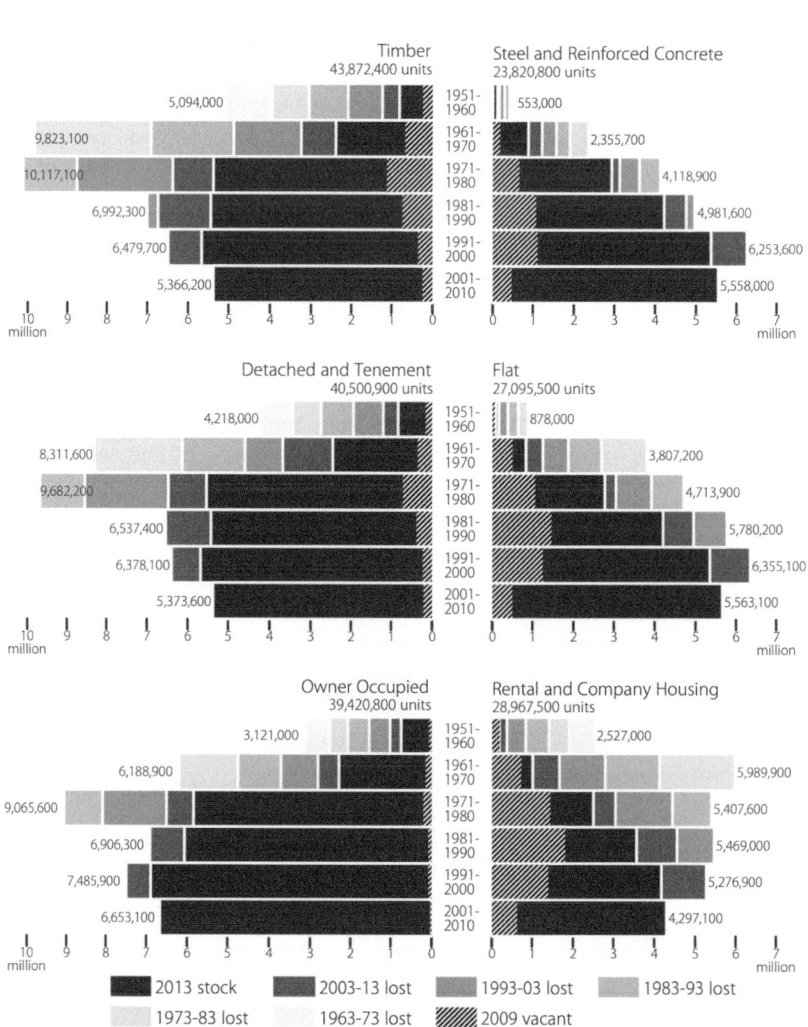

Renovation of condominiums

Full renovation: Skeleton Reform

Recently in Japan, a renovation technique known as Skeleton Reform has been gaining attention (Matsumura, 2016). Skeleton Reform refers to the large-scale renovation of condominiums from scratch, which is performed by retaining the existing structural framework and common parts such as structural columns and beams and removing all mechanical equipment and interior fittings. In addition to permitting free selection of interior layout, decoration and equipment, all the invisible piping, electrical equipment, insulation, and so on can be completely renewed and replaced thanks to this technique.

After purchasing an old condominium building, with the application of the Skeleton Reform approach, the dwellings can be completely modified to the level of a newly built condominium, allowing free modifications in room arrangement and other aspects.

Figures 12.3 through 12.4 demonstrate how an old condominium unit, narrow and deep, has been significantly modified; the interior space is opened up by removing the walls and by modifying the room arrangement. The builder removed all the inner walls, ceiling and floor finishing, equipment and mechanical facilities, leaving the basic structure intact (Figure 12.3-1), and performed an overall renovation of their residence. Note that the fact that the unit is an 'end' unit gives added possibilities for room reconfiguration. In this project, like virtually all reinforced concrete multifamily buildings in Japan, a raised floor of 30–40 cm was used in the initial construction. During renovation, this floor system was removed and replaced by a new raised floor (Figure 12.3-2). In this case, Mitsui Fudosan Reform signed a contract with the general contractor, who brought in subcontractors to complete the job, similar to the way new construction projects are managed. Our research indicates that multi-skilled workers who can cover a variety of tasks are used in renovation projects, where the project scale is smaller than in new construction. The unit was renovated in 2–3 months (Figure 12.4).

Figure 12.3-1, 12.3-2
Skeleton Reform: emptied space and the raised floor

Figure 12.4
Before and after plans of a dwelling in a Skeleton Reform project

Renovation using the NEXT-Infill system

In Japan, there are various limitations in the renovation of old condominium buildings. In addition to the obvious issue of construction cost, such limitations include a long construction period, noise, waste, and other factors. Construction noise sometimes causes conflicts in the neighborhood, and the disposal of waste must also be considered.

To solve such issues, it is necessary to find measures to shorten the construction period and to minimize the amount of construction work on site as much as possible. The NEXT-Infill system has been developed for this purpose.

The system was originally studied for the renovation business of Sekisui Chemical Company and developed under the leadership of Mr. Adachi in 2002. However, it was not adopted because the superiority to the conventional way was not evaluated positively by Sekisui, leading Mr. Adachi to start a new company to further develop the product based on reduction of time and cost. He continues to develop access to the market. Approximately 100 residences have applied this system so far. By the application of this system, it is possible to reduce the construction period, reduce the construction costs, prevent the quality deterioration of woodworking and minimize work on-site.

The NEXT-Infill system includes only seven standard wooden parts (Figure 12.5) which are produced in a factory. These parts can be combined to make partition walls between rooms, wall-liners against the existing walls, column and beam covers, and as 'hung' ceiling coverings. Standardized base panels are produced by combining these seven parts. The base panel is composed and formed by the H-liners and the cross pieces; they are completely packaged by connecting and fixing the three H-liners with grooves with the six cross pieces of varying lengths (Parts #278, 293, 500).

These packaged base panels are designed such that their length can be adjusted on site, in consideration of the variable dimensions of the existing structure.

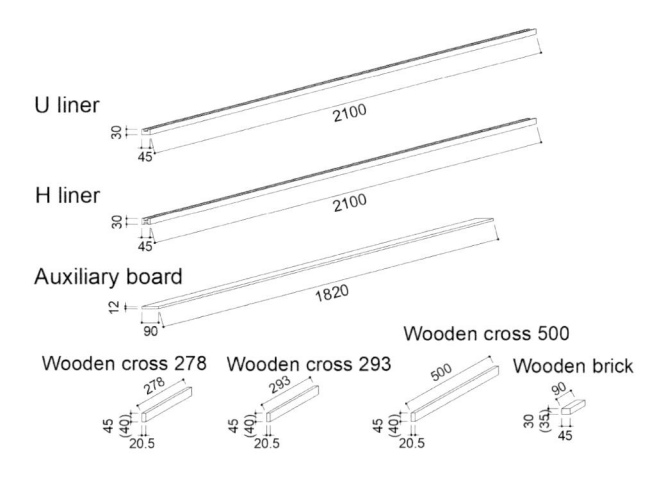

U liner 2100
H liner 2100
Auxiliary board 1820
Wooden cross 278
Wooden cross 293
Wooden cross 500
Wooden brick

Figure 12.5
Seven wooden parts manufactured in a factory

The advantage of the NEXT-Infill system is its accurate and rapid constructability. It is enabled by its minimum basic components and its good performance which allows the simplest and varied assembly. When constructing a wall or wall liner, first, the space around the wall is fixed with the U liner, and then it is reinforced by the Wooden cross part 278, and on such reinforcement the Base Panel is installed last. As the heights of the ceilings of the dwellings where NEXT-Infill is used vary, the height can be freely adjusted by using the cross piece 500. Each of the panels are connected with the cross piece 293 to complete the entire wall (Figure 12.6).

Figure 12.6
The con-
struction
method
of walls

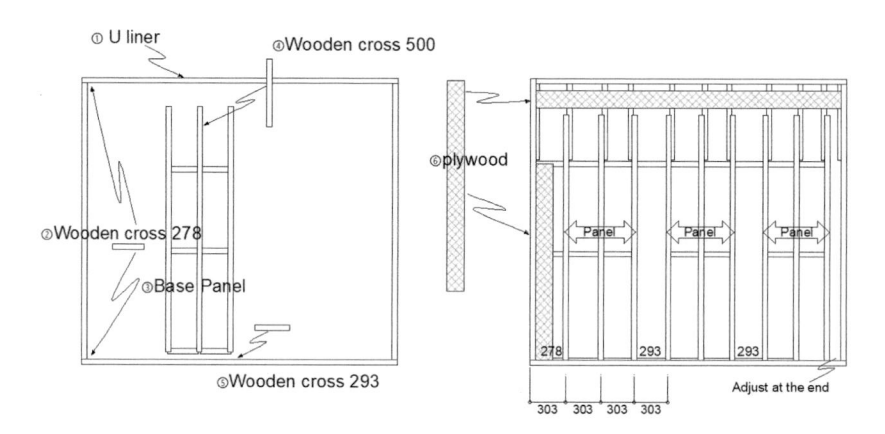

In cases where the wall requires structural strength, the reinforcement can be applied by using and attaching the stiffener to the H-liner and the cross piece, and also the intersection between walls, and walls to ceiling, can be simply constructed (Figure 12.7 and 12.8). Moreover, the (standard) electric wiring and electric box can be installed by using the H-liner and the cross pieces.

Figure 12.7
Structural reinforcement, intersection of walls and ceiling

Figure 12.8
Image during installation

A typical electrical "spider" wiring system is used, with conventional electrical parts prefabricated per project/per room for Adachi. The "box" is attached to the ceiling in the middle of the room, and the wires are run down the partitions before the gypsum board is installed. Once installed, there is no access to the wires (except perhaps a little door in the ceiling near the connector part). Wires are color coded (switches, convenience outlets, ceiling fixtures, and red from the main circuit breaker of the apartment).

Earlier versions of NEXT-Infill had a special floor panel subsystem under which horizontal water piping and other utilities were installed. That is not used today; instead, industry standard raised floors are installed, provided by other manufacturers. The before and after floor plans show that the WC, bathtub and kitchen all moved. The piping serving these 'wet' spaces are above the concrete structural slab. As usual in Japan, no concrete slab waterproofing was applied. This is based on an assumption that water leakage doesn't occur in drainage lines. In case it should occur, it is covered in insurance policies.

Although installation of the base panel can be managed by a single worker, the worker usually brings an assistant in most cases. Usual construction period is two months in total, in which cleaning out and installing base panels takes four days for each on average.

The NEXT-Infill system can also be applied on new residences. A condominium building in Ota City (Tokyo), which was completed in September 2020, has 13 residences on four floors, which adopted this system for the infill work. The space of one residence is remarkably opened and the NEXT-Infill system has been applied in the partition walls between all rooms (Figure 12.9, 12.10 and 12.11).

Figure 12.9
A completed NEXT-Infill project

Figure 12.10
A new condominium project using NEXT-Infill (Ota City)

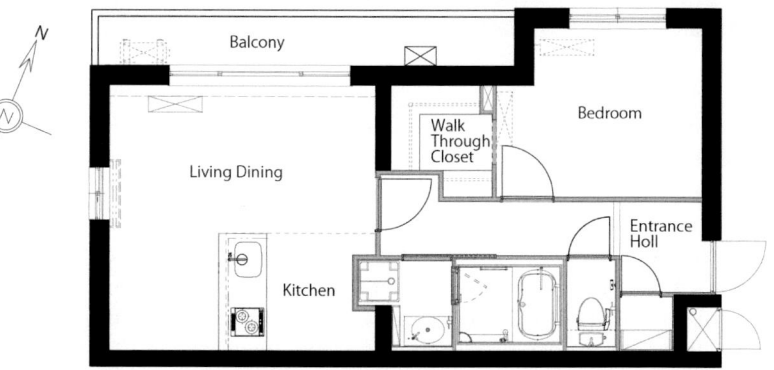

Red lines show where the NEXT-Infill system was installed

Figure 12.11
After completion of a new project using NEXT-Infill

Renovation of public rental apartments

This and the next section, under the context of the shift from a 'flow' to a 'building stock activation' market, focuses on the housing type of rental flats. We introduce several projects that aim to bring new life into vacant buildings with the active participation of the residents.

MUJI x UR Danchi Renovation project: products for renovation of public housing units

UR and 'Danchi'

UR (Urban Renaissance Agency) is a semi-governmental organization whose mission is to engage in urban and housing development. UR is also responsible for managing 720,000 rental dwellings all across Japan, which the organization started to supply as JHC (Japan Housing Corporation) in 1955 to solve the huge housing shortage during post WWII reconstruction. JHC developed a number of multifamily housing estate projects ('Danchi') in urban neighborhoods, and the development spread to the suburbs of many cities.

From the viewpoint of that development period, housing blocks supplied until the early 1960s were relatively close to downtown and have already been demolished and new housing constructed in their place, exploiting the locational potential of the sites. These redevelopment projects were a combination of building at higher densities by UR, and new construction on surplus parcels of land by private developers. On the other hand, some suburban estates developed after the late 1960s and farther from urban centers are experiencing more difficulties in making needed investments to reactivate the buildings, due in part to the aging of the residents and an increase of vacancies, both of which present serious challenges in these older developments.

Earlier Danchi projects were developed under the regulation to conform to the rule of 4-hour access to daylight on the first (ground) floor even in winter, which resulted in vast open spaces between buildings. Although Danchi buildings surrounded by rich nature used to be an ideal neighborhood for young households with children, as the population aged, these environments were not attractive any longer, in part because they had no elevators. Given the access types of these projects – with two dwellings sharing a common stair per floor – installing an elevator at each stair was considered too expensive.

Despite the stagnation in these projects, suburban Danchi are now being re-evaluated by some of the younger generation. The MUJI x UR Danchi Renovation is one of the projects to be established under this new situation and is explained in what follows.

Concept of the project

MUJI is a retail brand dealing with a wide variety of products including household goods, apparel and food (www.muji.com/jp/ja/store). The MUJI x UR Danchi Renovation project compares itself to 'dishing up favorite "food" in a "lunchbox". Residents can choose and add MUJI's products based on the concept of 'Utilize,' 'Change,' and 'Customize.' The MUJI x UR Danchi Renovation Project is based on an approach to invite the residents into design tasks meaning that residents select MUJI's products and put them in the renovated unit.

Utilize: The MUJI x UR Danchi Renovation Project intends to enable tenant residents to arrange the unit in their own way. Kitchens can be somewhat changed in location as well as layout. Air conditioning units are typically installed at the initiative of the tenants in Japan. Sometimes aged wooden columns and finishing carpentry in RC structures are inherited and preserved as design elements in contrast to white renovated interiors, and closets are preserved as large display storage units which can be used as desk spaces. Being old-fashioned can be valued for the younger generation today (see Figure 12.12 and 12.13).

Change: A variety of products have been originally prepared for the project apart from MUJI's original product offerings. Island kitchens to encourage communication, narrow, ceiling hung unit shelf systems (hung from the ceilings, preventing overturning during earthquake), lightweight semitransparent sliding doors, soft and tough tatami mats made of hemp are examples.

Customize: The project suggests the way of life by changing room layouts in accordance with the lifestyle and life stages of the residents by using furniture and fittings. Unit shelving is an existing merchandise of MUJI, to be utilized as storage partitions, selected and installed by tenants (sometime with help from friends or professional installers).

Modular design coordination

One of the distinctive features of the project is that the infill system is developed by the collaboration of MUJI and UR. It is responsible to confirm modular design coordination in every corner of the dwelling unit. Up to this point, tenants are invited to take part in decision making in the given condition. This is in contrast to what is happening in private rental apartment renovations, discussed in the next section.

The 'MUJI Unit Shelf' (mentioned above), long available in the open market, is a key product to help achieve variable and changeable room layout whose size is coordinated with the height of doors and kitchen. MUJI manufactures almost 7000 items. Storage boxes, baskets, household electric appliances and small articles are designed to fit together (see Figure 12.13).

Figure 12.12
Change of floor layout (www.muji. net/ie/ mujiur/plan/ plan01.html)

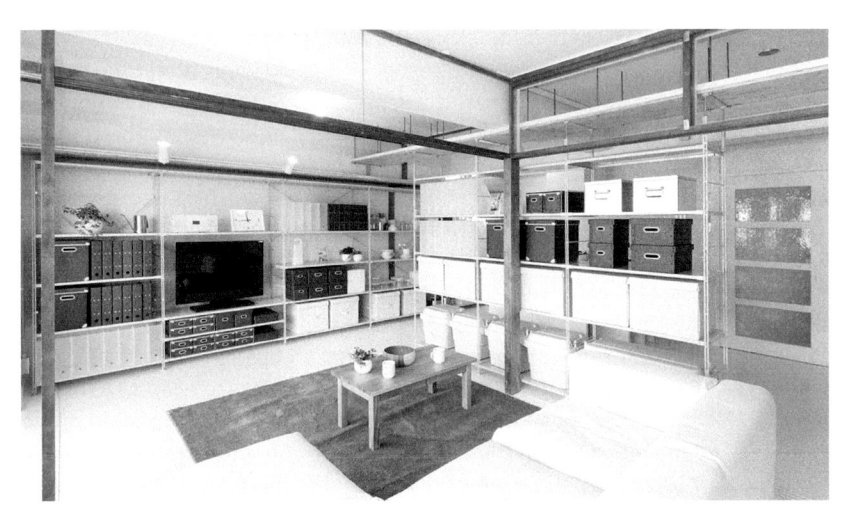

Figure 12.13
Unit shelf working as a moderate partitioning (www.muji. net/ie/ mujiur/plan/ plan01.html)

Renovation of private rental apartments

DIY renovation movement: enhancing value of old rental apartments and the area by 'do it together' – an approach to welcome the residents into the design process

In contrast to the MUJI x UR Danchi Renovation approach, in the field of private rental apartments there is a recent movement that the prospective tenant is invited to be part of the renovation team through the entire process, or most of it. This is a result of long-held discontent on the part of tenants of private rental dwellings; tenants were prohibited from even driving a nail in a wall to hang a painting. The 2011 earthquake may have triggered a change in attitude of the building owners to be more open to tenants taking care of their own spaces. The movement is often led by some unique building owners who have inherited old apartment properties from their predecessors.

Case 1

Yoshiura building: creating a new cycle by DIY in the building stock

The following projects are characteristic examples of a more widespread trend in Japan, discussed at length in *Open Architecture for the People* (Matsumura, 2020). The Yoshiura Building was built in 1973 in Fukuoka City. It has 40 rental housing units whose vacancy ratio used to be as high as 20%. Most residents were aging, and the rent defaults reached 10 million JPY in total. It was a kind of negative legacy from the older generation of buildings, when newer buildings were expected to yield higher rent just for that reason.

In 2013 Mr. Takanori Yoshiura inherited the property which his grandfather had built on farmland. As soon as the inheritance process was completed, he decided to make four showrooms, one of which had no fixtures and equipment. By the fact that the empty 'skeleton' units were leased quickly, he was convinced of the market for 'skeleton rental apartments.'

Unlike the standard process, the owner of the skeleton rental apartment building designs a unit together with the prospective tenant with support of an architect. The building owner provides the budget equivalent to three years' rent. In case the monthly rent is 50 thousand JPY ($465), the budget is set at 1.8 million JPY ($16,720). Out of that budget, 1.6 million JPY ($14,850) is usually required for plumbing fixtures, water and electric installations, and raised floors.

The process follows three steps: (1) Study of design and room layout alternatives by the tenant, the designer and the building owner; (2) Once agreed to, the major renovation work is undertaken by professionals; (3) This is followed by DIY work by the tenant. The owner promises to spend 1.8 million JPY ($16,720), but that is usually not enough for the entire completion of the dwelling. The tenant can keep the total expense within the amount promised by doing some work by themselves. Exactly what the tenant does depends on the plan for the dwelling renovation and their skills. The tenant is given the initiative to determine the way of using the remaining 0.2 million JPY ($1850); any shortage is to be covered by the tenant. In this way, the tenant reduces their costs by doing some of the work themselves (DIY) (Figure 12.14).

Figure 12.14-1, 12.14-2 **Before and after the DIY renovation (www.yoshiura-build.jp)**

In this building, piping for water and drainage had been routed under the concrete slab (in the ceiling space of the unit below), which was usual in old buildings. During the renovation, the placement of kitchen, bath and toilet can be changed as long as the gradient in drainage pipes connected to the pipe shafts are set under the newly raised floor (Figure 12.15).

Figure 12.15
New piping connected to the base building vertical pipe shaft

Figure 12.16
DIY shop and material storehouse on the ground floor of the building

The tenant DIY-er is encouraged to utilize the DIY shop and material storehouse on the ground floor of the building (Figure 12.16). A two-months' rent-free period is offered to complete the DIY work. In most cases the tenant moves into an unfinished unit and continues the work while living in it.

Mr. Yoshiura points out that tenant DIY-ers have more attachment to their own dwellings and tend to live there longer. Tenants' DIY enhances the value of the dwelling unit, and higher rent is expected by the successive tenant.

Case 2

Corpo Edoyashiki: DIY as a tool of community design

There is also a movement that DIY activities are introduced into community design (the urban design level).

DIY approach where renovation investment cannot be recovered

Corpo Edoyashiki in Kurume City is a rental housing complex of 48 units built in 1978 by a private company. It had long faced a high vacancy rate and population aging due to its inconvenient location.

The Danchi property was purchased in 2015 by an investment company, Vintage no Machi (VM), with a plan for building renovation and community design (see Figure 12.17). Dr. Katsumi Yoshihara, head of VM, looks back on the policy shift of the project from investing for renovation to enhancing the community with DIY activities. The main reason for the shift was the financial difficulty stemming from Kurume's location where the renovation investments could not be recovered from rent increases alone.

Figure 12.17
Corpo Edoyashiki (www. space-r. net/rent-page/ edoyashiki/ story)

In one of the buildings in this Danchi development, there is a unit which a group of skilled craftsmen occupies as a shared office. The group is composed of a variety of professionals: a gardener, carpenter, plasterer and realtor. They are there to lead DIY activities in the estate, helping to build outdoor decks and to beautify the common landscape (Figure 12.18). A dwelling unit renovated by the group also serves as a showroom and consultation center for the neighbors who are planning DIY renovation in their own units elsewhere in the development.

Figure 12.18
**Outdoor
deck by DIY
team (www.
space-r.net/
rent-page/
edoyashiki/
story)**

Through the project, called *SpaceRDesign*, the management firm of the Corpo Edoyashiki came to use a combination of three design methods to revitalize the housing estate:

1. DIY for cultivating residents' emotional attachment to the building and the neighborhood.
2. Renovation for enhancing the value of the built environment.
3. Landscape design to show the community's prosperity to the neighborhood.

According to the concept, DIY renovation by residents corresponds to a combination of (1) and (2); redesigning outdoor spaces with craftsmen's group (2) and (3) methods.

Change of social backgrounds

DIY home improvement center as an infrastructure for DIY-ers
The number of DIY home improvement centers in Japan has been steadily increasing, which helps DIY-ers with tools and materials. Starting with no home improvement centers in 1975, the number in 2020 is close to 5000 nationwide. The sales accounts reached 4 trillion JPY ($37.6 billion) in 2020, one fourth of which is occupied by the 'DIY goods and materials' division. The internet also offers a tremendous amount of DIY know-how as well. The support system for DIY-ers is rapidly being enriched.

Exclusion of restoration duty

It is natural that introducing enhanced tenants' DIY leads to eliminating the requirement that tenants restore the unit to the condition in which they found it at lease termination. In DIY apartments, tenants are instead recognized as partners in improving the value of property, instead of thinking of tenants as those whose living leads to its deterioration.

Affected by the current state of increasing DIY apartments, the Ministry of Land, Infrastructure and Transport released guidelines for rental agreement of tenants' DIY dwellings in 2014. In case the new agreement is adopted for a given project, tenants themselves can renovate their units according to their own preferences at their own expense, while the building owners can lighten the burden by leasing the units without fixing them up.

> The possibility of a new kind of industry is in the renovation market rather than new building market at the least in Japan, I think. I will give you one example. Nowadays in Japan, the younger generation has less resistance to living in second-hand condos than my generation who much prefer new to second-hand. Therefore, the market of second-hand condos is enlarging. Some young singles, couples and families buy second-hand condo housing units at a cheaper price and invest in the renovation as they like. 'Tool Box' company (see www.r-toolbox.jp/) is one typical example of a new business model corresponding to such a new tendency of the market. It can be called a 'select shop of the building components and materials on the website' for the residents who will realize their own taste in living space by their own selection of infill components and sometimes by using DIY. It is not the business for the mass market such as IKEA and Home Depot. It is a smaller shop which has its own taste and its own fans. Although I don't expect much in the way of new infill hardware systems nowadays, I do expect such a new business style of infill for the people.
>
> (Private correspondence in January 2021, with Professor Shuichi Matsumura, Professor of Architecture, University of Tokyo, and author of *Open Architecture for the People*, Routledge, 2020)

Conclusions

Despite the difference of housing type, these projects show the current changes of decision-making arrangements for continuous reuse of the building stock and the built environment in Japan. These changes are occurring under the shift from flow to housing stock activation market, under the pressures of a rapidly aging population, and a serious oversupply of obsolete housing units.

In the rental multifamily housing field, the process of planning and building is beginning to be opened to residents and the community. In the condominium field (units for sale), where strong sole ownership often stagnates common businesses, project managers with strong initiative are required. These changes will fulfill the demand for variety in housing in the future.

References

Matsumura, Shuichi (2016). *Theory and Practice of Architectural Renovation.* Tokyo: Ichigaya Shuppansha Publishing.

Matsumura, Shuichi (2020). *Open Architecture for the People: Housing Development in Post-War Japan.* London and New York: Routledge.

Sato, Koichi et al. (2017). *A Guide to the Industry of Architecture.* Shokokusha Publishing, Tokyo.

Chapter 13

Dualities of interior decoration companies in China

Li Shanshan

Introduction

Chinese interior decoration companies play a significant role in both housing construction and maintenance, as well as the realization of the residential Open Building approach in the market of large housing projects in China. On further scrutiny, China's contemporary decoration market is characterized by its duality. On the one hand, standardization and personalization interact; the scheme of fitting out a new-built community relies upon high standardization, whereas people's individual demands are reflected in the refurbishment of existing dwellings. On the other hand, while the traditional mode of on-site manual labor remains dominant, the revolution characterized by industrialization and off-site prefabrication coupled with advanced logistics and enterprise software is inexorably finding its way into the market, as this chapter concludes.

This chapter approaches this duality primarily from the perspective of interior decoration companies. It reveals the phenomenon, interprets the duality's cause, then discusses their effect on Open Building practices. This chapter is based on a critical review of the extant literature regarding marketing strategies and practices of decoration companies, in addition to their reliance on prefabrication and industrialization in fitting-out interior living space per dwelling. Moreover, the chapter draws on professional interviews carried out with six companies that are focused on providing comprehensive decoration services, as well as nine companies working in the refurbishment market. (Table 13.1). The aim is to uncover the duality characteristic in China's decoration (infill or fit-out) market, as well as to analyze Open Building's prospective development in the Chinese context from this perspective.

Part 1: Two kinds of services provided by decoration companies

Throughout the entire interior decoration market, two different services are offered by current companies. One service is targeted at newly built housing projects, in which the inhabitants are unknown during the design stage. The

DOI: 10.4324/9781003018339-16

Table 13.1 Description of investigated companies

New-built market	Description
Company N1	It provides examples which represent how a decoration scheme is typically devised.
Company N2	Its decoration standard divides the inhabitants into 12 family types, then concludes on the highlights of the suite layout and decoration per type.
Company N3	It is the first practitioner of industrialized decoration.
Company N4	It has developed ten prefabricated systems.
Company N5	It is recognized for the productive performance in so-called industrialized decoration.
Company N6	It is recognized for the productive performance in so-called industrialized decoration.

Refurbishment market	Description
Company R1	It pursues a high degree of customization and concentrates primarily on large suites in congregated housing and luxurious single-family villas.
Company R2	It is characterized by cost-effective performance and 'simple' fashion. It is managed as an affiliated institute of a rental-agent business, as well as a real-estate platform to provide basic yet fast refurbishment packages for both the dwelling-for-rent market and self-owned housing.
Company R3	Its business scope has been extended to office buildings and commercial space.
Company R4	It concentrates on research and development of their own materials and products.
Company R5	It shows the typical procedures of a whole-dwelling decoration service.
Company R6	It charges a high 'design and service fee' per suite. It extends its after-sale warranty to 10 years for concealed work.
Company R7	It charges a labor fee for serious damage of work done out of the quality-guarantee duration.
Company R8	It provides two standard infill packages in the refurbishment of individual dwellings.
Company R9	It focuses on integrated bathroom units' design, manufacture and installation, and serves individual clients.

(Source: the author)

decoration design type is subject to the decisions and preferences of both the developers and construction companies. The other service pertains to individual dwellings fit-out; in the majority of cases these companies refurbish them in accordance with the users' personalized demands, which directly reflects the users' financial situation, living habits and stylistic tendencies. These services have different goals, thus accounting for their distinct operational strategies and establishing the foundation of the apparent duality. As a context for the further discussion, this section interprets the reason for both modes' emergence and survival.

Service for mass decoration of fully fitted housing

There is an established history of decoration companies dealing with the finishing of public buildings. Their market in the housing sector was opened up over the past two decades (2000–2020), accompanied by advocacy for and development of fully furnished housing being delivered to the market. This presents a history of standardization, as well as combining the design of the infill and support (or base building). In 1999, a document was approved by the General Office of the State Council of the People's Republic of China, which was forwarded to affiliated organizations and local governments nationally. This document was developed by the Ministry of Housing and Urban–Rural Development alongside six other housing-related agencies, comprising 35 recommendations regarding 'housing industrialization,' through which well-completed decoration was initially advocated by the authority.[1] The fully furnished decoration business was stimulated in the housing field, involving not just existing companies but new participants. Subsequently, in 2002 a specification was implemented that included the collation of technical points, providing a form of practical direction, with many local regulations subsequently being introduced. The policy orientation promoted the requirement of fully furnished dwelling supply, while stimulating companies to develop corresponding services.

Alongside the compulsory regulations, the nature of the real estate industry is the pursuit of profit, absorbing full decoration into the process, while rationalizing associated services provided by interior decoration companies. Investigations in various districts have revealed that fully furnished interior decoration services dramatically increase dwelling sales prices, which both expands the return on investment for decoration as well as creating more generous profits than anticipated. For example, statistics pertaining to new community construction projects in Nanjing in 2016 is evidence that the dwelling price per square meter increased from 2000RMB to 7000RMB ($300–1060) having already been fitted out (Jia Chunfeng, 2016). Consequently this appears to be attractive, particularly among districts with low residential construction rates.

Complete decoration services are accompanied by government subsidies and high public esteem in the majority of instances, thus making costly approaches widely acceptable. In addition, with the significance of energy-saving and ecologically sustainable performance having progressively received acknowledgement, such performance is now cited as an important standard for green building assessment.[2] High star-rated projects are entitled to acquire corresponding financial subsidies. This is regulated by the central government, which in 2012 was set at 45 and 80 RMB per m^2 for two-star and three-star projects respectively.[3] Meanwhile, the majority of regions have released their own incentives and compensation policies in response to national policy direction. Besides compensation that may be calculated in numbers, what absorbs developers is the ability to earn a degree of reputation and subsequently attain higher brand value in addition to better building opportunities.

A number of encumbrances have hindered full decoration from being accepted without hesitation, with two facts being significant. One is that it evokes greater doubts, dissatisfaction, disputes and even litigation from inhabitants. The second is that it extends the construction period, thus delaying the pursuit of benefits in the subsequent projects. To overcome such obstacles, standardization and prefabrication are perceived as significant tools for acceleration and quality improvement, which is clarified further below.

Services for individual dwellings

From the mid-1980s, housing property was transformed from being state-owned welfare to the status of a self-owned commodity, thus encouraging people to expend greater time, energy and money for their private dwellings, particularly with regards to interior decoration. This requirement bred product suppliers who fulfilled material requirements (Figure 13.1) and provided corresponding installation services, alongside refurbishment teams comprised of experienced workers who are trained to deal with the relatively

Figure 13.1
A typical plumbing parts store in China (photo Stephen Kendall)

complex and professional work required, such as piping and wiring. These two entities have occupied a prominent position in relation to decoration activities; the 'product supplier + decoration team' mode has been adopted by the majority as a priority.

However, deficiencies have increasingly been revealed. Firstly, tremendous responsibility was placed on the residents, compelling their visits to numerous product showrooms and construction sites. This involved not just intricate decisions and the comparison of materials and goods, it is also related to supervisory incompetence during the construction process which exhausted inhabitants. This is to say nothing of the transportation and management of workers across various trades or construction fields. Secondly, the decoration teams exhibited varied levels of skills and financial credit, which affected inhabitants' satisfaction. Moreover, their frequent regional mobility eliminated the prospect of after-sales service. A secure third platform was urgently required, with its establishment hastening the emergence of decoration companies during the 1990s,[4] which delivered a one-unit-at-a-time fit-out service and connected the three parties of product supplier, decoration worker and client.

Decoration companies' fundamental operational mode is the purchase of materials and goods at a discounted trade price, followed by selling them to customers as decoration finishing and assorted services. However, each company's specific emphasis differs. Some pursue a high degree of customization and concentrate primarily on large suites in congregated housing and luxurious single-family villas, for example Company R1. Others are characterized by cost-effective performance and 'simple' fashion. A typical example in this regard is Company R2, a company managed as an affiliated institute of a rental-agent business, as well as a real-estate platform that provides basic yet fast refurbishment packages for both dwelling-for-rent market and self-owned housing. Alongside dispersed decoration for individuals, certain companies devote themselves to completely furbished housing projects and other building types, for instance Company R3, whose business scope has been extended to office buildings and commercial spaces. Certain counterparts have concentrated on research and development of their own material and products, alongside manufacturing and sales, for example Company R4 who recommends wall panels and furniture from its own product-line.

The merits of decoration companies are conveyed primarily by the fact that they liberate users from the complex decoration process, providing them with a quality-guaranteed result and dependable pre-and-after-sale service. Additionally, consumers' materials and goods expenditures are decreased due to bulk purchasing. Such attributes have received 30% acceptance of inhabitants(Investigation, 2016). Nevertheless, suspicion has arisen simultaneously. An investigation in Nanchang revealed three reasons that generated people's criticism of decoration companies: use of inferior materials; extended construction period, as well as ineffective performance or commitment to after-sales service (Xiao Yating, Xu Peishu, 2015). A survey in Shangqiu identified similar results, while unreasonable deposit and contract clauses, exaggerated advertisements and insufficient enterprise qualifications were also mentioned (Yang Xia, 2017). Regardless, the expression of skepticism has not hindered the phenomenon of interior decoration firms' increasing acceptance, nor their normalization process.

Discussion: different essences of the two services

Two types of services have been found to coexist within China's housing interior decoration market, each characterized by varying initiatives and aims. The government has advocated the first service type, with its attainment primarily being affected by policy orientation and developers' choices, where the individual typically has no right to have a say. The second is initiated due to individual households having their personal, specific and sometimes unique requirements. This is principally restricted by the customer's economic and aesthetic preferences. The differences contribute to their varying attitudes towards standardization and individuality, alongside their diverse acceptance of innovation; this is the basis of the discussion in Part 2.

Part 2: the balance of standardization and individuality

The mass decoration of new-built housing and refurbishment of existing individual dwellings is characterized by a different balance regarding standardization and individuality. The former is underpinned by users' common requirements yet pursues diverse results through subdividing clients into 'market segments' emphasizing each segments' characteristics. The latter responds to individual preferences, while summarizing their commonalities as a business strategy in order to simplify the operational processes. Furthermore, these two 'directions' are reflected in the practice of Open Building as the pursuit of capacity for change, the delineation and separation of design tasks between the communal areas of a building and individual (independent) dwellings, alongside the emphasis on housing quality improvements over time.

Full-decoration housing: the reliance on standardization and pursuit of diversity

How a new-built community is fitted out is to a certain extent determined by the real estate developer, being declared in their bidding or commissioning document. Therefore, there is limited space for the interior decoration company to play with. The following example conveys how a decoration scheme is typically devised. It concerns a high-rise residential building with a total area of 25575.59 m² (275,288 ft²). It is comprised of 164 dwelling units with four different dwelling area standards of 156 m² (1680 ft²), 147 m² (1582 ft²), 123 m² (1324 ft²) and 91 m² (980 ft²), with each having a distinct sub-division of the interior space. The project was fitted out according to three schemes: Scheme A for 156 m² dwellings, Scheme B for 147 m² dwellings, as well as Scheme C for 123 m² and 91 m² dwellings. The schemes' variations are represented primarily in the main surface colors used, combined with several variations in terms of details, appliances and cabinets, the brand and model number of which are determined by the real-estate company from their partner companies.

The interior decoration company's development was in accordance with three principal procedures. Initially, reflecting the anticipated property price, Rank A was selected as the decoration standard, which set the decoration cost as limited to between 1100 and 1300 RMB/m² with corresponding instructions released concerning which parts were to be decorated, while precisely stipulating each detail and what kinds of products were to be provided. Secondly, the decoration style was proposed based on a survey of potential clients, indicating the principal color, molding types, arrangement of sanitary fixtures in bathrooms, layout of closets, while being adopted as the reference for rectifying product selection errors. Thirdly, with the first two steps' results having been declared in the bidding documents, the selected interior company (Company N1) completed the specific design scheme for the real-estate company's approval (Figure 13.2).

Reliance on standardization has been revealed through the commonly applied procedures outlined above, combined with the constraints placed on individuality which are prominently conveyed by the adoption of decoration standards and prediction of potential clients. The former is proposed

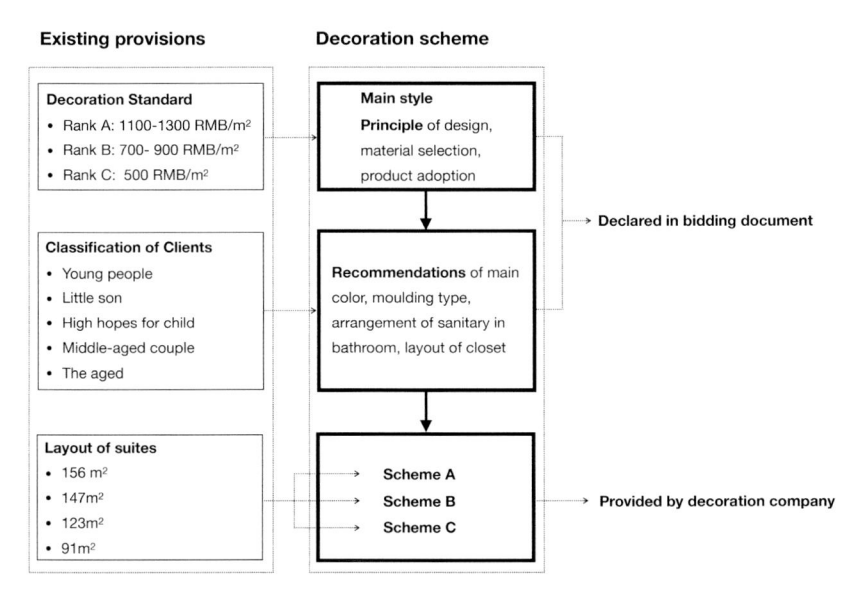

Existing provisions   **Decoration scheme**

Decoration Standard
- Rank A: 1100-1300 RMB/m²
- Rank B: 700- 900 RMB/m²
- Rank C: 500 RMB/m²

Main style
Principle of design,
material selection,
product adoption

····> Declared in bidding document

Classification of Clients
- Young people
- Little son
- High hopes for child
- Middle-aged couple
- The aged

Recommendations of main
color, moulding type,
arrangement of sanitary in
bathroom, layout of closet

Layout of suites
- 156 m²
- 147m²
- 123m²
- 91m²

Scheme A
Scheme B
Scheme C

····> Provided by decoration company

Figure 13.2
**Procedures
of a typical
interior
design**

to regulate costs, although the principles of design, materials selection and product adoption determined in the meantime touch even on certain details that emphasize the gap between 'ranks.' For example, regulations stipulate that the concrete ceiling of the main living space may only be whitewashed in Rank C, while for Level A the living room, dining room and main bedroom are permitted to have a suspended ceiling and LED lighting strips, with the other bedroom or study room decorated with a plaster crown molding. The latter provides more detailed instructions. This is exemplified in the decoration standards of Company N2, which divided the inhabitants into 12 family types, then concluded on the highlights of the suite layout and decoration per type, including the specific type of main sanitary fixtures in the bathroom. Normally, such regulations are devised from in-depth research into consumer group's preferences as well as the real-estate firm's extensive experience, which represents the common requirements, while inhabitants' individual preferences have no place in the process. Ultimately, a single scheme is characterized by total uniformity, within which may be found information covering all details of the residences.

The concept of decoration menus

Certain efforts have been made to afford individuals with greater choice. Towards the end of the 20th century, the concept of decoration menus was advocated within both policy documents and by researchers who were convinced that neither the fixed decoration scheme nor 'raw' dwelling approach provided desirable solutions. Thus, they predicted that fitting-out a housing project from menu-based selections would become the new trend (Chen Yeming, 1998). The generally recognized procedures may be broadly defined as having four steps: the invitation of several design institutes to provide a variety of choices; exhibition of sample rooms with price quotations; formulation of a decoration order reflecting clients' choices; completion of the installation (Li Peide, 2001). The menu theoretically provides a selection reflecting the most common requirements, alongside an individual selection presenting personality and permitting alternatives (Wang Feng, 2001). A typical approach is to 'formulate several menus with different decoration styles and prices, and to preserve some selections of color, size and pattern in each design' (Ma Chunjie, Hu Xiaomin, 2003). To vividly express potential achievements, multi-media technology was introduced, followed by BIM as a display approach (Yu Xia, 2013). A near-simultaneous phenomenon during this period were experimental activities emerging within the Shenzhen, Beijing and Shanghai markets (Li Juanjuan, Tang Lei, 2001). Taking Shanghai as an example, in 2000, 3000 dwellings were furnished according to inhabitants' menu order, while the number expanded tenfold over the subsequent year (Chen Min, Yu Jie, 2013). This attempt attracted certain developers' establishment of special product lines, for example 'UNI' by Quli Real Estate, 'Mia' by the Sunshine 100 company, as well as 'Meihaojia' of Vanke company.

During this period, certain studies were provided by researchers which advocated the reduction of menu selection and even raised a degree of suspicion regarding its necessity. Both developers and construction companies realized that this mode placed encumbrances upon them. Each procedure of setting the options, recording the client's choice, producing individual price quotations, as well as construction in accordance with various schemes necessitates several times more work compared with the traditional mode of decorating the entire project using a single decoration scheme. Work efficiency was dramatically impacted, while quality was negatively affected; this goes against the fundamental objective of complete decoration (Ma Ying, 2004). In addition, client's satisfaction has not been enhanced. On the contrary, the individualized results created greater prospects for clients to doubt and complain about whether the realized decoration was constructed in accordance with their selection without any alteration or error and if the cost was reasonable compared with the neighbors. Such questions emerge in an endless stream. The more choices offered through the menu, the more items touched by the decoration, the greater the disputes that were expected to be faced. Irrespective of the extent of the menu's all-encapsulating nature, it is inevitable that the client's requests will be unfeasible to implement as desired. Additionally, it was discovered that interior decoration was not among the top 15 factors affecting people's selection of a housing project (Yue Pan, Long Hao, 2018). Either to accelerate the building process or to escape from inevitable troubles, a consensus emerged that the menu-based decoration approach was inadvisable as a strategy. Therefore, after 2004, the research on menu decoration declined and its associated practices gradually ceased.

The refurbishment of individual dwellings: the way towards individuality and standardization as complementary strategies

Various interior decoration companies have established whole-dwelling refurbishment businesses, aimed at providing a one-stop service for individual refurbishment in existing buildings, encapsulating the design, material purchase and transportation, construction and maintenance. Renovation items are freely determined by the clients, for example replacement of obsolete windows and cast-iron radiators, or installation of air purifying systems to protect against the long, smog-plagued winters. Overall, each family's (infill) decoration scheme is completely individualized, with the outcomes potentially differing entirely. Practically, the no-material provision mode, wherein all the building materials are purchased by the client, as well as the half-material-provision mode, through which the client provides the majority of the principal materials while the interior decoration company has responsibility for purchasing the remaining materials and for installation, have been devised to maintain greater freedom of choice (Li Jie, Dai Xiangdong, 2010). With the two modes being premised on all-inclusive provision with a certain degree of simplification, this section is focused on the whole-dwelling decoration mode to ascertain how individualized achievement is produced. The analysis shows that the relevant companies investigated follow almost identical basic procedures, albeit with some diversity in details. Company R5's experiences are drawn on as the major body of evidence here, although the distinctions in other aspects is indicative of the diversity. The operational procedures of Company R5's whole-dwelling decoration service generally consist of pre-service, design and construction, in addition to after-sales guarantee, as presented in Table 13.2.

It is difficult to trace the process of people's selection between alternative companies; it may be attributed to colleague recommendations who possess relevant experience or housing agendas, as well as online searches in certain instances. Ultimate decisions always follow shopping around and comparison. The pre-service task is to a certain extent equivalent to sales promotion. The consultant and sometimes interior designer introduce their characteristics, particularly with regards to environmental performance, product brands, cost-effectiveness and special offers, as a means of enticing clients by making a favorable impression. Furthermore, the clients are presented with an experience shop (Figure 13.3) and guided around the on-going construction site (Figure 13.4) to provide an intuitive feel. Meanwhile, they assist with the rough calculation of the total price having listed the potential costs generated due to supplementary services, for example piping system renovation. This stage concludes with the security deposit.

Table 13.2 The operational procedures of Company R5's whole-dwelling decoration service.

Stages	Procedures	Service provided	Main roles	Payment
Pre-service	Information provision	• On-site investigation of experience shop and sample projects to show the materials, product and realization; • The introduction of service packages for sale, including the price, service items, alternative products.	Consultant	
	Package selection	The client reserves a service package		10,000RMB as deposit
Design and construction	Preliminary design	• Interior space is measured. • General dimensions of main furniture items are provided by client. • Decoration scheme is proposed and improved.	Interior designer	
	Decoration scheme determination	• The feasibility of design scheme is confirmed on site, the additional items which are not included in service package are declared, and extra fee is calculated. • The materials and products are determined by the client's selection. • Official contract is signed.	Interior designer Project manager Forman Consultant	95% of total payment (deposit included)
	Cement work	• Auxiliary material is transported to the site: including sand, cement, tubes for piping and wiring, plaster, putty, etc.; • Demolishing and reconstruction of piping and wiring systems; • Waterproofing; Installation of the framework of suspended ceiling and partition	Plasterer Forman Project manager	

(continued)

Table 13.2 Cont.

	Bricklaying work	• Main material is transported to the site, including flooring and ceramic tile.	Bricklayer
		• To cover the surface of bathroom and kitchen with the ceramic tile;	Forman
		• To measure the accurate dimension of kitchen and order the cabinets;	Project manager
		• To paint the wall with putty and then coatings;	
		• To cover the surface of suspended ceiling and partition;	
		• To lay the floor;	
		• To measure the accurate dimension of wooden doors.	
	Woodwork	• Customized products are transported to the site;	Carpenter
		• To install the interior doors;	Forman
		• To install the sanitary equipment in bathroom;	Project manager
		• To install cabinets and appliances in kitchen.	
	Delivery	• To clear the construction site.	Project manager	Final payment
		• The client inspects the decoration result and signs for acceptance.	
After-sale service	Quality guarantee	Quality guarantee service is provided:	Workers
		• 1 year for the main products	Product supplier
		• 2 years for the basic construction (wall and floor);	
		• 5 years for the hidden elements (piping and wiring)	
		• Maintenance beyond the period is charged for the cost of material and product and is free from labor fee.	

(Source: by the author according to a consultant, an interior designer and a site manager of Company R5)

Figure 13.3
An 'experience shop' showing the alternatives of heating equipment (photo by the author)

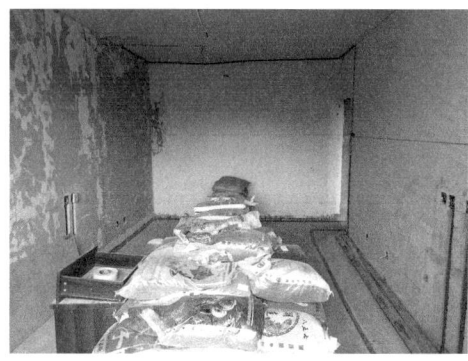

Figure 13.4
An on-going site (photo by the author)

Regarding R5, the design service generally includes color matching of finishes, general furniture layout, alongside arrangement and positioning of power sources and water supply. Furthermore, the interior designer has responsibility for declaring additional items which generate extra fees prior to construction, as well as examining the design's feasibility and appropriateness to the existing situation. Their work exceeds questions of style, incorporating finance and construction elements, with this amount of service typically being called 'design and service.' Among various companies, charges for such work differ markedly. In certain circumstances when charges per dwelling are made, 1000 RMB ($152) was the lowest price while 22,000 RMB ($3345) was the highest. Alternatively, certain companies charge according to the usable area, for example 80 RMB ($12) per square meter.

> Design service is charged separately. If your requirement is simple, we charge 1000 RMB per dwelling unit. It cannot be called a design fee, but expense for design and service. That is to say, I need to visit the project and to deal with possible problems. The drawings we provide are interior layout. Renderings will bring an additional expense. We have some clients with oversimplified needs such as laying the floor and painting the walls. We also encountered professional clients who design by themselves. In these two extreme cases, the design fee is exempted. But I still come to the site regularly. That is my service attitude.[5]
> We have three price-levels of 12,000, 15,000 and 22,000 RMB per dwelling, depending on the professional level of the designer. Correspondingly, we provide a whole set of services. The design touches every detail. As the client's selection of material and products is completely free, the designer even accompanies them to the showroom with professional assistance.[6]

Construction covers an expansive scope of cement work, bricklaying work and woodwork, which is in accordance with typical on-site construction. Correspondingly, the main roles in relation to construction are the site manager, who controls the entire process, as well as the trades people who carry out the various forms of work activities. The former is responsible for ensuring cooperation between the varied kinds of workers, while the latter are engaged in specific construction tasks. They are grouped and incorporated into specific geographical divisions, with their working schedule being assigned centrally. Both of these roles within Company R5 are screened and recruitment is undertaken from the experienced labor force. Employees are retrained and assessed every three months following their employment.

Nevertheless, it has been identified that certain firms of a limited magnitude only employ a foreman, who is then authorized to enlist plumbers, bricklayers and carpenters; these are typically his relatives and acquaintances, who are provided with the company's detailed specifications and who take responsibility for the installation results. This mode compresses management expenses by saving on the requisite insurance and housing fund costs when employing workers directly.

> In a decoration project, we normally need at least three main tradesmen – plumbers, bricklayers, carpenters, each performing his own function. All our craftsmen are self-trained by our company. Their insurance and housing fund are submitted periodically by the company too. At present, they are assessed every three months. People failing two times will be fired.[7]

Two phenomena reveal the characteristics of refurbishment and therefore merit further explanation. Firstly, the procedure of changing wiring and piping is pervasive, although the new wiring and piping layout is not predesigned by the designer who simply marks the power and data termination and fixture positions; rather it is determined on site by the plumber and electrician. That is primarily due to the specific situation of associated walls, particularly the arrangement of reinforcing bars, making it difficult to investigate prior to the project's initiation. In practice, the builders' different conventions and methods are manifested vividly in the varied and sometimes distinct results. Particular companies are accustomed to arranging new piping along the walls, whereas others reduce the necessary length by allowing the new lines to cross some spaces in shallow grooves cut into the concrete floor (Figure 13.5 and 13.6).

> We do not provide construction drawings for piping reorganization because it normally makes no sense. Even if I fixed the specific position for each line, it has to be changed if it turns out that steel reinforcing bars are in the way. This situation is frequently found but cannot be predicted.[8]

Secondly, demolishing an existing wall, whether it is load bearing or not, is usually declined by the investigating companies. A lack of demolition qualifications is the major reason which makes them refuse the task without hesitation. Moreover, the situation whereby an official inspection

Figure 13.5
An example of arranging new piping along the walls and in grooves cut in the existing floor (photo by the author)

Figure 13.6
An example of arranging new piping across the floor of a space without cutting grooves (Photo by the author)

and approval procedure must necessarily be followed to acquire permission is not just complex, it is also time-consuming, which affirms such a decision. This prudent approach positively affects the structural safety and integrity of a building, albeit restricting the fulfilment of people's individual requests. This phenomenon has been practiced smoothly until now without provoking excessive opposition. This demonstrates that to a certain extent, reorganization of the interior subdivision of space is neither the sole nor main means through which the clients can express their individuality. Additionally, the users' requirements typically cover a wider scope of finishing, detail and products.

Company R5's after-sales service is the most representative. It guarantees free maintenance for one year on its main products, two years for basic construction such as walls and floor, as well as five years for concealed project work which refers to piping and wiring. Services beyond the warranty period are charged solely for material costs. Analogous provisions were implemented broadly across the majority of companies as indicated during the interviews, although slight variations were apparent in a minority of cases. For example, Company R6 extended its warranty to ten years for concealed work. Company R7 charges a labor fee for serious damage on any out of the quality-guarantee period.

It should be noted that this mode of interior decoration necessitates in general five laborers and 30 days' work.

Regarding the conventional services that have been clarified above, these may be summarized as 'offering alternatives,' denoting the manner in which a decoration firm fulfils clients' requirements. This enables them to possibly choose an appropriate decoration company, a desirable service mode, a series of favorable materials as well as finished products. Despite the achievements potentially being highly customized, mass-produced furniture with standardized dimensions can prove to be an obstacle. As a supplementary strategy, a collection of companies providing a personalized furniture service was established in 2004 (Hao Yuanyuan, Zhang Bingning, 2018). In previous decades, their service scope has evolved from doors and closets to wardrobes, from a single space to an entire dwelling unit or house, while an array of corporations have explored multiple product lines covering various product categories (Top Design, 2018). Its rapid growth is evidenced by the statistic showing personalized furniture selection accounts for 35% of the home furnishing and building material market share, while the whole house customization mode has been established as one of three prominent directions.[9] In contrast with the standardized results, personalized furniture fit more effectively to specific users' living habits as well as the detailed context of the dwellings. Stubborn problems, for example electrical sockets being hidden by closets or the residual space being insufficient for a table, have been resolved to a certain extent, while decoration style and furniture's harmonization have been enhanced. Meanwhile, this represents the extreme pursuit of individuality.

In terms of the objective of satisfying people's individual demands, certain similarities were apparent among the thousands of refurbishment activities, which generates a mode of standard infill packages. As a business strategy, this incorporates those fixed services that are regularly applied during individualized decoration projects alongside best-selling goods, thus posing a restricted selection. For example, Company R8 provides two packages of 97,930 ($14,890) and 53,930 RMB ($8200) respectively (Table 13.3). Both concentrate on painting walls, laying flooring, as well as re-equipping the kitchen and bathroom, while including an equivalent selection of products. The principal difference pertains to the brand of material and products for selection, in terms of whether imported or domestic manufacturers predominate. This simplifies the procedures through compressing the alternatives and diversity. Taking wall boards as an example, just three brands and two colors are

Table 13.3 Standard infill packages

Service package	Basic price	Maximal area (measured by building area)	Products	Renovation of piping and wiring (measured by dwelling floor area)	Tax	Extra area (measured by building area)
1	97,930 RMB	70m²	Domestic product predominated	145 RMB/m² for demolition 150 RMB/m² for new construction	Included	1399 RMB/m²
2	53,930 RMB	60m²	Imported product predominated			899 RMB/m²

(Source: by the author according to investigations with a consultant of Company R8)

optional. Moreover, the stove and range hood type were predetermined and fixed. This strategy has been effectively adopted among numerous firms, which all offer packages comprising near-equivalent decoration scope and kinds of products, besides marginal differences in terms of specific hardware and small appliances (Figure 13.7). This mode permits specific products' selection in the package, alongside increase of extra items with an additional fee. The objective here is not individuality, rather it is quality and convenience. Once more, this conveys how clients' perspectives of individuality are typically rational, with high standards and convenience being prioritized over personal expression.

Figure 13.7 A kitchen fitted out by standard infill package (photo by the author)

Discussion: contrast of attitudes towards individuality and the evolution of the Open Building concept

The decoration of newly built housing and the refurbishment of existing dwellings reflects varied attitudes towards the relationship between standardization and individuality. One is underpinned by standardization and attempts to fulfil the diversity requirement, whereas the other aims at satisfying individuality while applying *interface standards* (not standard products) as a tool for simplifying the selection process. The alleviation of the tension between these two 'forces' is also conveyed in the Open Building approach, inspiring exploration of its connotations within the Chinese context.

In John Habraken's (1972) book *Supports: An Alternative to Mass Housing*, he observed that the absence of inhabitants' initiative resulted in the unbearable uniformity of cities and large housing projects, in addition to a shortage of housing and more expensive housing. He subsequently advocated the support–infill distinction as an approach to re-establishing the 'natural relationship' between people and their immediate environment. This required establishing the independence of each dwelling in large housing projects. Meanwhile, with regards to rapid development of industrialization, the proposed distinction and separation of design tasks (support and infill) was aimed not to create personalized products – rather it sought the integration of standardized manufactured goods into aggregated infill packets for each independent dwelling, each of which may differ yet possess equal efficiency in realization. Hence, the support concept was conceived on the basis of two seemingly contradictory principles; the pursuit of independent dwellings (infill), utilizing industrialized (non-project specific) parts organized and installed per-dwelling (a kind of construction process), alongside the construction of supports, which serve the common needs of all independent dwellings.

The notion of supports and related concepts was introduced to China as Support Housing during the 1980s (Bao Jiasheng, 1988), Open Building during the 1990s (Xu Wencai, 1991), followed by a transition into Long-life Sustainable Housing during the 2000s (Liu Dongwei et al, 2009). The first generation, encapsulated in the 1985 Wuxi Experimental Project, concentrated on the capacity of the support to accommodate the interior space's variable subdivisions. Its definition of infill was limited to the position of non-load bearing interior division walls. During the second generation, exemplified by the Cuiwei Community in 1994 (led by Ma Yunyue and Zhang Qinnan), a number of interior decoration companies were consciously involved in the exploration of the infill package's diversity, comprising both the varied partition types as well as the core kitchen appliances and bathroom sanitary fixtures. The scope of infill was extended further during the third generation of Little Universe in 2012, in addition to its subsequent pilot projects. The majority of items filling in empty spaces were covered: the interior walls with wallpaper and connected moldings were involved; the kitchen and bathroom were entirely fitted out. The infill package incorporated numerous other product types, although the selection offered was relatively small. During the most recent projects, dwellings were recognized having an almost identical appearance.

Research into Open Building is in accordance with the overall context of architecture and housing in China. Three main issues directly affect both support design and infill decisions in the aforementioned three phases: the shift of housing property from welfare to commodity; the transition of the principal aim shifting from quantitative satisfaction to qualitative improvement; advocacy of industrialization, prefabrication and fully furnished dwellings by the central government and subsequently local authorities. Even so, if the social context's constraints are deviated from momentarily, and concentrating on the phenomenon's emergence, it is clear that throughout the four-decade development, the infill's scope has been dramatically extended while its degree of variety has been markedly compressed up to now. Essentially, as the abundance of industrialized products increases, the inhabitants' individuality diminishes, as of this writing.

Accompanying this tendency is the recognition of people's determination to attain individualized results, which accords appropriately with their personal and original concept of dwelling. Certain researchers were convinced that consumers may be persuaded in case the layout and predetermined decoration of the dwelling was sufficiently reasonable and advanced (Liu Minnan, 2007). As a result, it may be stated that occupants' inner disposition and taste was primarily presented in their selection of furniture, lighting fixtures, curtains, carpets, decorative ornaments and even dinnerware for the dinnertable (Wang Yimin, 2003), thus advocating simplified and standardized decoration and individualized ornaments (Li Lixin, 2003). Likewise, a perspective that has reached strong consensus has acknowledged the significance of personalized requirements, although not in dwelling layout or major interior design decisions. This strategy seems to be reasonable since it has revealed in an investigation that in the case of standard decoration or refurbishment, people's expenses on the 'soft part' is 1.5 times that of the 'hard and fixed part' (Feng Shanshan, 2016).

This view is critically challenged by certain investigations and social phenomena which demonstrate how personal preferences are difficult to satisfy in a predetermined and finished dwelling, where only the selection of furniture is made possible. It has been broadly established that prior to occupancy, residents will seek to renew even those dwellings completed to a high standard and that are occasionally up to date. Even in the demonstration project of long-life sustainable housing, people's disgruntlement about what is being offered is unavoidable. In July 2013, 15 months from the occupancy of Little Universe which was generally deemed to be the foremost and prominent Open Building project in China at that time – particularly in its dwelling layout and product selection – an investigation was launched focusing on 25 families. Eight families (32%) expressed their intention to undertake refurbishment, whereas the others suppressed their change aspirations merely because of restrictions of time, energy, economy and expertise (Miao Qing et al., 2014). The saying that 'no "refined" dwelling escapes from second decoration' is not at all groundless. Additionally, a survey of 113 Beijing-based families who had renovated their present dwelling determined that 21 items within the dwelling's main body were touched, with the top three being whitewashing of the walls and ceilings, laying of the floor and alteration of the bathroom's sanitary fixtures.[10] From this, the capacity for changing the dwelling itself as opposed to just replacing a closet or bed turns out to be of necessity.

In recent years, ignorance of individual demands has been found to be an obstacle preventing fully finished dwellings from being widely accepted, thus drawing a certain amount of attention. In a study of 1000 potential homebuyers, 71% complained about the limited choice offered by existing 'refined' dwellings (Gong Liming, Si Yantao, 2016). A survey in Liaoning indicated that one of the most prominent reasons preventing the interviewees from purchasing refined dwellings was the restrictions on their personal preferences.

The majority of individuals anticipated that they would decorate their dwellings in accordance with their personal desires and tastes, while the majority of projects provided two alternatives at most (Wang Xing, 2013). This issue has been criticized nationally. In a 2018 survey in Fuzhou, 75% of 100 interviewees attributed 'cannot be decorated according to my desire' to their resistance against fully furnished housing (Gao Weixing et al., 2018). A questionnaire investigation in southern Jiangsu gave evidence that 70.77% of the 561 responders ascribed the principal problem of refined dwellings to their inability to fulfil people's personal preferences, while 65.95% were convinced of the necessity of being able to express one's individual preferences in dwellings' interior spaces (Zhao Qinxian, 2017).

People's individual preferences do in fact generate refurbishment services for individual dwelling units. Nevertheless, this has neither drawn much attention nor is widely practiced in the field of either Open Building or housing so far. This fact runs counter to the original concept of Open Building which takes the inhabitant's stubborn pursuit for their own and usually special requirements of dwelling as its essence.

How this affects people's satisfaction and living experiences will be revealed more comprehensively and clearly below.

Part 3: Traditional mode of wet work and developments toward prefabrication

The construction of both new-built dwellings and existing dwelling refurbishment is still reliant upon on-site 'wet work'[11] to a significant extent. This work concerns the finishing of all surfaces and particularly the fitting out of kitchens and bathrooms with cabinets and sanitary fixtures. Construction typically accords with the sequential order of cement work, bricklaying work, woodwork and product installation, as outlined in the previous section. Despite a large number of mass-produced products being involved in this process, the vast majority of the work is still completed through field operations, with the strategy to achieve the compression of the construction period being the management of simultaneous operations involving various trades.

Refurbishment projects repeat a similar story which may be perceived as a hobbled version. A similar situation within the two fields to a certain extent represents China's contemporary situation regarding the construction mode in the decoration field. This applies to 'industrialized' products manufactured for 'the market' and adopted for any project, meanwhile depending on traditional on-site 'wet work' as opposed to installation of products industrially produced and only requiring 'dry' installation or assembly on-site.

This phenomenon generates a yet unanswered question: how does the field of interior decoration move toward industrialization? How we reply to this is dependent on how terms are defined. One group of researchers believes that industrialization equates simply to the application of products produced in an industrial mode (made for the market). A prominent example is research into refitting dwellings using an industrialized method. This has summarized the requisite goods and items within the principal dwelling space, aiming to provide consensus on a product provision standard, covering types, required performance, expected size and life-expectancy (Chang Xiaoxue, Hu Huiqin, 2018). Under this concept, if measurements for widely used kitchen cabinets and interior doors (Figure 13.7) are made on-site, then produced in the factory, then returned for installation alongside other standard products which are factory produced, purchased on the market and then installed on-site without modification – it may be concluded that industrialization has already for a long time significantly affected the interior decoration field. Nevertheless, when the main procedures' operation modes are investigated, how cement mortar covers the renewed piping (Figure 13.8), how walls are leveled and painted with coatings, how the site is dominated by the necessary cement and sand for wet work, as well as how dust and noise pollution affect the field, it may

Figure 13.8
A wall with the renewed piping to be covered by cement mortar and drainage pipes serving the dwelling unit above needing to be hidden by a lowered ceiling (photo by author)

be concluded that there is considerable way to go before achieving more complete industrialization.

The following section concentrates on industrialization in the latter sense of the term, investigating its current application for both new-build housing decorations and existing dwelling refurbishment.

Industrialization relating to new-built housing

The process of fitting out dwellings with the 'dry method' comprises just a limited fraction of the market, although it is increasing. Around the mid-2010s it was recognized as 'industrialized decoration,' followed by 'prefabricated furbishment' since the 2016 policy change. In contrast with the traditional mode, its main characteristic is considered to be high level of off-site kitting or preparation of industrialized products and their installation/construction mode using trained installer teams. Its emergence can be attributed to two realities. Firstly, traditional methods' shortcomings have approached the limits of tolerance; the resulting quality cannot be effectively guaranteed; negative environmental effects have resulted, while there is always a long-term construction period necessary for completion which consumes considerable labor, the price of which has increased dramatically. Secondly, industrialized products which are manufactured for the market as opposed to a specific project have expanded significantly, as well as the competence to provide the requisite material, logistics and technical support.

This has enticed some companies to devote themselves to related research and practices, for example with Company N3 being the first practitioner from 2000 (Huang Yiru et al., 2011), Company N4 developed ten prefabricated systems (Yan Jian et al., 2018), while Company N5 and Company N6 have been recognized for their productive performance. The following paragraphs consider the activities and operations of Company N6 (Company N5 – Henenghome – is discussed in Chapter 14).

Company N6 was established in 2015, engaged in the principal business of selling building materials, building decorations, as well as strengthening of aged structures. Immediately following the company's establishment, it entered the prefabricated decoration business to offer construction services and technical assistance. Up until the present, they have completed almost ten related projects, the great majority of which are financially subsidized. During their recent Chaoqingzhizhu Community project (Figure 13.9), 160 dwelling units with a total area of 33,600 m² (361,667 ft²) were fitted-out within six months. Eight types of products were involved, including unit bathroom, kitchen, partitions, floor heating, raised floor, cabinets, water supply and separation of piping from the structure. Alongside this innovative assembly mode, the company has maintained its traditional construction methods, which continue to account for around 50% of their activities.

These two companies' experiences and interviews with their managers have revealed the existing situation of industrialization, which may be characterized according to two aspects.

Figure 13.9
An exterior view of Chaoqing-zhizhu Community Project (photo by the author)

First, the innovative and advanced methods remain in the process of being accepted, with the stronger impulse coming from the central government. Indeed, the major demand in both examples is associated with government subsidized housing. The explanation as to why limited acceptance has been seen among developers is partially linked to their established habits and behavior. To alter these habits requires nothing less than overturning the entire design and construction processes associated with traditional methods. Interior designers have begun stepping into the architectural field, in order to modify the dimensions in accordance with the dimensional modules of the industrialized products. Meanwhile, numerous labor processes usually completed by the plumber, the carpenter and the bricklayer have been replaced by the installer, combined with the change that an increasing 'value added' is completed in the factory. The potential economic loss to traditional players is a further daunting aspect. The evident increase in costs to acquire the same finishing inevitably compresses the potential client group, some of whom have been found to complain about the undesirable experiences stemming from having a raised floor and hollow, non-load-bearing partitions. The majority of developers instinctively want to avoid potential risk. The government has proposed compulsory requirements to promote industrialization during particular projects' bidding stage, as well as offering financial subsidies for constructions to fulfil related standards (Table 13.4).

Secondly, the realized projects included various 'integrated products,' suggesting a dearth of practical regulations concerning industrialization in the decoration process. Until the current time, single companies capable of providing comprehensive technical systems and solutions remain a minority (Wei Suwei, Miao Qing, 2019). The two typical companies explained above

Table 13.4 Compulsory requirements and financial subsidies to promote industrialization (prefabrication) in the main cities

City	Target (proportion of new-built prefabricated building)	Compulsory requirements	Financial subsidies
Beijing	30% by 2020	Government subsidized housing, community in excess of 50,000 m² in the 7 main districts and in excess of 100,000 m² in the rest area have to be prefabricated.	3% extra area; no value-added tax
Shanghai	all buildings inside inner ring and 50% of buildings in the rest by 2016		100RMB/m²; 3% increase of floor area ratio
Guangdong	35% new-built buildings in PRD, 30% in central district of prefectural-level cities and 20% in the left by 2025		2 million RMB maximum for specific performance
Jiangsu	30% by 2020		1.5 to 2.5 million RMB per project
Zhejiang	30% by 2020	All the new-built dwellings in the central district of cities and towns have to be fully equipped before delivery.	A reduction of retention money of quality guarantee and property maintenance; an increase of floor area ratio
Hubei	30% by 2025	All the new-built public rental housing have to be prefabricated from July 1st of 2017; All the new-built housing in four cities have to be fully equipped by 2020.	
Shandong	40% by 2025	All the new-built public rental housing and projects invested by the government have to be prefabricated.	A reduction of retention money
Sichuan	40% of prefabricated building by 2025; 70% of fully finished housing by 2025		A reduction of business income tax; an increase of floor area ratio; subsidies for research fee

Table 13.4 Cont.

City	Target (proportion of new-built prefabricated building)	Compulsory requirements	Financial subsidies
Fujian	35% by 2025	All the projects of residential, educational, medical and office building invested by the government have to be from 2019.	A reduction of tax; an increase of floor area ratio
Shanxi	30% by 2025		50% reduction of value-added tax; an increase of floor area ratio

(Source: by the author according to relevant policies by 2019)

provide 12 and eight main integrated products respectively. Among these product types, the unitized bathroom and kitchen has a longer history, alongside the suspended ceiling system which being applied as a traditional technique relying on wet work has received more acceptance, while the remainder remain questionable. The current regulation[12] provides an assessment standard and corresponding score for the integrated kitchen, integrated bathroom, dry-work (raised) floor, as well as separation of piping from the structure, although such regulations have not been declared compulsory options. Correspondingly, the simplest and most well-accepted products are extensively selected to fulfil the minimum standard for authentication. However, the products – the application of which may enhance the level of industrialization – are seldom observed in practice. In 2019, the Technical Standard for Interior Assembled Decoration has been proposed as an industry standard,[13] which recommends products for industrialized decoration projects. It is anticipated that the standard's full release will positively affect the market's regularization over the near term, although the path towards a national and compulsory standard remains long and tortuous.

Prefabrication for refurbishing existing dwellings

Influenced by relevant practices for new-built communities, certain researchers have started exploring the application of industrialized products combined with the dry-work mode for refurbishing individual dwellings. Indeed, the realization of a limited number of projects has been seen during the process of experimentation, with those having foremost impact being listed as follows.

In 2015, Professor Zhou Jinmin refurnished her own 90 m^2 (969 ft^2) dwelling in Shanghai. The renovation involved separation of piping from the structure, application of industrialized products (unit bathroom, integrated kitchen, raised floor, lightweight partition and storage units), while relying primarily on installation services offered by both product suppliers and decoration companies. Given that industrialized products' supply has not been effectively developed, the construction process was pervaded by exploration and discussion. Irrespective of sufficient design preparation, in-depth comprehension of existing goods alongside corresponding construction processes, modifications and repeated work remain unavoidable. As a result, the construction period has clearly been extended compared with traditional wet construction, with the entire process necessitating over a year's work. Nevertheless, the integrated bathroom installation required just eight hours work carried out by two laborers, indicating its advantage to a certain extent (Zhou Jinmin et al., 2017).

Between 2014 and 2016, Tsinghua University renovated 35 dwellings, which are relatively standardized among the 700 dwelling units in their faculty dormitory. The renovation approach included: suspended ceilings to obscure the heating systems; additional wall boards fixed against two to three existing walls, with metal studs to hold the electrical and data connection boxes; laying PVC synthetic boards on the existing floor with ceramic tiles, thus altering the interior atmosphere while avoiding any structural damage; changing the piping into a drainage mode on the same floor; installation of an integrated (unit) bathroom and kitchen (Jiang Yong et al., 2017a). Each bathroom's renovation necessitated 51.5 hours of labor by two craftsmen, including eight hours for piping changes, 31.5 hours for bathroom unit installation, in addition to 12 hours for associated components' installation. During construction, 37 unanticipated problems arose, impacting the installation speed and achievement (Jiang Yong, 2017b).

As a product supplier, Company R9 was established in 2017, with the company focusing on integrated (unit) bathroom design, manufacture and installation. The product comprises thousands of components. The design and construction logic revolve around: applying a support framework, in the cavity of which the piping is arranged, while above this a flat floor including drains is installed; installing the framework on the existing walls, combined with the prefabricated wall boards on which the necessary holes for equipment were prepared; arranging the wiring and appliances against the ceiling, below which the prefabricated ceiling boards were installed; installation of the remaining components, for example partitions and sanitary fixtures. The entire process requires four hours in the factory. The products have been applied during a few refurbishment projects of existing dwellings. Following an ordinary process of client consultation, alongside field measurement, the configuration layout and renderings may be produced within ten minutes. The components in their entirety were assembled in the factory and transported to the site. The installation of a 1.92 m² (21 ft²) and a 3.6 m² (39 ft²) bathroom in high-rise buildings required seven and four days respectively, while a 2 m² case in a bungalow necessitated five days of installation labor.[14]

The three examples provided have indicated suppliers' capacity to deliver the requisite service, as well as the capacity of various trades to complete the installation, while also revealing some clear hindrances. Both practitioners involved in the first two whole-dwelling renovations have an established and constant concentration in the field of industrialization and prefabrication. They possess architectural background and in-depth comprehension of associated techniques, which has facilitated and guided installers and helped to resolve unanticipated problems. Their robust relationships with the suppliers ensured appropriate selection and supply of products and components.

Inquiries were undertaken to establish whether ordinary decoration companies are capable of adopting an industrialized mode. Their explanations below reveal the confusion in their perspectives regarding the challenging future that this innovative working method poses as a mainstream strategy for refurbishing individual dwellings.

> It is possible to use integrated (unit) bathroom in the decoration of public buildings. But in dwelling refurbishment, we have to rely on the traditional methods. We may try if you have your own supply channel of the integrated unit, which are not available in our company.[15]
>
> We have never practiced the construction of separating the piping from the structure. We can only deal with the traditional mode at the moment, which arranges the piping in slots cut into the structure and bonds them with cement mortar. The slot is usually 2 cm wide (.8 inches). It almost has no influence on the structural stability. The proposal to arrange at least some of the piping along the existing walls and to cover them with metal studs and gypsum board will narrow the interior living space. Meanwhile, the expense will be increased dramatically.[16]

Discussion: is industrialization equivalent to Open Building?

The industrialized decoration method as discussed so far is strongly connected to Chinese Open Building practices, especially over the past decade. Indeed, in certain researches, these two concepts have even been confused. To provide clarity, it is necessary to explore two questions. One concerns whether industrialized decoration assists with realizing the independence of each dwelling within a communal building; the second is whether the procedure of individual change has been simplified over the course of time. Both questions may be partially answered according to the practices of Company N5. The company is competent in manufacturing diverse results per product type. Considering Company N5's wall surface products as an example, the calcium silicate board is the sole panel material, although numerous patterns have a strong likelihood of being realized. This company's 2019 illustrated book presents 25 series with various styles, containing hundreds of design figures. Furthermore, to realize the customized pattern is not just possible but is actually more convenient compared with the existing wet-work mode. Any picture with sufficient resolution can be easily printed on the wall board, regardless of whether it is a landscape or an ancient poem. Regardless, specific customers seldom take advantage of this service in practice, because the private-ordering mode inevitably raises the issue of expenses as noted above, thus making it less acceptable.

Concerning the second question, prefabricated decorations' construction is much simplified, which is also confirmed by the experience of Company N5. It is reliant upon a small group of just 40–50 installers, who provide technical support as opposed to specific services in particular cases. The vast majority of their installers have experience of traditional decoration. Having participated in one project, they gain the capability to work independently. This phenomenon reconfirms that prefabricated products' installation is not a highly specialized and complex skill. Nevertheless, the procedure for attaining individual change is not dramatically reduced.

Taking the movement of an electrical socket as an example – which is one of the most common requirements – it may be theoretically realized that by replacing the entire board with a new one with a proper socket hole, the old board could be collected for recycling. However, the reality is that this is rarely done due to the additional expense incurred, complex nature of the process, as well as lack of a reclamation process. Consequently, even during projects which ought to be refurbished effectively, this change continues to be realized via the traditional mode of cutting a hole for the new socket and repairing the abandoned hole before finishing the entire wall with wallpaper.

Moreover, industrialized products prevent people from undertaking changes in certain instances. In a post-occupancy investigation of an Open Building project, it was revealed that imported bolts were necessary, combined with skilled craftsman, in order to hang a painting on the partition constructed from light steel studs and gypsum board (Miao Qing, 2014). The raised cost prevented the inhabitants from undertaking an ordinary, simple change which should have been something to be straightforwardly realized by themselves. Such criticisms generally arise in relation to residential dwellings decorated in accordance with the industrialization concept.

From this perspective, even if the capacity of the support may be set aside as a problem to be solved during design and construction, the pathway in China for developing an infill industry through offering infill packages in fully independent units of occupancy at competitive prices remains difficult, despite the success reported by Company 5. This transition is dependent not just on the development of techniques, some of which have been explored in this chapter. More importantly, this marks a revolution in the operation and management mode of the entire market. Perhaps the governmental certification of infill companies will assist with securing the market, promoting both developers and consumers' confidence in this new manner of working.

Acknowledgment

This research was supported by a grant from the National Natural Science Foundation of China (No. 51908019).

Notes

1 The title of the document is 'Some suggestions aiming at propelling housing standardization and improve its quality.' It is the No. 72 document of General Office of the State Council in 1999.
2 Assessment standard for green building (GB/T 50378-2014).
3 According to the 'Implementation documentation to accelerate the development of green building' which is the No. 167 document released by Ministry of Finance of the People's Republic of China in 2012.
4 According to statistics of the 15 most influential corporations in 2019 which were evaluated by *China Internet Weekly*, 13 of them were established in the 1990s, while 11 corporations between 1996 and 1999.
5 According to an interior designer in Company R5.
6 According to an interior designer in Company R6.
7 According to an interior designer in Company R5.
8 Ibid.
9 It was realized by You Intelligence in July 2017. www.iyiou.com/intelligence/insight50261.html
10 According to an investigation by the author. The result was presented in the Open Building Session of UIA 2017 Conference, Seoul.
11 In the Chinese interior decoration field, wet work refers to construction procedures that have to be completed on site with mortar or other cohering material. The typical wet-work items include sealing floors and walls with water-proofing, plastering, tilling, etc.
12 Standard for assessment of prefabricated building. (GB/T 51129-2017)
13 The consultant draft has been released on March 27, 2019. According to relevant notification on the official website of Ministry of Housing and Urban-Rural Development of the People's Republic of China (www.mohurd.gov.cn/).
14 A presentation given by one of the executives of Company R9 in the symposium on architectural renovation and industrialization of housing, which was held in Tsinghua University, Beijing, China, on December 8, 2019.
15 According to an interior designer of Company R6.
16 Ibid.

References

Bao Jiasheng (1988). *Support Housing*, Nanjing: Phoenix Science Press.
Chang Xiaoxue, Hu Huiqin (2018). Research on refitting the interior space & application of parts in the old residential buildings. *Architectural Journal*, S1, pp. 56–60.
Chen Min, Yu Jie (2003). Overall decorated house. *Housing Science*, 4, pp. 46–48.
Chen Yeming (1998). Towards restricted individualized decoration. *China Real Estate Information*, 1, p. 32.
Jia Chunfeng (2016). Fully furnished dwelling: the inevitable direction of housing development. *Doors & Windows*, 11, p. 248.
Feng Shanshan (2016). The cost on decoration of dwelling. *CFO World*, 7, pp. 23–25.

Gao Weixing, Xu Qian, Lin Gengping (2018). Status survey and coping strategy of fully furnished housing in Fuzhou, *Fujian Architecture & Construction*, 9, pp. 129–132.

Gong Liming, Si Yantao (2016). A study on the development of fully furbished housing. *Doors & Windows*, 3, pp. 233, 235.

Habraken, N. J. (1972). *Supports: An Alternative to Mass Housing*. New York: Praeger.

Hao Yuanyuan, Zhang Bingning (2018). Rational thinking over the current development of custom furniture industry. *Furniture & Interior Design*, 7, pp. 13–16.

Huang Yiru, Zhou Xiaohong, Yin Rourui (2011). Practice of residential interior fabricated diversification and localization. *Interior Architecture of China*, 2, pp. 222–223.

Jiang Yong, Zhu Ning, Liu Mingzheng, Wang Qiang, Yuan Ruhai, Jin Rongshan (2017a). A study on the applied technology of integrated bathroom units in apartment renovation. *Architectural Journal*, 2, pp. 69–73.

Jiang Yong, Zhu Ning, Liu Mingzheng, Wang Qiang, Yuan Rumei (2017b). Industrialised technique system used in the refurbishment of existing dwelling. *Urban and Rural Development*, 5, pp. 70–72.

Li Jie, Dai Xiangdong (2010). Research of Chinese decoration pattern in present time. *Furniture & Interior Design*, 5, pp. 84–85.

Li Juanjuan, Tang Lei (2001). Apply menu decoration in new-built housing projects. *Shanghai Building Materials*, 4, pp. 11–13.

Li Lixin (2003). Design strategy and management for full decoration residence. *Housing Science*, 10, pp. 35–37.

Li Peide (2001) Menu decoration will be launched in China. *Builder's Monthly*, 4, pp. 51.

Liu Dongwei, Gong Tiejun, Yan Yingjun, et al. (2009). LC housing system and demonstration projects based on the concept of long-term effectiveness. *Architectural Journal*, 8, pp. 1–5.

Liu Minnan (2007). Trend analysis and optimized countermeasures of overall-finished housing. *Journal of Tongji University (Natural Science)*, 3, pp. 326–329.

Ma Chunjie, Hu Xiaomin (2003). After the application of menu decoration. *Urban and Rural Development*, 2, pp. 62–63.

Ma Chunjie, Hu Xiaomin (2003). After the application of menu decoration. *Urban and Rural Development*, 2, pp. 62–63.

Ma Ying (2004). The comprehensive of full decoration of housing in practice. *China Housing Facilities*, 1, pp. 6–8.

Miao Qing (2014). An investigation and analysis of the living situation in CSI housing, Tongji University, Master Thesis.

Miao Qing, Zhou Jingmin, Hao Xue (2014). Evaluating the infill construction system of Yashi Hejin Housing and analysis of residential factual conditions and users' satisfaction. *Architectural Journal*, 7, pp. 40–46.

Top Design (2018). Study on the development tendency of customization industry in 2018. *Furniture & Interior Design*, 02, pp. 34–37.

Wang Feng (2001). Menu decoration of community. *Anhui Architecture*, 4, p. 27.

Wang Xing, Tian Tian, Zhou Lin (2013). The constraints of the implementation of fully furnished dwellings and solutions. *Liaoning Economy*, 11, pp. 54–55.

Wang Yimin (2003). Discussion on finishing of commercial housing. *Shanxi Architecture*, 7, pp. 78–79.

Wei Suwei, Miao Qing (2019). Present situation and prospect of the assembled interior decoration. *City & House*, 1, pp. 17–20.

Xiao Yating, Xu Peishu (2015). A research on the interior decoration market in Nanchang. *Business*, 22, pp. 261–263.

Xu Wencai (1991). Open housing in China. *Architectural Journal*, 11, pp. 10–13.

Yan Jian, Lu Xiaobiao, Wang Peng (2018). Practice and exploration of fabricated interior decoration. *Construction Science and Technology*, 10, pp. 88–92.

Yang Xia (2017). An analysis on the current situation and development of decoration market in Shangqiu. *Light Industry Science and Technology*, 1, pp. 103–104.

Yue Pan, Long Hao (2018). To select a house is equivalent to selecting the location?. *Insight China*, 16, p. 56.

Zhao Qinxian (2017). An investigation and analysis of the fully furnished housing in Southern Jiangsu. *Housing and Real Estate*, 32, pp. 10–12.

Zhou Jinmin, Miao Qing, Chen Jingwen (2017). Research on infill reformation system for existing housing. *Architecture Technique*, 3, pp. 54–57.

Chapter 14

Developments toward a residential fit-out industry: the key to a sustainable housing stock

Stephen H. Kendall

The office building-to-condominiums conversion project at the corner of 78th Avenue and Central Park features a breakthrough approach for developers to make money while offering home buyers a way get just what they want, at the price they can afford, in just a few weeks after signing a contract. What's unique about the development is that the developer is offering a 'net-zero' building with empty units and providing a list of fit-out companies each of which offers the service of installing everything needed to make the empty space ready for the condo buyer to move in. No longer will buyers have to wait many months in a building experienced as constantly under renovation.

Because of the new approach, the design of each dwelling is entirely independent and can be changed later without disturbing any other unit in the building, above or below it. Because of this, the building is truly sustainable: it can be regenerated cell-by-cell for one hundred years as demographics change and as new consumer-oriented technologies come into the market.

The competitive fit-out companies each offer a certified service of installing state-of-the-art cabinets, finishes, energy-efficient equipment and floor plans matching each buyers' preferences. For example, if you want a large open kitchen next to the family room, with a powder room next to that, you can get that. Or, you can have a formal dining room separated from the living room and kitchen. If you plan to have your aging parents to come to live with you in a few years, this to can be planned for, by adding another bathroom and even a separate entry. These are only some of the choices these companies offer, each with its certification and brand.

This is possible because of a totally new approach to gut-remodeling and marketing: separated design of the base building and fit-out. The developer has obtained approval for construction, with specific places for attaching the buildings' utility infrastructure with that of each condo unit. Each empty unit is set up with the capacity to accommodate a substantial

DOI: 10.4324/9781003018339-17

range of layouts and lifestyles. Each fit-out company provides the kit to fill in the unit, just-in-time and to the exact specifications selected and at the exact price and schedule agreed to.

This idea brings together the efficiencies of off-site factory production for the fit-out, controlled logistics and supply chain management, and on-site multi-skilled installation teams. The fit-out companies use their own advanced computer visualization tools and cost estimating software to quickly 'build' a virtual model of the unit, providing a virtual walk-through and immediate cost information. The drawings can be printed out, and the buyer can go home and discuss the plans around their dining table. This process can be repeated several times until the buyer is happy, a contract is signed, and a few weeks later they can move into their new home.

Soon, the same developer will announce another development – this time a new 15-story rental building in a quickly rejuvenating part of the city. In this case, the developer has selected her preferred fit-out company, which uses a web-based menu selection and design process, where renters can work on alternative layout ideas on their laptop, starting with a base design with an established rental rate, before going to the company showroom to make final decisions, which may include either choosing a more simple fit-out (reducing the rent) or a more elaborate scheme.

(A fictitious news article in the real estate
section of the local newspaper)

The future of large residential projects belongs to a fit-out industry

This chapter presents the case for a residential fit-out industry, and how it will change the culture of the residential building industry. It gives an abbreviated history of developments in this direction, including the world's most advanced fit-out company, and concludes with some of the reasons that progress in this direction has been slow to happen.

A residential fit-out industry consists of certified companies, operating in a local market region, delivering everything that can be decided independently per dwelling as a single-source service under a unified design-production-installation contract. The service of these companies involves organizing all of the work and products per dwelling unit, accounted for per unit. In new construction, this service engages a project's critical path when decisions are to be made about the specifications of each dwelling, whether by the developer or by the future occupant, but after the support or base building has been designed, is already under construction or may be nearly complete. The key is that the base building design is not dependent on the fit-out decisions. In the reactivation or conversion of existing buildings – either upgrading residential properties or converting buildings to residential use – the service offered is to fill in fully 'gutted' spaces one-at-a-time, on time, quietly and on budget. In reactivating existing buildings, all 'common' infrastructure elements, including the mechanical, electrical and plumbing (MEP) parts of the base building will have been upgraded and reconfigured as needed for long-term capacity (not just a one-off renovation), ready for each unit's fit-out to be installed and connected to base building infrastructure.

Fit-out companies prepare well-organized 'packages' or assemblies of parts off-site. These packages, along with the coordinated delivery of other parts straight from manufacturers or suppliers, are delivered to the site and brought into the empty space in the needed sequence through a balcony window by a boom truck or, on tall buildings, using a boom lift (also used for window washing), or via the elevator and through the unit's front door. Once inside, they are installed by a multi-skilled team of workers who stay with the job until it is finished. Only minimal cutting of parts is required thus producing very little on-site waste, debris and noise. Such companies will compete on service and quality, on their ability to use the latest enterprise management software and the latest consumer-oriented products from the market, and their ability to deliver on time and on budget. They deliver at various price points, and hand over a user's manual and multi-year maintenance agreement to each new occupant.

Working this way means an end to choreographing separate subcontractors, with all the familiar scheduling and quality control problems. This new mode of operation means implementing true teamwork into residential construction. Fit-out company product solutions are truly systematic, which does not mean uniform solutions but quite the opposite, because good systems enable rather than block variety.

A complete fit-out will include everything behind (and perhaps including) the front door. In this latter case the fit-out is everything making that space habitable – the thousands of discrete parts including parts for making walls, doors and door frames and hardware, all wiring, piping and plumbing fixtures, lighting, cabinets, and so on. The space may even be rented, and the fit-out purchased. The fit-out may even include part of the buildings' façade directly related to each independent dwellings' floor plan (as in NEXT21 reported on later and in Chapter 8).

A question of business structure and culture

In contrast to this vision, the building industry today is, after more than 100 years, still dependent on organizing ad hoc contracts among many subcontractors each delivering labor and products to complete the specified work. This is the mode of operation whether talking about an entire building or a single unit of occupancy. The conversion of existing buildings to new uses and new construction are similarly burdened. As more subsystems have come into residential construction over time, each with its own specialized trade, this mode of operation has become the Achilles' Heel of construction and its regulation. Partly as a result, most large general contractors have become project managers with no workforce of their own, allowing them to apply downward pressure on subcontractors to lower project costs. While this may be a prudent business model for general contractors and subcontractors in an industry that is notorious for its up- and down-swings directly related to swings in the general economy – hiring when the market is hot and laying off workers when business is slow – it is no longer reliable, is unable to deliver affordable housing, nor does it deliver acceptable quality.

Because the existing building industry has been unable to break out of its obsolete habits and mode of operation, a fit-out industry of many competitive, certified companies is likely to come into being by outside actors entering the stage because they see untapped opportunities with fresh eyes. This is the case with Henenghome in China reported in Chapter 13 and later in this chapter.

There is precedent for this. IBM, for example, developed a culture and a clear set of corporate rules, well suited for handling the demands of clients of its mainframe computers. But when the personal computer came into existence, and individuals rather than corporations became the customer base, IBM was awkward and slow to adapt. Its rules did not match the new realities. Dell and Apple were born with business models targeted to the individual consumer. Henry Ford had the insight that a market existed for something better than horse-drawn carriages. The automobile industry with its supply chains was born. A ubiquitous infrastructure of roads, highways, expressways and all the ancillary land-use functions associated with transportation followed, coming into being to support the automobiles and trucks being produced.

Sometimes, established companies recognize this and move internally to activate something like this process. They create subsidiaries or divisions, sometimes known as 'skunkworks,' to try out new models of business operation, to meet new challenges and opportunities. This happened in the commercial construction sector, when large construction companies spawned new divisions specializing in tenant fit-out work for the office and shopping center markets. The same thing happens in architecture firms, when market opportunities are recognized by either the acquisition of new niche companies or hiring new people to spearhead a new corporate posture.

In the same way, some company will develop a successful residential fit-out service, which will stimulate competition and which in turn will lower costs and will put residential base buildings, as a new kind of infrastructure, in demand as the pragmatic basis for a regenerative building stock.

A short history infill or fit-out systems development

The full story of efforts to bring complete residential fit-out services per dwelling to the market has yet to be written. Nevertheless, this chapter offers a brief history, and concludes with a number of lessons learned about why a residential fit-out industry is slow to emerge.

The ubiquity of commercial fit-out starting perhaps in the 1960s with the emergence of such companies as Herman Miller, Steelcase, Haworth and others is well known. Yet, in spite of this fact, this phenomenon has not yet been studied as it deserves to be, a shortcoming due in part to the lack of industry-wide statistics on this level of intervention.

The European part of the story of residential fit-out begins in the Netherlands. In the early 1970s, Nijuhis Toeleverinjg BV began delivering its 4DEE infill system (see Figure 14.1). Then in the mid-1970s, Bruynzeel, a major producer of kitchens, developed a demountable partition wall system (Brunzyeel Inbouwpacket) that was used in a few support projects in the Netherlands and in the UK (PSHHAK, 1979) and in a large project in Lunetten

Waaruit bestaat de
4 dee Inbouw.

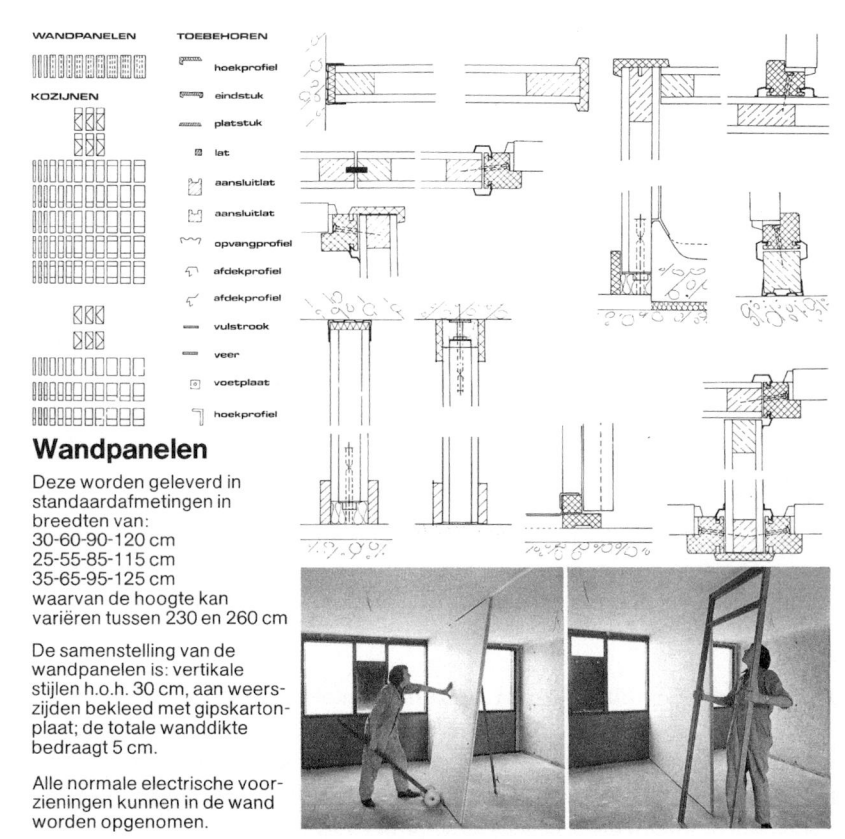

Wandpanelen

Deze worden geleverd in standaardafmetingen in breedten van:
30-60-90-120 cm
25-55-85-115 cm
35-65-95-125 cm
waarvan de hoogte kan variëren tussen 230 en 260 cm.

De samenstelling van de wandpanelen is: vertikale stijlen h.o.h. 30 cm, aan weerszijden bekleed met gipskartonplaat; de totale wanddikte bedraagt 5 cm.

Alle normale electrische voorzieningen kunnen in de wand worden opgenomen.

Figure 14.1
Nijhuis 4DEE system (source: archival company brochure)

Figure 14.2
**Bruynzeel
delivery
truck (photo
by the
author)**

Figure 14.3
**Bruynzeel
partition
system
installation
(photo by
Frans van
der Werf)**

designed by Frans van der Werf in 1982 (see Figures 14.2 and 14.3). Also in the early 1970s, a company named Dura had developed an approach using a raised floor under which all horizontal piping could be installed, separated from the support, as well as a 'wall liner' system behind which electrical and other conduits could be routed, all part of its infill system. They called it 'open building,' the name which eventually was adopted by the OBOM research group at Technical University Delft. Studies of infill packages were made in the early 1980s (for example, Wilma made a study of infill packages). In 1984, the Stichting Open Building (Foundation for Open Building) was formed to advance this mission. Also, starting in the mid-1980's, Espirit and Interlevel

Figure 14.4
**Interlevel
floor system
(source:
archival
company
brochure**

were companies exploring infill systems (see Figures 14.4 and 14.5). These early efforts are briefly documented (Boosma et al., 2000; Fassbinder and Proveniers, 1992).

A few pioneering architects were learning to design, and general contractors were willing to construct Support projects in the Netherlands in the early 1980s that did not cost more than the traditional way, although there was heavy resistance. Economic studies demonstrated that Supports could in fact cost less (Dekker, 1982). This in itself was a breakthrough, because builders were generally reluctant to change their habits and give up what they saw as their way of assuring control and profit – the completion of an entire project from foundation to setting the tiles and the fixtures and cabinets in the bathrooms. When given a set of drawings with the infill taken out, they had the tendency to make cost proposals for construction that did not fairly represent the true value of a building without its infill.

MATURA's origins

In 1986, a group of Dutch colleagues steeped in the theory of separating Support and Infill met to take steps toward developing a commercial infill system. The discussion focused initially on modular coordination, at the time under serious discussion in the Dutch building industry, as the key to infill system development. This group included John Habraken, Age van Randen,

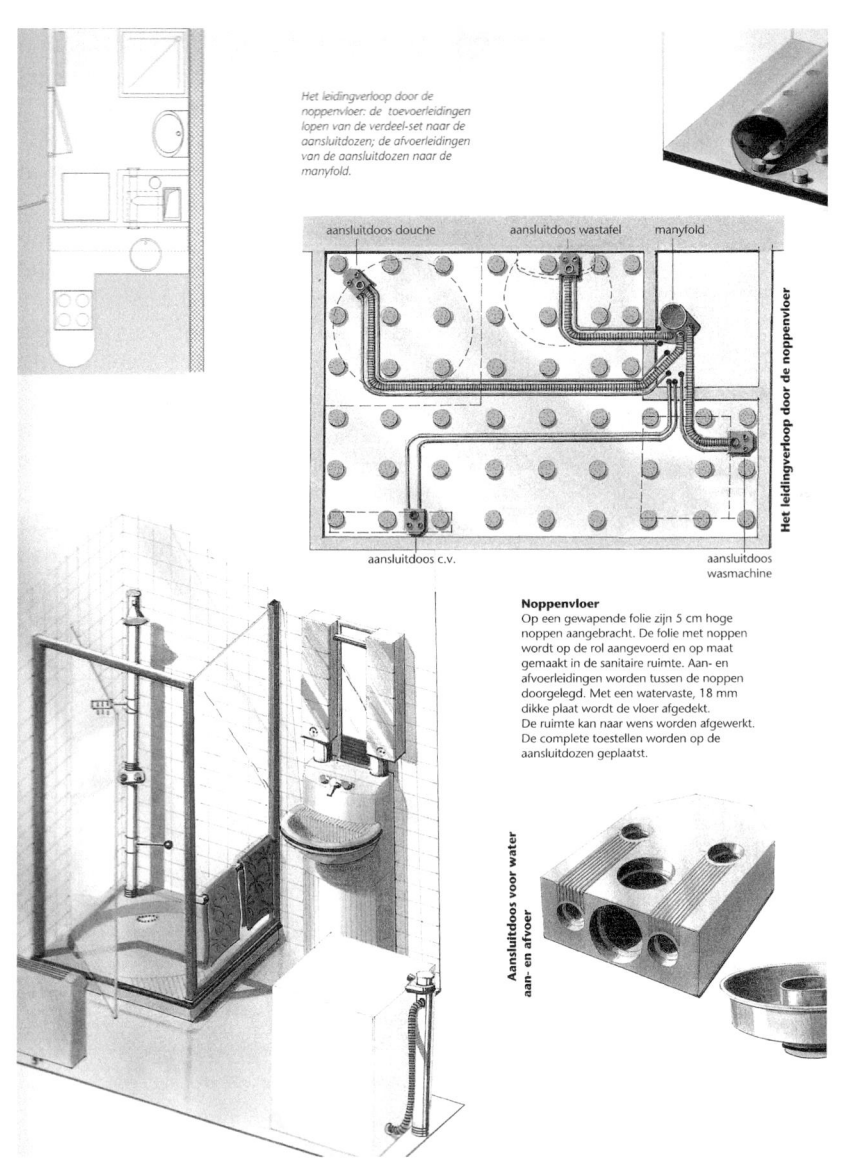

Figure 14.5
**Espirit
system
(source:
archival
company
brochure)**

Het leidingverloop door de
noppenvloer: de toevoerleidingen
lopen van de verdeel-set naar de
aansluitdozen; de afvoerleidingen
van de aansluitdozen naar de
manyfold.

aansluitdoos douche   aansluitdoos wastafel   manyfold

Het leidingverloop door de noppenvloer

aansluitdoos c.v.   aansluitdoos
                                               wasmachine

Noppenvloer
Op een gewapende folie zijn 5 cm hoge
noppen aangebracht. De folie met noppen
wordt op de rol aangevoerd en op maat
gemaakt in de sanitaire ruimte. Aan- en
afvoerleidingen worden tussen de noppen
doorgelegd. Met een watervaste, 18 mm
dikke plaat wordt de vloer afgedekt.
De ruimte kan naar wens worden afgewerkt.
De complete toestellen worden op de
aansluitdozen geplaatst.

Aansluitdoos voor water
aan- en afvoer

Frans de Vries, Jan van Vonderen, Frans van der Werf, Rens de Groot and
Dirk Smit.

Soon thereafter, in 1986, the OBOM research group (Open Building
Development Model) was founded at TU Delft on the initiative of Professor
Age van Randen. Its goal was to work out the pre-competitive technical and
regulatory issues for the emergence of an infill industry. It focused heavily
on the disentanglement of the utility installations (mechanical, electrical and

plumbing systems), separating these installations on the different decision levels (Support and Infill) and also developing basic principles for installation pathways in both. With regular exchanges and consultations with partners in industry and discussion with regulatory bodies, a number of basic principles were formulated for the complete independence of infill from supports. These studies were published in a number of Dutch language reports.

In 1987, Infill Systems BV was incorporated, to carry the university-based research into commercial reality. Patents for two key elements of the MATURA Infill System were applied for: the 'Matrix Tile' and the 'Base Profile' (Figures 14.6 and 14.7). Following extensive studies and mock-ups, the first trial installation of the system was initiated, with investments coming from the partners of the company.

The MATURA Infill System was intended to offer an alternative to filling-in empty spaces in buildings for dwellings in both new construction and the reactivation of older apartments, at a price equal to conventional methods while offering a faster and less disruptive service, decision flexibility to the building owner and choice to occupants. The value proposition was based on two key products and proprietary software, patent protected by Infill Systems BV. These products were intended to be key parts of an 'open system' with most parts of each infill package available in the open market of building products (piping, wiring, sanitary and kitchen equipment, cabinets, partitions, doors, etc.). In 1990, Infill Systems BV granted a license to use the system to MATURA Netherlands.

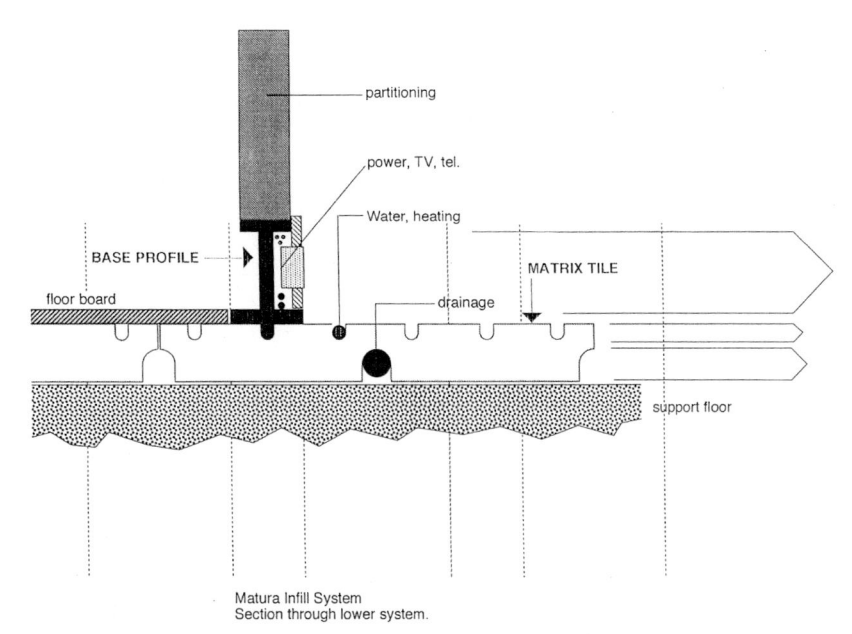

Figure 14.6 The MATURA 'lower system' concept: matrix tile and base profile. 0-slope gray water drainage piping using the siphonic drainage system was installed under the Matrix Tiles as shown

Matura Infill System
Section through lower system.

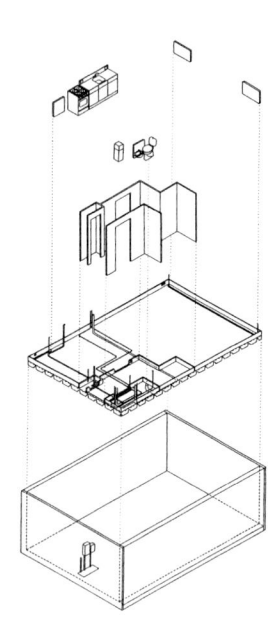

Figure 14.7
An exploded view of the MATURA system: empty shell space, proprietary lower system to manage horizontal piping and wiring, upper system from the open market

Description of the MATURA® Infill System

A MATURA information brochure gave a description of its product/service:

> Given an empty shell for a dwelling unit, MATURA® offers a fully prefabricated and adaptable infill system for residential construction. It includes spatial partitioning as well as all technical installations and kitchen and sanitary equipment, providing a fully equipped and habitable dwelling unit.
>
> The MATURA® Infill System:
>
> • Is a so-called 'Open System,' utilizing subsystems and parts that are readily available on the market like wall systems, doors and door frames, various wall finishes, as well as equipment for kitchens and bathrooms. It also can accommodate new developments of such 'off the shelf' products. All these subsystems are integrated into an adaptable whole by means of two newly developed elements: the 'MatrixTile' and the 'Base Profile.'These new elements provide flexibility in design, fast installation on the site, and changeability in the future.
>
> • Is based on a radically new distribution of technical conduits made possible by the Matrix Tile and the Base Profile. Interfaces among conduits (for sewage, water, heating, electricity etc.) and between conduits and walls are minimized. Each conduits' deployment in space follows specific rules of positioning in the Matrix Tile grid, by means of which it can run freely without interference with other

systems. Moreover, all conduit deployments are independent of the Support structure of the building. All this assures extremely rapid installation of the technical systems serving the dwelling unit.

- Fits in any given physical context. Installation does not pose special demands on the support structure and the facades. Thanks to the free distribution of conduits the position of vertical shafts does not determine floor plans any longer. This makes the MATURA® Infill System particularly attractive for renovation projects.
- Responds to user needs. The systematic deployment of all parts makes future adaptation to user needs easier. Users can arrange outlets for electricity, telephone, and television at any time.
- Is installed unit by unit by a well-trained team of two or three workers. A single team installs the complete infill package for one dwelling unit in a short time. This means that large- scale projects with uniform floor plans are no longer a prerequisite for efficient residential construction. By employing several teams at the same time in one project, each doing a different floor plan, more units can be filled in simultaneously.
- Utilizes proprietary software. This software allows the quick translation of a floor plan into a technical design of all subsystems needed for its realization. The technical design, in turn, automatically feeds a database that steers the selection and dimensioning of all parts needed for one unit and determines their packaging in the container from where the infill unit is installed on the site. Included in the software is proprietary know-how concerning the dimensional coordination of all parts allowing these parts to be cut to size before they reach the building site.
- Offers advantages for all parties involved:
    - For builders: Faster installation on the site. Shorter time needed for interior finishing, less overhead, fewer logistics problems.
    - For clients: Free choice of floor plans per unit. Determination of floor plans only a few weeks before installation. Choice of different wall systems, doors and doorframes, wall finishes, and kitchen and sanitary equipment.
    - For users: Possibility to determine their own floor plan; Future adaptation of the floor plan and technical systems to changing needs; Easy adaptation and augmentation of outlets for electricity, telephone, and television corresponding to the chosen arrangement of furniture in any room.
    - For manufacturers: Any technical subsystem in the MATURA® Infill System (including kitchen and bathroom equipment) can be replaced by a newer or preferred version without interference with other subsystems. Therefore, improved or alternative subsystems can be offered swiftly and economically as part of the total infill system.

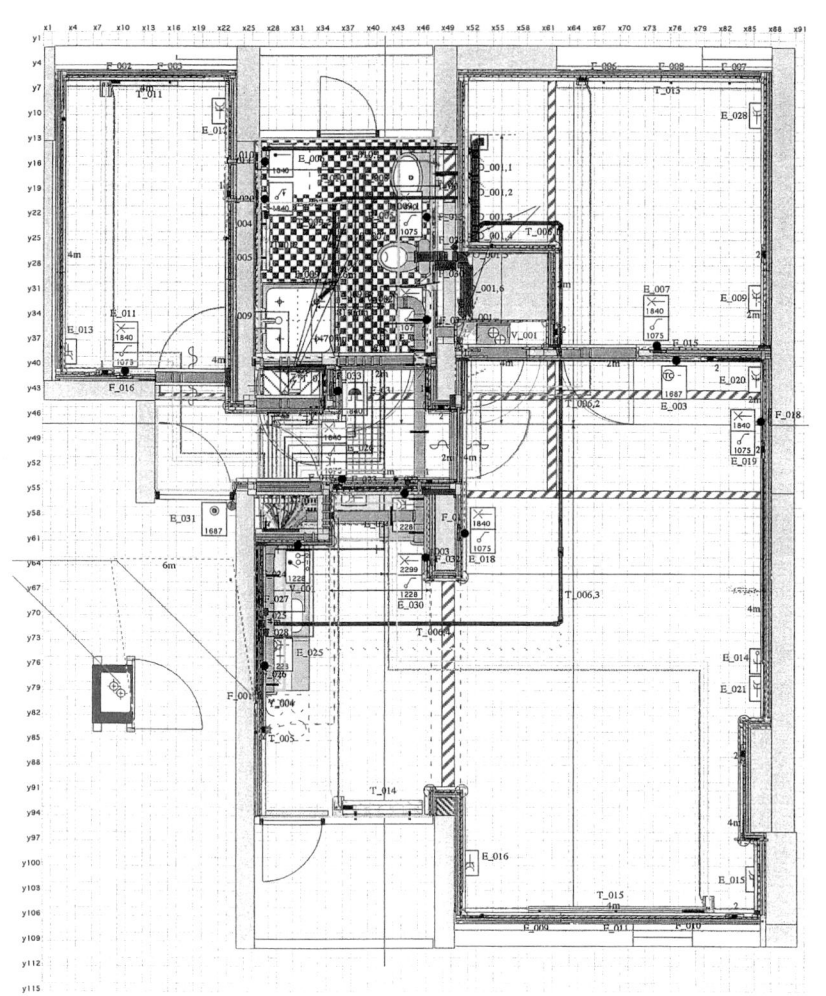

Figure 14.8
**An example
of a MATURA-
CADS
output**

27_*zien_alles*

Projekt 110 renovatiewoningen te Voorburg
Technisch Ontwerp
Prinses Beatrixlaan 152   Maart 1996
Schaal 1:50
MATURA INBOUW Tel.: (076) 542 47 74

The MATURA ® Infill System (was) made available for licensing by Infill Systems BV which held worldwide rights. These rights particularly related to the deployment of technical conduits for drainage, gas, ventilation, heating, water, electricity, electronics etc., by means of the Matrix Tile and the Base Profile. Infill Systems BV also held rights to the software used for technical design and related data. MATURA ® is a registered trade name.

In 1988, the first application of MATURA in a for-sale dwelling unit was completed, followed the next year by another. In 1989, MATURACADS, a computer program to manage the ordering of all parts of a MATURA infill packet was developed, providing output to the fabrication facility for accurate

Figure 14.9
Lower system installed in the Voorburg renovation project

cutting of parts per infill packet (Figure 14.8). Investors were sought and initial funding was obtained to set up a business structure (MATURA International) with an international market ambition.

In 1990, Infill Systems was asked to bid on the renovation of a single apartment unit in a housing estate in Voorburg built in the 1960's that needed to be upgraded. A study showed how this upgrading could be done for the entire block of housing owned by the housing association, in a cost-effective way 'one-unit-at-a-time' (Dekker, 1989). It was called 'cellular renovation.' This installation was done successfully (the author was invited to take part in the installation) (see Figure 14.9). A total of 20 such packets were installed there over the next few years, some in the renovation of the older apartments, some in new supports added to the housing association's property.

But in 1995, funding from investors was withdrawn for various reasons, and MATURA Nederlands ended in 1998, after delivering infill packets for 100 dwelling units. Since that time, post-occupancy surveys have indicated no problems with the system.

Why the MATURA Infill System was discontinued

Opinions vary on the question of why the system was discontinued, evidence for which is contained in an unpublished 186-page report (Kendall, 2015), based on in-depth interviews with many of the principals involved in the development and use of the system, including investors.

Conclusions drawn from the interviews include, in no particular order:

1. MATURA (both the products and the company) was far ahead of its time.
2. The company did not have a sufficiently convincing business plan to attract sustained investments.

3. The developers were focused on technical perfection of its proprietary technical products, rather than on the less technical but nevertheless crucial problem of opening a new market of delivering complete infill packages, while developing the products step-by-step as lessons were gained by experience.

4. Demand was not there nor was demand developed through an aggressive marketing strategy. The company owners simply believed that there would be a market demand, given the state of the Dutch housing market at that time, other similar developments, and the vocal interest expressed in the concept. However, demand never developed from large housing associations who controlled much of the rental housing stock, or from individual buyers; developers of new projects were not yet ready to invest in 'empty' base buildings, in which decisions would be made later about fit-out for each dwelling unit; in regard to the renovation of the existing stock, developers were not ready to risk signing contracts with a single-source company to deliver infill, for which there was no competition. There was legitimate concern that the two proprietary products might not continue to be available later when repair or replacement was needed.

5. The Dutch building industry (including its regulatory, financing and legal structures) was not ready to accept the concept of a single-source infill company instead of the conventional use of multiple subcontractors under a general contractor.

John Habraken, one of the partners in Infill Systems BV, had the following assessment in 2020.

Housing in the Netherlands was (and still is) entirely based on professional networks that are more than a century old. Nobody wanted to change these old ways of working – technical detailing, cost estimation, government regulations and so on – that all were based on predetermined floor plans that drove the entire decision-making process, either in new construction or renovation. These traditions persist.

Building contractors and project managers were busy organizing and overseeing the sequence of specialized subcontractors. They understood that they would be without jobs when each housing unit was done in the new way proposed by MATURA. Technical and managerial know-how in those days was more primitive compared to today, and professionals were used to an outdated and complicated culture.

The two patent-protected products were considered clever but also a risk. Like any truly new product for which there were no substitutes on the market, everyone wanted to know if they would still be available when there was a need to renovate the dwelling units later.

The desire to deliver a perfect and advanced integrated system demanded long-term investments for the development of market demand and efficient production to serve it. But the construction industry thinks short term, pulls out of the market when there is a recession, firing the workers, and goes back into business when the market goes up.

In hindsight, a state-of-the-the art technical system, using familiar subsystems from the market and a more pragmatic approach focused on logistics and management might have been a more reasonable starting point for going into business. This might have avoided the risks and gained acceptance, allowing new specialized products replacing older versions to be introduced later to improve the service.

Yet, even if a more pragmatic approach had been taken, there is a good chance that nobody would have wanted to risk adopting an alternative way of working while the ongoing ways, based on government subsidies and a rising national economy, continued to allow everyone to make money. The housing industry is the only major industry that continues to make things whose quality decreases and costs rise. No other industry could survive doing this.

MATURA 2

Starting in 2009, Age van Randen, one of the co-inventors of the proprietary MATURA products (Matrix Tile and Base Profile) began to rethink these products, developing a variation on the Matrix Tile and an entirely new and independent product called CableStud. They were now considered separate products, not necessarily used together (see Figure 14.10). Frans de Vries, one of the original partners of MATURA, held the patents, and gave a license to GYPROC which brought CableStud to the market in the Netherlands and the Benelux and as PlacoPlatro in France. Neither company fulfilled its contractual obligation to sell the agreed upon quantity of the product, and the licenses were withdrawn. In 2020, a Dutch steel building company took the license for CableStud, renaming it WallHubb (www.WallHubb.nl).

In 2012, Frans de Vries and the author made efforts to sell the know-how of CableStud and Matrix Tile in China for a lump sum, displaying full-scale mock-ups in the International Housing Exposition in Beijing that year. No takers were found. The CableStud patent was granted for the United States in 2014, with no success in bringing it to market (at this writing).

Developments toward Open Building and a fit-out industry in Japan

One could say that the idea of infill appeared quite early in Japan. Osaka is one of the big cities in the Kansai Region (the western part of Japan) which has a long history of urban housing. From around the end of the Edo Period (1603–1867) until the Second World War there was a housing system called 'Hadakagashi.' In the Hadaka-gashi system, the building framework, roof, exterior walls and external fittings belonged to the owner of houses, and

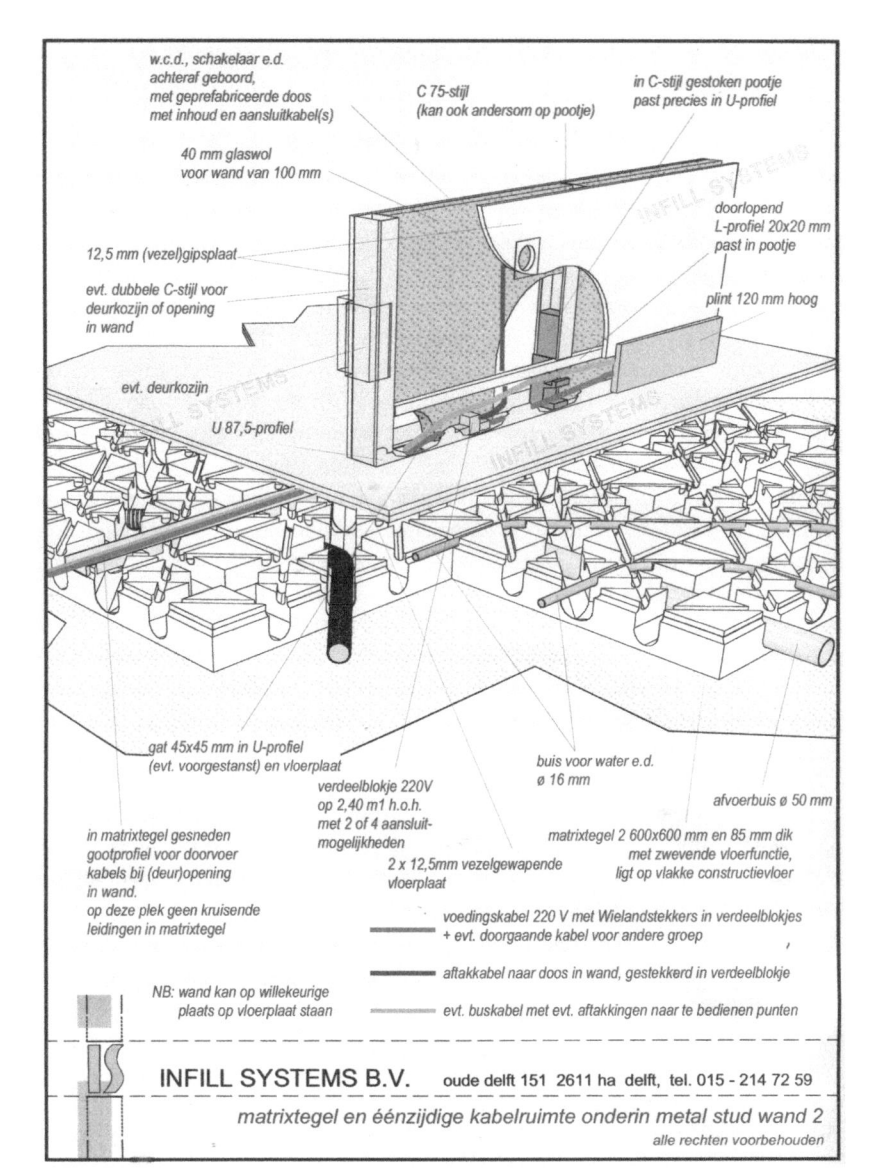

Figure 14.10
**Drawing
of the new
Matrix
Tile and
CableStud**

tenants fixed their own infill such as interior fittings, tatami mats, ceilings and internal equipment by themselves. About 80% of houses in Osaka were 'rented,' and most of them were said to be supplied by the Hadaka-gashi system. Many of these row houses included a store facing the street as well as a dwelling space behind and upstairs. The Hadaka-gashi system was not only a housing system satisfying these diverse needs, but also such a reasonable system that difficulties would be averted between owners and tenants when making repairs on the interior of a house.

There needed to be some conditions for the widespread use of the Hadaka-gashi system. Firstly, technological requirement of compatibility of the infill like tatami mats or fittings had to be satisfied. In those days, there were several kinds of room arrangement systems all over Japan. Two representative kinds were the 'Edo-ma' system in the eastern part of Japan, for example in Edo (now Tokyo); another was 'Kyo-ma' system in the western part of Japan, for example Osaka and Kyoto. In the Edo-ma system the measurement between the center of pillars is a multiple of a certain module. In the Kyo-ma system the measurement between the face of one pillar and that of another pillar is a multiple of a certain module. In the Edo-ma system, if the size of a room changes, the sizes of tatami mats and fittings have to be changed, and the infill is not compatible even in the same house. On the other hand, in the Kyo-ma system, the infill is compatible with rooms of any size, even in different houses.

The second requirement for the Hadaka-gashi system is an industrial condition of distribution of the infill parts such as tatami mats and fittings. The system made it possible to standardize the sizes of tatami mats and fittings. While ready-made infill appeared on the market, the business of recycling used infill was conducted. Therefore, tenants were able to rearrange rooms or to move to a new house with great ease, taking their tatami mats with them. This was therefore an excellent system suitable for urban areas with high mobility. Historical studies show that the ready-made infill produced in Osaka was sold even in cities like Kyoto where Hadaka-gashi system was not necessarily common (Takada, 2001).

The work of the SAR was first introduced to Japan in 1972 (Toshi-Jutaku, September 1972, pp. 8–52). At that time the whole picture of the work of the SAR was not always understood. In the mid-1970s Professors Kazuo Tatsumi and Mitsuo Takada at Kyoto University developed a concept called 'Two-Step Housing,' making a distinction between the social (collective) part of a large housing project and the individual (dwelling unit) part. The Two Step Housing System (TSHS) was a proposal that includes not only a physical housing system but also a spatial housing system and a social housing system. This system was created by simplifying the Government Aided Housing System (GAHS) (Tatsumi and Takada, 1978). GAHS was based on Tatsumi's paper (Two Aspects of Housing Policy, 1975) that discussed the role of the public sector and the private sector in housing. This paper advocated the reorganization of Japan's social housing in which the public and private housing were divided. GAHS proposed a housing system that integrated the social housing system, the spatial housing system, and the physical housing system, with a system-theoretical consideration. However, this system was ideological and too complex to be feasible. TSHS was a simplification, aimed to increase its feasibility. It was inspired by the Hadaka-Gashi housing supply system noted above. As a result, it became very similar to Professor Habraken's Supports concept. A number of pilot projects were realized followed by a number of TSHS projects over the succeeding years in the Kansai region (Osaka and Kyoto) between 1983 and 1998 (Tatsumi and Takada, 1978; 1980).

At the University of Tokyo, under the leadership of Professor Yositika Utida, another path of development was occurring also in the mid-1970s, in which the principle of differentiating parts of a building based on their expected useful life was developed. Two key initiatives resulted. One was KEP (Kodan Experimental Project), initiated by the governmental Housing and Urban Development Corporation. The other was the Century Housing System, begun in 1980 by the Ministry of Construction. The Ministry of International Trade and Industry (MITI) also took initiatives to build experimental projects following the principle of separating a skeleton from its infill. These efforts were followed by a substantial number of other S/I (skeleton/infill) projects built in the market, by private sector companies as well as public entities (this is summarized in Chapter 8).

In 1989, two large Japanese companies (Shimizu Construction Company and Haseko Development Company) approached Infill Systems BV in the Netherlands with interest in licensing the MATURA Infill System for introduction into the Japanese market. After intensive efforts, studies by Japanese plumbing experts of the 0-slope gray-water drainage piping enabled by the Matrix Tile, and a full-scale mock-up put together in an empty warehouse space in Tokyo, this effort ceased.

An important breakthrough came in 1994 with the construction of NEXT21, initiated by the Osaka Gas Company (see Figure 14.11) under the leadership of Professor Utida. It continues to be a project in which new

Figure 14.11
NEXT21
(photo courtesy Osaka Gas)

concepts for urban living are implemented. It was an important step in Open Building in Japan. The skeleton was designed by one team; a dimensional coordination system was developed by another team to coordinate independently designed infill; a façade system was developed by still another team, offering a 'kit-of-parts' to be used by each architect designing an independent dwelling infill; and 13 different architects each designed a dwelling unit in the skeleton, using the façade system according to the needs of each dwelling's layout. Since it was first built, many changes have been made by different architects, some units have been combined, others reorganized, and innovations in heating and air conditioning systems have been installed. The project continues as a place for experimenting with both the social and technical aspects of the Open Building approach (NEXT21, 1994; NEXT21, 2005).

In 1997, the Urban Development Corporation (formerly the Japan Housing Corporation) launched an R&D program called KSI (Kodan Skeleton and Infill) Housing (see Figure 14.12). Kodan was a Japanese term for UDC that builds public housing. At their UDC Technology Center, they showcased six infill systems, each representing a different approach, by a variety of private companies or consortia of companies. These were completed in 1999 and opened to the public. Two are shown here (see Figures 14.13, 14.14). Also shown is the long history of R&D of the UDC, to 2000 (see Figure 14.15).

An early initiative to develop an integrated infill system for the Japanese multi-family market was undertaken in 2005 by an architect (Mr. Yoshikazu Adachi) working with Sekisui Chemical's housing division. Adachi later left Sekisui to start his own company, called Next Infill. Currently, the company licenses its product to real estate developers, but has delivered a very small number of infill packets so far. This is reported on in more detail in Chapter 8.

An expected turning point in making S/I housing more widespread in Japan occurred with the passage of the Long-Life Housing Law of 2009, by the Japanese Diet (central government). This is reported on in detail in Chapter 8. Yet its results are disappointing from the viewpoint of Open Building. Developers have not wanted to follow the Long Life requirements, especially those of anti-seismic performance and high durability of reinforced concrete, which raise prices above their competitors. This suppresses demand; people have never heard the name "Long Life Housing" in the market and don't value the law's requirements.

One commentator familiar with the long history of developments toward Open Building in Japan made this assessment:

Condominiums constructed with a reinforced concrete structure started to be built in 1962 when the 'Act on Building Unit Ownership' was established. This type of housing has a 60-year history and today there are now more than 6.65 million housing units in existing condos in 2019 according to government statistics. It makes a rather big market of renovation of units' infill. It includes partial renovation as well as

Figure 14.12
**KSI-Kodan
skeleton and
infill experi-
mental
housing**

gut rehabilitation of each unit. Also, it includes the renovation by the resident's order as well as the renovation after/before the change of the owner and resident in the re-sale market. In this renovation market, various types of existing companies such as general contractors, house builders, house makers, inclusive building component and material makers, etc. are entering to do the infill renovation. From the technical and organizational point of view, most of them apply conventional construction methods.

In the case of new condominium construction, all the infill works are under the unified construction contract for the entire building (not separated as skeleton and infill contracts) and managed by general contractors. Usually in such cases, interior work in each dwelling unit

Figure 14.13
**UDC infill
with flexible
layout even
for the water
use spaces**

Infill Experimental Housing

Room 203

UDC Infill with flexible layout even for water use space

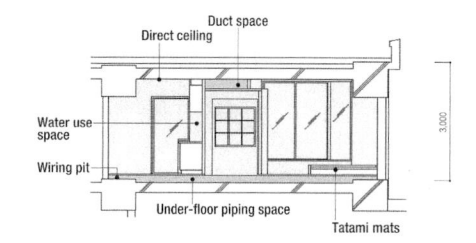

Designed by Urban Development Corporation

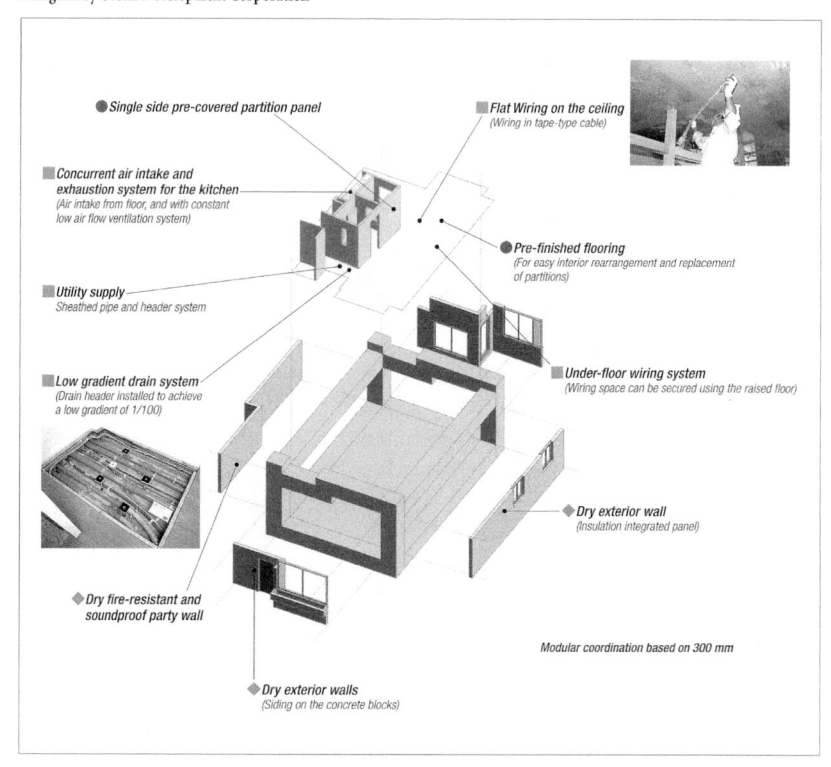

is done by not one infill contractor with multi-skilled installers, but by using several types of sub- contractors under the general contractors' management. There is nothing new from the Open Building viewpoint.

As far as the 2009 Act for the Promotion of Long-Life Quality Housing (LQH) is concerned, I had been involved in this project since the beginning.

Figure 14.14
**Infill compo-
nent parts
of eight
companies**

Room 202

Infill Component Parts of 8 Companies

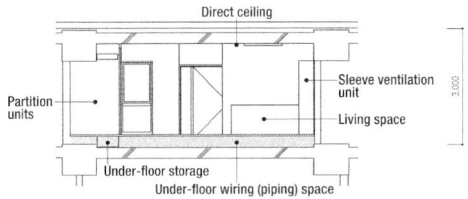

Provided by Mitsui Construction Co., Ltd. / Bridgestone Corporation / Nippon Sheet Glass Environment Amenity Co., Ltd.
Mitsubishi Plastic, Inc. / Top Housing System Co., Ltd. / Tokyo Electric Power Company / Matsushita Electric Works, Ltd. / Uniteboard Co., Ltd.

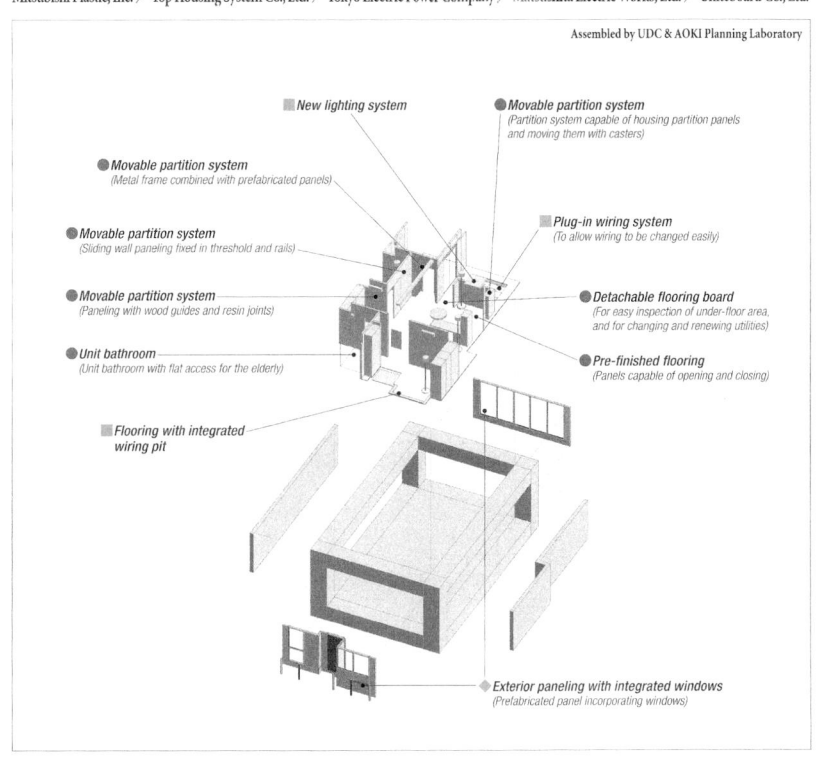

In 2019, I chaired the advisory committee about how to make the market use this system more. The official report of the committee made clear the following fact. Namely, in the detached house new building market the occupancy rate of the certification system based on the Act was 24.1% in 2010 and 25.1% in 2018. We cannot find any progress. In the multi-family dwellings new building market (for-sale condominiums and rental apartments), the adoption rate was 0.5% in 2010 and 0.1% in 2018 – a

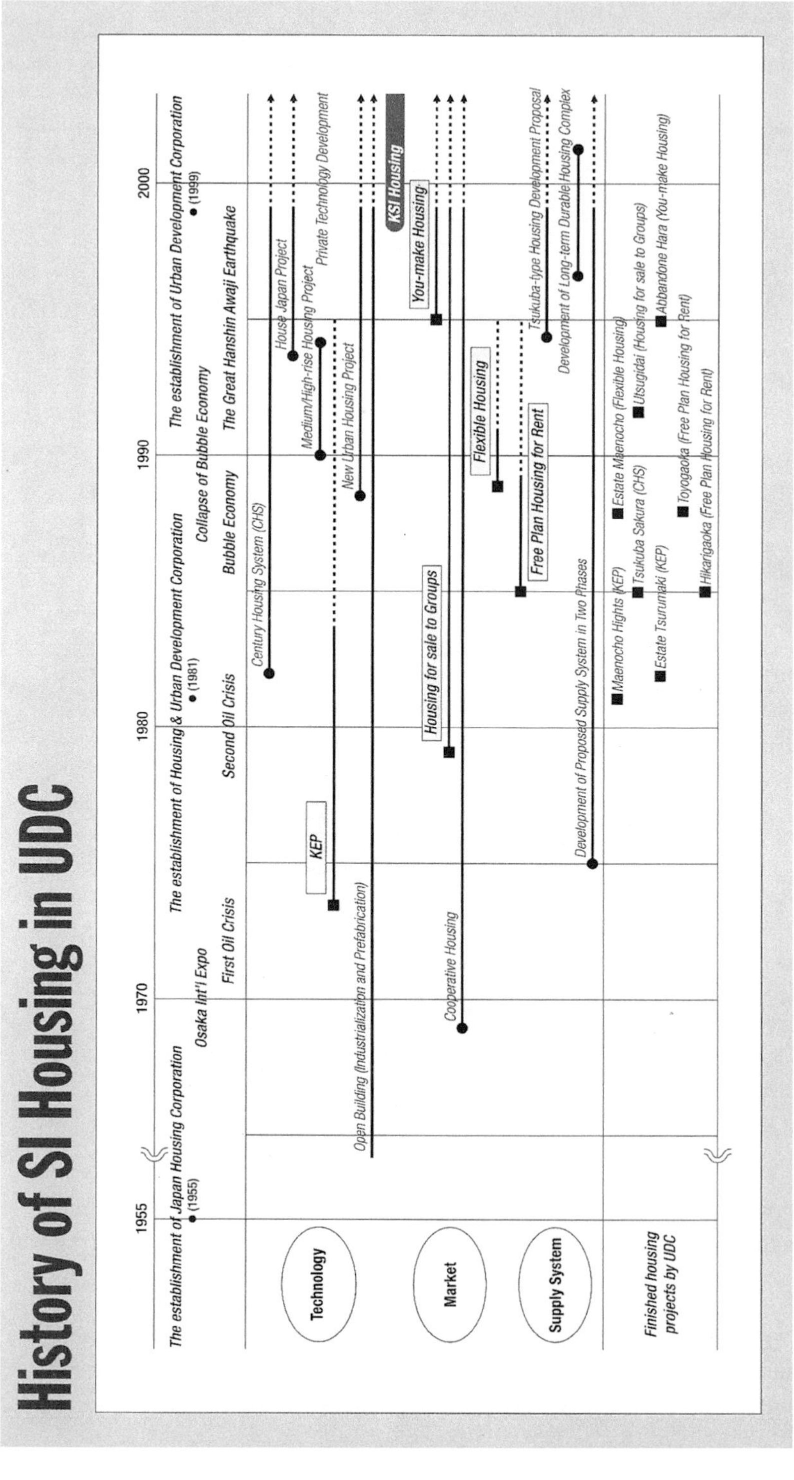

History of SI Housing in UDC

Figure 14.15
History of SI housing in UDC

very small portion of a large market. This reveals that few consumers know the name 'Long Life Quality Housing.' This act started to include the renovation of existing houses, condos and flats in 2014. But the occupancy rate of the certification system is much less than that in the new building market. Therefore, at least so far, it cannot be influential on the emergence of Open Building or an infill industry in Japan. I hope the expected actions following our committee report will help to increase the market's use of the law's incentive program and make it become more influential in the near future.

(Professor Shuichi Matsumura, Department of Architecture, University of Tokyo, in a personal exchange with the editor, December 2020)

Henenghome: the worlds most advanced infill system

One fit-out company in China is especially advanced. This company was briefly introduced in Chapter 13 as Company N5 (www.henenghome.com).

The company's president started in business developing and selling software to manage hotel reservations (now used in 75% of Chinese hotels) and manufacturing a pharmaceutical for children (now used by most hospitals). He later got into real estate development. Around 2008, seeing a market in the interior decoration business, he started this company that now supplies thousands of complete infill packages to public rental housing projects in several large cities in China, and is also supplying the single-family luxury market and the for-sale condominium market, healthcare and educational facilities. They produce many thousands of infill units each year. They also have their own manufacturing facilities to make everything from metal studs of various sizes, all panel materials for walls and floors, doors and steel door frames, door hardware, etc. Their 'quick-connect' water piping system does not require licensed plumbers. They complete a small apartment in seven days – from a raw space to installed furnishing – with a trained multi-skilled installation team of four workers (see Figures 14.16 – 14.22).

Their logistics strategy is to deliver as much as possible from their own factories. They deliver exactly the right quantity of each subsystem, with each delivery bar coded as to which building, which floor and into which dwelling unit a given bundle of parts is to be delivered.

By mid-2020, after just five years in full operation, the company had completed over 80,000 apartment units, 4000 hotel rooms and over 60,000 m^2 (646,000 ft^2) of public buildings including hospitals, schools, commercial chain stores, offices and renovation of existing buildings. Some clients are government controlled, such as public housing projects. Projects like residential condominiums, schools, hotels, gyms and hair salons are all privately owned. By 2020, about 90% of their work was in new construction, about 10% in improving existing buildings. They recognize that improving existing buildings is a bigger market, so they intend to expand in that market.

In 2020, they had five factories in China, each with the production capacity of 50,000 apartment units per year, with a supply radius of 300 km

Figure 14.16
Sequence of installation stages over seven days of a Heneng-home infill system (courtesy Heneng-home)

Figure 14.17

(185 miles). This supply ability allows them to be competitive in renovating existing buildings, and beginning in 2020, they began to face customers directly in showrooms.

They are using technologies such as big data, cloud computing and AI to connect their BIM+ERP+MES system – what they call their HENENG digital fabrication platform. They have developed their own design software (based on BIM – Building Information System), which allows designers to freely design (they have over 2000+ wall surface patterns and finishes to choose from: wood, fabric, marble etc.) and avoid worrying about drawing details of their infill system (the software does that itself). When the design is finished, it automatically generates orders to their Enterprise Resource Planning (ERP) system and sends the orders directly to their production line (MES or Manufacturing Execution System) without any human interference. This means all data comes from the same origin; the same model is used from design to manufacture to installation and maintenance; and every project

Figure 14.18

Figure 14.19

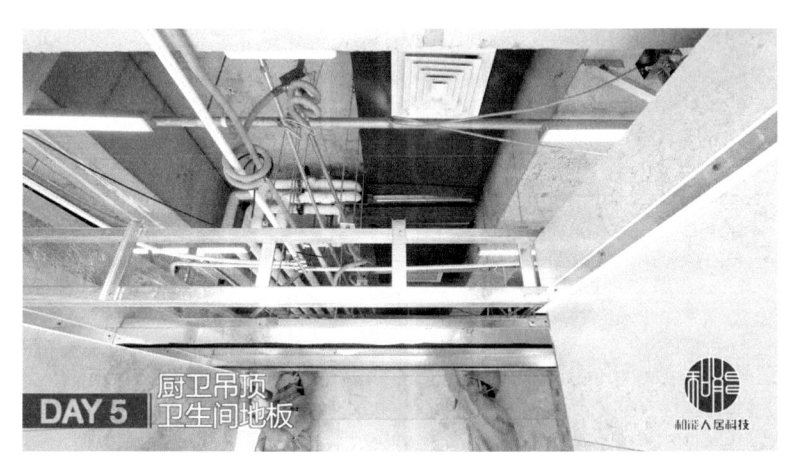

Figure 14.20

Figure 14.21

Figure 14.22

has a digital twin. This combination of both the digital and industrial world maximizes efficiency and connects the whole industrial supply chain.

The company has 102 patents and a 100% factory production rate. For large-scale projects they save 50% time; on small scale projects they save 75% time. Also, they save 65% on material waste, and the repair rate is lowered 95% compared to traditional construction method. They are now in version-3 of their software and logistics system. As noted in Chapter 11, the developers they work with save money and time using their services.

The executive director of Henenghome, in private correspondence with the author, said 'Some traditional construction companies are trying to do what we do, but it is hard for a construction company to transform their whole system from construction management to production. It is

two different fields and it takes time to shift to a new mode. The market
is huge; we hope there are more companies to join us so we can make
the industry better together.'

Lessons learned: why a residential fit-out industry is slow to emerge

For many years Open Building enthusiasts have suggested that the Open
Building approach makes a fit-out industry desirable and possible. But it
never happened.

The many hundreds of successful residential Open Building projects
that are already on record show that the Open Building approach applied
to residential architecture does not depend for success on advanced fit-out
systems. The variety of examples shown in Part 1 and in other published
books and reports shows that there are many reasons to adopt the Open
Building approach, and that they take various architectural, social/organiza-
tional and technical forms. But progress is slow.

It is a familiar fact that productivity in the building industry has declined
over the past half-century. The proposition made here is that to successfully
turn around the outdated professional housing culture and to improve productivity, commercially successful fit-out systems and competitive companies
delivering them are needed. And, in the long-run, keeping a national housing
stock up-to-date and sustainable requires the availability of many certified
fit-out companies, as Chapter 7 argues.

The proposal to separate fit-out design from support or base building
design and to make each dwelling unit fully independent was usually
considered to be too expensive compared to the traditional mode of tying
the design of the support to the initial fit-out design, uniform or not. Despite
evidence to the contrary (the yearly expenditures on remodeling residential
buildings often equals investments in new construction) no one believed that
change or variety at the level of the individual dwelling was important to consider, even though no one argued against the idea that being able to decide
on your own dwelling design was a good idea.

So, it is not surprising that it is only in the last decade that pioneering companies have appeared, in several countries, to offer the service of delivering
and installing each residential unit as an integrated, single-source and separate
task. Some of the more significant examples have been presented at the beginning of this chapter. These few companies have based their business models
not on the fragmented construction industry model of organizing labor and
materials per project, but on an industrial systems model. But as the chapters
in Part 2 show, even the passage by national governments of long-life housing
guidelines and laws has not made much difference, at least not yet.

A fit-out industry based on an industrial model – the basis of the success in
the automotive and other complex consumer products' industries – is rooted

in the understanding that a robust system is not a limitation on variety but enables variety and does so efficiently. An example in the building industry is the 'steel framing system.' Using this model enables production to meet a massive demand of individualized requests, each somewhat different but all based on a few key interface, logistics and software standards, and a few key organizing products, that may be proprietary to each company.

We can now say, based on the evidence so far mainly from developments in China, that fit-out systems based on an industrial model can be economically competitive. But they operate with a great deal of 'head-wind.' How much the success of the Chinese example is dependent on their particular socio-economic situation needs to be carefully studied.

The following, in no particular order, suggests why a residential fit-out industry is slow to emerge in the multi-family housing market.

Demand is either suppressed or nonexistent

- In the U.S., the banking and real estate development industries, along with the Government Sponsored Enterprises, have intentionally taken the power of self-determination away from people who buy homes. Standardization is an institutional priority, and it (standardization) has been sold to buyers as something that they should like. It's ironic. Once upon a time, people thought that becoming a homeowner gave you special rights to participate in decisions about your own home as well as the community. Now when you buy a home (in a Home Owners Association or condominium community), all the decisions are made by the long-gone developer who commissioned the Covenants, Conditions & Restrictions and whoever got elected to the Board of Directors. 'People have been convinced that they should give up their own freedom and control so that they can prevent their neighbor from having either – and they are so afraid of their neighbors (perhaps due to fear of increasing diversity) that they think this is a prudent way to do things' (from an exchange with Evan McKenzie, author of *Privatopia* and *Beyond Privatopia*).
- Households are usually too stressed and busy to make all the decisions involved in dwelling fit-out design the way things work today and can't imagine how it would even be possible or affordable. They can't be blamed for thinking this.
- Most consumers have come to expect someone else to decide on the fit-out for them even if they think they could afford it; most consumers therefore want finished dwellings (but start changing them soon after moving in anyway); most consumers have been (subtly) taught to think of their dwelling as a 'product' to be bought and sold, not something to cultivate according to their individual preferences (although the strength of the DIY market, IKEA and other product/services in which buyers like to 'add value' seem to suggest otherwise).

No supply

- There is no concept of separated design tasks in multi-family residential design and construction. The legal separation of residential property ownership into base building and fit-out is lacking (see below);
- Companies like IKEA, which already offer CAD design services for kitchens and bathrooms, etc. and deliver RTA (ready-to-assemble) parts of partial dwelling unit infill (but only parts classified as furnishings, appliances and limited equipment), are profitable with their current scope of services and have no incentive to expand into the MEP (mechanical, electric/plumbing) domain and other code-constrained and building-industry controlled parts of infill;
- The design/build industry – otherwise flourishing in the U.S. – has no imagination to enter the market with integrated infill 'product/solutions.'
- Installers of MEP (mechanical, electrical and plumbing) systems remain divided by product type and trade jurisdictions. They are resistant to develop integrated 'installation' services or otherwise cooperate for fear of losing jobs and because they profit from the current conflict-prone and dis-integrated situation.

Technical entanglement

- Multifamily residential infill has more MEP per cubic meter and more service points of various kinds than, for example, offices, and except in the most complex parts of hospitals and laboratories.
- Conventional MEP service distribution pathways do not respect the independence or autonomy of dwelling units (e.g. drainage pipes serving one unit still are distributed in the ceiling of dwellings below) and are still buried and inaccessible, including inside non-bearing stud-and-gypsum-board walls and wood-framed floor systems.
- MEP systems are relatively new in the long history of building technology and are changing faster and becoming more complex than other technical subsystems such as structure and enclosure. Their installation entanglement inhibits replacement by more advanced products when they become available, without undue disruption and cost. When all-electric houses become the norm (when we finally stop dependency on natural gas) it will be very difficult because of buried MEP systems;

Legal/regulatory/financing obstructions

- Multi-family, single-family attached or detached homeowner associations (HOAs) establish rules to keep neighborhoods 'uniform' in an effort to prevent property depreciation or drop in home values as a result of unkempt homes or unmanicured lawns.
- California Civil Code §1351 (f) defines 'condominium' as 'an undivided interest in common in a portion of real property coupled with a separate

interest in space called a unit, the boundaries of which are described on a recorded final map, parcel plan, or condominium plan in sufficient detail to locate all boundaries thereof.' Yet, legal clarity is absent vis-à-vis what is 'movable'/'immovable' ('trade fixtures' vs. 'fixtures') as noted above.

- Building permits for new residential projects require 'integrated' building design, driven by floor plans and details of every part of a building which must be recorded for regulatory review prior to construction permitting.
- Certificates of occupancy for new construction in many jurisdictions require that a bathroom and a kitchen are in place. While not an absolute obstacle (as evident, for example, in the projects in Finland) this goes against the idea of an empty space waiting for infill decisions for complete floor plans, and only encourages the entanglement mentioned above.
- Standardization is an objective of developers, investors, lenders, insurers and regulators, because it is more predictable. Variety is problematic and variety decided per dwelling unit is considered high risk and very troublesome.
- Decision-flexibility vis-à-vis an infill level – already well understood for non-residential lending and regulation – is unknown and arguably of little benefit to developers in the residential market, given the rest of the development process.

The building industry lags in adopting 21st century methods

- The building industry is beginning to embrace the power of automation, 'kitting,' bar-coding, and integrated but nimble data management. This process of adoption, however, still sees the 'multifamily residential building' as a unitary product. It still has not recognized the importance of two separate design and production tasks in this market.
- Unlike the U.S. Navy or auto industry, as examples, the building industry at large is not yet recognizing the benefits of 'hybrid workers' and 'minimal manning,' or the use of cross-trained and therefore smaller crews (Unseem, 2019, p. 58). In part this can be explained by the relatively low wages workers earn (usually with no benefits), the swings in the market that lead to lay-offs and then rehiring when the market heats up, and their relatively low skill levels and the widespread acceptance of low-quality construction by the market.
- Modularity in the building industry is too narrowly defined and too 'coarse-grained.' Everyone thinks of 'modular construction' as large, fully completed rooms or even larger elements made off-site in virtually the same way and using the same materials and products that would be used if built on-site. No one thinks about modular and dimensional coordination, most needed when tasks are separated, serving as a planning and design tool already well-understood in the building products sector where competitive manufacturers of discrete products

depend on dimensional and interface agreements and standards made at an industry level (e.g. in piping, cabling and other subsystems).

These observations mean that the professional class – worldwide – sees no advantage in a residential fit-out industry at present, with the exception, perhaps, of the case of Henenghome in China. In most cases, the existing players in the building industry make money now and do not see advantage and only assume greater risk trying a new way.

Future prospects

The reason the book focuses on an infill or fit-out industry in its last sections is that as long as society excludes households from a direct (e.g. disintermediated) relation to their habitation, Open Building will be unable to expand more broadly. Users of offices and shopping centers, laboratories and other so-called 'flexible' buildings have economic power. Users in large housing projects, whether 'social housing' or 'for-market' projects, are, to a large extent, passive recipients, are often too harried with the pressures and uncertainties of everyday life to deal with the disjointed and expensive housing process that really does not want their active engagement in any case, and therefore have no active decision role.

But there are, at this writing during the COVID-19 pandemic, significant pressures for developers to 'peer into the future as they build for today.' An essay in the *New York Times* business section (Williams, 2021, emphasis in original) is one example of a dawning recognition that current methods don't work anymore:

> A century ago, developers didn't give the future much thought; but today, they don't have the same luxury. A combination of pandemic disruptions and constantly changing technology has brought the hazy, distant horizon much closer .... this shortening shelf-life has left architects, developers and investors in a conundrum: **How do you build for today without becoming obsolete tomorrow?** ... the core problem is that commercial construction (including multifamily residential) is an industry producing highly durable goods in a world that is asking for greater flexibility with changing tastes and economic conditions .... the specter of unanticipated change will color future projects. Going forward, developers will be asking how much flexibility they have.

If this is to be believed, the spread of residential fit-out companies worldwide is just a matter of time. This new kind of industry will do its largely invisible work inside buildings – fitting them out for dwelling units, live–work spaces, or whatever the project allows in terms of possible mixed uses. This will be a specialized industry with nimble companies delivering systematic product/solutions that can go into a wide variety of building types, and that develop their place in the local culture and economic habits.

The businesses operating in this new residential-focused industry will be market driven, will use the most advanced logistics and supply chain organizations, supported by advanced building information management tools. The argument that each building is different and therefore there is no way to systematize the process of fitting them out one at a time will no longer be relevant, given highly sophisticated digital tools for recording existing conditions and sending these to the production floors of off-site fabricators and product bundlers.

In the beginning, developers will hire these companies to save time and money. In time, these companies will enable occupants to customize their spaces, selecting products and equipment from large catalogues of options – from floor plan to cabinet pulls and everything in between – constantly updated with the newest products. If users prefer, they can hire designers to assist them, or use the design services of fit-out company showrooms. Or, the developer can decide on the fit-out for each unit of occupancy when they are ready for lease or sale, thus avoiding the problem of predicating the entire projects' design, budgeting, approvals and construction processes on dwelling unit designs. Confident that fit-out service companies are available, a developer's decision to separate and defer decisions on unit interiors will help them avoid risk and will lower costs, including the problem of making contracts with suppliers and subcontractors too soon and being forced to negotiate for many change orders and rework to respond to dynamic markets, evolving regulations and advances in technical subsystems and consumer-oriented products.

In this new way of organizing project delivery, many products and product 'bundles' will be tested and will obtain UL 'system' approvals (Underwriter Laboratory certification in the U.S. or similar agencies in other countries), assuring buyers, developers and public officials that the fit-out packages meet building standards and can be approved as 'systems' (for which there are precedents) rather than needing a separate regulatory approval process for each fit-out package. This will streamline the inspection process as well.

This new kind of business will relieve developers of many of the risks they now face when they try to meet a varied and fluctuating market demand. In a time when society is undergoing dramatic disruption (now it is the COVID-19 pandemic) and buildings are being altered to accommodate new uses and use patterns, this fit-out capability is of critical importance. After all, the building process – and dealing with individual customers – is just a bothersome way to make a profit for most building companies for whom real estate buying and selling is more profitable. And custom builders, who are used to dealing with individual users, can expand their market, offer services at a range of price points, and expand their market share.

Meanwhile, architects can focus on architecture as a contribution to the public sphere and forget about tying that work to the bothersome design of floor plans. A new architecture may emerge from this new possibility.

In our age, culture develops by technical innovation serving the individual. It is the way we got private cars, home telephones, televisions, cameras, computers, cellphones, washing machines, high-efficiency boilers for heating and various air conditioning systems, etc., all offered at various price points. In each case, economists and the public thought the new product was too expensive for the average citizen to afford it. I personally remember it when the television was invented. Everyone thought only rich people could afford it but ten years later there were more television sets than home telephones, just as earlier no one thought normal people could afford a car, until Ford made it possible. I remember that one economist in the Netherlands told me: 'you architects must stop trying to design cheaper houses; you must design better houses; the money will come when people want them.' In all these cases people gained individual power over their daily lives and their mode of living.

It took me a very long time to learn this lesson. I kept saying 'the inhabitant must have decision making power'; but professionals as well as politicians did not listen and saw no advantage for themselves. Now, when fit-out systems can deliver more for less money the user will get the same power over their daily living circumstances that these other products offer. Politicians, managers, sociologists and even designers will say they always wanted that.

Many of us dream in various ways of a culture based on local consensus free from upper level, top-down rules. That is what is gained when housing is the result of Open Building.

(Private exchange with John Habraken, November 2020)

References

Boosma, Koos, van Hoogstraten, Dorine and Vos, Martijn (2000). *Housing for the Millions: John Habraken and the SAR (1960–2000)*. Rotterdam: NAI Publishers.

Dekker, Karel (1982). Supports can be less costly. *Dutch Architect's Yearbook*.

Fassbinder, Helga and Proveniers, Adri (1992). *New Wave in Building: A Flexible way of Design, Construction and Real Estate Management*. Van Gorcum: Eindhoven University of Technology.

Kendall, Stephen (2015). Notes toward a history of the matura infill system (unpublished manuscript).

NEXT21. (1994). SD Special Edition #25. *NEXT21*. Tokyo: Kajima Institute Publishing Company. (in Japanese)

NEXT21 Editing Committee (2005). *NEXT21: All about the NEXT21 Project*. Osaka: Osaka Gas Company.

PSHHAK (1979). In Hatch, Richard. (1984). *The Scope of Social Architecture*. New York: Van Nostrand Reinhold (pp. 48–52).

Takada, Mitsuo (2001). Tradition of 'Hadaka-gashi' System in Osaka and the New Generation Housing System 'Flex Court Yoshida', *Traverse: Kyoto University Architectural Journal*, 2. Available at: https://issuu.com/traverse-architecture/docs/traverse2 (English)

Tatsumi, Kazuo (1975). Two aspects of housing policy, Jutaku (Housing). *Japan Housing Association*, 24(9). (Japanese)

Tatsumi, Kazuo and Takada, Mitsuo (1978). A proposal of 'government aided housing system.' *Study on Urban Problems*, 30(330), pp. 49–65.

Tatsumi, Kazuo and Takada, Mitsuo (1980). Development of 'Two Steps Housing System' for urban multi-unit housing: New development of government aided housing system. *Study on Urban Problems*, 32(357), pp. 58–81.

Toshi-Jutaku. (1972, September). pp. 8–52. Tokyo: Kajima Institute Publishing.

Unseem, Jerry (2019). The end of expertise. *The Atlantic*, July, p. 58.

Williams, Kevin (2021). The ever-shrinking shelf-life of buildings. *New York Times*. February 24.

Postscript

A personal note

Stephen H. Kendall

In 1963, in my senior year of high school, I had to write a book report for an English class. I found Jane Jacobs *The Death and Life in Great American Cities* (Jacobs, 1961) in my father's bookcase, and despite its hefty size, I completed the assignment and got good marks for the effort. I was living at that time in New Concord, a small college town in southeastern Ohio (population 2000) where my father was teaching violin and conducting the orchestra at a small liberal arts college, at the foothills of Appalachia, so the story she told was not an everyday reality to me. I had visited New York City once a few years before, and had visited Columbus, Ohio, a mid-size mid-western city a few times. But that was the extent of my urban experience during my first 18 years. Yet something in what Jacobs saw and wrote stuck with me.

A few years later, in architecture school in Cincinnati, Ohio during the tumultuous 1960s, I began what became a lifelong interest in the pulse and grit of everyday urban living environments where so much of the real life of cities happens. This was happening in the context of an architectural education that was still steeped in the Bauhaus Basic Course, but which soon departed from that to include studies of Alexander's Pattern Language. Outside of the classroom, I watched the fine-grained changes made to ordinary houses and apartment buildings in the older German settlement of brick row houses on the edge of downtown which was struggling with poverty and creeping gentrification. My co-op work experiences that were part of that architecture program took me to live in Philadelphia, New York City, Boston, and 12 weeks of hitch-hiking around Europe in 1968. These experiences gave me added opportunities to see the tension between the everyday environment and the heroic examples of modernist architecture. I was interested in this because I was a carpenter before entering architecture studies (I had already built or worked on a number of residential-scale buildings and would continue to do small design/build jobs) and wanted to see how things got built, but also partly because something from Jane Jacob's book still lived in my con-sciousness. In the preface of her book, she wrote: 'The scenes that illustrate this book are all about us. For illustration, please look closely at real cities.

DOI: 10.4324/9781003018339-18

While you're looking, you might as well also listen, linger, and think about what you see.'

A decade later, while pursuing a graduate degree in architecture and urban design at Washington University in St. Louis, I took a course on 'Housing' and was introduced to John Habraken's writings. I had the chance to hear him give a lecture in 1974, on his work at the SAR in the Netherlands, at a design methods conference in London. This was the beginning of what turned out to be a lifelong friendship and intellectual journey. He argued that the kind of healthy built environment we generally appreciate most (that is, the sort of real everyday neighborhoods Jacobs wrote about) could not come into existence and prosper without the direct action of people living there. No matter the power or insights of experts (certainly still needed), without action (control) by people, we would inevitably find ourselves living in rigid built environments that would still change (it's only natural) but in which a building stock, designed exclusively by experts steeped in 'form follows function' (who of course were educated to believe in the superiority of their knowledge) would invite conflict and waste. Environments designed exclusively by experts in this way could, Habraken wrote, never attain the kind of natural fine grain that we instinctively are drawn to in well-worn but well-loved places we visit on vacations and architectural tours. He showed how architects could do better – could help cultivate (but not design) the ordinary – when they would realize that they couldn't have the entire world to themselves. He spoke about, developed and showed methods and skills needed by architects to participate effectively in this ongoing reality. That's when the principle of separating design tasks first became palpable to me, with design methods to show how to make it work.

Further reading at that time (including John Turner's *Housing for People*, 1976) revealed to me that a lack of agency on the part of ordinary people on their immediate environments could also result from an imbalance of economic and political forces. We could have a tyranny of experts (Lieberman's *The Tyranny of the Experts*, 1970, and Goodman's *After the Planners*, 1973), and/or peoples' induced passivity – perhaps, in part, cultivated by the expert class so they could remain in control – that could very well result from the harried lives people lived (Stefan Linder, *The Harried Leisure Class*, 1970).

I think these writings and my everyday experiences also connected to my father's observations on teaching methods. He was a violin teacher who led the introduction of the Suzuki approach to music education into the U.S. He wrote once about his attitude and approach to his teaching:

> In the event that these notes (on methods) seem to be preoccupied with technique and mechanics, it should be understood that in every instance the technique must be a means to better musicianship without which all efforts would be sterile. Momentarily, for problem solving, we may separate the technical from the expressive, but it is never to be completely isolated and should not remain apart for long.

This made instinctual sense to me. As a carpenter, I was interested in how things work (therefore methods), but also the quality of everyday environment, craftsmanship and beauty. Everywhere I looked walking around (eventually in 31 countries, in both formal and informal settlements), I tried to distinguish questions of quality from questions of method or approach and political power. This distinction could not be explored in practice at that time, although I did manage to become a registered architect and worked in a small firm designing hospitals, schools and houses. After five years of that, I jumped ship into an academic path, where a focus on methods was more likely to be accepted as a legitimate endeavor. Little did I realize at the time that a focus on methods and in particular the Open Building approach would prove to be a difficult career path in academia.

Reading research studies and books, teaching, writing, using big-box DIY stores for my own work as a small-time builder, talking to developers, builders, architects and regulators, it was clear that more money was being spent on fine-grained alterations of existing residential environments than was being invested in any given year in new construction, which was too often coarse and banal and 'locked-in' in a way that resisted incremental change. I also came to realize that 'planned' environments, and those organized under 'homeowners' associations' or 'common interest developments' (McKenzie, 1994) as they are known in the U.S., were having a pernicious effect. In their effort to manage complexity and uncertainty, they were rapidly spreading and supplanting the kinds of everyday neighborhoods that exhibited the natural process of incremental change that Jacobs and Habraken, among others, helped me to see and admire. Ironically, people seemed ready to buy-in to these rigid environments and to accept limits to their own agency and freedom in order to make sure others also could not exercise their freedom to modify their places of living.

So, if people (across income groups) already exhibited direct agency in shaping their immediate environments, but there is also evidence of widespread thwarting of such change, *what could be ways to enable and facilitate the apparently natural tendency toward the granularity that characterizes the most sustainable places?* And, if the evidence was that supposedly enlightened governance systems such as HOA's and condominiums in fact throttle gradual adaptation, what would be effective ways to organize more dense living environments to support a good balance of forces – community aspirations and individual agency – what Habraken called the 'natural relationship?'

Jane Jacobs told us that 'experts of the time did not respect what foot people knew and valued.' She argued in favor of local wisdom and community visions. She later told Roberta Brandes Gratz (an author):

> There are two kinds of change, and you can symbolize them on the land; there is the kind of change in which the topsoil is being built up, and it is being made more fertile and is good husbandry of the land. The land

is changing when you do that, but it is positive change. Then there's the kind of change that's definitely change – that's erosion. Gullies are being dug into the land, and the topsoil is being carried away and it's being made infertile. The fact that it's change doesn't mean it's progress. It's ruin. But people were, for a long time, brainwashed into the idea that every sort of change in a city was progress. 'Well, yes, it's bad but that's progress.' No, that's erosion.

It was interesting that Habraken, like Jacobs, used the analogy of the land and gardening in his writings. Using the metaphor of the gardener, he said that 'cultivating the ordinary' is, in effect, the mark of environmental wisdom. Being an architect who appreciates architecture of high quality and who is at heart a methodologist, he also was contrarian enough to assert that architects could learn to cultivate excellence in the ordinary fabric of built environment (what he later came to call 'Thematic Design'), rather than introduce invasive, foreign species of their own invention. Out of this insight, he developed design methods for architects to use in practice and explored teaching methods at MIT focused on Thematic Design. I used much of his insights in methods in my 35-year teaching and consulting career, both before and after studying with him for my Ph.D. at MIT in a mid-career leave from my teaching in the mid-1980s.

It was only after almost three decades of focusing on the Open Building approach in my teaching and writing that I came to understand that it is relatively easy for students to learn how to develop the technical and design skills associated with Open Building. I taught such skills in the design of housing and healthcare facilities, in the U.S, China, Italy, Republic of China, South Africa and Japan, and managed to publish a sizable number of published papers and research reports on this work and to give lectures around the world. I remain convinced that these skills are very important for students to have and to bring into their professional careers.

But it finally dawned on me that this was not enough, just before I retired. If I could do it all over again, I would put a stronger emphasis in my teaching on what Jacobs and Habraken and others refer to as the quality of the commons. I would teach students to methodically examine how such everyday environments work and incrementally change – to explore their patterns, types and systems – and achieve excellence. Professor Jia Beisi and I were able to explore this approach in a workshop at the School of Architecture at Harbin Institute of Technology in China in 2012, based on Habraken's ideas of Thematic Design, first worked out in his teaching at MIT (when I was his teaching assistant) and later discussed in a book *Conversations with Form* (Routledge, 2014) and a website (www.thematicdesign.org).

In 2017, with John Dale, FAIA, another former student of Habraken's and a practicing architect, I helped launch the Council on Open Building (www.councilonopenbuilding.org). Its mission is to make the Open Building approach normative for design professionals. It focuses on building up professional design methods and skills as shared, not proprietary knowledge, rather than on what is good or bad architecture. This has been instructive: it has clarified for me the extent to which methods – ways of working – remain largely implicit in architectural practice. To the extent that this remains the case, the profession will be hamstrung in arguing the case for its relevance in changing times, not to mention facing difficulties in developing the specific design skills required to make the Open Building approach conventional.

References

Goodman, Robert (1973). *After the Planners*. Clearwater, FL: Touchstone.

Habraken, John (2014). *Conversations with Form*. London: Routledge.

Jacobs, Jane (1961). *The Death and Life in Great American Cities*. New York: Random House.

Lieberman, Jethro K. (1970). *The Tyranny of the Experts*. New York: Walker & Co.

Linder, Stefan (1970). *The Harried Leisure Class*. New York: Columbia University Press.

McKenzie, Evan (1994). *Privatopia*. New Haven, CT: Yale University Press.

Turner, John (1976). *Housing for People: Towards Autonomy in Building Environments*. New York: Pantheon.

Glossary of Open Building terms

Base building (sometimes called support, primary system, or skeleton): A base building is a complete architectural infrastructure (not a structural skeleton), with capacity for variable size and layout of units of occupancy, ready for independent fit-out. It consists of all spaces and building elements that are common to all units of occupancy. These common elements generally include the building's structure, enclosure (or most of it), elevators, fire egress stairs (and perhaps corridors), and all common or shared MEP systems serving independent units of habitation. Walls or parts of walls separating units of occupancy (called demising walls in the U.S.) are considered to be part of the base building once fixed but are generally able to be changed without disturbing the permanent base building.

Capacity: Capacity means that something can accommodate something else, often an unknown something. This is a familiar concept; for example, when we walk into a room in an apartment we are considering buying, we think to ourselves 'I could use this room as a home office or perhaps a bedroom'; or 'We're thinking of our future family needs, so I'm wondering if I can add a second bathroom and divide this big room into two bedrooms'; or 'I wonder if I could buy the apartment next door when my elderly parents come back to live with us, since we don't want to move.' We are doing an informal capacity analysis or exploration when we think this way. Beyond this informal way, more formal and precise methods are available and needed to assure clients of the proposed design. In architectural terms, a building that offers capacity will have a 'higher level' configuration of spaces and physical forms that can accommodate a variety of configurations on a 'lower level.' That means that the configuration on the lower level (e.g. infill walls and piping) can change without forcing change on the higher level (the system of physical elements belonging to the base building decisions), but a change on the higher level will force an adjustment to the lower level. In the context of the separation of base building and fit-out, capacity refers to a range of variations in floor plan and use within the constraints of a given base building.

Certified fit-out company: A business offering the service of designing and fitting out a legally defined space in a base building, under a unified contract with all the installers and products required (i.e. not the use of independent subcontractors), assuring a good product/service delivered on time for the agreed upon price. A certified company meets recognized performance standards governing all similar companies in a given governmental jurisdiction.

Design methods for Open Building: The built environment as an autonomous and complex living entity that we want to cultivate (it will be there whatever we professionals do) raises questions of the skills we need to do so successfully. Once we recognize that we must cooperate and interrelate among designers working on a common task, **Design Methodology** – the study of how we design and the development of new and more effective **Ways of Working** – becomes an urgent and necessary subject. For instance, the straightforward and reasonable question of how we can find out whether an empty base building can allow the kind of unit designs that we (and our client) value triggers various methodological responses (e.g. capacity analysis). How we can best reach and **notate agreements about shared form** (e.g. themes and types and dimensional constraints) in a given urban fabric is a methodological question as well. A few methodological design tools are already available, such as capacity analysis, the use of zones, sectors, basic variants and band grids, and the principle of sharing values and reaching agreements about such elements of architecture as typology, patterns, systems, variants and structure.

Disentanglement: Organizing technical systems in such a way that a change of one will not cause harmful ripple effects on other parts. In Open Building terms, this also means that the parties controlling each technical system will avoid conflict with other parties, when one party changes the parts they control. One example of disentanglement is avoiding burying in inaccessible ways those parts which change frequently. Another example is avoiding placing parts (e.g. drainage piping) serving one unit of occupancy in the ceiling space of an occupancy below it. Disentanglement therefore has both a technical and a legal/territorial meaning.

Disintermediation: Disintermediation is the removal of intermediaries from a supply chain, or 'cutting out the middlemen' in connection with a transaction or a series of transactions. In the context of the Open Building approach, disintermediation is the natural outcome of infill or fit-out companies offering complete single-source services directly to consumers or developers, bypassing the normal intermediaries such as multiple contractors and subcontractors, and even multiple layers of regulations.

Fit-out (sometimes called infill or secondary system): Refers to what is decided independently for each unit of occupancy. A fit-out system is the integrated bundle of products and services used to fill in a 'serviced' space in a building, to make it ready for use or habitation. Fit-out includes everything installed within the legal (and fire) boundaries of a single unit of occupancy; that is, within the walls or floors separating that unit of occupancy from other such units. The fit-out bundle includes the MEP (mechanical, electrical and plumbing) systems specific to and within the occupied space, as well as walls, doors, cabinets, plumbing fixtures, lighting fixtures, and most if not all surface finishes. The fit-out might include some of the façade (e.g. windows) if legally defined to be part of the unit of habitation. Whether part of a buildings' façade is fit-out or base building is a technical as well as a cultural question; whether the fit-out includes the bathroom is another question to be resolved.

Infrastructure: Infrastructure is the general term for the basic physical systems of a business, region, or nation. Examples of infrastructure include transportation systems, communication networks, sewage, water, and electric systems. In respect to the Open Building approach, infrastructure is the hierarchical organization of basic elements of a complex system in which higher levels of the system dominate lower levels, but lower levels are free to change or be replaced by more up-to-date parts performing the same function. For example, electrical service constitutes an infrastructure system in itself. From the power generation facility to the laptop or electrical appliance, there are many 'levels' each deployed, owned, leased and managed by a different party, crossing many territorial boundaries, and each capable of being replaced with higher-performing parts while maintaining the entire system's functionality. The same can be said for a public water supply, or a public sewage/waste-water system, all dependent on good interfaces between levels of intervention.

Levels: The concept of levels is directly related to the design of infrastructure systems. For example, urban designers 'operate on another level' than the architect. In this case, the built environment is divided in two groups of things: those that are decided about by the urban designer and those that are the concern of the architect. This distinction is evident in explaining what happens when things change on one level or another. The architect designs a building within the context established and documented by the urban designer. She must respect, for instance, the layout of streets and rights-of-way and the division of lots in the block, and for example, certain patterns, themes and typologies. But within that context, she is free to act and make her own variations. She can change the design of the building in many ways. Indeed, different architects can build different buildings in different places in an urban tissue but will share the street network and the types and patterns that are meant to yield coherent variety, explicitly notated in the urban designers' plan. Although the urban design constrains their work, they are free within those constraints to do their own thing. However, when the street network must be changed for whatever reason, the buildings may have to adjust. The urban designer cannot act without effecting the designs of the architect. The relation, therefore, is asymmetrical and hierarchical. Change on the level of the building does not affect the higher level of the urban design but change in the urban design affects the lower level of the buildings. This is the meaning of a hierarchical structure of the built environment. Other levels can be found, such as base building (a higher level) and fit-out (a lower level).

Open Building: The international movement committed to making the Open Building approach normative. Open Building design seeks to deal with the proper separation and distribution of design tasks in their hierarchical organization. This is the essence of the built environment as a living, regenerative organism. This is also the essence of infrastructure design. Separation of design tasks is an essential aspect of built environments that sustain themselves and yet continue to evolve. The same principle can be applied to many kinds of projects, including laboratories, shopping centers, medical and educational facilities, large residential projects, campuses and neighborhoods. One of the reasons to separate design tasks is to reduce costs and distribute risk; another is to enable work at various levels to proceed simultaneously; another is to enable independent units of occupancy to change, without disturbing other units of occupancy or the shared infrastructure. This requires that each unit of control (e.g. a dwelling unit in a building, or a building in an urban tissue) is in fact fully independent, technically and legally.

Sharing thematic qualities: When design tasks are separated (a basic principle of the Open Building approach), and yet variety within coherence is desired from the work of multiple players over time, shared values are essential. We might call these conventions. For example, in urban design, it makes sense that certain patterns, themes and typologies are agreed upon to be shared – to harmonize various interventions, each of which can make its own variation on these shared architectural values. We might call this thematic design. Historic fabrics that have sustained themselves for centuries are good examples (think of Boston's Back Bay; Amsterdam's canal environment; Bologna's arcaded streets; Kyoto's historic Machia neighborhoods, etc.), contemporary urban tissues less so because we have developed an unfortunate tendency to emphasize how each intervention can be as different as possible from the next; the only thing bringing about coherence then being coercive regulations.

Index